RECONSTRUCTING MACROECONOMICS

The authors treat macroeconomic models as composed of large numbers of micro-units or agents of several types and explicitly discuss stochastic dynamic and combinatorial aspects of interactions among them. In mainstream macroeconomics, sound microfoundations have meant incorporating sophisticated intertemporal optimization by representative agents into models. Optimal growth theory, once meant to be normative, is now taught as a descriptive theory in mainstream macroeconomic courses. In neoclassical equilibria, flexible prices led the economy to the state of full employment, and marginal productivities are all equated. Professors Aoki and Yoshikawa contrariwise show that such equilibria are not possible in economies with a large number of agents of heterogeneous types. The authors treat equilibria as statistical distributions and not as fixed points. They employ a set of statistical dynamical tools via continuous-time Markov chains, and statistical distributions of fractions of agents by types available in the new literature of combinatorial stochastic processes, to reconstruct macroeconomic models.

Masanao Aoki is Professor Emeritus in the Department of Economics at the University of California, Los Angeles. He is past President of the Society for Economic Dynamics and Control, a Fellow of the Econometric Society, and a Fellow of the IEEE Control Systems Society (inactive). Currently, Professor Aoki is Vice President of the Society for Economic Science with Heterogeneous Interacting Agents and a member of the editorial board of the *Journal of Economic Interaction and Coordination*. A past Associate Editor of the journal *Macroeconomic Dynamics*, published by Cambridge University Press, Professor Aoki also served as Editor of the *Journal of Economic Dynamics and Control* and the *International Economic Review*. He is the author or editor of a dozen books, including *Modeling Aggregate Behavior: Fluctuations in Economics*, which won the 2003 Nihon Keizai Shinbun-Center for Japanese Economics Research Prize for best book in economics by a Japanese scholar (Cambridge University Press, 2002); and *New Approaches to Macroeconomic Modeling* (Cambridge University Press, 1996).

Hiroshi Yoshikawa is Professor of Economics at the University of Tokyo. He received his Ph.D. from Yale University in 1978 and has also taught at Osaka University and the State University of New York at Albany. Professor Yoshikawa is the author of seven books, one of which received the Nikkei Award and another of which received the Yoshino-Yomiuri Award, in addition to a textbook in macroeconomics and the frequently cited *Macroeconomics and the Japanese Economy* (1995). He is a member of the Council on Economic and Fiscal Policy of the Japanese government's Cabinet Office, and he served in 2002 as president of the Japanese Economic Association.

Japan-U.S. Center UFJ Bank (formerly Sanwa) Monographs on International Financial Markets

The UFJ Bank (formerly Sanwa Bank) has established the UFJ Bank Research Endowment Fund on International Financial Markets at the Center for Japan-U.S. Business and Economic Studies of the Stern School of Business, New York University, to support research on international financial markets. One part of this endowment is used to offer an award for writing a monograph in this field. The award is made annually on a competitive basis by the selection committee. The winning published titles and proposals are listed below.

1991, Richard C. Marston, University of Pennsylvania. *International Financial Integration: A Study of Interest Differentials Between the Major Industrial Countries*, ISBN 0-521-59937-7

1992, Willem H. Buiter, University of Cambridge; Giancarlo Corsetti, University of Bologna; and Paolo A. Pesenti, Federal Reserve Bank of New York. *Financial Markets and European Monetary Cooperation: The Lessons of the 1992–1993 Exchange Rate Mechanism Crisis*, ISBN 0-521-49547-4, 0-521-79440-4

1993, Lance E. Davis, California Institute of Technology, and the late Robert E. Gallman, University of North Carolina, Chapel Hill. *Evolving Financial Markets and International Capital Flows: Britain, the Americas, and Australia, 1865–1914*, ISBN 0-521-55352-0

1994, Piet Sercu, University of Leuven, and Raman Uppal, London Business School. *Exchange Rate Volatility, Trade, and Capital Flows under Alternative Exchange Rate Regimes*, ISBN 0-521-56294-5

1995, Robert P. Flood, International Monetary Fund, and Peter M. Garber, Brown University. *Speculative Attacks on Fixed Exchange Rates*

1996, Maurice Obstfeld, University of California, Berkeley, and Alan M. Taylor, University of California, Davis. *Global Capital Markets: Integration, Crisis, and Growth*, ISBN 0-521-63317-6, 0-521-67179-5

1997, Pravin Krishna, Johns Hopkins University, *Trade Blocs: Economics and Politics*, ISBN 0-521-77066-1

Continued on page following Index

Reconstructing Macroeconomics

A Perspective from Statistical Physics and Combinatorial Stochastic Processes

MASANAO AOKI

University of California, Los Angeles

HIROSHI YOSHIKAWA

University of Tokyo

CAMBRIDGE
UNIVERSITY PRESS

32 Avenue of the Americas, New York NY 10013-2473, USA

Cambridge University Press is part of the University of Cambridge.

It furthers the University's mission by disseminating knowledge in the pursuit of
education, learning and research at the highest international levels of excellence.

www.cambridge.org
Information on this title: www.cambridge.org/9780521831062

© Masanao Aoki and Hiroshi Yoshikawa 2007

First published 2007
First paperback edition 2011

A catalogue record for this publication is available from the British Library

Library of Congress Cataloguing in Publication data
Aoki, Masanao.
Reconstructing macroeconomics : a perspective from statistical physics and combinatorial
stochastic processes / Masanao Aoki, Hiroshi Yoshikawa.
p. cm. – (Japan-U.S. Center UFJ Bank monographs on international financial markets)
Includes bibliographical references and index.
ISBN-13 978-0-521-83106-2 (hardback)
ISBN-10 0-521-83106-7 (hardback)
1. Macroeconomics – Mathematical models. I. Yoshikawa, Hiroshi, 1951– II. Title. III.
Series.
HB172.5.A583 2006
339.01´51923 – dc22   2006016287

ISBN 978-0-521-83106-2 Hardback

To Chieko and Fumie for their support and encouragement.

M.A.

To Setsuko and Momoko who make it all worthwhile.

H.Y.

Contents

Contents

Contents xiii

Preface by Masanao Aoki

In the last ten years or so, I have devoted my research efforts to revising the commonly adopted frameworks for modeling and analysis by mainstream macroeconomists. Results of my initial thoughts and proposals were published in 1996, followed by another book in 2002. In these two books I explained my proposed methods for modeling and analyzing stochastic dynamic interactions among economic agents of possibly many different types, and how to analyze aggregate behavior and associated fluctuations. The two books are mostly exposition of concepts and techniques and had only a few suggestive economic examples.

I have realized that more substantive examples are needed to convince mainstream macroeconomists of the usefulness of my approaches. This book, jointly written with Hiroshi Yoshikawa, integrates the methodologies and approaches in these two earlier books with much more detailed analysis of more substantive and substantial macroeconomic examples.

As the subtitle of the book makes clear, our approaches have two components: (1) continuous-time Markov chains to model stochastic dynamic interactions among agents and (2) combinations of stochastic processes and non-classical combinatorial analysis, called combinatorial stochastic processes.[1]

In (1) a version of Chapman–Kolmogorov equations called master equations describes how states of the models evolve stochastically over time. In this sense this part is devoted to applications of some of the concepts and methods from statistical physics. In (2) some concepts and results from the combinatorial stochastic process field are applied to describe stochastic dynamic processes of formation of clusters or groupings of heterogeneous agents and probability distributions of cluster sizes. We show by examples that macroeconomic properties of models emerge from the interaction of a large number of economic agents as an interacting whole.

---

[1] Jim Pitman of the Department of Statistics, University of California, Berkeley, has used this phrase in his lecture notes (2002).

There are always dangers of mechanical applications or attempts to import tools and concepts from outside economics proper without good reason. Axel Leijonhufvud warned against these.[2] We are aware of this danger and confident that we have avoided it in this book.

For your information here is a bit of my intellectual meander to writing this book. I remember vividly my shock when I first encountered representative agent models at an NSF workshop.[3] I was very puzzled by this representative agent assumption that many papers were using. I kept asking myself "what about interactions among agents?"

Acknowledgments

Preliminary versions of some of the material in this book were reported at the annual Wehia meetings held at Genoa, Marseilles, Maastrict, Kiel, Trieste, and Kyoto; a conference paper at the complexity conference at the University of Salerno; a paper given at the 2005 annual meeting of the Society of Computational Economics, Washington, DC; a conference paper at the Stern School of Business, New York University; a conference paper at the LABORatorio Revelli Center for Employment Studies in Torino; a workshop paper at the University of Bologna; two Nikkei conference papers in Tokyo; seminar talks at the New School, New York; the University of Siena; the University of Ancona; Summer School of Trento University; Catholic University of Piacenza; University Messina; the Center for International Research on the Japanese Economy; and the University of Tokyo, among others. I thank the meeting organizers for the opportunities to present my ideas as they matured.

My special thanks to the Center for International Research on the Japanese Economy, Faculty of Economics, University of Tokyo, for hosting my several visits to work on the book manuscript with my coauthor.

The initial computer simulation program for the model in Chapters 6 and 7 with multi-sector ultrametric distances for pools of unemployed was written by Vitali Kalesnic, a former research assistant of mine in the Department of Economics, UCLA. The program was later revised and expanded by graduate students at the University of Tokyo, Shinsuke Ikeda, Yutaka Suga, and Futoshi Narita, under supervision of my coauthor. I thank them all for their help.

---

[2] See M. Aoki and A. Leijonhufvud (1976), "Cybernetics and Macroeconomics: A Comment," *Econ. Inquiry* **XIV**, 251–258. In rereading his comments I am amazed how insightful and current his comments and warnings are if "cybernetics" is interpreted broadly enough to include current efforts by some econophysicists.

[3] I had been contemplating changing my specialization to economics, and the late Jacob Marshak kindly invited me to observe research in economics first-hand. I had training in physics and systems theory but none in economics.

Preface by Hiroshi Yoshikawa

Macroeconomics has gone astray. I suspect that many economists, or at least half of macroeconomists who are old enough to know the "Old Macroeconomics," feel that way. In the past 30 years, macroeconomics has become less relevant.

The mainstream macroeconomics today begins with optimization of the representative consumer. The real business cycle (RBC) theory is the foremost example. The optimum growth theory once meant to be normative is now being taught as a descriptive theory. It is the neoclassical equilibrium theory. Preferences and technologies certainly move the economy. The prediction of the neoclassical doctrine seems often right for the very long run. However, saying that something moves eastward, and saying that it reaches the east end, are wholly different matters. Most of the time, the real economy must move on a bumpy road. It is misleading and wrong to analyze such problems as business cycles, unemployment, and deflation – the subject matters of macroeconomics – with the neoclassical equilibrium theory.

Contrary to the belief held by some economists, we need a new approach for macroeconomics, different from the standard equilibrium theory. The purpose of this book is to explain it. Having sound "microeconomic foundations for macroeconomics" has been long taken as building sophisticated optimization of an individual economic agent into a macro model. This agenda is on the wrong track. The new approach we advance in this book is based on the methods of statistical physics. It provides different and proper microeconomic foundations for macroeconomics, and by so doing, it revives the old Keynesian economics.

Attempts to build "the out of the mainstream" macroeconomics in the heyday of rational expectations and equilibrium theory have not been easy. However, I have been privileged to receive encouragement in my pursuits from two great economists. The late professor James Tobin, my dissertation advisor at Yale 30 years ago, had always inspired me. An important theme of this book is to provide foundations for "stochastic macro equilibrium," which he proposed in his AEA presidential address. Professor Robert M. Solow has also given me a number of constructive comments on my papers, and by so doing great encouragement.

This book won the UFJ Monograph Award. We are proud of it, and grateful to Professor Ryuzo Sato and other committee members for their helpful comments and encouragement. We are also grateful to the Research Center for the Relationship between Market Economy and Non-market Institutions, a Center of Excellence (COE) program in the Graduate School of Economics at the University of Tokyo, for its financial support. Messrs. Shinsuke Ikeda, Futoshi Narita, and Yutaka Suga, graduate students at the University of Tokyo, did simulations in Chapters 6 and 7 and gave very detailed comments on every page, often saving us from errors. Ms. Momoko Inui provided excellent assistance. We thank them all. Now, the book has been done. I hope that it will contribute to reconstructing macroeconomics.

This book contains some material that appeared in earlier publications, and we would like to thank the publishers of the following journal and books for their kind permission to reproduce portions of this material.

Mankiw, N. G., "Real Business Cycles: A New Keynesian Perspective," *Journal of Economic Perspectives*, American Economic Association, 3, 1989, 84.

Davis, S. J., J. C. Haltiwanger, and S. Schuh. *Job Creation and Destruction*. Cambridge, Massachusetts: MIT Press, 1996/2004, 88 and 100.

Feller, William. *An Introduction to Probability Theory and Its Applications*, 3rd ed., Vol. 1. Hoboken, New Jersey: John Wiley & Sons, 1968, 87.

Gates, Bill. *Business @ The Speed of Thought: Using a Digital Nervous System*. New York: Warner Books, 1999/2003/2004, 118.

Rostow, W. W. *The World Economy: History & Present*. Austin, Texas: University of Texas Press, 1978, 107.

1

Introduction: A New Approach to Macroeconomics

In his 1844 essay, "On the Influence of Consumption upon Production," J. S. Mill endeavored to refute the belief that, "A great demand, a brisk circulation, a rapid consumption (three equivalent expressions) are a cause of national prosperity." In this book, we take up the old belief and propose that aggregate demand *does* matter in the determination of total output. The argument requires a drastic turn in macroeconomic, theory and introduces new methods. The purpose of this book is to explain the new approach. Readers will see how new methods and concepts broaden the scope of macroeconomics and shed new light on old problems such as demand deficiency, inflexible prices, business cycles, and asset prices.

The idea that demand matters was, of course, established by Keynes (1936) – indeed, macroeconomics used to be synonymous with Keynesian economics. Alas, no more! Keynes' principle of effective demand – that aggregate demand determines the level of aggregate production or output – is in stark contrast to the neoclassical doctrine that aggregate output is determined solely by supply factors such as factor endowments and technology, and that demand is relevant only with respect to composition of outputs. Despite its empirical attractiveness, Keynesian economics has long been charged with lacking *microeconomic foundations*. The need for microeconomic foundations meant that the optimization of agents had to be explicitly considered in models.

Many economists have come to believe that the first principle of economics is the optimization of economic agents such as household and firm. This principle and the notion of equilibrium – namely equality of supply and demand – constitute the core of the neoclassical theory. To some, this is the only respectable economic theory on earth. For example, Lucas (1987) concluded his Yrjo Jahnsson Lectures as follows:

The most interesting recent developments in macroeconomic theory seem to me describable as the reincorporation of aggregative problems such as inflation and the business cycle within the general framework of "microeconomic" theory. If these developments succeed, the term "macroeconomic" will simply disappear from use and the modifier "micro" will become superfluous. We will simply speak, as did Smith, Ricardo, Marshall and Warlras, of *economic*

1

theory. If we are honest, we will have to face the fact that at any given time there will be phenomena that are well-understood from the point of view of the economic theory we have, and other phenomena that are not. We will be tempted, I am sure, to relieve the discomfort induced by discrepancies between theory and facts by saying that the ill-understood facts are the province of some other, different kind of economic theory. Keynesian "macroeconomics" was, I think, a surrender (under great duress) to this temptation. It led to the abandonment, for a class of problems of great importance, of the use of the only "engine for the discovery of truth" that we have in economics. Now we are once again putting this engine of Marshall's to work on the problems of aggregate dynamics. (Lucas, 1987, 107–108)

Thus, over the last 30 years, economics has attempted, in one way or another, to build maximizing microeconomic agents into macroeconomic models. To incorporate these agents into the models, the assumption of the representative agent is usually made. These exercises lead one to neoclassical macroeconomics. The real business cycle (RBC) theory (e.g., Kydland and Prescott, 1982) praised by Lucas (1987) is the foremost example.

In this book, we argue that the standard approach represented by RBC is misguided, and that a fundamentally different approach is necessary to analyze the *macroeconomy*. Such an approach is based on *statistical physics and combinatorial stochastic processes*, which are commonly used in physics, biology, and other natural sciences when one studies a system consisting of a large number of entities. Contrary to Lucas's assertion, we *do* need "some other, different kind of economic theory" when we study the macroeconomy.

As the founders of the neoclassical economics such as Walras, Marshall, and Pareto explicitly recognized, neoclassical theory is built on concepts and methods imported from classical Newtonian mechanics. Interestingly, Marshall was aware of the limitations of his method. At age 78, in the preface to the eighth edition of his *Principles of Economics*, he wrote:[1]

The Mecca of the economist lies in economic biology rather than in economic dynamics. But biological conceptions are more complex than those of mechanics; a volume on Foundations must therefore give a relatively large place to mechanical analogies; and frequent use is made of the term "equilibrium," which suggests something of statical analogy. This fact, combined with the predominant attention paid in the present volume to the normal conditions of life in the modern age, has suggested the notion that its central idea is "statical," rather than "dynamical." But in fact it is concerned throughout with the forces that cause movement: and its key-note is that of dynamics, rather than statistics. . . .

The main concern of economics is thus with human beings who are impelled, for good and evil, to change and progress. Fragmentary statical hypotheses are used as temporary auxiliaries to dynamical – or rather biological – conceptions: but the central idea of economics, even when its Foundations alone are under discussion, must be that of living force and movement. (Marshall, 1920, xii–xiii)

---

[1] This idea, an emphasis of biological analogy in economics, dates back to his earlier writing (see Marshall, 1898).

Marshall knew that his method, based on the assumption "other things being equal," is suitable for analyzing a single market but faces difficulty in the analysis of the macroeconomy because "gradually the area of the dynamical problem becomes larger; the area covered by provisional statical assumptions becomes smaller" (Marshall, 1920, xiii). Marshall was much more cautious than Lucas (1987); however, he lacked the method required to achieve his goal!

In physics, during the late nineteenth century, a fundamentally new approach called statistical mechanics had been advanced by Maxwell, Boltzmann, Gibbs, and others to study an entity consisting of a large number (typically 10^{23}) of units. Curiously, the method and concept of statistical mechanics have escaped economists' eyes for more than a hundred years though they perfectly fit the purpose of studying the macroeconomy as distinguished from microeconomic behavior.

Indeed, the macroeconomy consists of a large number of heterogeneous interacting agents. For example, the number of households is of the order of 10^7; the number of firms is of the order of 10^6. In analyzing a system composed of such a large number of units, it is meaningless and impossible to pursue precise behavior of each unit, because the economic constraints on each will differ, and objectives of the units are constantly changing in an idiosyncratic way. This does not mean that economic agents do not behave rationally or do not optimize their objective functions. They certainly do. Their rationality may be bounded, but this is not essential for macroeconomics. The point is that precise behavior of each agent is *irrelevant*. Rather, we need to recognize that microeconomic behavior is fundamentally stochastic, and we need to resort to proper statistical methods to study the macroeconomy consisting of a large number of such agents. The starting point of statistical mechanics was the recognition that it was impossible and meaningless to pursue precise motion of an individual molecule in a gas. Macroeconomics must be built on the same premise.

We also need to reconsider the notion of *equilibrium*. That microeconomic behaviors are all accompanied by *fluctuations* is of fundamental importance. Traditional economic theory abstracts from microeconomic fluctuations. Thus, the outcome of optimization by an economic agent is given by a deterministic "point" in some set or space. Accordingly, macro equilibrium is also given by such a point. The Walras–Arrow–Debreu general equilibrium model is an example. In this model, prices clear the way for aggregation of micro-equilibria of many agents into a macro-equilibrium, because microeconomic fluctuations are assumed away, and equilibrium is given by a deterministic point.

In contrast, the new approach leads us to a new concept of "equilibrium." Specifically, equilibrium is a *probability distribution* over a set of points, not a single point. Most importantly for the purpose of macroeconomics, productivities across sectors/firms *never* equalize (Salter, 1960). In equilibrium, we have a number of productivity levels in the economy, rather than a unique level of productivity. We will explain this in Chapter 3. We then find that demand plays a crucial role in the determination of the aggregate level of production or output, as the old Keynesian economics claims. Simply stated, high aggregate demand mobilizes production factors to high productivity sectors and thereby raises the level of total output. Okun (1973) made a similar point in his effort to explain Okun's Law. One of the goals of this book is to shed new light on Keynesian economics from this angle.

First, however, we must explain the new approach. Typically one analyzes the behavior of microeconomic agents in sophisticated dynamic models. Consider the consumer in the Ramsey model. The Ramsey (1928) model was once called the "optimum growth model" and was meant to be normative, not descriptive. However, as the economic profession has turned macroeconomics into the neoclassical equilibrium theory such as RBC, the Ramsey model is now taken as a descriptive model, and is usually taught as such (Blanchard and Fischer, 1989)

The Ramsey consumer maximizes the discounted utility sum under the constraint of lifetime income. Suppose households in the economy are, in fact, Ramsey consumers. However, there are a large number (10^7, for example) of households in the economy, and as we pointed out earlier, both their perceived lifetime constraints and their objectives are changing in idiosyncratic ways. For example, some may unexpectedly experience unemployment, which changes their constraints, while others may suffer from illness, which tilts their utility functions. Facing new situations, 10^7 households are continuously revising their best strategies.

This problem has been recognized by some. For example, Dixit and Pindyck (1994), after advancing their model of investment, note the following challenge for macroeconomic analysis:

In the economy as a whole, different consumers have different thresholds and different historically determined initial positions relative to these thresholds. They are also subject to different (idiosyncratic) shocks as well as some common (economy-wide) shocks. (Dixit and Pindyck, 1994, 424–425)

Macroeconomic theory that deserves its name must resolve these problems.

It is useful to come back to the Ramsey model and explain the problem explicitly. The behavior of the Ramsey consumer who maximizes the discounted utility sum under the lifetime income constraint can be described in the well-known phase diagram (Figure 1.1). This analysis is routine for every macroeconomist or even graduate student. Now, economists are so accustomed to the deterministic Ramsey model that they are prone to use the optimal trajectory (shown by dotted lines in Figure 1.1) as the potential time path of consumption. This is not the actual time path of consumption chosen, however. Because the consumer's preferences and constraints keep changing stochastically, the optimal path also keeps changing. At each point in time, given the level of capital stock or assets, the consumer chooses the optimal consumption point on the newly revised optimal trajectory. In Figure 1.1, the optimal trajectories and the corresponding optimal

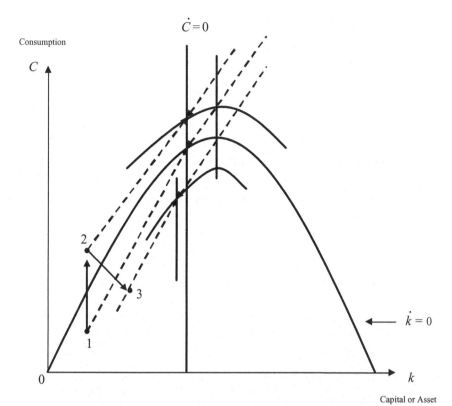

Figure 1.1. The Behavior of a Ramsey Consumer in Stochastic Environment.
Note: The explanation of this phase diagram can be found in any advanced textbook of macroeconomics such as Blanchard and Fischer (1989).

consumption points (points 1, 2, and 3) at time t_1, t_2, and t_3 are shown. The time path of consumption in this case is a line that goes through three points 1, 2 and 3 (shown in bold in Figure 1.1). In general, reflecting incessant shocks to both preferences and constraints, the optimal path of consumption would show zigzags. Note that shocks to preferences and constraints that affect the optimal consumption, as described in Figure 1.1, are basically microeconomic shocks, though they may reflect macroeconomic shocks. We, therefore, *never* know what those shocks are. Additionally, we have 10^7 consumers in the economy who all face different idiosyncratic shocks. Therefore, we have 10^7 different zigzag paths of consumption!

Table 1.1 shows means and standard deviations of changes in consumption and income across 768 Japanese households. Rate of change in consumption over half a year (April–September 1981) is *on average* 1.4 percent. For the same period, the average growth rate of income is −0.9 percent. However, the standard deviations of growth rates of consumption and income across 768 households

Table 1.1. Changes in Micro Consumption and Income:
Means and Standard Deviations across 768 Japanese
Households (April–September 1981)

	Food consumption	Total consumption	income
(1) Means	0.028	0.014	−0.009
(2) S.D.	0.179	0.309	0.440
(3) C.V.*	6.400	22.100	48.900

Source: Hayashi (1986)
* Coefficient of variation is standard deviation divided by mean ((2)/(1)).

are 30.9 percent and 44.0 percent, respectively. Large values of the coefficient of variation are striking. These figures show a great diversity of income and consumption patterns across households. They demonstrate that the representative consumer is imaginary. What is the bottom line? It is hopeless and meaningless to try to pursue the exact behavior of each economic agent. At the same time, it is wrong to associate the behavior of the macroeconomy with that of an individual economic agent.

The standard approach (RBC) takes the opposite position, relying heavily on the precise behavior of the representative economic agent. Prescott (1986), for example, advocates his own RBC by saying that

Economists have long been puzzled by the observations that during peacetime industrial market economies display recurrent, large fluctuations in output and employment over relatively short time periods. Not uncommon are changes as large as 10 percent within only a couple of years. These observations are considered puzzling because of the associated movements in labor's marginal product are small.

These observations should not be puzzling, for they are what standard economic theory predicts. For the United States, in fact, given people's ability and willingness to intertemporally and intratemporally substitute consumption and leisure and given the nature of the changing production possibility set, it would be puzzling if the economy did not display these large fluctuations in output and employment with little associated fluctuations in the marginal product of labor. (Prescott, 1986, 9)

Prescott's argument is based on the premise that macroeconomic phenomenon can be understood in terms of the behavior of the representative agent. Many economists take this premise for granted even if they do not entirely accept RBC. That is why they take "micro foundations" so seriously in macroeconomics.

Some economists have explicitly criticized the standard approach based on the representative agent. Kirman (1992), for example, in his paper "Whom or What Does the Representative Individual Represent?" argues as follows:

There is simply no direct relation between individual and collective behavior.... Trying to explain the behavior of a group by that of one individual is constraining. The sum of the behavior of simple economically plausible individuals may generate complicated dynamics, whereas constructing one individual whose behavior has these dynamics may lead

GDP

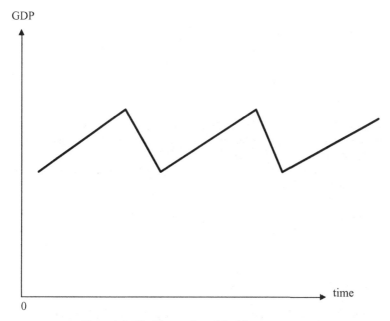

0

time

Figure 1.2. The Fluctuation of the Macroeconomy

to that individual having very unnatural characteristics. . . . In particular, I will argue that heterogeneity of agents may, in fact, help to save the standard model. . . . The way to develop appropriate microfoundations for macroeconomics is not to be found by starting from the study of individuals in isolation, but rests in an essential way on studying the aggregate activity resulting from the direct interaction between different individuals. (Kirman, 1992, 117–136)

Suppose that the macroeconomy fluctuates as shown in Figure 1.2. The standard approach attempts to explain these fluctuations by constructing a microeconomic model that produces similar fluctuations under appropriate aggregative shocks. It means that the behavior of the representative economic agent facing such shocks resembles Figure 1.2. To understand the point, consider the consumption of durable goods. If durability of consumables *were* constant, and if the timing of purchases of such consumables *were* synchronized, then *aggregate* consumption may be explained by the standard approach based on the representative agent. However, even in this simple example, the assumptions are actually too unrealistic. In many cases, as Kirman (1992) argues, the requirement that the microeconomic behavior mimics that of the macroeconomy is too harsh and constraining. We must begin our analysis on the assumption that the behavior of macroeconomy and that of microeconomic agent do not mutually correspond.

Summers (1991) made a similar point in his critical study of empirical macroeconomics. He took up the influential works of Hansen and Singleton (1982, 1983). Their works resulted in the rejection of a particular relationship between consumption and asset prices. Summers pointed out that although the two authors took the estimated parameters seriously, they may have rejected the representation of the household sector by one consumer with an additively separable utility function and constant relative risk aversion.

Davis, Haltiwanger, and Schuh (1996), in their study of job creation and destruction, made a similar point. On business cycles, they argue as follows:

> Prevailing interpretations of business cycles stress the role of aggregate shocks and downplay the connection between cycles and the restructuring of industries and jobs. Several aspects of gross job flow dynamics do not fit comfortably with prevailing views. Rather, the empirical evidence points to the need for a richer view of business cycles that highlights their connection with the restructuring process. (p. 83) . . .
>
> The focus on aggregate shocks leads economists to adopt a macroeconomic framework characterized by representative producers and consumers. That is, the production side of the economy is modeled as one firm whose economic behavior is thought to represent the average of all firms. Likewise, the consumption side of the economy is modeled as one household whose economic behavior represents the average of all households. This framework typically abstracts from differences in business cycle behavior among households and sectors, and among employers within sectors. (p. 85)

Why is the theory based on the representative agent wrong? Because micro agents differ so much. To demonstrate these differences, Davis and colleagues show employment growth rate distributions at (1) two-digit industry level and at (2) plant level. They are reproduced here as Figures 1.3 and 1.4, respectively. The distribution of industry-level growth rates is highly concentrated (Figure 1.3). This fits comfortably with a standard macroeconomic framework (RBC) that is built on the representative agent and stresses aggregate shocks. However, Figure 1.4 uncovers the enormous variance of *plant-level* growth rates (note Figures 1.3 and 1.4 are of the same scale). It demonstrates that the apparent high concentration of growth rates based on aggregated data is deceptive. In reality, there is a great variance among micro agents or units. Given these observations, Davis, Haltiwanger, and Schuh (1996) criticize the theories of representative consumers and producers and draw the conclusion that we need "a richer view of business cycles that highlights their connection with the restructuring process."

Now, the major reason these criticisms have failed to change the minds of many economists and lead them to abandon the assumption of the representative agent is, we suspect, that if it is abandoned, there is no alternative unifying principle or method to handle such complex situations with many heterogeneous agents. This book explains that there are, in fact, such principles and methods that fit the purpose of macroeconomics. Generally, the fundamental method we advocate in this book is an approach based on statistical physics and combinatorial stochastic processes.

The point that the behavior of a macro system cannot be directly inferred from the behavior of a micro unit is common knowledge in other disciplines, particularly in natural sciences. In physics, no one denies the law of motion

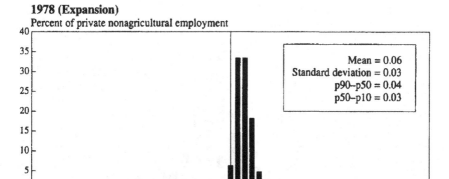

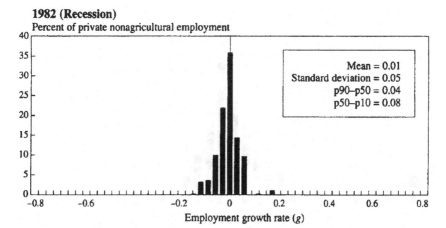

Figure 1.3. Two-Digit Industry-Level Growth-Rate Distributions: 1978–1982.
Source: Davis S J, Haltiwanger J C, and Schuh S (1996), 88.
Note: (p90–p50) is the 90th employment percentile minus the 50th employment percentile. (p50–p10) is the 50th employment percentile minus the 10th employment percentile.

The growth-rate distributions show the number of occurrences of each observed employment rate weighted by each industry's employment. The bars thus indicate the share of employment associated with each rate.

In this figure, the growth rate (g) is measured as the change in employment divided by the average of current and lagged employment. (Technical Appendix.)

for a micro unit; however the law does not really help our understanding of *macro* system, which consists of a large number of micro units such as atoms or molecules. In his classic lecture *"What is Life?"* Schrödinger (1944), a physicist and one of the founders of the quantum mechanics, made the following observation:

... we know all atoms to perform all the time a completely disorderly heat motion, which, so to speak, opposes itself to their orderly behaviour and does not allow the events that happen between a small number of atoms to enrol themselves according to any recognizable

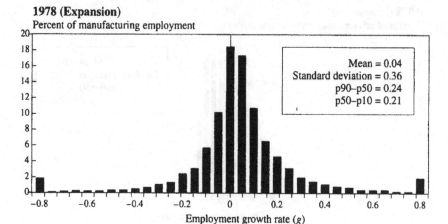

1978 (Expansion)

Percent of manufacturing employment

Mean = 0.04
Standard deviation = 0.36
p90–p50 = 0.24
p50–p10 = 0.21

Employment growth rate (g)

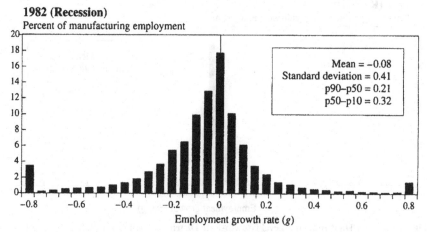

1982 (Recession)

Percent of manufacturing employment

Mean = –0.08
Standard deviation = 0.41
p90–p50 = 0.21
p50–p10 = 0.32

Employment growth rate (g)

Figure 1.4. Plant-Level Employment Growth-Rate Distributions: 1978 and 1982.
Source: Davis S J, Haltiwanger J C, and Schuh S (1996), 100.
Note: (p90–p50) is the 90th employment percentile minus the 50th employment percentile. (p50–p10) is the 50th employment percentile minus the 10th employment percentile.

The growth-rate distributions show the number of occurrences of each observed employment rate weighted by each plant's employment. The bars thus indicate the share of employment associated with each rate.

In this figure, the growth rate (g) is measured as the change in employment divided by the average of current and employment. (Technical Appendix.)

laws. Only in the co-operation of an enormously large number of atoms do statistical laws begin to operate and control the behaviour of these *assemblées* with an accuracy increasing as the number of atoms involved increases. It is in that way that the events acquire truly orderly features. All the physical and chemical laws that are known to play an important part in the life of organisms are of this statistical kind. (Schrödinger, 1944, 10, p. xii)

Schrödinger pointed out that we must understand "life" this way, which has proved correct. Recall the old Marshall saying that "the Mecca of the economist lies in economic biology rather than in economic dynamics."

The behavior of a micro unit is always subject to stochastic fluctuations, and it is beyond our capacity to pursue its exact behavior. An individual firm or household is like an atom. Evidence presented in Table 1.1 and Figures 1.3 and 1.4 illustrates that microeconomic behavior is very diverse. Despite such diverse and erratic micro behavior, we can expect the orderly behavior of a macro system consisting of a large number of micro units – the law for macro systems is statistical. Schrödinger's observation applies not only to physics and chemistry but also to economics. This book explains how fruitfully an approach based on statistical physics can be applied to macroeconomics.

The reader might think that stochastic (difference) equations are common tools in economics, and that the stochastic terms in these equations are meant to represent diversity of microeconomic agents. The standard method is, however, that we first consider microeconomic behavior of the representative agent, and then translate essentially microeconomic equations into macroeonomic equations simply by adding stochastic terms. The standard approach focuses on means and variances of the variables of interest in such a model. RBC is a primary example. We argue that this standard approach is invalid because macroeconomic regularities or statistical laws which Schrödinger noted emerge *not* from microeconomic behavior of the representative agent but from *stochastic interactions of a large number of agents*. Note that in the standard approach, the expected values of the variables we focus on usually represent the assumed microeconomic behaviors. We need a different approach. We also note that it is often necessary to look at *sample paths* and *probability distributions*, not just *moments*, of stochastic variables to understand the behavior of the macroeconomy.

Consider the economy consisting of many *different* Ramsey consumers once again. The economy is so complex that it is hopeless to describe the micro behavior of all the consumers. Luckily, we do not need to do this to know the behavior of the macroeconomy. At each moment in time, as a result of the Ramsey-type optimization subject to shocks to economic constraints and utility functions, some households increase their consumption while others lower theirs, as shown in Figure 1.1. It is then useful to classify the types of household, and to assume that household types change in a stochastic way. The number of types is arbitrary as long as it is countable.

From the beginning, we resort to a stochastic approach. We can usefully classify the types or states of microeconomic agents, and then analyze stochastic transitions of such types or states to draw important implications for the economy as a whole. Specifically, we can use continuous-time Markov chains or *jump Markov processes*. The models have countable states and are specified by sets of transition rates. As explained in Chapter 2, transition rates can be nonlinear functions of state variables, called state-dependent transition rates. Models with

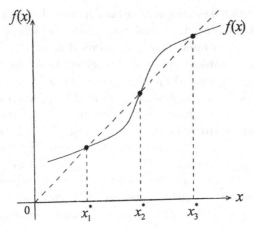

Figure 1.5. Multiple Equilibria
Note: x^*, which satisfies $f(x) = x$, is taken as "equilibrium"; see main text.

state-dependent transition rates may produce multiple stationary states and yield information on fluctuations about equilibria.

To get an idea of the difference between the standard approach and the one described in this book, let us study a model with multiple stationary states. The notion of multiple equilibria is common in economics. Suppose there are two stable equilibria x_1^* and x_3^* as drawn in Figure 1.5. Economists have discussed the selection of equilibrium in such a situation. Krugman (1991), for example, studies this problem in his "History vs. Expectations." In the stochastic approach, the case of multiple equilibria in deterministic models corresponds to the situation in which the potential has two local minima. The economy then stochastically fluctuates between x_1^* and x_3^* as shown in Figure 1.6. The problem of equilibrium selection then disappears; instead, the model provides a possible explanation of fluctuations of the economy (Aoki, 1995). This model will be explained in Chapter 4.

It is important to recognize that the microeconomic behavior has no resemblance to the macroeconomic fluctuations shown in Figure 1.6. Often, a mere aggregation of a large number of stochastic movements of micro units produces a certain macro fluctuation or pattern with no similarity to those of micro units. In such a case, we cannot deduce the behavior of the macro entity from that of the micro unit. This applies not only to natural sciences but also to economics. To study a system consisting of a large number of units such as the macroeconomy, we need a different approach.

To provide micro foundations for macroeconomics, one need not explicitly analyze optimizing behavior of individual agents. Instead one must use proper statistical methods suitable for the study of the macro system consisting of a large number of fluctuating micro units. We maintain that the so-called micro foundations for macroeconomics are not true micro foundations, but simply misguided.

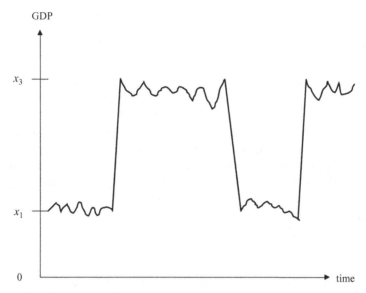

Figure 1.6. The Fluctuation of the Macroeconomy Corresponding to "Multiple Equilibria" in Figure 1.5

The purpose of this book is to advance and explain this new stochastic approach to macroeconomics and financial markets. Chapter 2 introduces the reader to these mathematical methods. The basic model used throughout this book is the *jump Markov process*. In the remaining sections of this chapter, we summarize the major results of our analyses from Chapters 3 through 10.

Equilibrium as Distribution – The Role of Demand in Macroeconomics

Chapter 3 proposes a new concept of equilibrium. We have seen that micro behaviors of individual households and firms are very diverse. To analyze the macroeconomy, we must explicitly consider these microeconomic fluctuations. As a consequence, we have distribution of responses by microeconomic agents as an equilibrium rather than a unique response by a representative agent. This, in turn, means that we have a probability distribution, not a simple "point" for macroeconomic equilibrium. In the standard analysis, because macroeconomic equilibrium is represented by a point in some space or set, its evolution is described by an ordinary differential equation. In contrast, our approach requires a partial differential equation to describe evolution of a macroeconomic equilibrium over time. This is the Chapman–Kolmogorov equation or master equation, to be explained in Chapter 2.

Chapter 3 explains that to give proper microeconomic foundations for macroeconomics is to specify transition rates for jump Markov process.

Specifically, we take up a simple binary choice model as an example of a macro model, and explain that the so-called Boltzmann–Gibbs type transition rates have sound microeconomic foundations. We also explain that the seemingly special binary (or more generally discrete) choice models are actually consistent with sophisticated (stochastic) dynamic optimization commonly used in economics. We clarify the difference between the standard approach and our approach by way of considering the well-known search model of Diamond (1982). An important difference is that in the model with multiple equilibria, as shown in Figure 1.5, the problem of *equilibrium selection* does not arise in our approach.

Chapter 3 also explains why aggregate demand affects total output. The standard approach focuses on price/wage rigidity. New Keynesian Economics (Mankiw and Romer 1991) is a primary example of such an approach. The explanation in this book is fundamentally different.

We begin with the observation that productivity differs across sectors/firms in the economy. Salter (1960), Mortensen (2003), and others have long acknowledged this fact. We show that productivity differential is not a puzzle, but a *necessity* in the macroeconomy. Following the method of statistical physics, we demonstrate that *in equilibrium*, the distribution of production factors across sectors/firms with different productivity is of the Boltzmann–Gibbs type:

$$\frac{n_i}{N} = \frac{e^{-\frac{Nc_i}{D}}}{\sum\limits_{i=1}^{s} e^{-\frac{Nc_i}{D}}}, \qquad i = 1, \ldots, s$$

where n_i is the amount of production factor used in sector i, N is its total endowment, c_i is the productivity coefficient in sector i, and D is the aggregate demand. The Boltzmann–Gibbs distribution means that when the aggregate demand, D, is high, production factors are mobilized to higher productivity. Okun (1973) makes a similar point, saying that workers climb a "ladder" of productivity in a "high-pressure economy."

Our notion of equilibrium is akin to what Tobin (1972) calls "stochastic macro-equilibrium." He argues that

(it is) stochastic, because random intersectoral shocks keep individual labor markets in diverse states of disequilibrium; macro-equilibrium, because the perpetual flux of particular markets produces fairly definite aggregate outcomes (Tobin, 1972, 9).

By way of affecting the transition rates of production factors, the real aggregate demand affects "stochastic macro-equilibrium," and consequently, the level of total output. We maintain that this is the proper microeconomic foundation for Keynes's principle of effective demand.

Uncertainty Trap, Policy Ineffectiveness, and Long Stagnation of the Macroeconomy

History shows us that the economy can be trapped in long stagnation. In the nineteenth century, the British economy suffered from the Great Depression for almost a quarter of century (1873–96). The Great Depression in the 1930s attacked the entire world. And since the beginning of the 1990s, the Japanese economy has stagnated for more than a decade. In every episode, various policies were discussed and experimented with. Yet the economy did not easily revive, and fell into a long stagnation. Certainly, in each case, there must have been policy mistakes. Granted, it appears that once the economy is trapped in a deep depression, the effectiveness of standard policy measures weakens.

In Chapter 4, we focus on a particular factor – *uncertainty*. Using a simple binary choice model introduced in Chapter 3, we show that great uncertainty *necessarily* weakens the effectiveness of macroeconomic policy, and that the macroeconomy may be stuck in "bad equilibrium." We certainly do not recommend that policy makers discard mainstream macroeconomics textbooks. However, in our view, the economy once facing great uncertainty *does* present economists and policy makers with real difficulties that the textbook remedies cannot easily handle. We extensively use mathematical methods explained in Chapter 2. Here, we briefly summarize the main results.

The standard analysis in macoeconomics begins with microeconomic experiments on the assumption of the representative agent. Suppose, for example, that the authority cut the interest rate. The microeconomic theory tells us that for the representative household or firm, a lower interest rate raises the optimal level of investment. Translating this result to macroeconomic analysis, one conjectures that *ceteris paribus*, *aggregate* investment would increase. This kind of analysis, including the IS/LM analysis, gives economists and policy makers sound guidance so long as the degree of uncertainty facing the economy is limited.

However, when the degree of uncertainty becomes significant, we must depart from the representative agent assumption, and seriously consider that the macroeconomy consists of a large number of economic agents. In this case, a stochastic approach is necessary. The combinatory aspect of the system plays a crucial role in the analysis of any system – either physical or social – consisting of a large number or entities. Though the standard economic analysis entirely ignores it, we show that it has important implications for macroeconomics. Specifically, the effectiveness of policy necessarily weakens as the degree of uncertainty rises. One might call this problem "uncertainty trap."

For example, once the economy is trapped into bad equilibrium as the degree of uncertainty rises, monetary policy becomes ineffective. Many economists argue that the Bank of Japan (BOJ) facing the zero nominal interest rate bound can still lower the real interest by generating inflationary expectations. In our model, it would induce more economic agents to find a shift from "bear" to "bull" advantageous. When uncertainty is insignificant, it certainly helps. This is a normal situation. However, when the combinatorial aspect cannot be ignored as the degree of uncertainty rises, policies that are effective in normal circumstances may not help.

In this way, *uncertainty* plays the key role. When uncertainty is insignificant, the economy fluctuates around the (unique) "natural" equilibrium, and policies are effective. In contrast, when the degree of uncertainty rises above a critical level, the economy may be trapped in a "bad" equilibrium, and standard macroeconomic policies *necessarily* become ineffective.

It is generally agreed that the performance of the postwar economy is better than that in the prewar period. Baily (1978) argues that better safety nets provided by the government in the postwar period have contributed to this outcome. Our analysis suggests that uncertainty is indeed a serious hindrance to the macroeconomy, and that once the economy faces great uncertainty, then the textbook remedies may not so readily work as we hope. Indeed, the "uncertainty trap" is what distinguishes "*depression*" from normal "*recession.*" We apply this analysis to the long stagnation of the Japanese economy during the 1990s, ineffectiveness of monetary policy in particular.

Slow Dynamics of Macro System: Inflexible Prices

The standard approach such as RBC is based on the premise that the microeconomic behavior of the optimizing agent mimics dynamics of the macroeconomy. In Chapter 1, we explain that this premise is wrong, and that the macro and micro behaviors are fundamentally different.

Chapter 5 focuses on a particular aspect of the macroeconomy – the speed of adjustment. The premise of the standard approach is that rational economic agents must respond quickly to any change in economic environment. It is taken for granted that this micro behavior translates into the macroeconomy. Thus, one expects the speed of adjustment in the economy as a whole also to be fast in normal conditions. In this way, the standard approach does not make any distinction between the speed of adjustment of micro agent and that of the macro economy.

Consider "prices" for example. Since the publication of Keynes's *General Theory* (1936), "inflexibile" or "rigid" prices have been always a focal point of macroeconomics. Modigliani (1944) was one of the first economists who coined the proposition that what distinguishes the Keynesian economics from the neoclassical economics is the assumption of inflexible prices (to be precise, rigid nominal wages in his case).

Many economists take inflexibility of prices as a sign of "irrationality." Aside from monopoly power or an institutional barrier such as regulation, healthy market forces should make prices flexible. In Chapter 5, we will explain that slow changes in price are a *necessity* in the macroeconomy. Slow dynamics is not confined to prices. It is, in fact, a generic property of any complex macro system.

To explain the "sluggish" behavior of the macroeconomy, Chapter 5 introduces the notion of "tree" and ultrametrics. The macroeconomy is composed of many different agents or sectors. It is organized into hierarchical layers, and has a tree structure whereby leaves of trees are basic clusters of agents. We show that the dynamics of a large system with such a structure is *necessarily* sluggish. The macroeconomy is a typical example. We then apply this analysis to dynamics of prices. We show that given input–output structure of the macroeconomy, there is no mystery in sluggish behavior of prices.

In Chapter 5, we explain another reason for slow dynamics in the macroeconomy. In the standard approach, it is assumed that a rational economic agent can swiftly find and move to his first-best or global optimum. This assumption may hold true, as a first approximation, for a well-organized financial market. However, in "real" economic activities, agents always face much more complex decision-making problems. Often the problem is not given in advance. To find the problem is, in fact, an important part of economic activity. Trial and error becomes a source of slow dynamics. Chapter 5 formalizes this idea.

Business Cycles

Chapter 6 analyzes a stochastic model of business cycles. Fluctuations of aggregate economic activities or business cycles have long attracted economists' attention. A glance at traditional literature such as Haberler (1964) reveals that all kinds of theories had already been advanced by the end of the 1950s, and the theme of business cycles remains prominent in macroeconomics today.

As typified by the RBC theory by Kydland and Prescott (1982), and the endogenous competitive business cycle theory by Grandmont (1985), economists often explain business cycle fluctuations as a direct outcome of the behavior of *individual agents*. This approach has been the standard in mainstream economics over the last 30 years or so. The more strongly one wishes to interpret aggregate fluctuations as something "rational" or "optimal," the more likely one is led to this essentially microeconomic approach. The aim of such an approach is to explain fluctuations as responses of the *representative agent* to changes in its economic environments. The consumer's intertemporal substitution, for example, is a device for achieving this goal.

Lucas (1987) is a model of this approach. On the basis of the representative agent assumption, he showed that, if aggregate consumption fluctuations of the magnitude experienced since World War II were eliminated completely, this would raise the level of utility by only $8.50 per person! Thus, he concludes that "economic instability at the level we have experienced since the Second World War is a minor problem."[2]

As we have argued, however, we need a different approach in macroeconomics. We must take seriously the fact that the economy consists of a large

---

[2] Fair (1989) in his review of Lucas (1987) points out that quite a different picture emerges when one considers a model in which business cycles are caused by demand failures. Referring to the 1980–82 recession, he estimates that, had real GNP grown at an annual rate of 3.0 percent from 1979 on, about $560 billion more in output would have been produced in the three years. He thus concludes that "this is a large lunch for everyone, about $2400 per person."

number of agents or sectors. In the real economy, perhaps agents intertemporally maximize their respective objective functions subject to constraints. However, their economic environments keep changing because of various idiosyncratic shocks. Plainly, an outcome of interactions of a large number of agents facing such incessant idiosyncratic shocks cannot be described by a response of the representative agent. Welfare calculation based on the representative agent as done by Lucas (1987) has no foundation.

We must explicitly consider the distribution of microeconomic behavior, which calls for a model of stochastic processes. In a seminal work, Slutzky (1937) proposed such a stochastic approach. Chapter 6 follows his lead to build a stochastic model of fluctuations. The model in Chapter 6 is a simple quantity adjustment model composed of a large number of sectors or agents. We use this simple model to demonstrate two main points. First, fluctuations of the aggregate economy endogenously arise as a natural outcome of the interactions of many agents/sectors. Second, the level of the aggregate economic activity depends on the structure of demand.

To obtain these results, we assume that productivities differ across sectors in the economy. In the standard analysis, resources are assumed to be instantaneously reallocated to attain the equality of productivity across sectors. Here, we explicitly assume that a reallocation of production factors takes time because thresholds for a change in behavior differ across agents, and as a result differences in productivity across sectors/firms persist. Resources are stochastically allocated to sectors in response to excess demand or supply. For simplicity, we assume that there is only one production factor, which we call labor. At each moment in time, there is either excess demand or excess supply in every sector, and this gives a signal for a reallocation of labor among sectors.

Suppose there are K sectors in the economy. We assume that sector i has productivity coefficient, c_i, which is exogenously given and fixed. To be specific, sectors are arranged in the decreasing order of productivity ($c_i > c_j$ if $i < j$). As explained in Chapter 3, given heterogeneous microeconomic objectives and constraints, thresholds for change in strategy differ across sectors/firms. Thus, differences in productivity among sectors persist. It takes time for productivities to equalize among sectors. Meanwhile, responding to excess demand or supply, the level of labor input n_i in *some* sectors changes, and the macroeconomic situation also changes.

The same excess demand or supply brings about a different reaction from each sector (or firm) because each faces an idiosyncratic economic environment or constraint. For the same reason, we do not know when the sector facing disequilibrium "reacts." It is stochastic. The notion of "holding time" (to be explained in Chapter 6) models the timing of stochastic reaction. We make only a reasonable yet weak assumption that a sector/firm facing excess demand possibly raises its production level, and *vice versa*.

When sector i changes its production level n_i, it affects both the aggregate output $Y = \sum_i c_i n_i$, and the sectoral demand pattern $s_i Y$ where s_i is sector i's demand share. In this way, the size of each sector n_i and the total output Y change stochastically over time. We can explore the behavior of the economy out of equilibrium, or of *sample paths* of the model.

Despite its simplicity, the stochastic behavior of the model turns out to be rather complex. To gain insight, we analyze a simple two-sector model. It can then be shown that, given differences in productivity and demand shares across sectors, *aggregate fluctuations arise endogenously out of simple quantity adjustments.*

Next, we consider the stationary probability distribution for the total output or GDP in the two-sector model. It can be shown that the expected value of aggregate economic activity depends on the pattern of demand. Specifically, the higher the share of demand for a high productivity sector, the higher the expected value of aggregate economic activity. Note that the level of aggregate economic activity is indeterminate in the equilibrium of a corresponding deterministic model because of its linearity. In a stochastic model, the higher the share of demand for high productivity sector, the more likely it is that the sector will face excess demand and raise its production level. Therefore, the higher the share of demand for high productivity sector, the greater the externality generated by an increase in the size of a sector, and consequently the higher the expected value of total output. This result provides a new perspective to *the principle of effective demand.*

We have seen that in our simple two-sector model (1) the sample path exhibits cycles or oscillations near the equilibrium, and (2) the share of demand for the high productivity sector is greater, the higher the expected value of aggregate economic activity. It is extremely difficult, however, to analyze the multi-sector model explicitly. We check the robustness of the two propositions which we analytically derived for the two-sector model by simulation for a K sector model ($K > 2$).

The simulations have confirmed the two major results obtained for the two-sector model. Beyond that, they also demonstrate the role of allocative disturbances in business cycles as emphasized by Davis, Haltiwanger, and Schuh (1996).

The real business cycle theory by Kydland and Prescott (1982) and the endogenous competitive business cycle theory by Grandmont (1985) are based on the representative agent. In those models, fluctuations of the macroeconomiy arise directly from behavior of the representative agent. However, the assumptions of particular values of crucial parameters or nonlinearity are arbitrary and devoid of any empirical support. These theories allegedly have the merits of showing that aggregate fluctuations are compatible with the Walrasian equilibrium. Throw out the obsession with the Walrasian equilibrium, and we realize that there is actually no merit in basing such a theory on the assumption of a representative agent.

The macroeconomy consists of a large number of heterogeneous economic agents. Aggregate fluctuations necessarily arise from interactions of these economic agents. Because of differences in productivity across sectors, demand plays an important role in the determination of the average level of total output. Because our model is extremely simple, we believe that the results are generic.

Labor Market Dynamics – A New Look at the Natural Unemployment and Okun's Law

Chapter 7 analyzes labor market dynamics by extending the simulation model of Chapter 6. There is a large body of literature devoted to labor market dynamics, including Blanchard and Diamond (1990), Mortensen (1989), and Pissarides (2000). In the existing literature, however, unemployed workers are differentiated at best by their reservation wages in search models, or by the length of unemployment. Their job experiences, human capitals, or geographical locations are not satisfactorily incorporated into models. Differences in job opportunities are not satisfactorily modeled either. As a consequence, *mismatches* between job opportunities and qualifications of job seekers can not be fully analyzed in such models.

Jump Markov process is an ideal tool to analyze these problems. In this chapter, we analyze labor market dynamics by adding pools of laid-off workers to the model presented in Chapter 6. We assume that there is unemployment. To present a simple model, we ignore quits and on-the-job searches, and assume that only the unemployed get jobs.

Signs of excess demand for good and services are used as a proxy for a profitability signal for each sector that wants to change its size of labor force accordingly. Firms with negative excess demand for their goods fire workers immediately. Firms with positive excess demands wish to hire workers, post vacancy signs, and go into overtime. If a sector has already posted a vacancy sign, then it hires one unit of labor and returns to normal time. Because the model is a continuous-time Markov Chain, only one sector can fulfill its wishes. Thus, there are asynchronous processes of firing and hiring.

Now, a vacancy may be filled from its own pool of laid-off workers, or from pools of related industries. When a sector hires a worker it does so randomly from a pool of workers of different clusters suitably weighted by the "ultrametric" distance explained in Chapter 5. This feature of the model is implemented by making clusters of different types of unemployed workers into a tree, and using ultrametrics to measure similarities of workers in different clusters. The clusters or sub-pools of unemployed have different probabilities of being picked. The highest probability is for the pool of the workers who are laid off from that sector. This corresponds to an observed fact that firms often recall laid-off workers as they become profitable again.

The model is similar to that in Chapter 6, but introduces unemployment and vacancy. Using this model, we examine three important stylized facts about the labor market: the natural unemployment, Okun's law, and procyclical productivity.

First, our simulations demonstrate that the Beveridge Curve – the negative relationship between unemployment and vacancy – depends on the level of total output, which, in turn, depends on the patterns of demand. This means that we cannot so clearly separate the "structural" or "natural" unemployment from unemployment due to demand deficiency. To put it differently, *the natural unemployment cannot be so clearly defined as we commonly think.*

Second, our simulations generate Okun's law – the relationship between changes in GDP and the unemployment rate. The value of the Okun coefficient, 3, has been a kind of puzzle because the existence of such increasing returns in the economy as a whole is questionable. Okun (1973) argues that, in addition to cyclical productivity change in each sector / firm, sectoral reallocation of resources plays an important role in explaining Okun's law. Our simulation analysis demonstrates that sectoral reallocation of resources among sectors with different productivity may indeed explain the apparent increasing returns implied by Okun's law.

Finally, our simulations demonstrate that the combination of productivity dispersion and demand shifts across sectors produces highly procyclical productivity in the economy as a whole.

Demand Saturation–Creation and Economic Growth

It is a standard view that demand, if it affects output in the short run, does not affect aggregate output in the long run. Economic growth is determined by supply factors. Chapter 8 explains a new model of economic growth by Aoki and Yoshikawa (2002). The model demonstrates that demand plays an essential role even in the process of the long-run economic growth.

In the standard literature, the fundamental factor restraining economic growth is diminishing returns to capital in production or R&D technology. Our model suggests that "saturation of demand" is another important factor restraining growth. In the less mathematical literature and casual discussions, the idea of "demand saturation" has been popular. Every businessperson would acknowledge saturation of demand for an individual product. In fact, if you plot a time series of production of any representative product such as steel or automobiles, or production in any industry, against time, then with few exceptions you will obtain an S-shaped curve.

The diffusion of such consumer durables as refrigerators, televisions, cars, and personal computers tell us that deceleration of growth comes mainly from saturation of demand rather than from diminishing returns in technology. Growth of production of a commodity or in an individual industry is bound to slow because demand grows fast in the early stage but eventually, out of necessity, slows.

Thus, the demand for some products grows much more rapidly than the GDP, whereas for others it grows much more slowly. Products/industries face different income elasticities of demand. The celebrated Engel's Law based on saturation of demand for food is one example.

Unfortunately, the existing literature on growth abstracts largely from this important fact that products/industries obey the law of demand saturation, and that each product/industry experiences a typical S-shaped life cycle. This, of course, is not to say that the appearance of new products and the disappearance of old ones have not been modeled. The so-called "creative destruction" and "quality ladder" literature (e.g., Grossman and Helpman, 1991; Aghion and Howitt, 1992) has analyzed such phenomena in growth models. However, in this line of research the old products disappear only through the introduction of new products. Unless new products appear, demand for the existing products remains the same. Therefore, it is possible for the economy to keep growing if it succeeds in raising productivity in the production of the existing commodities.

In sharp contrast, with saturation of demand, a raise in productivity of the "mature" products will not help to sustain economic growth. Put another way, in the existing R&D-based growth models the economy can keep growing if, for instance, the automobile industry keeps raising the quality of cars; whereas in the present model it cannot, because the demand for cars will become saturated in spite of quality improvement.

Similarly the product life cycle in the existing literature (e.g., Grossman and Helpman, 1991) is based on a production technology life cycle, while in our model it is based on a demand life cycle. In contrast to the "creative destruction" that occurs in the existing literature, growth in the demand for the existing commodities in our analysis of "saturation" necessarily slows whether or not new commodities appear. It would be absurd to argue that the growth in the demand for food decelerated, as Engel found, because manufactured products appeared; nor did the demand for cars approach its ceiling because personal computers were invented. Rather, the law of demand saturation endures.

Within the same industry, new and old products are often close substitutes, for example black/white and color TVs, or personal computers of different vintage; and old products gradually disappear as new ones appear. Thus, the "creative destruction" story nicely fits the growth of an *industry*. The R&D race among competing firms as it is modeled in the standard endogenous growth literature certainly plays an important role. Technical progress described in the existing literature concerns close substitutes, as those models explicitly state. However, as we argued above, the same story does not necessarily hold true for different industries. The model presented in Chapter 8 takes the logistic growth of an individual product/industry as a "stylized fact," and presents a formal model of growth built on this "stylized fact." An obvious implication of the logistic growth of an individual product/industry is that the economy enjoys high growth if it successfully keeps introducing new products or industries that temporarily enjoy a high growth in demand. In this model, innovation or "technical progress" leads to the introduction of new commodities or sectors that enjoy a high growth in demand, and by so doing sustains the economic growth of the economy as a whole.

It is important to recognize that the demand-creating innovation in our model is different from the standard total factor productivity (TFP), or an "upward shift" of the production function. In the standard "quality ladder" models and the "creative destruction" literature such as Grossman and Helpman (1991), Caballero and Jaffe (1993), and Young (1998), innovation or technical progress raises total factor productivity by replacing old commodities with new ones, simply because new commodities are assumed to have greater value than old ones. Again, whereas this seems to hold true for the commodities that are basically the same but of different vintages, it does not make much sense for wholly different products such as cars and personal computers. Personal computers do not necessarily command higher value than cars. In short, the standard literature models the dynamics of close substitutes, while the Aoki–Yoshikawa model stresses the importance of demand saturation and creation of wholly different products or industries.

Innovations in the economy facing the law of demand saturation contribute to growth in a way that is different from an "upward shift" in the production function. That TFP does not necessarily capture the significance of technological progress is pointed out by Gavin Wright:

The identification of 'technological progress' with changes in total-factor-productivity, or with the 'residual' in a growth-accounting framework, is so widely practised that many economists barely give it a passing thought, regarding the two as more-or-less synonymous and interchangeable.... Even with extensive quality adjustments, TFP is not generally a good index of technology. If a genuine change in technological potential occurs in a firm, an industry, a sector, or a country, in any plausible model this change will affect the mobilisation of capital and labour in whatever unit is involved. In the new equilibrium, inputs as well as outputs will have changed; the ratio between these may convey little if any useful information about the initiating change in technology. (Wright, 1997, 1562)

We share Wright's concern. The economy always mobilizes resources and accumulates capital whenever it finds goods or sectors for which demand grows rapidly. In fact, in the present model the elasticity of capital in the production function is equal to one (the so-called AK model). Therefore, the economy grows whenever capital accumulates. But capital accumulation is constrained by a saturation of demand. Innovation creates goods/sectors for which demand grows rapidly, elicits capital accumulation, and thereby ultimately sustains economic growth.

Innovation or technical progress in our model creates a major new product or industry that commands high growth of demand and thereby elicits capital accumulation and sustains economic growth. Schumpeter (1934), in his famous book *Theory of Economic Development*, distinguishes five types of innovations: (1) the introduction of a new good, (2) the introduction of a new production method, (3) the opening of a new market, (4) the conquest of a new source of supply of raw materials, and (5) the new organization of industry. His first and third types of innovations as an engine for growth seem to be most naturally interpreted in terms of the kind of model presented in Chapter 8.

Robert Solow emphasizes the importance of the "medium-run" analysis as a challenge to modern macroeconomics:

One major weakness in the core of macroeconomics as I have represented it is the lack of real coupling between the short-run picture and the long-run picture. Since the long-run and the short-run merge into one another, one feels they cannot be completely independent. There are some obvious, perfunctory connections: every year's realized investment gets incorporated in the long-run model. That is obvious. A more interesting question is whether a major episode in the growth of potential output can be driven from the demand side. (Solow, 1997, 231–2)

In short, the integration of the Keynes principle of effective demand for the short run and growth theory for the long run remains a central theme in macroeconomics. Our model to be explained in Chapter 8 may provide a constructive step toward solving this problem.

The Types of Investors and Stock Market

Chapter 9 examines a stock market by using a jump Markov process to model entries, exits, and switchings of trading rules by a large number of interacting participants in the market. The combinatory aspect plays an essential role in this model. We examine stationary distribution of clusters of agents by strategies. Potentially, the number of types of investors is infinite. However, when behaviors of market participants are positively correlated, a majority (about 92 percent) of the market participants can be shown to belong to two large groups of agents with two different trading rules. In other words, although market participants potentially have many different strategies, two dominant trading rules spontaneously emerge. Thus, contributions of the remaining 8 percent or so of participants can be ignored in examining the market behavior as a whole.

Given this result, we assume that there are two types of investors, *chartists* and *fundamentalists*. Market excess demand and price dynamics are examined in this framework. We show that the fluctuations of stock price become greater when chartists dominate than when fundamentalists are the majority in the market. Furthermore, we show a possibility for *power laws* with the exponent close to 3 for returns on stock. The significance of this result will be explained in Chapter 10.

Stock Prices and the Real Economy

The final chapter explores the difference between the asset market and the real economy. The standard approach attempts to explain asset prices based on the assumption of the representative agent. The so-called consumption-based asset pricing model is a primary example of such an approach. In Chapter 10, we argue once again that the representative agent assumption is fundamentally flawed. Drawing on the recent advancement of "econophysics" on financial markets, we argue that in contrast to the neoclassical view, there is in fact a wedge between financial markets and the real economy.

In the neoclassical macroeconomic theory, the following relationship between the rate of change in consumption, C, and the return on capital, r, must hold in equilibrium:

$$-\left[\frac{u''(C)\,C}{u'(C)}\right]\left(\frac{\dot{C}}{C}\right) = \frac{1}{\eta(C)}\left(\frac{\dot{C}}{C}\right) = r - \delta$$

Here, the elasticity of intemporal substitution η is defined as

$$\frac{1}{\eta(C)} = -\frac{u''(C)\,C}{u'(C)} > 0.$$

This equation says that the rate of change in consumption over time is determined by η and the difference between the rate of return on capital, r and the consumer's subjective discount rate, δ. This equation, called the *Euler equation*, is derived as the necessary condition of the representative consumer's maximization of the Ramsey utility sum.

Within this framework, many economists have attempted to explain the "excess volatility" shown by Shiller (1981) and LeRoy and Porter (1981). Using the same representative agent model, Mehra and Prescott (1985) also presented the "equity premium puzzle." Their analyses all rest on the assumption that the rate of change in consumption (the real economy) and the asset return (financial market) are tightly linked by the above Euler equation. However, as we will explain in Chapter 10, the probability distributions of the growth rate of real variables such as real GDP and financial returns are fundamentally different. Specifically, it is now well established that the probability distribution of changes in stock prices r follows the following power law with the exponent $\alpha = 3$:

$$P(|r| > x) \propto x^{-\alpha}, \quad \alpha = 3.$$

On the other hand, the probability distribution of the growth rate of GDP, g, is exponential:

$$P(g) \propto \exp\left(-\gamma\,|g|\right).$$

This fact implies that *we cannot use the standard Euler equation based on the representative agent assumption for explaining asset prices.*

In Chapter 10, we use a particular type of model, a truncated Lévy flight, and show that power laws and exponential distribution emerge depending on parameters. Specifically, when the number of micro growth events within a period is small, exponential distribution can emerge. Conversely, when the number of micro growth events within a period is large, power-law distributions can emerge. Thus, given the model, to account for the stylized fact, we must assume that within a given period, the number of micro growth events is relatively small in the case of real economic activities, whereas it is large in the case of asset prices. Here, we must take this proposition as an assumption, and leave it for further research. However, we believe that we can reasonably argue that the frequency of multiplicative shocks is much higher for asset prices than for real micro economic activities. In conclusion, we have a good deal of empirical observations to reject the standard asset price model based on the representative consumer, and at the same time, a plausible theoretical reason to believe that the real economy and asset markets are different creatures.

Summing Up

Throughout this book, we advance the following propositions.

1. Micro behaviors of the representative agent do not mimic the behavior of the macroeconomy. Macroeconomic phenomena are the outcomes of interactions of a large number of economic agents such as households and firms.
2. Equilibrium in the macroeconomy is better described by a probability distribution than by a "point" in some space or set. Jump Markov process is a powerful tool to analyze dynamics of the macroeconomy. Partial differential equation (the Chapman–Kolmogorov equation) or master equation to be explained in Chapter 2 describes its time evolution.
3. Productivity always differs across sectors and firms in the economy. At each moment of time, we have a distribution of productivity across sectors or firms. This distribution of productivity depends on the level of aggregate demand. High aggregate demand mobilizes resources to high productivity sectors, and thereby raises the level of total output. Aggregate demand plays a role similar to temperature in physical system.
4. Uncertainty weakens the effectiveness of macroeconomic policies. The economy may lapse into the "uncertainty trap." It is the presence of great uncertainty that distinguishes "depression" from normal cyclical "recession."
5. "Sticky" prices/wages are often attributed to particular behavior of micro agents. However, such micro behaviors as menu costs are arbitrary. In fact, without any dubious assumption on micro behavior, sticky prices/wages generically emerge out of interactions of many agents/sectors in the economy with complex "tree" structure.
6. Sectoral reallocations of resources generate aggregate fluctuations or business cycles. Aggregate demand affects total output by way of mobilizing production factors. This is the proper microeconomic foundation for Keynes's principle of effective demand.

7. The Beveridge Curve – the relationship between unemployment and vacancy – depends on demand. This means that we cannot separate the "structural" or "natural" unemployment from unemployment due to demand deficiency. It, in turn, means that we cannot so clearly define the "natural" unemployment rate as we usually think.

8. The combination of productivity dispersion and cyclical demand shifts across sectors produces procyclical productivity in the economy as a whole. This naturally explains Okun's law.

9. Demand is important not only in the short run, but also in the process of economic growth. We argue that the crucial factor restraining economic growth is saturation of demand. The ultimate factor generating economic growth is demand-creating technical progress.

10. The asset market and the real economy are different creatures. Specifically, we obtain different probability distributions for financial returns and real economic growth, one a power law, the other an exponential. We provide an explanation for the generic mechanism that produces the difference between the two.

2

The Methods: Jump Markov Process and Random Partitions

The new approach to macroeconomics and financial markets outlined in Chapter 1 requires mathematical methods and concepts that are quite different from those commonly used in economics. This chapter introduces them to the reader.

Phenomena we can analyze using the methods explained here share one or more of the following three features:

1. A finite but large number of micro units or agents interact.
2. Different "types" of agents are present.
3. New and unknown types of agents, products, or technologies may appear; that is, the number of types of agents, products, or technologies may not be fixed nor known in advance.

To analyze these phenomena, we must depart from the standard methods of model construction and analysis in mainstream economics. Specifically, in this book, we formulate models as *continuous-time Markov chains*, also known as *jump Markov processes*. This approach gives us new insight, and often yields more information on the behavior of the macroeconomy than the traditional approach can offer.

The standard approach in "micro-founded" macroeconomics formulates complicated intertemporal optimization problems facing the representative agent. By so doing, it ignores interactions among nonidentical agents. Also, it does not examine a class of problems in which several types of agents simultaneously attempt to solve similar but slightly different optimization problems with slightly different sets of constraints. When these sets of constraints are not consistent, no truly optimal solutions exist.[1] In this book, we explicitly introduce and deal with a group of *heterogeneous* agents and focus on interactions among those belonging to different subgroups called clusters. Roughly speaking, we deemphasize the role of precise optimization of an individual unit while

---

[1] This is analogous to *frustrated systems* in condensed matter physics.

emphasizing the importance of proper aggregation for understanding the behavior of the macroeconomy.

The experiences in disciplines outside economics such as physics, population genetics, and combinatorial stochastic processes that deal with a large number of interacting entities amply demonstrate that details of specification of optimizing microeconomic agents (units) frequently diminish as the number of agents becomes very large. Only certain key features or parameters such as correlations among agents matter in determining aggregate behavior. Our models, analyses, and simulations in subsequent chapters will show that this observation or insight holds true in economics as well.

Two Classes of Methods

The methods we use generally fall into two broad categories. One deals with stochastic dynamics, and the other with the formation of clusters and random combinatorial analysis.

Stochastic Dynamics. *Stochastic dynamics* examines behavior of the model *over time* and extracts dynamic properties of stochastic models. The key method is to solve evolution equations for probability distribution such as the *Chapman–Kolmogorov equation*, or *master-equation*, and the *Fokker–Planck equation*. Stationary solutions of the master equation give us stationary or equilibrium behavior of the model. In some cases, we can rigorously solve the master equation. However, in many cases, we must resort to approximation. For example, we can use probability generating functions or use Taylor expansions to solve master equations. Or, in certain cases, we must be satisfied only with information on moments by solving cumulant generating functions. Fluctuations around equilibria are obtained by solving the associated Fokker–Planck equation.

Random Cluster Formation. The second class of methods, *random cluster formation*, deals with *combinatorial* aspects of agents forming clusters. This has to do with the sizes of configurations or state spaces. Using these methods, we can examine the size distribution or *frequency spectrum*.

2.1. First Class of Methods: Stochastic Dynamics

We first introduce the notion of states, or configurations, to dynamic phenomena under examination. To paraphrase Bellman (1961), states are sets of information that are sufficient to determine future time evolution of probability distributions of model configurations, given whatever information on external influences that affects model behavior. In Markov models, states may be subsets in some Euclidean spaces, or may be graphs. In some cases, states may be organized as *trees* which have hierarchical layers of branches and leaves. In Chapter 5, we will see that trees are, in fact, extremely useful for understanding "slow" dynamics of macro systems including the macroeconomy. Slow dynamics of prices is a primary example.

We start our modeling by specifying how interacting agents behave at the microeconomic level. Then we explain how clusters of agents behave by describing their behavior in terms of aggregated state variables. Stochastic description in terms of macroeconomic variables may involve deterministic laws and stochastic fluctuations around them.

Here is a simple example of state. Suppose agents have binary choices, or there are two types of agents. The two choices may be represented by 0 and 1, for example. The state of n agents is

$$\mathbf{s} = (s_1, s_2, \ldots, s_n)$$

where the choice by agent i is denoted by $s_i = 1$ or $s_i = 0$, $i = 1, 2, \ldots, n$. A set of all possible values of $\mathbf{s}$ is called *State* Space, S.

This vector $\mathbf{s}$ gives us a complete picture of who has chosen what. This is the microeconomic state at a point in time. We may then proceed to investigate the dynamic process of how agents revise their choices over time by considering rewards and costs facing agents, and possibly *externalities* among agents as well.

In many cases, we need not model the collection of agents with this much detail. For example, identities of agents who have chosen 1 may not be necessary if we care only about the fraction of agents with choice 1. Then, $\sum_i s_i/n$ is the information we need, and not individual s_i. At this level of description, the vector (n_1, n_2), where n_i is the number of agents with choice $i = 0, 1$, is a state vector. This state vector shows fractions of two types of agents.[2] In such a case, if the total number of agents n is fixed, then the scalar variable n_1 or the fraction $f_1 = n_1/n$ serves as the state variable. Then, we may proceed to specify how this "demographic" or fractional information of choices by agents evolves with time.

Jump Markov Process

We are interested in the time evolution of the states. In this book we choose the *jump Markov process* as our basic stochastic process, which neatly allows us to model dynamic economic phenomena involving agents making discrete choices such as either raising or cutting expenditures. In general, these choices may be subject to *externality* such as fashion, fads, bandwagon effects, or the state of the macroeconomy.

As we pointed out above, in many cases, *details of microeconomic behavior of an individual agent (namely, who did what) are irrelevant in macroeconomics.* Thus, most microeconomic behavior can be well approximated by a dynamic

---

[2] This is nothing but the empirical distribution in statistics. It is relevant to *exchangeable sequences*, in which the order of appearances of 1 and 0 is not relevant.

discrete choice model. Some readers might think that discrete choice models are too special with only very limited applications. That is not true. In Chapter 3, we will explain that discrete choice models are actually consistent with dynamic optimization commonly used in macroeconomics.

Now, we can think of groups of economic agents by associating types with the decisions or choices. Agents change their types when their decisions or behavioral rules are altered. In *open* models, agents of various types may enter or exit; the total number of agents is not fixed. These changes are stochastic, and may occur at any time, not necessarily at an equal time interval. In other words, agents act asynchronously.

The stochastic behavior of agents is modeled by specifying *transition rates* of continuous time (jump) Markov processes. A particular jump Markov process is determined uniquely when we specify transition rates of a countable number of states. After reaching a state, the process stays there for a random duration of time called *holding* or *sojourn time*.

Here is an example for which agents face binary choices (0 or 1). We can take the number of agents making choice 1, n, as the state variable. The state space is then $\{0, 1, 2, \ldots, N\}$, where N is the total number of agents in the model. It is exogenously fixed for simplicity of presentation. This model may be interpreted as a random walk, or birth–death, model in probability textbooks because n changes at most by ± 1 in a small time interval. The changes are interpreted as one agent changing his mind, taking a step to the right or left on a line.

Using the notation $q(a, b)$ to denote the transition rate from state a to state b, the transition rates from state n to $n \pm 1$ may be specified by

$$q(n, n+1) = (N-n)\eta_1 \left(\frac{n}{N}\right), \quad \text{and} \quad q(n, n-1) = n\eta_2 \left(\frac{n}{N}\right). \quad (2.1)$$

where η_1 and η_2 are some positive rate functions. Generally, parameters λ and μ are present as birth and death rates. Here, for simpler exposition, we set $\lambda = \mu = 1$.

The first equation in (2.1) specifies the transition rate of an increase in the number of agents making choice 1 from n to $n+1$ $(0 \leq n < N)$. It depends naturally on the number of agents currently making choice 0, that is $N - n$. The function $\eta_1(\frac{n}{N})$ considers the presence of externality. When η_1 is an increasing function of n/N, for example, it means that changes in economic decision from 0 to 1 are encouraged as the share of agents making choice 1 rises, and vice versa. Similarly, the second equation specifies the transition rate for state n to $n - 1$ $(1 \leq n \leq N)$. In this case, one person changes the strategy from 1 to 0. This transition rate then depends naturally on the number of agents currently making choice 1, that is n. With η's set to some constant, (2.1) becomes a well-known birth–death or entry–exit process in elementary probability textbooks.

Example: Pure Death Process with Immigration. *A simple example of the above is obtained by setting the first transition rate to a positive constant, and setting the* *second transition rate in (2.1) to $q(n, n-1) = \mu n$, where μ is some positive constant:*

$$q(n, n+1) = \alpha, \quad and \quad q(n, n-1) = \mu n.$$

This transition rate, together with the initial condition $n(0) = n_0$, defines a death process with immigration, that is entry from outside the model. Note that "immigration" from outside is, by definition, independent of n. This example will be used later several times for illustrating other technical points in this chapter. ∎

Example: A Business-Cycle Model. *Suppose there are N firms in the economy, and there are K levels of production. Each agent chooses one of K levels of output, presumably as a result of some optimization problem. Here for simpler explanation, we keep N fixed and set K to 2; that is, the level of output is either high, denoted by y^*, or low, denoted by y ($0 < y < y^*$). Call firms with high production rate type 1, and low production rate type 2. The total output of this economy, or GDP, is*

$$Y = ny^* + (N-n)y = N\left\{y + x(y^* - y)\right\}, \quad (2.2)$$

where $x = n/N$ is the fraction of type 1 firms in the economy. There are many firms, so x can be regarded as a real number ($0 \le x \le 1$). When x fluctuates between 0 and 1, so does Y between Ny and Ny^*.

The transition rates are given by (2.1). Suppose one type 2 firm decides to increase output from y to y^*. Over a short time interval, Δt, this happens with probability $q(n, n+1)\Delta t + o(\Delta t)$. When one type 1 firm decides to reduce output from y^* to y, this happens with probability $q(n, n-1)\Delta t + o(\Delta t)$ in the next Δt time interval.

Transition rates in this example are called state-dependent because the factors $\eta_1(x)$ and $\eta_2(x)$ in (2.1) represent such effects of externalities as introduced by Diamond (1982). Chapter 3 will explain a particular type of transition rate called the Boltzmann–Gibbs type. Then in Chapter 4, we will use this model again to analyze the role played by uncertainty in the macroeconomy. ∎

Setting Up the Master Equation

Once transition rates such as (2.1) are specified, a particular jump Markov process is defined. Its behavior over time is the dynamics for the joint probabilities of states. Dynamic equations can be derived by accounting for the probability fluxes into and out of a specified state over a small interval of time. To be specific, we use the *backward Chapman–Kolmogorov equation* to do this accounting of probability flows. The Chapman–Kolmogorov equation describes time evolution of probability distribution of states.

In this book, we call this equation *master equation* for short. This name is used in physics and other disciplines such as chemistry, biology, and ecology. It is an appropriate name because everything of importance we need to know about the dynamic behavior of models can be deduced from this equation. In particular we can derive dynamics for the first few moments of the state variable.

We call the dynamics for the first moment (mean) *aggregate dynamics* because it roughly corresponds to macroeconomic dynamics. We also derive the dynamics for the fluctuations of state variables about the means, that is the second moment (variance). It is given by *the Fokker–Planck equation*.

In generic form, the master equation is stated as a partial differential equation for the probability of state vector $\mathbf{s} \in S$:

$$\frac{\partial P(\mathbf{s}, t)}{\partial t} = \sum_{s'} q(\mathbf{s}', \mathbf{s}) P(\mathbf{s}', t) - P(\mathbf{s}, t) \sum_{s'} q(\mathbf{s}, \mathbf{s}'), \qquad (2.3)$$

where the sum is taken over all states $\mathbf{s}' \neq \mathbf{s}$, and $q(\mathbf{s}', \mathbf{s})$ is the transition rate from state $\mathbf{s}'$ to $\mathbf{s}$. The first term on the right-hand side of equation (2.3) sums up probability flows "into" state $\mathbf{s}$ from all the other states whereas the second term sums up the same probability flows "out of" state $\mathbf{s}$ to others. Thus, equation (2.3) simply says that the rate of *change in probability that a state is in* $\mathbf{s}$, *is nothing but the difference between the inflows of the probability fluxes into state* $\mathbf{s}$ *and the outflows*. Schematically, the master equation can be written as

$$\frac{\partial P(\mathbf{s}, t)}{\partial t} = \text{(Inflows of Probability Fluxes into } \mathbf{s})$$

$$- \text{ (Outflows of Probability Fluxes out of } \mathbf{s}).$$

Setting the left-hand side of equation (2.3) to zero yields the equation for *the stationary or equilibrium probabilities of states*; by definition, a change in probability distribution becomes zero. It is called the full balance equation in Kelly (1979). If we require that each pair of terms is zero in (2.3), we obtain

$$q(\mathbf{s}', \mathbf{s}) P^e(\mathbf{s}') - q(\mathbf{s}, \mathbf{s}') P^e(\mathbf{s}) = 0, \qquad (2.4)$$

where superscript e indicates the equilibrium probabilities. This is a special case of full balance. It is known as the *detailed balance condition*. The detailed balance condition is only a sufficient condition for the equilibrium probabilities, not a necessary condition. When the state space is a tree, the detailed condition always holds (see Kelly, 1979 or Aoki, 2002, 18).

Example: Pure Death Process with Immigration. *Let α be the rate of immigration (innovation) and μ be exit (death). For simplicity, we assume each n agent or unit exits independently. A straightforward probability flux accounting gives the master equation*

$$\frac{\partial P(n, t)}{\partial t} = \alpha P(n - 1, t) + \mu(n + 1) P(n + 1, t) - (\alpha + \mu n) P(n, t) \quad (2.5)$$

with the initial condition $P(n, 0) = \delta_{n, n_0}$. That is, there are initially n_0 units in the model. Inflows into $P(n, t)$ arise from an immigration in state $n - 1$ which is $\alpha P(n - 1, t)$, and a death in state $n + 1$ which is $\mu(n + 1) P(n + 1, t)$. Likewise, flows out of $P(n, t)$ arise from an immigration and a death in state n which is

$(\alpha + \mu n) P(n, t)$. *Note that the death rate depends on population or n whereas "immigration" is by definition independent of n.*

By setting the right-hand side of (2.5) to zero, we obtain the equation for the equilibrium distribution $P^e(n)$ for the death–immigration process:

$$\mu(n+1)P^e(n+1) = (\alpha + \mu n)P^e(n) - \alpha P^e(n-1). \qquad (2.6)$$

We will later show that this equation can be solved recursively to illustrate that $P^e(n)$ is a Poisson distribution with mean α/μ. ∎

Solving the Master Equation

To derive nonstationary behavior, we need to solve the master equation explicitly. For simple cases, we can derive aggregate (mean) dynamics easily. Here, we consider the above example of pure death process with immigration.

Example: Pure Death Process with Immigration. *The expected value of n can be directly obtained from (2.5) without the help of the probability generating function. We multiply the master equation (2.5) by n, and sum over $n = 0$ to $n = \infty$ with $P(-1, t) = 0$. Then we obtain*

$$\sum_{n=0}^{\infty} n \frac{\partial P(n, t)}{\partial t} = \sum_{n=0}^{\infty} \alpha n P(n-1, t) + \sum_{n=0}^{\infty} \mu n(n+1) P(n+1, t)$$

$$- \sum_{n=0}^{\infty} n(\alpha + \mu n) P(n, t)$$

$$= \alpha \sum_{n=0}^{\infty} (n-1) P(n-1, t) + \alpha \sum_{n=0}^{\infty} P(n-1, t)$$

$$+ \mu \sum_{n=0}^{\infty} (n+1)^2 P(n+1, t) - \mu \sum_{n=0}^{\infty} (n+1) P(n+1, t)$$

$$- \alpha \sum_{n=0}^{\infty} n P(n, t) - \mu \sum_{n=0}^{\infty} n^2 P(n, t).$$

The first and second moments of n are, by definition,

$$\langle n \rangle = \sum_{n=0}^{\infty} n P(n, t) \quad and \quad \langle n^2 \rangle = \sum_{n=0}^{\infty} n^2 P(n, t).$$

Noting that $P(-1, t) = 0$ and

$$\sum_{n=0}^{\infty} n \frac{\partial P(n, t)}{\partial t} = \frac{\partial}{\partial t} \left[\sum_{n=0}^{\infty} n P(n, t) \right],$$

we can rewrite the above equation as

$$\frac{d\langle n\rangle}{dt} - \alpha\langle n\rangle + \alpha + \mu\langle n^2\rangle - \mu\langle n\rangle - \alpha\langle n\rangle - \mu\langle n^2\rangle = \alpha - \mu\langle n\rangle.$$

If we denote the first moment or the expected value of n, $E(n) = \langle n\rangle$, by

$$\phi = E(n) = \langle n\rangle,$$

we have just found that it is governed by the following ordinary differential equation:

$$\frac{d\phi}{dt} = \mu\phi. \tag{2.7}$$

This equation is a simple aggregate dynamic equation. It has α/μ as the correct asymptotic value of the mean. Note that the right-hand side of equation (2.7) is equal to the difference of the expected rightward move, α, minus the expected leftward move, $\mu\phi$. ∎

We have directly derived the dynamic equation for the mean for the pure death process with immigration. For more complicated models, however, this straightforward method does not work so we need to use other methods. There are at least three ways for solving the master equations for the probability distributions, or for the moment expressions: (1) probability generating function, (2) cumulant generating function, and (3) Taylor expansion.

Probability Generating Function. To gain information on the probability distribution and its moments, we can use probability generating functions.

Definition: Probability Generating Function. *Given the probability that state is in $k \geq 0$ at time t, $P(k, t)$, the probability generating function is defined as*

$$G(z, t) = \sum_{k=0}^{\infty} z^k P(k, t) \tag{2.8}$$

The probability generating function is useful because once we know it, we can easily find the time evolution of moments. For example, the first moment or means $E(k)$ of stochastic variable k ($k = 1, 2, \dots$) is defined as

$$E(k) = \sum_{k=0}^{\infty} k P(k, t).$$

By comparison, we know that this is equal to

$$\left.\frac{\partial G(z, t)}{\partial z}\right|_{z=1} = \sum_k k z^{k-1} P(k, t)\Big|_{z=1} = \sum_k k P(k, t) = E(k).$$

That is, we obtain the first moment as the first derivative of the generating function with respect to z. The problem to solve the master equation, therefore, boils down to obtaining the generating function.

Example: Pure Death Process with Immigration. *Here, we illustrate the method for the death immigration process. In this case, the master equation is given by equation (2.5). Multiply both sides of (2.5) by z^n and sum it over n ($n = 0, 1, 2, \dots$), and we obtain*

$$\sum_n \frac{\partial z^n P(n, t)}{\partial t} = \sum_n \alpha z^n P(n-1, t) + \sum_n \mu(n+1)z^n P(n+1, t)$$
$$- \sum_n (\alpha + \mu n)z^n P(n, t).$$

Hence, we derive the partial differential equation for $G(z, t)$:

$$\frac{\partial G(z, t)}{\partial t} = \mu(1-z)\frac{\partial G}{\partial z} + \alpha(z-1)G, \tag{2.9}$$

with the initial condition ($n = n_0$ at time 0); that is $G(z, 0) = z^{n_0}$ In deriving (2.9) we note that

$$\sum z^n P(n-1, t) = zG, \qquad \sum (n+1)z^n P(n+1, t) = \frac{\partial G}{\partial z},$$

and

$$\sum nz^n P(n, t) = z\frac{\partial G}{\partial z}$$

up to initial condition terms.

Once this partial differential equation is solved, we can recover $P(k, t)$. An easy way to solve (2.9) is to eliminate the second term by transforming $G(z, t)$ as follows:

$$G(z, t) = e^{\kappa(z-1)}H(z, t) \quad \text{with} \quad \kappa = \frac{\alpha}{\mu}.$$

Equation (2.9) then becomes

$$\frac{\partial H}{\partial t} = \mu(1-z)\frac{\partial H}{\partial z}.$$

This simplifies to

$$\frac{\partial Q}{\partial t} = \frac{\partial Q}{\partial w}$$

where we define

$$Q(w, t) = H(z(w), t) \quad \text{with} \quad \frac{dz}{dw} = \mu(1-z), \quad \text{or} \quad w = -\frac{1}{\mu}\ln(z-1).$$

Now, the solution of this last equation is

$$Q(w, t) = \Phi(w + t)$$

for some differential function Φ, since

$$\frac{\partial Q}{\partial t} = \Phi' \quad \text{and} \quad \frac{\partial Q}{\partial w} = \Phi'.$$

This function is determined by the initial condition that $G(z, 0) = z^{n_0}$. Substituting these back into $H(z, t)$ and $Q(w, t)$, we easily obtain

$$G(z, t) = \exp\left[\frac{\alpha}{\mu}(z - 1)\right] \gamma(z, t : \alpha)$$

where γ is seen to approach 1 as $t \to \infty$. (The reader is invited to derive the expression for γ.) Thus, in this example, the generating function converges to the following equation:

$$G(z, t) \to \exp\left[\frac{\alpha}{\mu}(z - 1)\right] \quad when \quad t \to \infty. \tag{2.10}$$

This means that in the limit of time going to infinity, the probability of k agents present in the model is given by the stationary distribution

$$P(k, t) \to \frac{e^{-\frac{\alpha}{\mu}}\left(\frac{\alpha}{\mu}\right)^k}{k!}. \tag{2.11}$$

Equation (2.11) verifies our earlier remark that the stationary distribution obtained from the detailed balance equation for the death–immigration process is a Poisson process with rate α/μ.

Now, differentiate equation (2.10), and set z equal to 1, and we obtain the following result:

$$\frac{d}{dz}\left\{\exp\left[\frac{\alpha}{\mu}(z - 1)\right]\right\}\Bigg|_{z=1} = \frac{\alpha}{\mu}\exp\left[\frac{\alpha}{\mu}(z - 1)\right]\Bigg|_{z=1} = \frac{\alpha}{\mu}. \tag{2.12}$$

From equation (2.12), we know that α/μ is the asymptotic first moment, or means for the death–immigration process. This example verifies our earlier remark that the generating function enables us to find the expected value:

$$\frac{\partial G(z, t)}{\partial z}\Bigg|_{z=1} = E(k(t)). \quad \blacksquare$$

Cumulant Generating Function

Definition: Cumulant Generating Function *Cumulant generating function $K(\theta, t)$ is defined as follows:*

$$K(\theta, t) = \ln G(e^{-\theta}, t)$$

that is, the log of the probability generating function $G(z, t)$ with substitution $z = e^{-\theta}$.

Again, we consider the pure death process with immigration.

Example: Pure Death Process with Immigration. *By using $K(\theta, t)$, we can derive from equation (2.9) the following equation:*

$$\frac{\partial K}{\partial t} = \alpha(e^{-\theta} - 1) + \mu(1 - e^{-\theta})\frac{\partial K}{\partial \theta}.$$

See Aoki (2002, 69, 75). In this example, the first two cumulants, $K_1(t)$ and $K_2(t)$, are the means and variance. Since $K(\theta, t) = K_1\theta + \frac{1}{2}K_2\theta^2 + \cdots$ the coefficients are such that they satisfy

$$\dot{K}_1(t) = \alpha - \mu K_1$$

$$\dot{K}_2(t) = -2\mu K_2 + \mu K_1 + \alpha. \tag{2.13}$$

In general, the set of ordinary differential equations for the cumulants may not terminate at some finite stage. However, for the present example, K_1 and K_2 constitute a set of two ordinary differential equations that do not involve any higher order cumulants. Setting the left-hand side of (2.13) to zero, we obtain the stationary values

$$K_1^e = \frac{\alpha}{\mu}$$

and

$$K_2^e = \frac{\mu K_1^e + \alpha}{2\mu} = \frac{\alpha}{\mu}.$$

That is, both mean and variance are equal to α/μ, which is correct for the Poisson random variable.

Taylor Expansion. Another method of solving master equations is the Taylor expansion. This method expands a nonlinear master equation in Taylor series. The expansion is to be done with respect to some size parameter, which is typically the number of agents in the model. Let S be the size parameter. We use S to express the stochastic state variable n as

$$n(t) = S\phi + \sqrt{S}\xi \tag{2.14}$$

where variable ϕ is the mean of $n(t)/S$ and ξ is a random variable with mean zero and finite variance. Note that ϕ is not stochastic but a real number. Equation (2.14) implies the following relations:

$$n(t) + 1 = S\phi + \sqrt{S}\left(\xi + \frac{1}{\sqrt{S}}\right)$$

$$n(t) - 1 = S\phi + \sqrt{S}\left(\xi - \frac{1}{\sqrt{S}}\right) \tag{2.15}$$

It may be more informative to rewrite (2.14) as

$$\frac{n}{S} = \phi + \frac{1}{\sqrt{S}}\xi.$$

Equation (2.14) gives a good approximation when probability distributions, which are the solution of the master equation, have sharp peaks. Probability distributions with broad peaks may require special care or more terms of expansion (see Van Kampen, 1992, 251 for details).

Example: The Pure Death Process with Immigration. *We specify the transition rates as*

$$w(n, n+1) = \gamma(n) \quad and \quad w(n, n-1) = \rho(n).$$

Using these transition rates, we rewrite the master equation (2.5) as

$$\frac{\partial P(n, t)}{\partial t} = \gamma(n-1)P(n-1, t) + \rho(n+1)P(n+1, t)$$

$$- P(n, t)\{\gamma(n) + \rho(n)\}. \tag{2.16}$$

We next define

$$\pi(\xi(t), t) = P(n(t), t) \tag{2.17}$$

for $\xi(t)$ in (2.14). Then, we note that

$$\frac{\partial P}{\partial t} = \frac{\partial \pi}{\partial t} + \frac{\partial \pi}{\partial \xi} \frac{d\xi}{dt}. \tag{2.18}$$

We also note that given equation (2.14),

$$\frac{d\xi}{dt} = \sqrt{S} \frac{d\phi}{dt}, \tag{2.19}$$

holds for n fixed.

Equations (2.18) and (2.19) give us

$$\frac{\partial P}{\partial t} = \frac{\partial \pi}{\partial t} - \sqrt{S} \frac{d\phi}{dt}. \tag{2.20}$$

If we rewrite the time scale from t to τ by $t = S\tau$, equation (2.20) becomes

$$\frac{1}{S} \frac{\partial P}{\partial \tau} = \frac{1}{S} \frac{\partial \pi}{\partial \tau} - \frac{1}{\sqrt{S}} \frac{\partial \pi}{\partial \xi} \frac{d\phi}{d\tau}. \tag{2.21}$$

On the other hand, using equations (2.15) and (2.16) and the definition of $\pi(\xi, t)$, (2.17), we obtain

$$\frac{1}{S} \frac{\partial P}{\partial t} = \gamma \left(\phi + \frac{1}{\sqrt{S}} \xi - \frac{1}{S} \right) \pi \left(\xi - \frac{1}{\sqrt{S}}, t \right)$$

$$+ \rho \left(\phi + \frac{1}{\sqrt{S}} \xi + \frac{1}{S} \right) \pi \left(\xi + \frac{1}{\sqrt{S}}, t \right) - \beta \left(\phi + \frac{1}{\sqrt{S}} \xi \right) \pi(\xi, t)$$

$$\tag{2.22}$$

where

$$\beta \left(\phi + \frac{1}{\sqrt{S}} \xi \right) := \gamma \left(\phi + \frac{1}{\sqrt{S}} \xi \right) + \rho \left(\phi + \frac{1}{\sqrt{S}} \xi \right).$$

Now, we expand each term of the right-hand side of equation (2.22) in the neighborhood of ϕ to obtain

$$\frac{1}{S}\frac{\partial P}{\partial t} = \left[\gamma(\phi) + \gamma'(\phi)\left(\frac{1}{\sqrt{S}}\xi - \frac{1}{S}\right) + \cdots\right]\left[\pi - \frac{\partial \pi}{\partial \xi}\frac{1}{\sqrt{S}} + \frac{1}{2S}\frac{\partial^2 \pi}{\partial \xi^2} + \cdots\right]$$

$$+ \left[\rho(\phi) + \rho'(\phi)\left(\frac{1}{\sqrt{S}}\xi + \frac{1}{S}\right) + \cdots\right]\left[\pi + \frac{\partial \pi}{\partial \xi}\frac{1}{\sqrt{S}} + \frac{1}{2S}\frac{\partial^2 \pi}{\partial \xi^2} + \cdots\right]$$

$$- \left[\beta(\phi) + \beta'(\phi)\frac{1}{\sqrt{S}}\xi + \cdots\right]\pi. \tag{2.23}$$

The right-hand sides of equations (2.21) and (2.23) must be equal. Equating the co-efficients of $-\frac{1}{\sqrt{S}}\frac{\partial \pi}{\partial \xi}$ (i.e., of order $\frac{1}{\sqrt{S}}$) on the right-hand sides of these two equations, we pull out the dynamics for the mean or the first moment of n/s, ϕ, as:

$$\frac{d\phi}{d\tau} = -\rho(\phi) + \gamma(\phi). \tag{2.24}$$

For this pure death process with immigration we have

$$\gamma(\phi) = \alpha$$

and

$$\rho(\phi) = \mu\phi.$$

Equation (2.24) is then identical with equation (2.7):

$$\frac{d\phi}{d\tau} = -\rho(\phi) + \gamma(\phi) = \alpha - \mu\phi. \tag{2.25}$$

Therefore, the stationary value of ϕ, $\bar{\phi}$, is equal to $\frac{\alpha}{\mu}$, the same value that we have derived by other two methods.

The Fokker–Planck Equation

The Fokker–Planck equation gives the dynamics of the probability density function $\pi(\xi, t)$ of ξ, that is fluctuations around the mean or the first moment, ϕ. Once again, we can consider the Taylor expansion of the master equation for the pure death process with immigration, (2.23). Equating the coefficients of order $1/\sqrt{S}$ on the right-hand sides of equations (2.21) and (2.23), we obtain dynamics for the mean (24). Now, equating the terms with scale $\frac{1}{S}$ on both sides, we deduce the dynamics for π as

$$\frac{\partial \pi}{\partial \tau} = -\gamma'(\phi)\frac{\partial \pi}{\partial \xi}\xi + \gamma(\phi)\frac{1}{2}\frac{\partial^2 \pi}{\partial \xi^2} - \gamma'(\phi)\pi + \rho'(\phi)\frac{\partial \pi}{\partial \xi}\xi$$

$$+ \rho(\phi)\frac{1}{2}\frac{\partial^2 \pi}{\partial \xi^2} + \rho'(\phi)\pi$$

$$= -b'(\phi)\frac{\partial}{\partial \xi}(\xi\pi) + \frac{1}{2}\beta(\phi)\frac{\partial^2 \pi}{\partial \xi^2} + \cdots \tag{2.26}$$

where we define

$$b(\phi) = \gamma(\phi) - \rho(\phi).$$

We recall that

$$\beta(\phi) = \gamma(\phi) + \rho(\phi).$$

Equation (2.26) truncated at the second partial derivatives of π is called *the Fokker–Planck equation*. Recall that π is a probability density function of ξ, that is fluctuations around the mean of n/S, ϕ. The Fokker–Planck equation describes time evolution of π.

Suppose that π is stationary. Then, by setting the time derivative $\partial \pi / \partial \tau$ to zero in equation (2.26), we obtain

$$-b'(\bar{\phi}) \frac{\partial}{\partial \xi} (\xi \pi) + \frac{1}{2} \beta(\bar{\phi}) \frac{\partial^2 \pi}{\partial \xi^2} = 0$$

where b' and β are evaluated at the equilibrium value of ϕ, $\bar{\phi}$. By integrating this equation with respect to ξ we obtain

$$-b'(\bar{\phi}) \xi \pi + \frac{1}{2} \beta(\bar{\phi}) \frac{\partial \pi}{\partial \xi} = 0.$$

Note that because the sum or integration of probability flux is zero, the constant term after integration in the above equation becomes zero. Now integrating the above equation once again with respect to ξ we obtain the probability density function of ξ:

$$\pi(\xi) = const. \times \exp\left(\frac{b'(\bar{\phi})}{\beta(\bar{\phi})} \xi^2\right) = const. \times \exp\left(-\frac{\xi^2}{2\sigma^2}\right)$$

where

$$\frac{1}{\sigma^2} = \frac{\mu}{2\alpha} > 0.$$

Thus, *the stationary* density function of ξ (fluctuations around the mean $\bar{\phi}$) in this example is the normal density. The variance depends on two transition rates, μ and α, that is, the death rate and the immigration rate.

See Aoki (1996, Section 5.3, 2002, Chapter 7) for other examples of the Taylor series expansion method.[3] See also Van Kampen (1992) for details of the Taylor series expansion of master equation and related topics. We will use the Taylor series expansion to analyze a model of business cycles in Chapter 4.

---

[3] We can improve the expression of π up to $O(S^{-1})$ by taking more terms. See Aoki (1996, p. 123).

Potential Representation and Multiple Equilibria

The notion of *potential* is extremely useful in the analysis of stochastic dynamics. In particular, it clarifies our analysis when multiple equilibria exist for stationary distributions. It is easy to explain this notion with a simple example.

Example: Binary Choice Model. *For a binary choice process with transition rates of equation (2.1), n/N is the state variable, where n is the agent of type 1 and N the total number of agents. The detailed balance condition becomes the difference equation for the equilibrium probabilities. Solving it, we obtain the expression for this stationary probability, $P^e(n/N)$. It can be put into the form of an exponential distribution:*

$$P^e\left(\frac{n}{N}\right) \propto \exp\left\{-\beta N U\left(\frac{n}{N}\right)\right\}. \tag{2.27}$$

Here, U is called the potential *and is given by the sum of two distinct terms*

$$U\left(\frac{n}{N}\right) = -\frac{2}{N}\sum_{r=1}^{n} g\left(\frac{n}{N}\right) - \frac{1}{\beta}H\left(\frac{n}{N}\right) + O\left(\frac{\ln N}{N}\right), \tag{2.28}$$

where the terms on the right-hand side are explained in (2.29) and (2.31). The first term depends on g, which is defined by η_i functions in the transition rates (2.1):

$$\frac{\eta_1(x)}{\eta_2(x)} = \exp[2\beta g(x)]. \tag{2.29}$$

We set n/N as x for short. With the normalization $\eta_1(x) + \eta_2(x) = 1$, we have an explicit relation between $\eta_1(x)$ and $g(x)$:

$$\eta_1(x) = \frac{\exp(\beta g(x))}{\exp(\beta g(x)) + \exp(-\beta g(x))}. \tag{2.30}$$

This is known as the Boltzmann–Gibbs distribution. In Chapter 3, we will show that the positive parameter β introduced in expression (2.30) can be interpreted as a measure of uncertainty in the model. The more uncertain the consequences of particular choices by agents, the smaller the value of β. In the limit of $\beta = 0$, $\eta_1(x) = \eta_2(x) = 1/2$.

The second term, $H(x)$, is the Shannon entropy:

$$H(x) = -x\ln x - (1-x)\ln(1-x). \tag{2.31}$$

This arises from the combinatorial aspects of the binary choices in the model. For N large, we replace the sum in equation (2.28) with the integral to obtain

$$U(x) = -2\int^{x} g(y)dy - \frac{1}{\beta}H(x). \tag{2.32}$$

This potential function determines the stochastic dynamics of the model. For example, given stationary distributions, we can look for states with the highest probabilities. These are the states at which the potential is at local minima.

By taking the derivative with respect to x, we find that the potential is minimized at x which satisfies

$$g(x) = \frac{1}{2\beta}\frac{dH(x)}{dx} = \frac{1}{2\beta}\ln\frac{x}{1-x}. \tag{2.33}$$

This value of x can be shown to be identical with that of the critical point(s) of the aggregate dynamics. In other words, the critical points of the aggregate dynamics are the points at which the potential is locally minimized.

Anything that changes the g(x) function, such as changes in perception regarding profitabilities of alternative decisions, and government policy changes, will shift the equilibrium positions in (2.33). Changes in the equilibia, however, also depend on parameter value β. We can show that the smaller the value of β, the smaller the change in the equilibrium value for a given amount of changes in g(x). This point is elaborated in Chapter 4.

Dynamics about an Equilibrium Point

Let us continue with the above example of the binary choice model. Denote by $z = x - x^*$ deviation of x from its equilibrium value, x^*. The dynamics of this deviational variable can be expressed using the potential as

$$\frac{dz}{d\tau} = -\beta\left\{x^*(1-x^*)\frac{d^2U}{dx^2}\right\}z. \tag{2.34}$$

The sign of the second derivative of U is positive near the minimum of the potential. Thus, smaller values of β imply a sluggish deviational dynamics for x to return to x^*. The greater the uncertainty about the consequences of choices for agents, the more sluggish is a return to local equilibria. This method is applied to the problem of policy ineffectiveness in Chapter 4.

2.2. Second Class of Methods: Random Cluster Formation

We next turn to the second class of methods. Stochastic combinatorial tools[4] introduced in this section are used to show how agents form "clusters" and how the clusters evolve over time. A cluster is a group of economic agents. It can be a sector, an industry, or any other group of economic agents with the same choice or same set of attributes. We examine the dynamic processes of clusters. What dynamics emerge in the processes of formation and dissolution of clusters comprising interacting agents? What are the stationary distributions of fractions of agents of different types, namely, stationary distributions of the

---

[4] We borrow from the literature of population genetics such as Ewens (1972, 1990), Watterson (1974, 1976), Watterson and Guess (1977), and Zabell (1992), and of statistics and stochastic processes such as Kingman (1978a, b), Arratia, Barbour, and Tavaré (1992, 2003), and Pitman (2002).

sizes of clusters? What are the market shares of a typical largest cluster, second largest cluster, and so on? These are the questions we answer using the methods of this second class.

Dynamics of cluster formation is important because a multisector approach is often useful, even essential, in macroeconomics. In Chapter 6, we show that the multisector stochastic model gives indeed a new perspective to our understanding of business cycles. We will use a similar model for the analysis of labor market in Chapter 7.

Distributions of cluster sizes matter because a few of the larger clusters, if formed, dominate the market excess demands for goods. They would basically determine the nature and magnitudes of fluctuations of macroeconomic variables. The *Ewens Sampling Formula* is a useful tool for studying such a problem. It will be used extensively in our analysis of the financial market in Chapter 9.

Dynamics of Clustering Processes

Let us begin by considering how n agents or elements randomly form K clusters. For ease of exposition, we call a set composed of n objects an n-set. For example, $[n] := \{1, 2, \ldots, n\}$, is an n-set. For ease of exposition, we speak of n "balls" for agents or goods, and K "boxes" for clusters or types.

We consider how n balls are distributed in K boxes. If balls are randomly distributed in boxes, we can find the distribution of balls by simply counting the number of configurations of n balls in K boxes. The number of different patterns depends crucially on whether balls and/or boxes are distinguishable. In applications in macroeconomics, the specific identity of n balls (economic units) usually does not matter. Labels we assign to balls are then merely for convenience of reference. Permuting labels of balls leaves nothing of substance changed.

First, we consider the case where K boxes are distinguishable. When n indistinguishable balls are distributed into K distinguishable boxes, there are

$$\binom{n}{n_1, n_2, \ldots, n_K} = \frac{n!}{n_1! n_2! \cdots n_K!} \tag{2.35}$$

different patterns. Here, n_i is the number of balls in the ith box where $n_1 + n_2 + \cdots + n_K = n$. This is the number of configurations of $[n]$ into K labeled clusters. The distribution is given by *frequency vector*, defined as

$$\mathbf{n} := (n_1, n_2, \ldots, n_K).$$

In this case, we obtain the probability of $(n_1, n_2, \ldots, n_K)$ by simply dividing (2.35) by the total number of configurations, K^n.

In most applications, clusters are not randomly distributed, but rather formed by interactions of agents. As agents interact, new clusters form or some existing clusters break up into smaller ones. The dynamics of such cluster formations can be analyzed by a jump Markov process of frequency vector $\mathbf{n}$. We use a frequency vector $\mathbf{n}$ as the state vector in this analysis. As in the previous section, we need to specify a set of transition rates of the jump Markov process.

We consider simple "closed" dynamics, in which the number of agents, namely n, and the number of boxes, K, are both fixed over time. For example, consider the following transition rates for $\mathbf{n}$:

$$w(\mathbf{n}, \mathbf{n} - \mathbf{e}_i + \mathbf{e}_j) = f(n_i, n_j), \quad (i, j = 1, \ldots, K)$$

where $\mathbf{e}_j$ is a unit vector with the only nonzero component, 1, at the j-th position. This transition rate means that one agent changes its type from i to j (or leaves the ith sector moving into the jth sector). The right-hand side specifies that the rates are some function of the sizes of type i and j.

Given such dynamics, we can find the stationary distribution of clusters. One tractable way to find it is to impose *the detailed balance condition*. By definition, the number of agents under the stationary distribution, n^*, does not change over time.

Example: K-dimensional Pólya Distribution. *We consider the jump Markov process with the following transition rates:*

$$w(\mathbf{n}, \mathbf{n} - \mathbf{e}_i + \mathbf{e}_j) = \frac{n_i}{n} \frac{n_j + \theta_j}{n - 1 + \theta} \tag{2.36}$$

$$\text{where} \quad \theta_j > 0 \quad \text{and} \quad \theta = \sum_{j=1}^{K} \theta_j.$$

We can determine the stationary distribution of this Markov process, $\pi(\mathbf{n})$, from the detailed balance condition

$$\pi(\mathbf{n}) \, w(\mathbf{n}, \mathbf{n} - \mathbf{e}_i + \mathbf{e}_j) = \pi(\mathbf{n} - \mathbf{e}_i + \mathbf{e}_j) \, w(\mathbf{n} - \mathbf{e}_i + \mathbf{e}_j, \mathbf{n}).$$

This condition means that probability inflows and outflows between two states $\mathbf{n}$ and $\mathbf{n} - \mathbf{e}_i + \mathbf{e}_j$ cancel out each other. Using this condition, we obtain the following difference equation for $\pi(\mathbf{n})$:

$$\pi(\mathbf{n}) = \frac{\theta_i + n_i - 1}{n_i} \frac{n_j + 1}{\theta_j + n_j} \pi(\mathbf{n} - \mathbf{e}_i + \mathbf{e}_j).$$

Then, we can derive the stationary distribution as

$$\pi(\mathbf{n}) = \frac{n!}{\theta^{[n]}} \prod_{i=1}^{K} \frac{\theta_i^{[n_i]}}{n_i!}, \tag{2.37}$$

where $[\cdot]$ denotes an ascending factorial:

$$\theta^{[n]} = \theta(\theta + 1) \cdots (\theta + n - 1).$$

This stationary distribution (2.37) is known as the K-dimensional Pólya distribution. See Aoki (2002, 26), for the details.

In some cases, new entry and/or exits of balls (agents) occur. The Markov model can accommodate such "open" dynamics. In the economy, "something new" often appears, and "something old" disappears. "Something new" may be a newly invented goods, a new technology, a new behavioral pattern and so on. One might think that there is no way to define the probability that "something new" emerges or is discovered. In fact, we can formally analyze this problem by using our methods. Specifically the *law of succession* in the statistical literature addresses these questions as conditional probabilities of agents entering models from outside the existing types. See Zabell (1992) for an illuminating discussion. Here, we rely on recent works by Kingman (1993) and Pitman (2002). Their models can be approximated as birth–immigration models in the context of continuous time branching processes. We introduce their results into our models. See Feng and Hoppe (1998) for the mathematical setup.

In "open" model, the number of agents and/or types, namely n and/or K, varies as time passes. We can set up appropriate open model by specifying transition rates. As for entry of agents, there is a difference depending on whether a newcomer enters an existing cluster or forms a new cluster. When a newcomer always joins an existing cluster, n is variable but K is fixed. Specifically, in this case, consider the following transition rates:

$$w(\mathbf{n}, \mathbf{n} - \mathbf{e}_i) = \frac{n_i}{n},$$

$$w(\mathbf{n}, \mathbf{n} + \mathbf{e}_j) = \frac{n_j + \theta_j}{n + \theta}.$$

The former means that one type i agent exits from the market, and the latter means that one j type agent enters the market. Combining these two, we can obtain the same expression as (2.37) for the closed dynamics:

$$w(\mathbf{n}, \mathbf{n} - \mathbf{e}_i + \mathbf{e}_j) = w(\mathbf{n}, \mathbf{n} - \mathbf{e}_i)w(\mathbf{n} - \mathbf{e}_i, \mathbf{n} + \mathbf{e}_j) = \frac{n_i}{n} \frac{n_j + \theta_j}{n - 1 + \theta}.$$

Using these transition rates, we can describe entry of one new type agent as follows. Suppose that a newcomer at time t forms a new cluster of type h. This means that $n_h = 0$ holds up to time t. Substituting $n_h = 0$ into the transition rate of new entry, we have

$$w(\mathbf{n}, \mathbf{n} + \mathbf{e}_h) = \frac{\theta_h}{n + \theta}.$$

Thus, the transition rate that a new type agent comes in can be derived as

$$\frac{\sum_{h \in \phi} \theta_h}{n + \theta}, \tag{2.38}$$

where ϕ is a set of indices of empty boxes.

For the case where K is variable as well as n, we must redefine the state vector. The frequency vector $\mathbf{n}$ is not a state because its dimension varies over time. As we discuss later, a state of this type of dynamics can be represented by a "partition vector." But here, without giving an exact expression for the state vector, we deal with the dynamics by using a sequence expression along with time evolution.

Let $X_1, \ldots, X_n, \ldots$ be an infinite sequence of random variables taking on any of a finite number of values, say $1, 2, \ldots, K$. The subscripts on X are thought of as a time index, or the order in which samples are taken or agents enter the system.

Two sequences are such that they have the same probability if one is a rearrangement of the other, or the probability is the function of the frequency vector, $\mathbf{n} = (n_1, n_2, \ldots, n_K)$. The observed frequency counts, $n_j = n_j(X_1, X_2, \ldots, X_n)$, are sufficient statistics for the sequence, in the sense that probabilities conditional on the frequency counts depend only on the frequency vector;

$$\Pr(X_1, X_2, \ldots, X_n | \mathbf{n}) = \frac{n_1! n_2! \cdots n_K!}{n!},$$

where $n = \sum_{i=1}^{K} n_i$. Such a conditional probability is sometimes called the *law of succession*. Focusing on the prior probability of X_{n+1}, we have Johnson's sufficientness postulate,[5] that is,

$$\Pr(X_{n+1} = i | \mathbf{n}) = f(n_i, n).$$

Namely, the prior probability of X_{n+1} depends only n_i and n. Zabell (1992) specifies the probability as

$$\Pr(X_{n+1} = i | \mathbf{n}) = \frac{n_i + \alpha}{n + K\alpha} \qquad (2.39)$$

for some positive parameter α. Note that the sum of the probability from $i = 1$ to K is one, so there is no room for new type agents to enter the system.

Next, we consider the case with entry of a new type of agent. In this case, we take the limit of (2.39), letting K go to infinity and α to zero in such a way that $K\alpha$ goes to a positive limit θ. Then, we obtain the conditional probability of X_{n+1}:

$$\Pr(X_{n+1} = i | \mathbf{n}) = \frac{n_i}{n + \theta}, \qquad (2.40)$$

for some positive parameter θ. Note that the sum of the probabilities (2.40) from $i = 1$ to K is less than one, so that there is room for new type agents to enter the system. Namely, we obtain

$$\Pr(X_{n+1} = \text{new} | \mathbf{n}) = \frac{\theta}{n + \theta}. \qquad (2.41)$$

By comparing (2.41) with (2.38), we can see the difference that arises depending on whether K is fixed or not.

We use these probabilities for the dynamics of the sectoral economy in Chapter 6. For the case where the number of sectors, denoted by K, is fixed, we use

---

[5] so called by I. J. Good (1965) to avoid confusion with the notion of sufficient statistics.

the expression (2.39) with $\alpha = 0$ as the probability for economic agent to enter a sector, or exit from a sector. If K is not fixed and the emergence of a new sector is allowed, we use the expression (2.41) for the probability of emergence of a new sector in the economy. It allows us to analyze the situation in which "something new" appears and thus a new cluster is formed.

Partition Vector

In the previous section we studied the case where K boxes are distinguishable. In what follows, we study the case where balls (agents) and boxes (types) are both indistinguishable, or delabeled. In economics, firm size distribution is an example. In this example, both capital/labor (balls) and firms (boxes) are indistinguishable.

When boxes are delabeled, the only way we can count configurations of ball distribution is to count the number of boxes containing i balls, namely, a_i, $i = 1, 2, \ldots, n$. We encode the partition of $[n]$ as follows in this book.

Definition: Partition Vector *The partition vector is defined by*[6]

$$\mathbf{a} = (a_1, a_2, \ldots, a_n)$$

where the number of agents is given by

$$\sum_{i=1}^{n} i a_i = n,$$

and the number of categories is given by

$$\sum_{i=1}^{n} a_i := K_n \leq K.$$

Because the number of clusters is variable, we use the notation K_n rather than K. The inequality $K_n \leq K$ means that K is now the maximum possible number rather than the actual number of clusters. In other words, K_n is the number of occupied boxes (i.e., with nonzero balls). Therefore, K_n is possibly less than K.

In counting the number of configurations or arrangements with partition vector $\mathbf{a}$, the argument used in deriving (2.35) applies. In addition, the subsets (clusters) of the same size (cardinality) can be permuted among themselves without changing configuration. So the number of configurations is given by

$$N(\mathbf{a}) = \frac{n!}{\prod_{j=1}^{n}(j!)^{a_j} a_j!} = \frac{n!}{(1!)^{a_1}(2!)^{a_2} \cdots (n!)^{a_n} a_1! \cdots a_n!}. \qquad (2.42)$$

---

[6] Kingman (1980) and Sachkov (1996) call partition vectors by different names.

This new representation has roots in *exchangeable random partitions of a set of agents into clusters*, which arise in examining clusters or subsets of agents of the same types.

Now we can analyze the dynamics of cluster formation using the partition vector **a** as the state vector. By using the partition vector **a**, instead of the frequency vector **n** as the state vector, we can easily set up the formulation of open dynamics, because we do not have to specify which of the K types a newcomer joins ("boxes" are indistinguishable!). For example, we can consider the following transition rates for **a**:

$$w(\mathbf{a}, \mathbf{a} + \mathbf{e}_1) = \frac{\theta}{n + \theta}. \tag{2.43}$$

This transition rate means that one new type of agent enters an empty box with rate $\frac{\theta}{n+\theta}$. Another example is

$$w(\mathbf{a}, \mathbf{a} + \mathbf{e}_{j+1} - \mathbf{e}_j) = \frac{ja_j}{n + \theta}. \tag{2.44}$$

This means that one agent enters a cluster of size j, thereby increasing the number of clusters of size $j + 1$ by one, and reducing that of size j by one. The right-hand side specifies that the rates are proportional to ja_j, which counts the total number of agents in the clusters of size j.

For an exit case where one agent leaves a cluster of size j, the number of clusters of size $j - 1$ increases by one whereas that of size j decreases by one. The transition rate can be, therefore, written as

$$w(\mathbf{a}, \mathbf{a} - \mathbf{e}_j + \mathbf{e}_{j-1}) = \frac{ja_j}{n}. \tag{2.45}$$

For the case where an agent of one type of size j changes into another type of size j, the transition rate is

$$w(\mathbf{a}, \mathbf{a} + \mathbf{e}_{j+1} - 2\mathbf{e}_j + \mathbf{e}_{j-1}) = \frac{ja_j}{n} \frac{j(a_j - 1)}{n - 1 + \theta}. \tag{2.46}$$

We can make these expressions simple by defining $\mathbf{u}_j := \mathbf{e}_j - \mathbf{e}_{j-1}$, and $\mathbf{u}_1 := \mathbf{e}_1$. Then, (2.43), (2.44), (2.45), and (2.46) become

$$w(\mathbf{a}, \mathbf{a} + \mathbf{u}_1) = \frac{\theta}{n + \theta}, \tag{2.47}$$

$$w(\mathbf{a}, \mathbf{a} + \mathbf{u}_{j+1}) = \frac{ja_j}{n + \theta}, \tag{2.48}$$

$$w(\mathbf{a}, \mathbf{a} - \mathbf{u}_j) = \frac{ja_j}{n}, \tag{2.49}$$

$$w(\mathbf{a}, \mathbf{a} + \mathbf{u}_{j+1} - \mathbf{u}_j) = \frac{ja_j}{n} \frac{j(a_j - 1)}{n - 1 + \theta}. \tag{2.50}$$

Given such dynamics, we can find the stationary distribution of partition vector **a**, imposing the detailed balance condition.

Example: Ewens Sampling Formula. *An important example is the* Ewens Sampling Formula. *It is extensively used in population genetics. The transition rates for the Ewens Sampling Formula are given by (2.47), (2.48), and (2.49). The detailed balance condition is*

$$\pi(\mathbf{a})w(\mathbf{a}, \mathbf{a} + \mathbf{u}_{j+1}) = \pi(\mathbf{a} + \mathbf{u}_{j+1})w(\mathbf{a} + \mathbf{u}_{i+1}, \mathbf{a}). \tag{2.51}$$

Thanks to (2.48) and (2.49), (2.51) becomes

$$\pi(\mathbf{a})\frac{ja_j}{n+\theta} = \pi(\mathbf{a} + \mathbf{u}_{j+1})\frac{(j+1)(a_{j+1}+1)}{n+1}. \tag{2.52}$$

We can confirm that the following stationary distribution, $\pi(\mathbf{a})$, satisfies (2.52).

$$\pi(\mathbf{a}) = \frac{n!}{\theta^{[n]}}\prod_{j=1}^{n}\left(\frac{\theta}{j}\right)^{a_j}\frac{1}{a_j!}. \tag{2.53}$$

This stationary distribution is called the Ewens Sampling Formula. It is parameterized by a single positive scalar parameter θ, which controls the size of clusters K_n. We derive this formula via the methods of counting configurations in Appendix 2.1.

To understand the roles of the parameter θ in the Ewens Sampling Formula, we consider a case with $n = 2$ and $a_2 = 1$. In this simple case, we have

$$\Pr(a_1 = 0, a_2 = 1|n = 2) = \frac{1}{1+\theta}.$$

This formula shows that the probability for two agents to belong to the same cluster increases as θ becomes smaller. Alternatively, the probability of a case with $n = 2$ and $a_1 = 2$ is

$$\Pr(a_1 = 2, a_2 = 0|n = 2) = \frac{\theta}{1+\theta}.$$

In general, we can consider the case with n agents. Suppose that $a_j = 0$, $1 \le j \le n-1$ and $a_n = 1$, that is, n agents all belong to a single cluster. The probability of such a case is

$$\frac{\theta(n-1)!}{\theta^{[n]}} = \frac{(n-1)!}{(\theta+1)\cdots(\theta+n-1)}. \tag{2.54}$$

For small values of θ, this probability is close to 1.

In contrast, suppose that $a_1 = n$, and $a_j = 0$ for $2 \le j \le n$. The probability is then

$$\frac{\theta^n}{\theta^{[n]}} = \frac{\theta^{n-1}}{(\theta+1)\cdots(\theta+n-1)}. \tag{2.55}$$

Table 2.1. Signless Stirling Numbers of the First Kind $c(n, k)$

$n \backslash k$	1	2	3	4	5	6	7	8	9	10
6	120	274	225	85	15	1				
7	720	1764	1624	735	175	21	1			
8	5040	13068	13132	6769	1960	322	28	1		
9	40320	109584	118124	67284	22449	4536	546	36	1	
10	362880	1026576	1172700	723680	269325	63273	9450	870	45	1

$$\begin{cases} c(n, k) = c(n - 1, k - 1) + (n - 1)c(n - 1, k), \\ c(n, 1) = (n - 1)!, \quad \text{and} \quad c(n, n) = 1. \end{cases}$$

An approximate expression for $c(n, k)$ is given by

$c(n, k) = \frac{(n-1)!(\ln(n))^{k-1}}{(k-1)!} [e^{\gamma x} + \mathcal{O}(\frac{k}{(\ln(n))^2})]$ if $x := \frac{k-1}{\ln(n)} < 1$. See Hwang (1995).

It is nearly zero for small values of θ. Conversely, it is close to 1 when θ is much larger than n. In summary, given n agents, they tend to form one huge cluster of size close to n if θ is larger than n, whereas n agents tends to form n singletons if θ is close to zero. Therefore, the probability of the number of clusters, K_n, also depends on θ.

We can calculate the probability that the number of clusters, K_n, is k. Let us define $q_{n,k}$ as

$$q_{n,k} := \Pr(K_n = k \mid n). \tag{2.56}$$

According to the transition rate (2.47), a newcomer enters a new cluster with probability $\frac{\theta}{n+\theta}$, and enters an existing cluster with probability $\frac{n}{n+\theta}$. Therefore, we have a recursion of $q_{n,k}$:

$$q_{n+1,k} = \frac{n}{n + \theta} q_{n,k} + \frac{\theta}{n + \theta} q_{n,k-1}, \tag{2.57}$$

with boundary conditions (2.54) and (2.55),

$$q_{n,1} = \frac{\theta(n - 1)!}{\theta^{[n]}}, \quad \text{and} \quad q_{n,n} = \frac{\theta^n}{\theta^{[n]}}. \tag{2.58}$$

The solution to the recursion can be described as

$$q_{n,k} = \frac{\theta^k}{\theta^{[n]}} c(n, k). \tag{2.59}$$

Here, $c(n, k)$ are called *signless Stirling Numbers of the first kind*, which satisfy a recursion

$$c(n + 1, k) = nc(n, k) + c(n, k - 1). \tag{2.60}$$

It is interesting to see how this $c(n, k)$ depends on the values of n and k. We provide some examples of $c(n, k)$ in Table 2.1 to illustrate that $c(n, k)$ becomes very large for relatively small n and k. An approximate expression of $c(n, k)$ below Table 2.1 can be useful in application in macroeconomics. Suppose $n = 10^6$ as is often the case with the number of firms in the economy, then the number of types, k, can take 14 at most to satisfy the inequality that is necessary for the approximation. Such number of types is sufficient to analyze macro behavior of the market or economy. See Appendix 2.2 for details on $c(n, k)$.

Using (2.59), we can see how many clusters are formed by agents. To calculate the expected number of clusters conditional on the number of agents, $E(K_n \mid n)$, we can usefully apply the technique of generating functions. The generating function for the number of clusters, K_n, is

$$
\begin{aligned}
E(s^{K_n} \mid n) &= \sum_{k=1}^{n} s^k \Pr(K_n = k \mid n) \\
&= \sum_{k=1}^{n} s^k \frac{\theta^k}{\theta^{[n]}} c(n, k) \\
&= \frac{\sum_{k=1}^{n} (s\theta)^k c(n, k)}{\theta^{[n]}} \\
&= \frac{(s\theta)^{[n]}}{\theta^{[n]}}.
\end{aligned}
\tag{2.61}
$$

For the third equality, we use the generating function of $c(n, k)$, that is, equation (2.68) in Appendix 2.2. By differentiating (2.61) with respect to s and setting s to 1, we have

$$
E(K_n \mid n) = \theta \sum_{j=1}^{n} \frac{1}{\theta + j - 1}.
\tag{2.62}
$$

In this way, we can derive the expected number of clusters by generating functions. See Appendix 2.3 for another example of application of this method.

The randomness of the number of clusters, K_n, is a key difference between our open model and conventional macroeconomic models. In conventional macroeconomic models, agents are usually assumed to be identical. Even if they are assumed to be heterogeneous, the number and/or the share of agent types are assumed to be fixed over time. We maintain that these assumptions are untenable. The methods explained here resolve of these problems.

Poisson–Dirichlet Distribution: The Distribution of Order Statistics of Market Shares

Next, we consider *shares* of clusters and analyze their distribution. The distribution of shares are useful in such applications as market shares of firms, or shares of agents by their strategy.

There are several alternatives in defining shares x_j. In terms of the frequency vector $\mathbf{n}$, we can set shares x_j as

$$
x_j = \frac{n_j}{n}, \qquad j = 1, 2, \ldots, K_n.
$$

In this case, each cluster is distinguishable. This x_j means the share of j-th type or sector. In terms of partition vector $\mathbf{a}$, we can set shares x_j as

$$x_j = \frac{j a_j}{n}, \qquad j = 1, 2, \ldots, n.$$

Because clusters are not distinguishable in this case, we are interested in the number of agents in each cluster. This x_j means the share of clusters with j agents. We can interpret this x_j as the market share of firms whose size of employees is j, for example. In either case, x_j satisfies

$$\sum_j x_j = 1.$$

In analyzing the distribution of shares x_j, we allow the number of agents, n, and/or the number of clusters, K_n, to become infinite.

We follow Kingman(1993), and suppose that the probability density of x_j is given by

$$f(x_1, x_2, \ldots, x_{K_n}) = \frac{\Gamma(K_n \alpha)}{\Gamma(\alpha)^{K_n}} (x_1 x_2 \cdots x_{K_n})^{\alpha - 1}. \tag{2.63}$$

The corresponding cumulative distribution function of the shares x_j's is known as the *Dirichlet distribution* with parameter α, often denoted by $\mathcal{D}(x_1, x_2, \ldots, x_n; \alpha)$. As Kingman (1993, Sec. 9) remarks, the Dirichlet distribution is the simplest probability distribution over an n-dimensional simplex Δ_n. It is also the equilibrium distribution for a variety of evolutionary models where α is small and n is large.

Order statistics of shares, $x_{(j)}$, is defined by arranging and renumbering shares in nonincreasing order as

$$x_{(1)} \geq x_{(2)} \geq \cdots \geq x_{(n)}.$$

Order statistics has a well-defined limit distribution as the number of agents, n, goes to infinity, and α to zero in such a way that $K_n \alpha$ approaches some positive parameter θ. This limit distribution is called the *Poisson–Dirichlet distribution* denoted by $PD(\theta)$.

Using $PD(\theta)$, we determine approximate market shares of dominant types. For example, the sum of the shares of the first two largest clusters, $x_{(1)} + x_{(2)}$, alone may account for the majority, say 70 percent, for small values of θ. In Chapter 9, we use these approximations to analyze the macro-behavior of financial market in which heterogeneous agents use different strategies.

Appendix 2.1: Alternate Derivation of Ewens Sampling Formula

We can show an alternate derivation of the Ewens Sampling Formula via the method of counting configurations. In counting the number of configurations, we have assumed for partition vectors that any two boxes have no difference as long as they contain the same number of balls. However, we can differentiate boxes even though the two boxes contain the same number of delabeled balls. These differentiations of boxes are called "internal states," which represent, for example, the number of ways to place delabeled balls within a box. When each box containing j balls can assume one of m_j internal states, the number of configurations becomes

$$N(\mathbf{a}) = \frac{n! \prod_{j=1}^{n} (m_j)^{a_j}}{\prod_{j=1}^{n} (j!)^{a_j} a_j!}. \tag{2.64}$$

For example, expression (2.42) is the case where $m_j = 1$. Another important example is the case where $m_j = (j-1)!$. In this case, the number is given by

$$N(\mathbf{a}) = \frac{n!}{\prod_{j=1}^{n} (j)^{a_j} a_j!}. \tag{2.65}$$

This expression is known as Cauchy's formula, which is the number of cyclical permutations. Because partitions of $[n]$ can be expressed as products of cyclical permutations, the number of configurations is given by that formula. This formula can be understood by noting that a cyclical permutation of j symbols has j equivalent ways of expressing it, and a_j such permutations can be arranged in $a_j!$ ways, and these two considerations are independent.

To incorporate interaction of agents, we tilt the distribution by using the nonuniform weights $W(K_n)$ for partitions with K_n clusters, where

$$W(K_n) = \theta^{K_n} / \theta^{[n]}. \tag{2.66}$$

Recall that $K_n = \sum_{i=1}^{n} a_i$, and $\theta^{[n]} = \theta(\theta+1)\cdots(\theta+n-1)$. The denominator $\theta^{[n]}$ is needed to normalize the probability. This weight is the probability of each configuration in $N(\mathbf{a})$. Therefore, by multiplying (2.65) and (2.66), we arrive at the expression

$$\pi(\mathbf{a}) = W(K_n)N(\mathbf{a}) = \frac{n!}{\theta^{[n]}} \prod_{j=1}^{n} \left(\frac{\theta}{j}\right)^{a_j} \frac{1}{a_j!},$$

which is the Ewens Sampling Formula.

Appendix 2.2: Cluster Size Distribution and Stirling Numbers

Let $c(n, k)$ be the number of permutation of n symbols with k cycles. Because partitions of $[n]$ can be described as products of cyclical permutations, we can use this value in our analysis. It satisfies a recursion

$$c(n, k) = (n-1)c(n-1, k) + c(n-1, k-1), \tag{2.67}$$

because a permutation of $(n-1)$ objects with k cycles (products of k cyclical permutations) can be made into a permutation of n objects with k cycles by inserting the nth object after any of the $n-1$ objects, that is, in $(n-1)$ ways. In addition the nth object can be attached as a singleton (a cycle of size 1) to any permutations of $(n-1)$ objects with $(k-1)$ cycles. The number $c(n, k)$ is a signless Stirling number. Clearly $c(n, k) = 1$ for $n = 1, 2, \ldots$.

Next we define

$$x^{[n]} := x(x+1)\cdots(x+n-1).$$

This is called a rising or ascending factorial. This expression can be written as

$$x^{[n]} = x^{[n-1]}(x+n-1)$$
$$= (n-1)x^{[n-1]} + x \cdot x^{[n-1]}.$$

Note that this recursion has the same form as $c(n, k)$, (2.67). Thus, we obtain a generating function

$$x^{[n]} = \sum_{k=1}^{n} c(n, k)x^k. \tag{2.68}$$

The falling or descending factorial is defined by

$$(x)_n := x(x-1)\cdots(x-n+1).$$

If we substitute $-x$ for x here, we have

$$(-x)_n = (-x)(-x-1)\cdots(-x-n+1)$$
$$= (-1)^n x(x+1)\cdots(x+n-1)$$
$$= (-1)^n x^{[n]},$$

and

$$(-x)^{[n]} = (-x)(-x+1)\cdots(-x+n-1)$$
$$= (-1)^n x(x-1)\cdots(x-n+1)$$
$$= (-1)^n (x)_n.$$

Thus we see that

$$(x)_n = \sum_{k=1}^{n} s(n, k)x^k \tag{2.69}$$

where

$$s(n, k) = (-1)^{n-k} c(n, k).$$

Equation (2.69) is the generating function for $s(n, k)$, called the Stirling number of first kind.

Table 2.2. Stirling Numbers of the Second Kind $S(n, k)$

$n \setminus k$	1	2	3	4	5	6	7	8	9	10	Bell(n)
6	1	31	90	65	15	1					203
7	1	63	301	350	140	21	1				877
8	1	127	966	1701	1050	266	28	1			4140
9	1	255	3025	7770	6951	2646	462	36	1		21147
10	1	511	9330	34105	42525	22827	5880	750	45	1	115975

$$\begin{cases} S(n, k) = S(n-1, k-1) + kS(n-1, k), \\ S(n, 1) = 1, \quad \text{and} \quad S(n, n) = 1. \end{cases}$$

Bell Numbers: Bell $(n) = \sum_{k=1}^{n} S(n, k)$.

Because (2.69) connects a falling factorial to power of x by a triangular matrix, we can invert it to obtain

$$x^n = \sum_{k=1}^{n} S(n, k)(x)_k.$$

The expression $S(n, k)$ is called the Stirling number of second kind. It expresses the number of partition of $[n]$ into k clusters.

Tables 2.1 and 2.2 show the calculated numbers of Stirling numbers of the first and second kind. We can see that those values become very large for relatively small n and k.

Appendix 2.3: Application of Generating Function to Random Process of the Number of Types

Let us demonstrate the situation for which both the number of agents and the number of types, namely n and K_n, are random variables. We suppose that each element in the partition vector a follows independent Poisson processes. We then find the closed forms of the probability of n, and the expected value of K_n.

Let a_j, $j = 1, 2, \ldots$, be independent Poisson random variables with mean

$$\mu_j = \theta \frac{x^j}{j},$$

for some $0 < x < 1$ and positive parameter θ, that is,

$$\Pr(a_j = k) = \frac{\mu_j^k}{k!} e^{-\mu_j}, \quad k = 0, 1, \ldots.$$

We calculate the generating function for the components of partition vector a by

$$E\left(s_j^{a_j}\right) = \sum_k s_j^k \Pr(a_j = k) = \exp\{(s_j - 1)\mu_j\}.$$

Because every component is independent of each other, the probability distribution of **a** becomes the product of those for each a_j:

$$E\left(\prod_j s_j^{a_j}\right) = \exp\left\{(s_j - 1)\sum_j \mu_j\right\}. \tag{2.70}$$

Using the generating function (2.70), we can calculate the probability of the number of existing agents, n, and the expected value of the number of existing types, K_n.

For the probability of n, we set $s_j = s^j$ for all j. Then, (2.70) becomes

$$E\left(s^{\sum j a_j}\right) = E(s^n) = (1 - x)^{-\theta}(1 - sx)^{\theta}.$$

by noting that

$$\prod_j \exp\left(\frac{\theta x^j}{j}\right) = (1 - x)^{-\theta}.$$

Equation (2.70) is given by $(1 - x)^{-\theta}(1 - sx)^{\theta}$. This can be seen by taking the logarithm of both sides, and expanding $\ln(1 - x)$ in a power series in x. The expression is called the Kelly–Kendall identity (Aoki (2002, 158)). The coefficient of s^n of this generating function is the probability of the number of existing agents, n:

$$\Pr\left(\sum_{j=1}^{n} ja_j = n\right) = \binom{-\theta}{n} x^{-n} = \binom{\theta + n - 1}{n} x^n.$$

For the expected value of the number of existing types, K_n, we set $s_j = s$ for all j. Then, (2.70) becomes

$$E\left(s^{\sum a_j}\right) = E(s^{K_n}) = (1 - x)^{\theta}(1 - x)^{-s\theta}. \tag{2.71}$$

By differentiating (2.71) with respect to s and setting s to 1, we have

$$E(K_n) = -\theta \ln(1 - x).$$

In addition, the expectation conditional on n is given by

$$E(s^{K_n} \mid n) = \binom{s\theta + n - 1}{n} \bigg/ \binom{\theta + n - 1}{n} = \frac{\Gamma(s\theta + n)}{\Gamma(s\theta)} \frac{\Gamma(\theta)}{\Gamma(\theta + n)}. \tag{2.72}$$

By differentiating (2.72) with respect to s and setting s to 1, we have

$$E(K_n \mid n) = \theta[\Phi(\theta + n) - \Phi(\theta)] = \theta \sum_{j=1}^{n} \frac{1}{\theta + j}. \tag{2.73}$$

where $\Phi(\cdot)$ is the digamma function.

3

Equilibrium as Distribution:
The Role of Demand in Macroeconomics

We begin this chapter by reconsidering the notion of *equilibrium* in economics. In the standard analysis, optimization by an economic agent is followed by supply and demand; every economic agent or unit is always in his/her best position. The equality of demand and supply in the market then constitutes equilibrium. In the equilibrium, marginal utilities and productivities are equated to prices, and as a consequence, they are all equal. Lucas (1987) describes this equilibrium theory as *the* economic theory. In this framework, demand does not matter for the determination of the level of aggregate economic activity. It is determined by technology and factor endowments.

In the economy, micro units or economic agents certainly optimize. Some economists stress the limits of rationality of economic agents, and advocate "bounded rationality." However, in our view, the problem surrounding bounded rationality is *irrelevant* to macroeconomics. *More fundamental are micro fluctuations, uncertainty, and the limits to arbitrage in real economic activities.*

In standard economic theory, which ignores microeconomic fluctuations, the outcome of optimization by an economic agent is given by a "point" in some set or space; typically, a point is supported by a price vector. In this chapter, we explain that this approach is not valid because of microeconomic fluctuations.

Given the complexity of the macroeconomy, we must explicitly consider stochastic deviations of microeconomic behavior from its mean. In Chapter 1, we have seen that micro behaviors of individual households and firms are very diverse. Thus, we have *distribution* of responses by microeconomic agents as an equilibrium rather than a unique response by a representative agent. This means that the *no arbitrage condition for competitive market equilibrium* commonly assumed in economic theory can not be clearly defined unless the unrealistic risk neutrality assumption is made.

In fact, Lamont and Thaler (2003) convincingly argue that even in competitive financial markets such as the stock market, the Law of One Price does not always prevail; there are significant limits to arbitrage. After reviewing several case studies on violations of the Law of One Price, they draw the following conclusion:

What prevents arbitrageurs from enforcing the Law? . . . For many of the examples we have discussed, markets were free and open, and selling short was not particularly costly. So, why aren't the arbs doing their job? The answer is that violations of the Law do not generally create arbitrage opportunities (meaning sure profits with no risk), they just create good but risky bets. . . . The law of one price is the basic building block of most of financial economic theorizing. The logic of why it should hold is simple: if the same asset is selling for two different prices simultaneously, then arbitrageurs will step in, correct the situation and make themselves a tidy profit at the same time. The concept is so basic that Steve Ross (1987) has written that "to make a parrot into a learned financial economist, he only needs to learn the single word 'arbitrage.'" As the examples we have discussed illustrate, it may be necessary to teach the parrot at least a few new words: "limits" and "risk" immediately come to mind and, for the very talented parrot, perhaps "short-sale constraints." (Lamont and Thaler, 2003, 200–201).

Economists are trained, like Ross's parrot, to believe that no arbitrage condition is essential for equilibrium. In particular, marginal utilities and products are all equal to prices for the economy to be in equilibrium. However, even in competitive financial markets, there are significant limits to arbitrage. The case can be made much more strongly for the real economy. Consider the decision of whether to build a factory for producing a specific product in a particular site. There are no close substitutes for such an action, so arbitrage cannot be relied upon to set its implicit price correctly. Besides, as we pointed out earlier, there are microeconomic fluctuations. Thus, given the same objective functions and constraints, we still have *distribution* of actions among agents.

Now, given a distribution of responses by microeconomic agents, we have a probability distribution, not a point for the macroeoconomic equilibrium. In the standard analysis, because macroeconomic equilibrium is represented as a point in some space or set, its evolution is described by an *ordinary differential equation*. In contrast, in our approach, equilibrium is a distribution, and, therefore, we need a *partial differential equation* to describe evolution of a macroeconomic equilibrium over time. This is precisely the Chapman–Kolmogorov equation, or master equation explained in Chapter 2.

For macroeconomics, the most important implication of this new concept of equilibrium is that productivities across sectors/firms substantially differ at each moment. In standard macroeconomics, production factors are assumed to move instantly across sectors/firms to keep their marginal productivities equal. The existence of (uniform) adjustment cost modifies this statement only inessentially, so long as the adjustment cost is common across agents, as is usually assumed. In equilibrium marginal productivities must be equated, because if they differ, production factors can gain by moving across sectors/firms, contradicting the notion of equilibrium. The standard reasoning is that there should be no room for arbitrage in equilibrium.

We have argued that this is *not* the case for the real economy. The same difference in productivity actually entails different responses from different economic agents. Because the nature and degree of uncertainty faced by each agent differs, and adjustment costs differ across agents, there is a *range* of responses from economic agents. Such microeconomic behavior can be best approximated by the *jump Markov process* explained in Chapter 2.

In the first section, we first consider micro behavior in a stochastic framework. We maintain that to provide macroeconomics with proper micro foundations is to define transition rates in Markov models based on microeconomic behavior. We emphasize that because of microeconomic fluctuations, *equilibrium becomes a probability distribution rather than a point.* For macroeconomics, distribution of productivity across sectors/firms is most important. This is the theme of the second section. We will show that the distribution of productivity becomes a particular type, namely the Boltzmann–Gibbs distribution in equilibrium. This distribution is conditioned by the level of aggregate demand. When the aggregate demand is high, production factors are mobilized to sectors with higher productivity. This analysis provides proper microfoundations for Keynes's principle of effective demand.

3.1. Microeconomic Foundations

Given intrinsic heterogeneity of economic agents, and microfluctuations in objective functions and constraints of all the microunits, the best research strategy for us is to describe the macroeconomy as continuous-time Markov chains, that is Markov processes with at most countable states, also called jump Markov processes. In this approach, *to provide microeconomic foundations is to specify state space and transition rates for a jump Markov process that describe the behavior of economic agents.* In this section, we explain this in detail.

Some economists suggest that representative agent models such as the Ramsey model can actually accommodate heterogeneous economic agents. In our view, the "heterogeneity" in this case is extremely limited and artificial, and does not actually deserve the name of heterogeneity. Caselli and Ventura (2000), for example, make the assumption that consumers differ only in their preferences for public goods to show that the standard Ramsey model can accommodate such "heterogeneity." If differences in preference for public goods were the only source of heterogeneity among consumers, then certainly the challenge for macroeconomists would be much relieved! This is not the sort of heterogeneity we have in mind in this book. In reality, economic agents differ in every respect, and their behaviors are all subject to stochastic fluctuations. Thus, we need a stochastic approach from the outset. Let us begin with a simple binary choice model as an example.

Binary Choice Model

Suppose there are N economic agents in the economy. There are two possible levels of production, "high" and "low." This assumption simplifies our presentation, though theoretically, the model does not have to be binary so long as the number of "choices" (here, the levels of production) is at most countable for each agent. The reader might think that the binary choice model is special, and that its scope is limited in economics. However, we will later explain that the binary choice model actually accommodates sophisticated (stochastic) dynamic optimization commonly used in economics. We note again that the number of "choices" does not have to be two, but any positive integer. Given heterogeneity of a large number of agents, and the existence of micro fluctuations of preferences and technologies, the jump Markov process is the best approach.

Now, the "high" level of production is denoted by y^* whereas the "low" level by y ($0 < y < y^*$). If the number of economic agents which produce at the high level, y^*, is n ($n = 0, 1, 2, \ldots N$), their total output in the economy or GDP is

$$Y = ny^* + (N - n)y \tag{3.1}$$

where Y is the state of the macroeconomy in this model, and we are interested in the behavior of Y. We denote the share of economic agents which produce at y^* by x:

$$x = \frac{n}{N} \quad (n = 0, 1, 2, \cdots, N). \tag{3.2}$$

Using x, we can rewrite Y as follows:

$$Y = N\left[xy^* + (1 - x)y\right]. \tag{3.3}$$

Where n is large, x can be regarded as a fraction ($0 \leqslant x \leqslant 1$). Equation (3.3) shows that Y and x correspond to each other. Whereas x fluctuates between 0 and 1, so does Y between Ny and Ny^*.

Changes in x are assumed to follow a jump Markov process. For a short time Δt, there are three possibilities: no economic agent changes its production level, or one either raises or lowers its production level. The process is then characterized by two transition rates, one from state y to y^* and the other from y^* to y. Once these two transition rates are given, it is known that they uniquely determine the stochastic process, and consequently the (stochastic) dynamics it produces.

It is important to recognize that an economic agent's decisions stochastically change. Namely, some agents change their decisions even if the *macroeconomic environment remains unchanged*. They are microeconomic fluctuations. We are not able to explain why an economic agent changed his decisions because we never observe his preferences and constraints. Luckily, we do not need to know the reason an economic agent changed his decisions for macroeconomics; it is simply irrelevant. All we need to know is transition rates based on the observable macroeconomic variables.

The probability that one economic agent currently producing at the low level, y, raises its production to high level, y^*, depends naturally on the number of agents producing at y, that is $N(1 - x)$. Similarly, the transition rate from y^* to y depends on Nx. This is the same as a simple fact that the probability that a baby is born at each moment in time is higher in a society with greater population.

Assume in addition that transition rates are state-dependant, that is, $N(1 - x)$ and Nx are modified by factors $\eta_1(x)$ and $\eta_2(x)$, respectively. Specifically, the transition rate from y to y^*, r, is

$$r = \lambda N(1 - x)\eta_1(x), \quad \lambda > 0, \tag{3.4}$$

and, the transition rate from y^* to y, ℓ, is

$$\ell = \mu Nx\eta_2(x), \quad \mu > 0. \tag{3.5}$$

The transition rates r and ℓ depend not only on the number of economic agents in each state, namely $N(1 - x)$ and Nx, but also on $\eta_1(x)$ and $\eta_2(x)$. The factors $\eta_1(x)$ and $\eta_2(x)$ mean that the optimal strategy taken by each agent depends on the state of the economy, namely x or Y. For example, equation (3.4) means that a switch of strategy by an economic agent from "bear" who finds y as optimal, to "bull" who finds y^* as optimal, depends on the share of bulls. Equation (3.5) means that the same is true also for a switch of strategy from y^* to y. The state-dependant transition rates such as (3.4) and (3.5) mean the presence of *externality*. Diamond (1982) gives an example of such externality in a search model.

Here $\eta_1(x)$ and $\eta_2(x)$ are defined as

$$\eta_1(x) = X^{-1}e^{\beta g(x)}, \quad \beta > 0, \tag{3.6}$$

$$\eta_2(x) = 1 - \eta_1(x) = X^{-1}e^{-\beta g(x)}, \tag{3.7}$$

where

$$X = e^{\beta g(x)} + e^{-\beta g(x)}. \tag{3.8}$$

The expression X simply ensures that the sum of $\eta_1(x)$ and $\eta_2(x)$ is equal to one, as it must be. At first sight, (3.6) and (3.7) may look arbitrary or even odd. However, they are actually quite generic, and known as the Boltzmann–Gibbs type transition rates. The Boltzmann–Gibbs type transition rate is, in fact, one of the key concepts in statistical physics. In Section 3.2, we will discuss the Boltzmann–Gibbs distribution of productivity in the macroeconomy. In what follows, we explain how naturally (3.6) and (3.7) arise in microeconomic models of choice under uncertainty.

Microeconomic Foundations for Transition Rates

In our approach, to provide microfoundations means to specify transition rates of the jump Markov processes, which describe the behavior of economic agents. In the present example, the transition rates $\eta_1(x)$ and $\eta_2(x)$ in (3.6) and (3.7) are of the Boltzmann–Gibbs type. They arise in many contexts. Here, we offer two interpretations for them based on the microeconomic behavior of individual agents. The first is based on approximate calculations of the perceived difference of the expected utilities, or advantages of one choice over the other. The second interpretation is based on discrete choice theory such as Anderson et al. (1993) or McFadden (1974).

Representation of Relative Merits of Alternatives. Denote by $V_1(x)$ the expected "return" from choice 1, given that fraction x has selected choice 1. For clarity, think of the discounted present value of benefit stream based on the assumption that fraction x remains the same over some planning horizon. Define $V_2(x)$ analogously. Note that we treat V_1 and V_2 as random variables. In our example above, choice 1 is to produce at the "high" level or to be a "bull," and choice 2 is to produce at the "low" level or to be a "bear." As we will explain it shortly, $V_1(x)$ and $V_2(x)$ can be derived from (stochastic) dynamic optimization commonly used in economics.

Let $\eta_1(x)$ be the probability that V_1 is greater than or equal to V_2:

$$\eta_1(x) = P_r\{V_1(x) \geqslant V_2(x)\}. \tag{3.9}$$

We omit x from the arguments of V from now on.

Assume that the difference $\Delta V = V_1 - V_2$ is approximately distributed as a normal random variable with mean $g(x)$ and variance $\sigma^2(x)$:

$$\Pr(\Delta V = v) = \frac{1}{\sqrt{2\pi}\sigma(x)} \exp\left[-\frac{(v - g(x))^2}{2\sigma^2(x)}\right].$$

This distribution reflects microeconomic fluctuations. In the standard approach the economic agent knows which of V_1 and V_2 is greater, and therefore, we do not speak of the *probability* that V_1 exceeds V_2. We will later explain this point in detail by using a well-known search model of Diamond (1982).

We calculate the probability that the difference is nonnegative, namely choice 1 is preferred to choice 2:

$$\eta_1(x) = \Pr\{\Delta V \geqslant 0\} = \frac{1}{2}[1 + \text{erf}(u)] \tag{3.10}$$

where the error function is defined[1] by

$$\text{erf}(u) := \frac{2}{\sqrt{\pi}} \int_0^u e^{-y^2} dy.$$

Here, u is defined as follows:

$$u = \frac{g(x)}{\sqrt{2}\sigma(x)}.$$

---

[1]   See Abramovitz and Stegun (1968) for the error function.

Now, Ingber (1982) demonstrates that the error function can be well approximated by the hyperbolic function:

$$\operatorname{erf}(u) \approx \tanh(\kappa u), \quad \left(\kappa = \frac{2}{\sqrt{\pi}}\right).$$

The hyperbolic function $\tanh x$ is defined as

$$\tanh x = (e^x - e^{-x})/(e^x + e^{-x}).$$

This approximation is remarkably good and useful for $|u| < 1$, that is when the coefficient of variation is large. For example, for small $|u|$, we note that

$$\operatorname{erf}(u) = \kappa\left(u - \frac{u^3}{3} + \frac{u^5}{5} + \cdots\right),$$

whereas

$$\tanh(\kappa u) = \kappa\left(u - \frac{u^3}{2.36} + \frac{u^5}{4.63} + \cdots\right).$$

Noting $\tanh x = (e^x - e^{-x})/(e^x + e^{-x})$, we obtain

$$\operatorname{erf}(u) \approx \frac{e^{\kappa u} - e^{-\kappa u}}{e^{\kappa u} + e^{-\kappa u}}. \tag{3.11}$$

By defining β as

$$\beta = \sqrt{\frac{2}{\pi}}\left(\frac{1}{\sigma}\right), \tag{3.12}$$

we deduce from (3.10) and (3.11) the desired expression of the Boltzmann–Gibbs type (3.6):

$$\eta_1(x) = \Pr\{\Delta V \geqslant 0\} \approx X^{-1}\exp[\beta g(x)]$$

where $X = e^{\beta g(x)} + e^{-\beta g(x)}$.

This offers one interpretation of β that appears in the expressions of the transition rates (3.6) and (3.7). Equation (3.12) shows that β *is basically a measure of uncertainty*. For example, large variances mean large uncertainty in the expected difference of the alternative choices. Such situations are represented by small values of β. Conversely, small variances means more precise knowledge about the difference in the values of two choices. It is represented by large values of β. Given β, or the degree of uncertainty, we interpret $g(x)$ as the conditional mean of the "prospect" that choice 1 is better than choice 2, conditional on the fraction x has decided on choice 1.[2] These results will be extensively used in Chapter 4 to clarify the role of uncertainty in the macroeconomy.

[2]   Aoki (1996, Chapters 3 and 8) shows how β arises as a Lagrange multiplier to incorporate macrosignals as constraints. Parameter β is related to the elasticity of the number of microeconomic configurations with respect to macrosignals. Small values of β mean that the number of microeconomic configurations responds little when macroeconomic signals change. This is in accordance with the

Discrete Choice Theory and Extreme Value Distributions. We offer another interpretation of the Boltzmann–Gibbs type equations (3.6) and (3.7) based on discrete choice theory. Suppose we calculate the probability that the discounted present value one, V_1, is higher than value two, V_2, associated with alternative choices 1 and 2, respectively. Suppose further that we represent some of the incompleteness and impreciseness of information or uncertainty about consequences surrounding the value calculation by adding random terms to the present values as

$$\widehat{V}_1 = V_1 + \varepsilon_1 \tag{3.13}$$

and

$$\widehat{V}_2 = V_2 + \varepsilon_2.$$

One interpretation is that these ε's are noises to account for inevitable fluctuations in the present values. A second interpretation is to think of them as (additional) evidence to support a particular choice. Other interpretations are certainly possible. For example, McFadden (1974) speaks of common or community preference and individual deviations from the common norm in the context of utility maximization.

One quick assumption to obtain the Boltzmann–Gibbs type expression in the case of two alternative choices is to assume that

$$\varepsilon = \varepsilon_2 - \varepsilon_1 \tag{3.14}$$

is distributed according to

$$\Pr\left(\varepsilon \leqslant x\right) = \frac{1}{1 + e^{-\beta x}}, \tag{3.15}$$

for some positive β. With this distribution, a large value of ε supports more strongly the possibility that $V_1 > V_2$. Parameter β controls how *much* changes in x translate into changes in probabilities. With a smaller value of β, a larger increase in x, or more "evidence," is needed to increase the probability that favors choice 1. The larger the value of β is, the smaller increase in x is needed to change the probability by a given amount.

With the probability distribution (3.15), we immediately obtain from (13) the desired expression of the Boltzmann–Gibbs type (3.6):

$$P_1 = P_r\left(\widehat{V}_1 \geqslant \widehat{V}_2\right) = \frac{e^{\beta V_1}}{e^{\beta V_1} + e^{\beta V_2}} = \frac{e^{\beta g}}{e^{\beta g} + e^{-\beta g}}. \tag{3.16}$$

Here, we define g as

$$g = \frac{(V_1 - V_2)}{2}.$$

---

interpretation that when β is small, agents face large uncertainty in their choices (see Aoki, 1996, 216). A similar interpretation may be offered from the viewpoint of the hazard function (see Aoki, 2002, Section 6.2).

When V_1 and V_2 in (3.13) depend on the state of the macroeconomy, x, g becomes a function of x, $g(x)$. To reiterate, in this framework, a larger value of β implies a larger difference of $|P_1 - P_2|$. Namely, with a larger the value of β (little uncertainty), one of the alternatives tends to dominate.

We have provided two microeconomic foundations for the Boltzmann–Gibbs type transition rates, (3.6) and (3.7). Seemingly exotic transition rates (3.6) and (3.7) of the Boltzmann–Gibbs type have, in fact, very robust and generic microeconomic foundations. Yet, some readers might think that they hold only for simple binary choice models, and wonder how they are related to sophisticated dynamic optimization commonly used in economics. Transition rates such as (3.6) and (3.7) are, in fact, consistent with dynamic optimization.

To explain how the above analysis is related to dynamic optimization, we first give a brief discussion on value functions using a simple asset price model. Then, we discuss a well-known search model of Diamond (1982) as an example of general equilibrium model. The comparison between the Diamond model and its counterpart should make it clear how our approach differs from models based on the representative agent.

Value Function and Dynamic Optimization

In our discussion of microeconomic foundations for the Boltzmann–Gibbs type transition rates (3.6), (3.7), and (3.8), we had the value functions V (namely, V_1 and V_2 of equations (3.9) and (3.13)). Although we referred to V_i as the "expected return from choice i," some readers may not be sure how V_i are related to dynamic optimization commonly used in economics. To clarify the point, we consider a simple asset price model as a concrete example.

The asset value V satisfies the following equation:

$$rV = \rho + E\left(\frac{dV}{dt}\right). \tag{3.17}$$

Here, the first term on the right is the flow of rewards or revenues, and the second term is the expected capital gain. The symbol r on the left-hand side is the interest rate, which is assumed to be constant. The sum of flow return and the capital gains on the right-hand side must be equal to the yield or return to the asset on the left-hand side for the asset to be willingly held.

In the finance literature, the underlying stochastic processes are usually modeled by some diffusion processes. Here, the stochastic processes X_t underlying flow income ρ are jump Markov processes. The value function with infinite horizon *with the initial state a* is defined by

$$V_a = E_a \int_0^\infty e^{-rt}\rho(X_t)dt \tag{3.18}$$

where E_a denotes the expectation with the initial condition $X_0 = a$ of a jump Markov process $\{X_t\}$, $t \geqslant 0$. It is known that $V = (V_a : a \in S)$ is the unique bounded solution to

$$(r - W) V = \rho, \tag{3.19}$$

where W is the generator matrix of the jump Markov process with transition rate $w(i, j)$:

$$\Pr(X_{t+h} = j \,|\, X_t = i) = \delta_{i,j} + w(i, j)h + o(h). \tag{3.20}$$

That is, the matrix of transition rates, $P(t) = (p_{i,j}(t))$ satisfies the backward equation

$$\frac{dP(t)}{dt} = WP(t), \tag{3.21}$$

with $P(0) = I$.

We illustrate this asset price model using a simple example with two states, a and b, without resorting to the Ito calculus. The number of states does not have to be two so long as it is countable. This two-state jump Markov process is specified by the two transition rates $w(a, b)$ and $w(b, a)$. The former is the transition rate from a to b, and the latter from b to a. In a small time interval of duration Δt, then, the probability of state a changes to b with probability $w(a, b) \Delta t + o(\Delta t)$. In this case, the value function over an infinite horizon is given by

$$r V_a = \rho_a + w(a, b) (V_b - V_a) \tag{3.22}$$

and

$$r V_b = \rho_b + w(b, a) (V_a - V_b)$$

where the subscripts refer to the two possible states, a and b. For example, ρ_a is the flow revenue or dividend in state a. Recall that $w(b, a) = -w(a, b)$.

Solving equations (3.22) for V_a and V_b, we see that they are the weighted averages of the two present values of the flow revenues

$$V_a = \pi_a \frac{\rho_a}{r} + (1 - \pi_a) \frac{\rho_b}{r}, \tag{3.23}$$

and

$$V_b = (1 - \pi_b) \frac{\rho_a}{r} + \pi_b \frac{\rho_b}{r},$$

where the weights π_a and π_b are defined respectively by

$$\pi_a = \frac{r + w(b, a)}{r + w(a, b) + w(b, a)},$$

and

$$\pi_b = \frac{r + w(a, b)}{r + w(a, b) + w(b, a)}.$$

ρ_a/r is the present value of the streams ρ_a, and the same for ρ_b/r. In equation (3.23), the expression $1 - \pi_a$ gives the probability that state a changes to state b, while $1 - \pi_b$ gives the probability that state b changes to state a.

Now, V does not have to be an asset value, but any value function of alternatives. The point is that the outcome of any dynamic optimization, V, depends on the initial state. States a and b in the above example correspond to $x = n/N$ in the binary choice model we previously considered. Suppose V_a depends on two choices of economic agent, 1 and 2, because choices 1 and 2 affect flow returns ρ. Let us denote two possible values $V_1(a)$ and $V_2(a)$. $V_1(b)$ and $V_2(b)$ can be defined similarly. These value functions are basically $V_1(x)$ and $V_2(x)$ in equations (3.9) and (3.13).

It should be clear by now that value functions $V_1(x)$ and $V_2(x)$ in equations (3.9) and (3.13), and accordingly, the Boltzmann–Gibbs type transition rates (3.6), (3.7), and (3.8) in the binary choice model, are consistent with standard dynamic optimization. Put another way, *the apparently very simple binary choice model actually accommodates sophisticated dynamic optimization under uncertainty.*

In Chapter 4, we will explore the dynamics of the binary choice model, and make clear the role of uncertainty in the macroeconomy. Here, we clarify the difference between the standard approach and ours further. Specifically, to see how the difference arises in macroeconomic (or general equilibrium) models, we next consider a well-known search model of Diamond (1982).

Diamond Search Model

The Diamond model is a simple barter model with identical risk-neutral agents where trade is coordinated by a stochastic matching process. In this model, there are two types of agents: employed and unemployed. Let k be the number of employed, and n be the total number of agents. The fraction of the employed, k/n, or equivalently k, is used as the state variable by holding n fixed.

Each of the $n - k$ unemployed persons independently encounters a production opportunity that appears at the rate of $a\Delta t$ in a small time interval Δt. If the opportunity is accepted, it yields the unit output at the cost c. The cost c is a nonnegative random number with a known distribution function G. There is a reservation or threshold cost $c^*(k)$, to be determined endogenously. Above the reservation cost c^*, the opportunity is rejected as being too costly. When the opportunity is accepted, the person's status changes from being unemployed to being employed.

Each of k employed persons independently encounters a trading opportunity at the rate $b(k/n)$ per unit time. It is natural to assume that for each individual, the arrival of a potential partner is a Poisson process with arrival rate $b(k/n)$ since k/n is the fraction of the population searching for a trading partner. When an employed person encounters a trading opportunity, he forms a pair with another randomly selected employed person, the pair trade, each member of the pair consumes the output of the partner to receive instantaneous utility v, and their status changes from being employed to being unemployed. See Diamond (1982) for more explanations for these assumptions.

Production opportunities arrive to the unemployed at the rate a as a Poisson process. If undertaken, each production opportunity yields a unit of output with cost c. Only production with cost c^* or less will be undertaken. Thus, the transition rate from k to $k + 1$ is given by $(n - k)a\,G(c^*)$ where c^* is the reservation cost in the sense that only production with cost $c \leqslant c^*$ is undertaken. Because this reservation cost is a choice variable and depends on k/n, we will write it as $c^*(k/n)$, or as $c^*(k)$ for short.

For an employed agent, trading opportunities arrive as a Poisson process at the rate $\beta(k/n)$. This arrival rate (the matching rate) depends naturally on the number (or the fraction) of counterparts, that is employed persons k (or k/n). When employed agents meet, they trade, exchange, and charge their status to the unemployed. As a consequence, the number of employed decreases by 2, from k to $k - 2$. Thus, the transition rate from state k to $k - 2$ is equal to the arrival rate of trading opportunities, $\beta(k/n)$.

The Chapman–Kolmogorov equation or the master equation at time t for the probability of employed being k, $P(k, t)$, is

$$\frac{\partial P(k, t)}{\partial t} = r_{k-1} P(k - 1, t) + l_{k+2} P(k + 2, t) - (r_k + l_k) P(k, t) \quad (3.24)$$

where l_k is the transition rate for the leftward move from state k, and r_k is that of the rightward move. This is essentially the birth–death equation we have explained in Chapter 2. The only difference arises from the fact that the leftward move involves a step of two units, not a single unit, because a matched pair of agents – that is, two agents – change their status. As explained above, the transition rate for the rightward move is

$$r_k = (n - k)a G \left(c^*(k/n)\right) = n(1 - k/n)\,aG\left(c^*(k/n)\right) \quad (3.25)$$

while that for the leftward move rate is

$$l_k = \frac{k}{2}b\left(\frac{k}{2}\right). \quad (3.26)$$

Equation (3.24) corresponds to equation (3.3) in Diamond (1982), here reproduced as equation (D.3):

$$\dot{e} = a(1 - e)\ G(c^*) - eb(e). \quad (D.3)$$

In equation (D.3), e is the fraction of the population employed in the trading process or simply the "employed," and equal to k/n in our model.

Now, the reader must note the difference between equation (3.24) and equation (D.3). The Diamond model has two *types* of agents; the employed and the unemployed. However, in each group, there is only *the representative agent*. In other words, there are the representative employed, and the representative unemployed. *There are no microeconomic fluctuations* within each group. That is why the fraction of the employed e is given as a real number, and the evolution of e is described by an ordinary differential equation, namely equation (D.3).

In contrast, in our model, because of microeconomic fluctuations, the fraction e at each time is not determined. All we have is the *probability* that the fraction of the employed is e or k/n, that is $P(k, t)$. *To describe the evolution of this probability distribution, we need a partial differential equation.* This is nothing but the Chapman–Kolmogorov equation or the master equation, equation (3.24).

The Diamond model explicitly considers dynamic optimization of agents. Lifetime utility is the present discounted value of instantaneous utility, V. Because trade and production take place at discrete times t_i, lifetime utility satisfies

$$V = \sum_{i=1}^{\infty} e^{-rt_i} V_{t_i}. \tag{3.27}$$

Here, r is the discount rate. Individuals are assumed to maximize the expected value of lifetime utility with respect to the times of work (or the arrival of production opportunity) and consumption (or matching). In this model, the only decision to make is which production opportunities to undertake, or in other words, the determination of the reservation cost, c^*.

Diamond considers a simple dynamic programming problem with the expected present discounted value of lifetime utility for employed and unemployed, W_e and W_u, respectively. Then, the discount rate r times W_i ($i = e, u$) equals the sum of the flow of instantaneous utility and the expected capital gain from a change in status, namely either $W_e - W_u$ or $W_u - W_e$. Therefore, we have

$$r W_e = b(y - W_e + W_u)$$

and (D.5)

$$r W_u = a \int_0^{c^*} (W_e - W_u - c) dG(c).$$

These two equations are equations (D.5) in Diamond (1982) which we reproduce as equations (D.5) above. Here y is instantaneous utility of consumption (or the arrival of trading opportunity).

An unemployed person accepts any opportunity that raises expected utility. Thus, we have the reservation cost

$$c^* = W_e - W_u = \frac{by + a \int_0^{c^*} c \, dG}{r + b + aG(c^*)}. \tag{3.28}$$

Because b depends on the level of "aggregate demand" e, the reservation cost c^* depends on e, too.

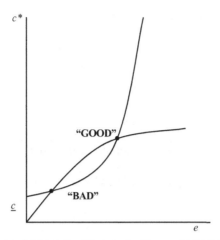

Figure 3.1. Multiple Equilibria in the Diamond (1982) Model.

For the steady state, the right-hand side of equation (D.3) is zero. Namely, the steady state satisfies the following equation:

$$a(1 - e)G(c^*) = eb(e). \qquad (3.29)$$

The share of employed e and the reservation cost c^* in steady state are, therefore, simultaneously determined by two equations, (3.28) and (3.29). In general, it is possible that we have multiple equilibria. Figure 3.1 reproduces a figure in Diamond (1982). The figure shows two equilibria; one is a "good" and the other a "bad" equilibrium.

The analysis in our model is parallel to Diamond's. We have already explained that the dynamic equation in the Diamond model, equation (D.3) which is an ordinary differential equation, corresponds to our Chapman–Kolmogorov equation which is the partial differential equation (3.24). In what follows, we show that the value functions and optimization (the determination of the reservation cost) in our analysis are also parallel to Diamond's.

Let $W_e(k, t)$ be the present discounted value of the lifetime utility of an employed person in state k at time t. Similarly let $W_u(k, t)$ be that of an unemployed person when the state is k. Because k is a random variable, we take the expectation of these random value functions after we derive the stationary distribution of k. We drop t from the argument of the value functions because dynamic programming involves an infinite horizon, and the problem is time-homogeneous.

Denote the discount rate by r. Value functions depend on the fraction k/n rather than on k directly. For shorter notation, however, we denote them simply by $W_e(k)$ and $W_u(k)$ for the employed and unemployed when the number of the employed is k. For an employed agent, we obtain

$$r W_e(k) = b\left(\frac{k}{n}\right)[v + W_u(k-2) - W_e(k)]$$

$$+ (n-k)\,a\,G\left(c^*(k)\right)[W_e(k+1) - W_e(k)]$$

$$+ \frac{k-2}{2}b\left(\frac{k}{n}\right)[W_e(k-2) - W_e(k)] \qquad (3.30)$$

for k between 3 and $n-1$. Similarly, for an unemployed agent,[3] we obtain

$$r W_u(k) = a\int_0^{c^*(k)}[W_e(k+1) - W_u(k) - z]dG(z)$$

$$+ (n-k-1)aG(c^*(k))[W_u(k+1) - W_u(k)]$$

$$+ \frac{k}{2}b\left(\frac{k}{n}\right)[W_u(k-2) - W_u(k)] \qquad (3.31)$$

for $k = 2, 3, \ldots, n-1$.[4] Equations (3.21) and (3.22) are parallel to Diamond's equations (D.5). The determination of the reservation cost, given these value functions, is analyzed by Aoki and Shirai (2000).

Our model and Diamond's are obviously quite similar, but there is actually a fundamental difference between the two. The apparent similarity must not hide this fundamental difference. The difference arises from the existence of *microeconomic fluctuations* in our approach. Diamond's model is a search model; that is, individual agent faces uncertainty and his behavior is stochastic. However, because the number of agents is assumed to be infinite, microeconomic fluctuations are assumed away in the limit. The seemingly innocuous continuum assumption, in effect, brings the representative agent into the model. As we pointed out earlier, in the Diamond model, there is the representative agent in each of two states (unemployment and employment). There are no microeconomic fluctuations; there are the employed and the unemployed. That is why the behavior of the macroeconomy can be described by deterministic equations in the Diamond model. Specifically, the share of employed e and the reservation cost c^* in steady state are simultaneously determined by two equations (3.19) and (3.20). Figure 3.1 shows two equilibria.

In the standard analysis like Diamond's, the important problem of *equilibrium selection* then arises; that is, which equilibrium, "good" or "bad" in Figure 3.1, is to be chosen. Krugman (1991) discusses this problem of equilibrium selection in his article "History vs. Expectations." History and expectations may play an

---

[3]   The probability intensity for the transition from state k to state $k+1$ is $(n-k)aG^*(c)$. Note that $(n-k-1)aG^*$ is the intensity for the event that one of other unemployed agents become employed while he remains unemployed. The intensity for him to become employed is aG^*. The transition from k to $k+1$ is simply the sum of these two possibilities.

[4]   There are boundary conditions, but we do not use them, so they are not mentioned here.

important role in such framework, but any sophisticated analysis on this issue cannot escape arbitrariness.

In contrast, in our approach, the problem of equilibrium selection does not arise. In this respect, our approach is fundamentally different from the standard approach of Diamond. Because of microeconomic fluctuations, we have a probability distribution which has two peaks rather than two points as shown in Figure 3.1. The economy keeps fluctuating with each of "good" and "bad" states having some positive probability. With the help of the *potential function*, the point is fully explained in Chapter 4.

In economics, it is often assumed that economic agents are represented by a continuum such as $[0, 1]$. For some purposes, it may be an innocuous assumption, or it may useful. However, we must be aware that a continuum assumption necessarily assumes away microeconomic fluctuations. We maintain that for the purpose of macroeconomics, it is not a valid assumption.

In summary, the comparison of the Diamond model and our approach makes clear the following points.

1. Value functions that determine transition rates are consistent with standard (stochastic) dynamic optimization.
2. In the standard approach, such as the Diamond model, microeconomic fluctuations are assumed away. As a consequence, the macroeconomic equilibrium is given by a point, that is, a real number. In the Diamond model, it is the share of employed, e. In contrast, in our approach, because of microeconomic fluctuations, we have a probability distribution as macroeconomic equilibrium. Evolution of macroequilibrium as a probability distribution is described by a partial differential equation instead of an ordinary differential equation – the Champan–Kolmogorov equation or the master equation. The fraction e is a random variable with positive variance around the mean.
3. As a consequence, even if we have multiple "equilibria" (more precisely, multiple basins of attraction of the potential function), the problem of equilibrium selection does not arise.

In the next section, we will explain the important implications of our approach for macroeconomics. In particular, we will shed new light on the role of aggregate demand and by so doing, clarify the meaning of Keynes's principle of effective demand.

3.2. Equilibrium in the Macroeconomy

We have seen that because of intrinsic heterogeneity of economic agents and the existence of microeconomic fluctuations, in general, we have equilibrium as a *distribution*, not as a point in the macroeconomy. In this section, we focus on distribution of productivity.

Differences in productivity remain in the economy at all times. In the standard reasoning, differences in productivity are taken as a sign of disequilibrium. They simply contradict equilibrium. This section explains that differences in productivity do not actually contradict equilibrium conditions, but rather it is a necessity that we have a distribution of productivity in equilibrium.

The equality of productivities across sectors/firms is the fundamental reason demand does not matter in determining the aggregate output. Demand affects only the composition of outputs. Conversely, the existence of *underemployment*, which is equivalent to inequality of the value marginal products across sectors, means that total output (GDP) can be increased by changing demand.

Suppose that there are n sectors in the economy, and that the amount of labor necessary to produce one unit of product in sector i is a_i. Labor is the only input. Taking the good in the least productive sector as a numeraire with p_i as the relative price of the ith good, we can arrange sectors in such a way that

$$\frac{p_1}{a_1} > \frac{p_2}{a_2} > \cdots > \frac{1}{a_n}. \tag{3.32}$$

Obviously, this order does not depend on the choice of numeraire. p_i/a_i is the *value* marginal product of labor in terms of good n; sector 1 is the most productive sector, sector 2 the second-most productive sector, and so on. One could interpret sector n as being the lowest productivity sector such as "household production (housework)," unemployment (job search) and "nonlabor force" status (leisure). Labor in each sector sums to a given total labor:

$$\sum_{i=1}^{n} L_i = L.$$

Given the demand for the product of the ith sector D_i, total output in the economy as a whole or GDP is

$$Y = \sum_{i=1}^{n-1} p_i D_i + \frac{\left[L - \sum_{i=1}^{n-1} a_i D_i \right]}{a_n} = \left(\frac{L}{a_n} \right) + \sum_{i=1}^{n-1} \left[p_i - \left(\frac{a_i}{a_n} \right) \right] D_i. \tag{3.33}$$

In the neoclassical equilibrium, the value marginal product is equated across sectors:

$$\frac{p_1}{a_1} = \frac{p_2}{a_2} = \cdots = \frac{1}{a_n}.$$

Therefore, we obtain

$$Y = \frac{L}{a_n}. \tag{3.34}$$

Total output is independent of demand, and depends solely on the endowment of the production factor, L, and technology, a_i.

However, when productivity differs across sectors, that is, when inequality (3.32) holds, an increase in D_i raises Y. Even a shift of demand increases Y. In short, Y depends on demand. In this case, we say that there is *underemployment* in the economy.

It is important to recognize that (involuntary) unemployment is merely a particular form of *underemployment*, and that underemployment, defined as differences in the productivity of production factors, is more important than unemployment for the proposition that demand affects total output. Not only in the textbook Keynesian model, but also in many recent models where demand plays a role in the determination of total output, underemployment – or equivalently the inequality of productivity across sectors – is assumed. For example, a combination of increasing returns and imperfect competition often leads us to the conclusion that demand matters (Matsuyama, 1995). However, such a combination is only a *sufficient* condition for underemployment.[5] The structures of the models in which demand plays a role are arbitrary, and therefore giving this or that example is of little significance.

For demand to play an essential role in the determination of aggregate output, the inequality of productivity across sectors/activities, or underemployment, is the generic condition. Why and how does the inequality of productivity persist? One might think that differences in productivity across sectors imply unexploited profit opportunities, and therefore that they contradict equilibrium. However, heterogeneous economic agents actually have different thresholds for a change in their strategies. In the previous section, we explained how uncertainty produces such heterogeneous responses among economic agents. As Lamont and Thaler (2003) pointed out, differences in productivity across sectors/firms do not actually mean the existence of unexploited profit opportunities, or opportunities for arbitrage, but merely "good but risky bets."

The kind of view we are advancing here is not foreign to labor economists, at least to some of them. Mortensen (2003), for example, documents wage dispersion observed for most economies, and summarizes his explanation as follows:

Why are similar workers paid differently? Why do some jobs pay more than others? I have argued that wage dispersion of this kind reflects differences in employer productivity. More productive employers offer higher pay to attract and retain more workers. Workers flow from

---

[5] In the model of Matsuyama (1995), for example, two technologies are assumed. One is constant returns to scale in the production of "leisure," the other in the production of the "consumption goods" enjoys increasing returns. In his model, GDP includes not only the consumption goods, but also leisure. The government expenditure G affects GDP because the government's propensity to spend on the consumption goods is higher than that of households. Thus, an increase in G tilts demand towards the sector that enjoys high productivity. Increasing returns are, however, essential for "involuntary unemployment" (see Weitzman, 1982).

less to more productive employers in response to these pay differences, and both workers and employers invest search and recruiting efforts in that reallocation process. Exogenous turnover and job destruction on the one hand, and search friction on the other, prevent the labor market from ever attaining a state in which all workers are employed by the most productive firms. Instead, a continuous process of reallocation of workers from less to more productive employers interrupted by transitions to nonemployment induced by job destruction and other reasons for labor turnover generates a steady-state allocation of labor across firms of differing productivity. Of course, the assertion that wage dispersion is the consequence of productivity dispersion begs another question: What is the explanation for productivity dispersion?

To this question, Mortensen's explanation is as follows:

Relative demand and productive efficiency of individual firms are continually shocked by events. The shocks are the consequence of changes in tastes, changes in regulations, and changes induced by globalization among others. Another important source of persistent productivity differences across firms is the process of adopting technical innovation. We know that the diffusion of new and more efficient methods is a slow, drawn-out affair. Experimentation is required to implement new methods. Many innovations are embodied in equipment and forms of human capital that are necessarily long-lived. Learning how and where to apply any new innovation takes time and may well be highly firm specific. Since old technologies are not immediately replaced by the new for all of these reasons, productive efficiency varies considerably across firms at any point in time. (Mortensen, 2003, 129–130)

Technical progress is certainly an important source of productivity dispersion. Remember that Schumpeter (1934), emphasizing the role played by *innovations*, went so far to argue that without productivity differentials – the source of "excess profits" – the interest rate would have to become zero! Salter (1960) in his careful study on productivity and technical change also made the following remark:

The real problems arise because this continuous change in techniques is allied to a slow adjustment process caused by durable capital equipment. In such circumstances the flow of new techniques outstrips the ability of the system to adjust, and a gap appears between potential technical change and actual technical change. This distinction may be most conveniently described by means of an empirical example. [Table 3.1] sets out two measures of labour productivity in the United States blast-furnace industry for selected years between 1911 and 1926.

The first column records the output per man-hour of modern plants constructed at each date; it approximates to what will be termed 'best practice' labour productivity since it relates to the most up-to-date techniques available at each date. The second column records the average performance of the industry, the conventional output per man-hour estimate. In this industry, average labour productivity is only approximately half best-practice productivity. If all plants were up to best-practice standards known and in use, labour productivity would have doubled immediately. In fact, a decade and a half elapsed before this occurred, and in the meantime the potential provided by best-practice productivity had more than doubled. This is not an isolated example; all the available evidence, some of which is presented in latter chapters, points to the crucial importance of this delay in the utilization of new techniques. (Salter, 1960, 6–7)

Table 3.1. Best and Average Practice Labour
Productivity in the United States Blast-Furnace
Industry, Selected Years from 1911 to 1926 (Salter, 1960)

Year	Gross tons of pig-iron produced per man-hour	
	Best-practice plants	Industry average
1911	0.313	0.140
1917	0.326	0.150
1919	0.328	0.140
1921	0.428	0.178
1923	0.462	0.213
1925	0.512	0.285
1926	0.573	0.296

Source: U.S. Bureau of Labor Statistics, *The Productivity of Labor In Merchant Furnaces* (Bulletin no. 474, December 1928).

Mortensen's (2003) argument cited earlier clearly echoes Schumpeter (1934) and Salter (1960). We cannot suppose that all the economic agents and production factors move instantaneously to the sector with the highest productivity. We must describe their behavior by the transition rates in the jump Markov process. Consequently, at each moment in time we have a range of productivity levels. Aggregate demand affects the aggregate output because it affects the transition rates of production factors across sectors/firms with different productivities.

It is important to recognize that productivity depends not only on technology but also on changes in "the utilization rates" of production factors. The utilization rate of production factor, in turn, depends on demand. John Stuart Mill noticed this over 150 years ago:

When we have thus seen accurately what really constitues capital, it becomes obvious, that of the capital of a country, there is at all times a very large proportion lying idle. The annual produce of a country is never any thing approaching in magnitude to what it might be if all the resources devoted to reproduction, if all the capital, in short, of the country, were in full employment.

If every commodity on an average remained unsold for a length of time equal to that required for its production, it is obvious that, at any one time, no more than half the productive capital of the country would be really performing the functions of capital. . . .

From the considerations which we have now adduced, it is obvious what is meant by such phrases as a brisk demand, and a rapid circulation. There is a brisk demand and a rapid circulation, when goods, generally speaking, are sold as fast as they can be produced. There is slackness, on the contrary, and stagnation, when goods, which have been produced, remain for a long time unsold. In the former case, the capital which has been locked up in production is disengaged as soon as the production is completed; and can be immediately employed in further production. In the latter case, a large portion of the productive capital of the country is lying in temporary inactivity.

From what has been already said, it is obvious, that periods of "brisk demand" are also the periods of greatest production: the national capital is never called into full employment but at those periods.[6]

We must expect a distribution of productivity in equilibrium. *Under employment defined above is, therefore, not a sign of disequilibrium but rather a state of equilibrium.*

Distribution of Productivity in Equilibrium – The Boltzmann – Gibbs Distribution

Given differences in productivity across sectors, we face the following important questions: What would a distribution of productivity in the economy be? And how would it depend on the aggregate demand? To answer these questions, we can follow the general procedure of statistical physics. In our view, this statistical procedure is nothing but the proper microfoundations for macroeconomics. In what follows, we show the equilibrium distribution is expected to be the Boltzmann – Gibbs distribution.[7]

Suppose that an economy consists of S sectors with size n_i, $i = 1, \ldots, S$. Here, n_i is the amount of production factor used in sector i. The endowment of production factor in the economy as a whole, N, is exogenously given. That is, we have the following resource constraint:

$$\sum_{i=1}^{S} n_i = N. \tag{3.35}$$

Note that N is akin to population rather than the labor force because it includes people who are engaged in "household production" or enjoying leisure. The output of sector i, Y_i, is

$$Y_i = c_i n_i, \quad (i = 1, \ldots, S). \tag{3.36}$$

Here, c_i is sector i's productivity, and is given. Productivity differs across sectors. Without loss of generality, we can assume

$$c_1 < c_2 < \ldots < c_S.$$

---

[6]   In spite of this statement, Mill (1844) did not regard the state of "full employment" desirable, for the following reason. "This, however, is no reason for desiring such times; it is not desirable that the whole capital of the country should be in full employment. For the calculations of producers and traders being of necessity imperfect, there are always some commodities which are more or less in excess, as there are always some which are in deficiency. If therefore the whole truth were known, there would always be some classes of producers contracting, not extending, their operations. If all are endeavoring to extending them, it is a certain proof that some general delusion is afloat. The commonest cause of such delusion is some general, or very extensive, rise of prices (whether caused by speculation or by the currency) which persuades all dealers that they are growing rich."(67) Here, Mill sounds like Hayek, Friedman, and Lucas!

[7]   The point was first made by Yoshikawa (2003). See also Boltzmann entropy in Aoki (1996, Sec. 3.2.2).

The total output in the economy as a whole, or GDP, Y is then

$$Y = \sum_{i=1}^{s} Y_i = \sum_{i=1}^{s} c_i n_i. \tag{3.37}$$

We assume that Y is equal to the aggregate demand, D, which is exogenously given:

$$Y = D. \tag{3.38}$$

From (3.37) and (3.38), we obtain

$$\sum_{i=1}^{s} c_i n_i = D \tag{3.39}$$

as another constraint. Here, D is exogenously given.

We are interested in the distribution of production factors across sectors, namely $n = (n_1, \ldots, n_s)$ or $n/N = (n_1/N, \ldots, n_s/N)$. Now, there are $N! / \prod_{i=1}^{s} n_i!$ ways or configurations for dividing N into size n_i, $(i = 1, \ldots, s)$. Assuming equiprobable configurations, we obtain

$$P(n) = \frac{\prod_{i=1}^{s} n_i!}{N!}. \tag{3.40}$$

The fundamental assumption of statistical physics is that the state, or $n = (n_1, \ldots, n_s)$, associated with the highest probability $P(n)$ is actually realized in equilibrium. The idea is similar to the method of maximum likelihood in statistics. It turns out that the equilibrium distribution is the Boltzmann–Gibbs distribution:

$$\frac{n_i}{N} = \frac{e^{-\frac{N c_i}{D}}}{\sum_{i=1}^{s} e^{-\frac{N c_i}{D}}}.$$

To show it, we must maximize probability (3.40) under two constraints, (3.35) and (3.39), with respect to n. For this purpose, we approximate the logarithm of $P(n)$ using the Stirling formula, $\log x! \cong x \log x - x$:

$$\log \prod_{i=1}^{s} n_i! \cong \sum_{i=1}^{s} n_i (\log n_i - 1). \tag{3.41}$$

Because $N!$ is a constant, we can ignore it for the purpose of maximization. Using (3.41), we set up the Lagrangean form:

$$L = \sum_{i=1}^{s} n_i (\log n_i - 1) + \lambda \left(N - \sum n_i \right) + \mu \left(D - \sum_i c_i n_i \right). \tag{3.42}$$

By maximizing L with respect to n_i, we obtain

$$0 = \frac{\partial L}{\partial n_i} = \log\ n_i - \lambda - \mu c_i, \quad (i = 1, \ldots, S) \tag{3.43}$$

or equivalently

$$n_i = e^{-\lambda - \mu c_i} \quad (i = 1, \ldots, S). \tag{3.44}$$

Summing (3.44) over i, we obtain

$$N = \sum_{i=1}^{s} n_i = e^{-\lambda} f(\mu) \tag{3.45}$$

where

$$f(\mu) = \sum_{i=1}^{s} e^{-\mu c_i}. \tag{3.46}$$

From (3.44) and (3.46), we obtain

$$\frac{n_i}{N} = \frac{e^{-\mu c_i}}{f(\mu)}. \tag{3.47}$$

This function $f(\mu)$ is called the *partition function* in physics. Multiplying (3.44) by c_i and summing over i, and noting (3.39) and (3.46), we obtain

$$Y = \sum c_i n_i = e^{-\lambda} \sum_i c_i e^{-\mu c_i}$$

$$= -e^{-\lambda} f'(\mu). \tag{3.48}$$

Note that

$$f'(\mu) = - \sum_i c_i e^{-\mu c_i}.$$

From (3.45) and (3.48), we obtain

$$\frac{Y}{N} = -\frac{f'(\mu)}{f(\mu)} = -\frac{d}{d\mu} \log\ f(\mu). \tag{3.49}$$

Integrating (3.49), we obtain

$$\log f(\mu) = -\frac{Y}{N}\mu + A \tag{3.50}$$

where the constant of integration A is

$$A = \log f(0) = \log S. \tag{3.51}$$

Thus, we can express the partition function as

$$f(\mu) = Se^{-(Y/N)\mu} = Se^{-(D/N)\mu}. \tag{3.52}$$

From (3.46) and (3.48), we define the average productivity $\bar{c}$ by

$$\begin{aligned} \bar{c} &= \sum_i \frac{n_i}{N} c_i \\ &= \frac{Y}{N} \\ &= -\frac{f'(\mu)}{f(\mu)}. \end{aligned} \tag{3.53}$$

Now, suppose we measure c_i in units of θ as

$$c_i = i\theta, \quad i = 1, \ldots, S. \tag{3.54}$$

That is, $\theta > 0$ is the basic unit in measuring productivity such as one dollar per hour, or if you like, one cent per minute.
Then

$$\begin{aligned} f(\mu) &= \sum_{i=1}^{S} e^{-i\theta\,\mu} \\ &\cong \frac{e^{-\theta\,\mu}}{1 - e^{-\theta\,\mu}} \end{aligned} \tag{3.55}$$

when $S \gg 1$.
Then, from (3.53), we can derive the following relation:

$$\bar{c} = -\frac{f'(\mu)}{f(\mu)} = \frac{\theta}{1 - e^{-\theta\,\mu}} \cong \frac{1}{\mu}. \tag{3.56}$$

The right-hand side of (3.56) can be obtained when we take a limit of $\theta/\left(1 - e^{-\theta\mu}\right)$ as θ approaches zero. Thus, we can interpret the Lagrangean multiplier μ as the inverse of the average productivity:

$$\mu = \frac{1}{\bar{c}} = \frac{N}{Y}. \tag{3.57}$$

Hence, from (3.46), (3.47), and (3.56), we finally obtain

$$\frac{n_i}{N} = \frac{e^{-\mu c_i}}{\sum e^{-\mu c_i}} = \frac{e^{-\frac{N c_i}{Y}}}{\sum e^{-\frac{N c_i}{Y}}}. \tag{3.58}$$

Because $Y = D$, (3.58) can be rewritten as

$$\frac{n_i}{N} = \frac{e^{-\frac{N c_i}{D}}}{\sum_{i=1}^{S} e^{-\frac{N c_i}{D}}}, \quad i = 1, \ldots, s. \tag{3.59}$$

Recall that the state vector $n^* = (n_1^*, \ldots, n_s^*)$ given by (3.59) is associated with the maximum probability $P(n)$ under macro constraints (3.35) and (3.39). It is called the Boltzmann–Gibbs distribution.

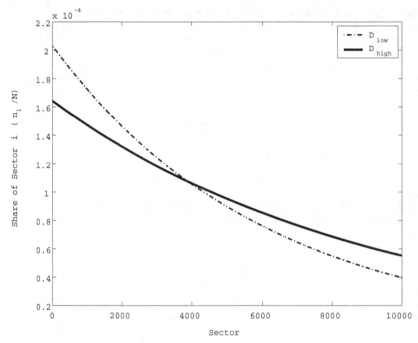

Figure 3.2. Distribution of Production Factors across Sectors with Different Productivity: The Boltzmann–Gibbs Distribution.

Note: $c_1 < c_2 < c_3 < \dots$, $c_i \propto 0.1 + 0.9 \times i/S$,
$S = 10^4$, $N = 10^8$, $D_{low} = 10^4$, $D_{high} = D_{low} \times 1.5$,

$$\frac{n_i}{N} = \frac{e^{-N c_i / D}}{\sum_{i=1}^{S} e^{-N c_i / D}}$$

When D rises, the Boltzmann–Gibbs distribution becomes flatter. An example given in Figure 3.2 shows it clearly. In this example, when D is low, the share of production factor in the lowest productivity sector (sector 1) is about five times as high as that in the highest productivity sector (sector 10,000). When D is high, the ratio declines from five to less than three, causing a flatter curve. Note that *aggregate demand D corresponds to temperature in physics.*

To be precise, aggregate demand relative to factor endowment, namely D/N, corresponds to temperature. For D itself is what physicists call an extensive (i.e., scale-dependent) variable whereas temperature is an intensive (i.e., scale-free) variable; D/N is intensive variable. *High aggregate demand relative to factor endowment corresponds to high temperature, and vice versa.* When the aggregate demand is high, production factors are mobilized to sectors/firms with higher productivity. Okun (1973) makes a similar point, saying that workers climb a "ladder" of productivity in a "high pressure economy." Here, we have provided a rigorous foundation for Okun's verbal argument.

The Old Keynesian Cross

The analysis in this section provides proper microfoundations for Keynes's principle of effective demand. Most economists take for granted that factor endowments are exogenous because they are physically given, and that they determine the total output. Keynes pointed out that factor endowments, if physically given, are *not* actually the fundamental determinant of total output because the utilization rates of those production factors are endogenous. The fundamental determinant is the aggregate demand rather than factor endowment.

Dispersions of utilization rates and differences in technology across firms/sectors entail distribution of productivity *in equilibrium*. The analysis parallel to that in statistical physics suggests that contrary to economists' erroneous belief in the "no arbitrage condition," it is actually *impossible* to obtain the unique marginal productivity in the economy as a whole. We have shown that the equilibrium distribution of productivity is expected to be the Boltzmann–Gibbs distribution. Just like temperature in physics, the aggregate demand determines the distribution of production factors across sectors with different productivity, and thereby the level of total output. *This is the foundation of Keynes's principle of effective demand.*

The present argument is akin to what Tobin (1972) calls "stochastic macro-equilibrium." He argues that

[it is] stochastic, because random intersectoral shocks keep individual labor markets in diverse states of disequilibrium; macro-equilibrium, because the perpetual flux of particular markets produces fairly definite aggregate outcomes. (Tobin, 1972, 9)

The concept of equilibrium distribution of productivity is similar to what Tobin called "a theory of stochastic macro-equilibrium."[8] By way of affecting the transition rates of production factors, the aggregate demand conditions "stochastic macro-equilibrium," and consequently, determines the level of total output.

The important question is what determines the aggregate demand, D in equation (3.59). This is, of course, what Keynes's *General Theory* is all about. Consumption function, multiplier, and so on are analytical tools for resolving this problem. Here, we can usefully recall the textbook old Keynesian analysis as shown in Figure 3.3. *Exogenous* demand, D_0 in the figure, determines the level of aggregate demand, D as $D_0/(1 - c)$ which corresponds to D in equation (3.59). D is equal to total output. Behind this old Keynesian cross, D affects the transition rates of production factors, and the distribution of productivity in stochastic macro-equilibrium. The textbook Keynesian cross and the IS-LM model are admittedly primitive. Though primitive, Blanchard and Fischer (1989)

---

[8]   See also Iwai (2001). He studies the dynamics of profits in the industry.

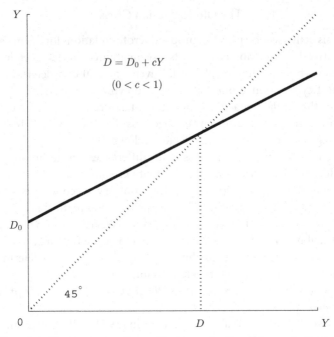

Figure 3.3. The Keynessian Cross – The Determination of Aggregate Output.

after a long excursion into the neoclassical paradigm acknowledge that they are "useful models." The old Keynesian model is useful because it is on the right track.

Differences in Productivity – A Glance at Data

Before we leave this chapter, we briefly examine actual differences in productivity in the economy. The Japanese Ministry of Labor used to compile the country's labor productivity statistics. These give us good information on *physical* labor productivity for the same production process in various firms in each industry. Figure 3.4 shows the distribution of labor productivity and wages across firms in the steel industry for 1971. We note that, given a small price dispersion for the same product, the *physical* labor productivity shown in Figure 3.4 would reasonably correspond to *value* productivity, and to the extent that production function can be approximated by the Cobb–Douglas type, *average* productivity shown in the figure corresponds to *marginal* productivity. We can see that the dispersion of productivity is much greater than that of wages which is documented by Mortensen (2003) and others. The productivity of the most efficient firm is more than 15 times that of the least efficient firm.

This is the dispersion of productivity across firms in the same industry. A similar dispersion is observed across industries. It is well known that higher

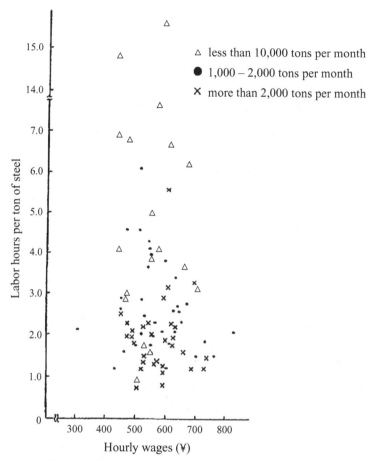

Figure 3.4. Distribution of Labor Productivity and Wages across Firms in the Japanese Steel Industry, 1971.
Source: Japanese Ministry of Labour, *Survey of Labour Productivity,* 1971.

physical productivity tends to be offset by lower relative price, and therefore that the dispersion of *value* productivity becomes smaller than that of *physical* productivity. Yoshikawa (1990), in fact, shows that high productivity growth of the Japanese export sector lowered the prices during the 1970s and 80s, and that it eventually brought about an appreciation of the yen. And yet, differences in value productivity across industries remain, or sometimes even widen, over time. Figure 3.5 shows the indices of the relative *value* productivity for the Japanese manufacturing industries (1978 = 100). If there were no productivity dispersion, the indices would be 100. One might naturally expect random fluctuations around 100, but in fact the dispersion appears cumulative: the value productivity of the electric machinery industry, for example, become 40 percent higher than the average obtaining during the period of 1978–97.

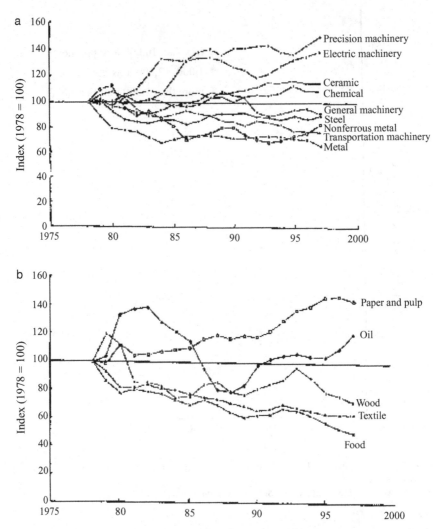

Figure 3.5. Differences in Productivity across Industries, 1975–2000.
Note: Value labor productivity for each industry shown in the figure is the product of the index of physical labor productivity compiled by the Japan Productivity Bureau and the Wholesale Price Index (WPI) compiled by the Bank of Japan (1978 = 100).

In summary, there is always a sizable dispersion of value productivity across firms and industries. This confirms Salter's (1960) early findings. Historically, the most significant productivity difference lay between agriculture and modern manufacturing industry in the early stages of development of most countries (Lewis, 1954; Ohkawa and Rosovsky, 1973). Productivity difference is not confined to developing economies. In the modern well-developed economy, we also must have a distribution of productivity *in equilibrium*. Aggregate demand affects the transition rates of production factor, a distribution of productivity, and consequently the level of total output.

3.3. Concluding Remarks

The problem of demand has been analyzed time and again in the context of Keynesian economics. The research efforts in the past two decades were summarized by Mankiw and Romer (1991) under the heading of "New Keynesian Economics." Unfortunately, New Keynesian Economics is, in our view, fundamentally misguided for two reasons.

First, most works of New Keynesian Economics take the aggregate demand as synonymous with nominal money supply: see, for example, Blanchard and Kiyotaki, 1987; Mankiw, 1985; and other works collected in Mankiw and Romer, 1991. It is not surprising to find Mankiw and Romer (1991, 3) saying that "much of new Keynesian economics could also be called new monetarist economics." In this framework, "demand" or nominal money supply affects real output so long as the nominal price is rigid. Thus, in this approach the primary agenda is to explain the rigidity or inflexibility of nominal price/wage in concurrence with "rationality" of economic agents. This is in accordance with that textbook cliché that Keynesian economics makes sense only when prices are rigid.

Effective demand in Keynes (1936) is, however, *real.* Long ago, Fisher (1933) pointed out that flexibility of price was not necessarily good for real demand. This was amply demonstrated by events that occurred during the long stagnation of the Japanese economy during the 1990s. The Bank of Japan, politicians, and economists all talked in unison about "fears of deflation." Nobody dared to argue that swifter price *declines* could have cured the economy. Here, once again we emphasize the importance of real demand, and cite Tobin:

The central Keynesian proposition is not nominal price rigidity but the principle of effective demand (Keynes, 1936, Ch. 3). In the absence of instantaneous and complete market clearing, output and employment are frequently constrained by aggregate demand. In these excess-supply regimes, agents' demands are limited by their inability to sell as much as they would like at prevailing prices. Any failure of price adjustments to keep markets cleared opens the door for quantities to determine quantities, for example real national income to determine consumption demand, as described in Keynes' multiplier calculus....

In Keynesian business cycle theory, the shocks generating fluctuations are generally shifts in *real* aggregate demand for goods and services, notably in capital investment. Keynes would be appalled to see his cycle model described as one in which "fluctuations in output arise largely from fluctuations in nominal aggregate demand" (Ball, Mankiw, and Romer, 1988, 2). The difference is important. (Tobin, 1993)

We have shown that *real* aggregate demand determinates total output by way of affecting a distribution of productivity in the economy.

The second reason New Keynesian Economics is misguided is methodological. To provide sound "microeconomic foundations," it analyzes microeconomic behavior in great detail. We have already argued that this is wrong. In the macroeconomy, we have a distribution of productivity in equilibrium, and this distribution is conditioned by real aggregate demand. We have shown that the distribution of productivity is the Boltzmann–Gibbs type in equilibrium. This is the proper microeconomic foundations for the Keynes's principle of effective demand.

4

Uncertainty Trap: Policy Ineffectiveness and Long Stagnation of the Macroeconomy

History shows us that the economy can be trapped in long stagnation. In the nineteenth century, the British economy suffered from the Great Depression for almost a quarter of century (1873–96). The Great Depression in the 1930s attacked the whole world. And since the beginning of the 1990s, the Japanese economy has stagnated for more than a decade.

In every episode, various policies were discussed and tried. Yet the economy did not revive, falling into long stagnation. Certainly, in each case, there must have been policy mistakes. Granted, it appears that once the economy is trapped into a deep depression, the effectiveness of standard policy measures weakens. Irving Fisher (1933), for example, in relation to his famous debt-deflation theory made the following argument.[1]

There may be equilibrium which, though stable, is so delicately poised that, after departure from it beyond certain limits, instability ensues, just as, at first, a stick may bend under strain, ready all the time to bend back, until a certain point is reached, when it breaks. This simile probably applies when a debtor gets "broke," or when the breaking of many debtors constitutes a "crash," after which there is no coming back to the original equilibrium. To take another simile, such a disaster is somewhat like the "capsizing" of a ship which, under ordinary conditions, is always near stable equilibrium but which, after being tipped beyond a certain angle, a tendency to depart further from it. (p. 339)

In this chapter, we focus on *uncertainty*. Using the simple theoretical model presented in Chapter 3, we show that mounting uncertainty *necessarily* weakens the effectiveness of macroeconomic policy. We certainly do not recommend policy makers to throw the mainstream macroeconomics textbooks away. However, in our view, the economy once facing great uncertainty *does* present economists and policy makers with real difficulties the textbook remedies cannot easily handle.

---

[1] Tobin (1975) presented a model in which the macroeconomy is locally stable, but is globally unstable.

Uncertainty is, of course, not new to economists. However, a new approach is necessary to make clear the real importance of uncertainty for the macroeconomy. To understand its importance, we must depart from the standard assumption of the representative agent, and once again take seriously the fact that the macroeconomy consists of a large number of heterogenous agents. We have already explained this point in the previous chapters. In what follows, we will show that the kind of approach we are advancing in this book sheds new light on the importance of uncertainty in the macroeconomy. The first section presents our model. The second section demonstrates the importance of uncertainty as a hindrance to macroeconomic policy. Finally, as a case study, the third section discusses the problems Japan faced in her long stagnation during the 1990s. Amid the stagnation, official short-term interest rates in Japan had fallen to zero; conventional monetary policy became impotent. Facing this unprecedented situation, many economists proposed alternative policies including *inflation targeting*. We critically examine these policy proposals, and conclude that they cannot solve the real difficulty *uncertainty* creates. Indeed, we suggest that whether the economy is caught in such *"uncertainty trap"* distinguishes *"depression"* from normal cyclical *"recession."* Finally, the fourth section offers brief concluding remarks.

4.1. The Model

The model we use is the binary choice model presented in Chapter 3. For convenience, we quickly summarize the model as follows. It is highly abstract, but is still useful in understanding policy ineffectiveness and long stagnation of the macroeconomy.

Suppose that there are N economic agents in the economy. There are K possible levels of production. Each agent, as a result of respective optimization, chooses one of K levels. To demonstrate our point, without loss of generality, we can assume that K is just two, with levels "high" and "low." This assumption simplifies our presentation, though theoretically, the model does not have to be binary so long as K is finite. In Chapter 3, we show that the apparently restrictive binary choice model is actually consistent with standard dynamic optimization.

The "high" level of production is denoted by y^*, and the "low" level by y $(0 < y < y^*)$. If the number of economic agents that produce at the high level, y^*, is n $(n = 1, \ldots N)$, then total output in the economy or GDP is

$$Y = ny^* + (N - n)y. \tag{4.1}$$

We denote the share of economic agents which produce at y^* by x:

$$x = \frac{n}{N} \quad (n = 1, \ldots, N). \tag{4.2}$$

Using x, we can rewrite Y as follows:

$$Y = N[xy^* + (1 - x)y]. \tag{4.3}$$

When N is large, x can be regarded as a continuous fraction ($0 \leq x \leq 1$). Equation (4.3) shows that Y and x correspond to each other. While x fluctuates between 0 and 1, so does Y between Ny and Ny^*.

Changes in x are assumed to follow a jump Markov process. For a short time Δt, there are three possibilities; no economic agent changes its production level, or one either raises or lowers its production level. The process is then characterized by two transition rates, one from state y to y^* and the other from y^* to y. Once these two transition rates are given, they determine the model, and accordingly the (stochastic) dynamics it produces.

The probability that one economic agent producing at the low level y raises its production to a high level y^* depends naturally on the number of agents currently producing at y, that is $N(1 - x)$. Similarly, the transition rate from y^* to y depends on Nx.

Transition rates are additionally assumed to be state-dependent in that $N(1 - x)$ and Nx are modified by $\eta_1(x)$ and $\eta_2(x)$, respectively. Specifically, the transition rate from y to y^*, r, is

$$r = N(1 - x)\eta_1(x). \tag{4.4}$$

And the transition rate from y^* to y, l, is given by

$$l = Nx\eta_2(x). \tag{4.5}$$

The transition rates r and l thus depend not only on the number of economic agents in each state, but also on $\eta_1(x)$ and $\eta_2(x)$. The factors $\eta_1(x)$ and $\eta_2(x)$ mean that the optimal strategy taken by each agent depends on the state of the economy, x or Y. Alternatively, η means the presence of externality in agents' behavior. For example, equation (4.4) means that a switch of strategy by an economic agent from "bear" who finds y as optimal, to "bull" who finds y^* as optimal, depends on the share of bulls. Equation (4.5) means that the same is true for a switch of strategy from y^* to y. Here, $\eta_1(x)$ and $\eta_2(x)$ are defined as

$$\eta_1(x) = X^{-1}e^{\beta g(x)} \qquad (\beta > 0) \tag{4.6}$$

$$\eta_2(x) = 1 - \eta_1(x) = X^{-1}e^{-\beta g(x)} \tag{4.7}$$

$$X = e^{\beta g(x)} + e^{-\beta g(x)}. \tag{4.8}$$

The expression X in (4.8) simply makes sure that the sum of $\eta_1(x)$ and $\eta_2(x)$ is equal to one as it must be. The above equations are quite generic, and called the Boltzmann–Gibbs type. In the first section of Chapter 3, we explained how naturally equations (4.6) and (4.7) arise in microeconomic models of choice under uncertainty. We also explained that they are consistent with standard intertemporal maximization.

The function $g(x)$ in (4.6) indicates how advantageous a switch of strategy from bear to bull is. The greater $g(x)$ is, the more advantageous a switch from bear to bull is, and *vice versa*. We assume that $g(x)$ becomes zero at $\bar{x}$. Note that

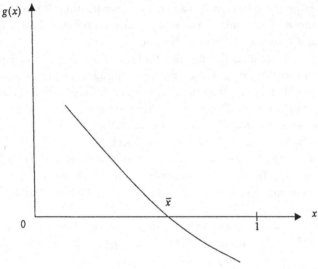

Figure 4.1. $g(x)$ Function.

at $\bar{x}$, $\eta_1(\bar{x})$ and $\eta_2(\bar{x})$ are both 1/2, and, therefore, that a switch from y and y^* and one from y^* to y are equally probable.

Obviously, the $g(x)$ function plays an important role. In fact, $g(x)$ describes *economic behavior*. Thus, we can make various assumptions on $g(x)$. The simplest assumption is that $g(x)$ has a unique stable critical value $\bar{x}$ as shown in Figure 4.1. In this case, when the share of bulls exceeds $\bar{x}$, more agents become cautious and find turning to bear advantageous.

Different assumptions are possible, of course. For example, we can assume that $g(x)$ has three critical values, say A, B, C as shown in Figure 4.2. In Figure 4.2, point B is a stable critical value whereas points A and C are unstable ones. If the share of bulls x is located between A and B, there is a (stochastic) tendency for x to approach B. However, if x exceeds C, more agents tend to turn to bull. The bandwagon effect is self-enforcing. In this sense, C is an unstable critical point. Similarly, if x becomes smaller than A, more agents tend to turn to bear. Again, A is an unstable critical point.

Note that most standard comparative static analyses in macroeconomics can be interpreted as shifts of the $g(x)$ function in our present analysis. We know that in comparative static analysis, we must focus on stable equilibrium. For the same reason, we focus on a stable critical value of the $g(x)$ function. Thus, for simplicity, let us assume for the moment a unique stable critical value for $g(x)$ as in Figure 4.1.

Take the IS/LM analysis as an example of standard comparative static analysis in macroeonomics. Suppose that a deteriorated expected profitability made the IS curve shift down. As a consequence, GDP or Y declines. This situation corresponds to the case where *given x*, more economic agents are likely now to find

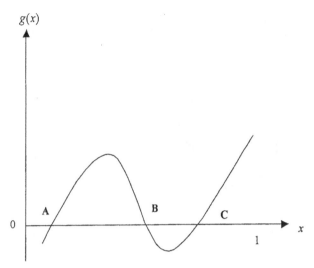

Figure 4.2. Three Critical Values.

advantageous to switch from bull to bear, namely the $g(x)$ function shifts down to the left as shown in Figure 4.3 (A). The stable critical point moves to the left accordingly. Next, suppose that the authority lowered the interest rate to fight against this recession. The LM curve moves downward to the right, leading Y to rise. This now corresponds to the case where, thanks to the expansionary monetary policy or lower interest rates, given x again, economic agents find it more advantageous to switch from bear to bull. The $g(x)$ function shifts up to the right as shown in Figure 4.3 (B). The economy returns from $\bar{x}_2$ to $\bar{x}_1$, that is, recovers from recession. In this way, a shift of $g(x)$ function in the present model corresponds to the standard comparative static analysis in a simple deterministic model.

Now, in the present stochastic framework, we have another important parameter in transition rates, namely β. The first section of Chapter 3 shows that β in equations (4.6) and (4.7) is a parameter that indicates the degree of uncertainty facing economic agents. Suppose, for example, that the payoff facing an agent is normally distributed. Then β is simply the inverse of its variance. Thus, when the degree of uncertainty rises, β declines, and *vice versa*. In the limiting case where β becomes zero, *regardless of* $g(x)$, both $\eta_1(x)$ and $\eta_2(x)$ become $1/2$. In this case, uncertainty is so great that economic decisions become equivalent to tossing a coin.

The Master Equation

Let us return to the model. The share of bulls, x, changes stochastically, and so does GDP (recall equaion (4.3)). Specifically, it follows the jump Markov process with two transition rates (4.4) and (4.5). We will analyze the dynamics of this model.

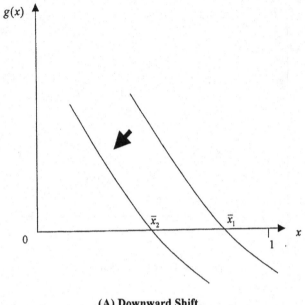

(A) Downward Shift

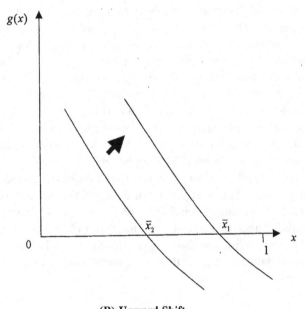

(B) Upward Shift

Figure 4.3. Shifts of the $g(x)$ Function.

The master equation or the Chapman–Kolmogorov equation is given by

$$\frac{\partial P(n, t)}{\partial t} = N\left(x + \frac{1}{N}\right)\eta_2\left(x + \frac{1}{N}\right)P(n+1, t)$$

$$+ N\left(1 - x + \frac{1}{N}\right)\eta_1\left(x - \frac{1}{N}\right)P(n-1, t)$$

$$- [Nx\eta_2(x) + N(1-x)\eta_1(x)]P(n, t). \qquad (4.9)$$

Here, $P(n, t)$ is the probability that the number of "bulls" or agents who produce at the "high" level, y^*, is n at time t. Note the following relations:

$$x = \frac{n}{N}, \quad x + \frac{1}{N} = \frac{n+1}{N} \quad \text{and} \quad x - \frac{1}{N} = \frac{n-1}{N}.$$

We analyze the master equation by the method of Taylor expansion explained in Chapter 2. First, we decompose a stochastic variable x (the share of bulls) into two components:

$$x_t = \phi_t + \frac{\xi_t}{\sqrt{N}}. \qquad (4.10)$$

Here, ϕ_t is the mean of x_t, $E(x_t)$, and, therefore, is not stochastic but is just a real number. The second component ξ_t is the stochastic deviation of x_t from its mean ϕ_t. By construction, the mean of ξ_t is zero. Note that both ϕ_t and ξ_t depend on time, and also that ξ is divided by $\sqrt{N}$ to normalize its standard deviation. Using ϕ and ξ, we can rewrite $P(n, t)$ as follows:

$$P(n, t) = P(Nx, t) = P(N\phi + \sqrt{N}\xi, t) = \pi(\xi, t). \qquad (4.11)$$

This relation defines the density function of a stochastic variable ξ at time t, $\pi(\xi, t)$. Then, by definition, we have

$$\frac{\partial P(n, t)}{\partial t} = \frac{\partial \pi}{\partial t} + \frac{\partial \pi}{\partial \xi}\frac{d\xi_t}{dt}. \qquad (4.12)$$

Now, at each moment of time, a realized value of x is given ($dx/dt = 0$) so that we have the following relation:

$$\frac{d\phi_t}{dt} = -\frac{1}{\sqrt{N}}\frac{d\xi_t}{dt}. \qquad (4.13)$$

Thus, substituting $d\xi_t/dt$ out in equation (4.12), we obtain

$$\frac{\partial P(n, t)}{\partial t} = \frac{\partial \pi}{\partial t} - \sqrt{N}\frac{d\phi_t}{dt}\left(\frac{\partial \pi}{\partial \xi}\right). \qquad (4.14)$$

Next, we rewrite the right-hand side of the master equation (4.9) using ϕ and ξ, and expand it around the expected value of x, ϕ by the Taylor series with respect to $1/\sqrt{N}$ up to the quadratic term (namely, $1/N$):

$$\frac{\partial P(n,t)}{\partial t} = N\left(\phi + \frac{\xi}{\sqrt{N}} + \frac{1}{N}\right)\left[\eta_2(\phi) + \eta'_2(\phi)\left(\frac{\xi}{\sqrt{N}} + \frac{1}{N}\right)\right]$$

$$\times\left[\pi(\xi,t) + \frac{\partial\pi}{\partial\xi}\left(\frac{1}{\sqrt{N}}\right) + \frac{1}{2}\frac{\partial^2\pi}{\partial\xi^2}\left(\frac{1}{N}\right)\right]$$

$$+ N\left(1 - \phi - \frac{\xi}{\sqrt{N}} + \frac{1}{N}\right)\left[\eta_1(\phi) + \eta'_1(\phi)\left(\frac{\xi}{\sqrt{N}} - \frac{1}{N}\right)\right]$$

$$\times\left[\pi(\xi,t) - \frac{\partial\pi}{\partial\xi}\left(\frac{1}{\sqrt{N}}\right) + \frac{1}{2}\frac{\partial^2\pi}{\partial\xi^2}\left(\frac{1}{N}\right)\right]$$

$$-\left[N\left(\phi + \frac{\xi}{\sqrt{N}}\right)\left(\eta_2(\phi) + \eta'_2(\phi)\frac{\xi}{\sqrt{N}}\right)\right.$$

$$+ N\left(1 - \phi - \frac{\xi}{\sqrt{N}}\right)\left(\eta_1(\phi) + \eta'_1(\phi)\frac{\xi}{\sqrt{N}}\right)\Bigg]\pi(\xi,t). \tag{4.15}$$

In this calculation, we used the following fact. When the number of bulls, $n = Nx = N\phi + \sqrt{N}\xi$, increases from n to $n+1$, the fluctuation or change of the stochastic variable ξ must be $1/\sqrt{N}$, because in that case, n increases by $\sqrt{N}\xi = \sqrt{N} \times (\frac{1}{\sqrt{N}}) = 1$. Similarly, when the number of bulls is $n-1$, the deviation of ξ_t is $-1/\sqrt{N}$. Note that we hold ϕ constant, and consider the deviation of ξ_t from its mean zero.

Now, look at the right-hand side of equation (4.15) as a power series of N: The maximum term is $N^{\frac{1}{2}}$, and other terms of lower order are N^0, $N^{-\frac{1}{2}}$, N^{-1}, $N^{-\frac{3}{2}}$, ... The term of the highest order, namely the term with $\sqrt{N}$, turns out to be as follows:

$$\sqrt{N}[\phi\eta_2(\phi) - (1-\phi)\eta_1(\phi)]\left(\frac{\partial\pi}{\partial\xi}\right). \tag{4.16}$$

We compare this term to the right-hand side of equation (4.14). For the respective terms involving $\sqrt{N}$ in equations (4.14) and (4.15) to be identical, the following relation must hold:

$$\frac{d\phi_t}{dt} = \dot{\phi}_t = \phi_t\eta_2(\phi_t) - (1-\phi_t)\eta_1(\phi_t). \tag{4.17}$$

The ordinary differential equation (4.17) determines the dynamics of the expected value of x, namely ϕ. Note that ϕ is not stochastic, and that its dynamics obeys an ordinary differential equation.

4.2. Uncertainty and Policy Ineffectiveness

We can understand the dynamics of the expected value of the share of bulls, ϕ, and accordingly GDP or Y by studying equation (4.17). The critical point of equation (4.17) is given by

$$\frac{\eta_1(\phi)}{\eta_2(\phi)} = \frac{\phi}{1-\phi}. \tag{4.18}$$

From equations (4.6) and (4.7), this equation is equivalent to

$$2\beta g(\phi) = \log\left(\frac{\phi}{1-\phi}\right). \tag{4.19}$$

The steady state ϕ satisfies equation (4.19). Recall the important fact that β in (4.19) indicates the degree of uncertainty facing economic agents. Specifically, when the degree of uncertainty rises, β declines, and vice versa. We then observe that when there is little uncertainty, namely β is very large, we can ignore the right-hand side of equation (4.19), and equation (4.19) becomes equivalent to

$$g(\phi) = 0. \tag{4.20}$$

Thus, when there is little uncertainty (large β), the expected value of x, ϕ, is equal to the zero of the $g(x)$ function in steady state. That is, ϕ is equal to ϕ^* which satisfies

$$g(\phi^*) = 0 \tag{4.21}$$

in steady state. If $g(x)$ looks like the one shown in Figure 4.1, then ϕ^* is equal to the unique stable equilibrium $\bar{x}$ in Figure 4.1.

In this case, x changes stochastically, but spends most of the time in the neighborhood of ϕ^*. Accordingly, GDP fluctuates stochastically but spends most of the time in the neighborhood of

$$Y = N[\phi^* y^* + (1 - \phi^*)y]. \tag{4.22}$$

As we explained above with respect to $g(x)$ function, the standard comparative static analyses hold without any problem in this case. If policy makers find the current *average* level of Y too low, for example, then they can raise fiscal expenditures or lower the interest rate. These policies would shift the $g(x)$ function upward to the right as shown in Figure 4.3 (B). The *expected value* of Y would increase since in the present case of low uncertainty (large β), it is basically determined by the zero of the $g(x)$ function (equation (4.21)).

When the degree of uncertainty rises, or equivalently β becomes small, the story gets much more complicated. Specifically, when the degree of uncertainty is high, (1) multiple equilibria may emerge, and (2) the response of the economy to *any* policy action *necessarily* becomes small. Standard macroeconomic policies face serious difficulties.

At this stage, it is useful to introduce the *potential* function. It is given by

$$U(x) = -2 \int^x g(y)dy - \frac{1}{\beta}H(x). \qquad (4.23)$$

The function $g(y)$ and β are the same as the ones in equations (4.6) and (4.7), and $H(x)$ is the *Shannon entropy* defined as follows:

$$H(x) = -x \ln x - (1 - x) \ln(1 - x). \qquad (4.24)$$

This entropy term is crucial to our subsequent argument. Recall that each of N economic agents faces a binary choice of being either a bull or a bear. $H(x)$ is nothing but the logarithm of the binominal coefficient ${}_N C_n$, namely the number of cases where n out of N agents are bulls. Using the Stirling formula that $\log N! \cong N(\log N - 1)$, we obtain

$$\log {}_N C_n = \log\Big(\frac{N!}{(N-n)!n!}\Big)$$

$$= N\Big[-\Big(\frac{n}{N}\Big)\log\Big(\frac{n}{N}\Big) - \Big(1 - \frac{n}{N}\Big)\log\Big(1 - \frac{n}{N}\Big)\Big]$$

$$= NH(x). \qquad (4.25)$$

The function $H(x)$ expresses the combinatorial aspect of our problem in which a large number of economic agents stochastically make binary choices. *It is this combinatorial aspect that the standard macroeconomics entirely ignores, and yet that plays a crucial role in the analysis of any system, either physical or social, consisting of a large number of entities.*

Let us keep this in mind, and go back to the analysis of the expected value of the share of bulls, ϕ. We have seen above that the steady state expected value of x, ϕ^*, satisfies equation (4.19). Thus, noting

$$\frac{dH(x)}{dx} = \log\left(\frac{1-x}{x}\right)$$

we can easily see that locally stable steady states of equation (4.17) are local minima of the potential function (4.23):

$$U'(\phi) = -2g(\phi) - \frac{1}{\beta}H'(\phi) = -2g(\phi) + \frac{1}{\beta}\log\Big(\frac{\phi}{1-\phi}\Big) = 0. \quad (4.26)$$

When β is large (little uncertainty), $U'(\phi) = 0$ is basically equivalent to $g(\phi) = 0$. Therefore, as long as the $g(x)$ function has a unique zero, the standard textbook results hold. When β is small, however, the expected value of x, ϕ, is not the zero of $g(\phi)$, but is determined by both $g(\phi)$ and $H'(\phi)/\beta$.

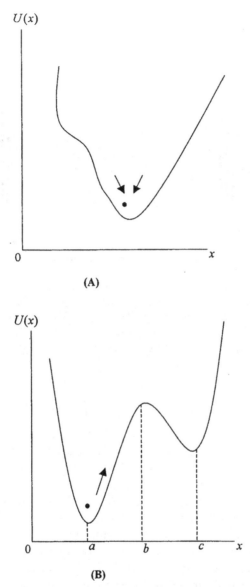

Figure 4.4. The Shape of the Potential Function and Fluctuations of the Economy.

Multiple Equilibria

The significant uncertainty (small β) creates various problems. First, even if $g(\phi) = 0$ has a unique stable root, $U'(\phi) = 0$ may have multiple stable roots. Figure 4.4 (A) shows the case of the unique local minimum while Figure 4.4 (B) shows the case of two local minima. Aoki (1995, 1996, Chapter 5) presents a numerical example. In that example, the shape of $g(x)$ looks

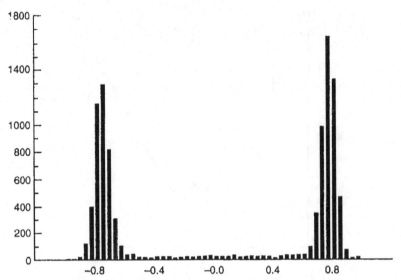

Figure 4.5. Simulation Result for the Case where the Potential Function Has Two Local Minima.
Source: Aoki, 1996. *Note:* In this simulation, $y = x - 1$ is measured horizontally.
In the text, the share of bulls, x, is between 0 and 1, but in this histogram y is between -1 and 1.

like the one in Figure 4.2, and it generates two stable roots for the following equation:

$$U'(x) = -2g(x) + \frac{1}{\beta} \log\left(\frac{x}{1-x}\right) = 0.$$

That is, the potential function $U(x)$ has two local minima as shown in Figure 4.4 (B). Figure 4.5 shows histograms of the values of x after 20 transitions in this simulation with 500 replications. With two stable equilibria, we clearly see a bimodal histogram with two well-defined peaks.

The dynamics just discussed is actually that mentioned as an example of multiple equilibria in Chapter 1 (see Figure 1.3). We stated there that unlike in deterministic models, we do not face the problem of equilibrium selection in the stochastic approach. The economy stochastically fluctuates, spending most of time in the neighborhood of two minima of the potential function. The simulation result shown in Figure 4.5 indeed demonstrates it very clearly. In passing, we can show that *the mean passage time*, t^*, for the economy to change from one equilibrium (say point a in Figure 4.6) to the other (point c in the same figure), depends on "the height of the barrier" between two minima in the potential function $U(x)$:

$$t^* \approx e^{\beta N(U(b)-U(a))}.$$

Figure 4.6 shows two cases. In Figure 4.6 (A), when the economy passes from a to c, it must cross the high barrier (large $U(b) - U(a)$). Thus, the mean

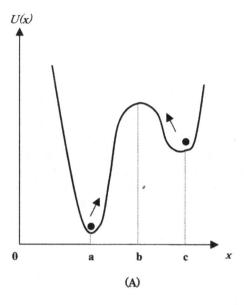

(A)

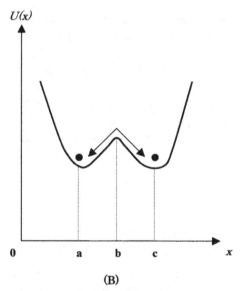

(B)

Figure 4.6. The Potential Function with Two Local Minima.

passage time from a to c, namely t_{ac}^*, is long. In contrast, since $U(b) - U(c)$ is small, the mean passage time from c to a, t_{ca}^* is short. Therefore, in this case, we have "asymmetric cycles." Using this model, Aoki (1998) explains "asymmetric business cycles" observed by Neftci (1984). Figure 4.6 (B) shows another possibility in which both $U(b) - U(a)$ and $U(b) - U(c)$ are equally small. In this case, the economy passes from a to c, and from c to a, both with the relatively short mean passage time.

In summary, suppose the $g(x)$ function that describes economic behavior has a unique *stable* equilibrium. When uncertainty is negligible (β is large), the potential function has a unique minimum as shown in Figure 4.4 (A). However, when uncertainty becomes significant (β is small), we cannot ignore the combinatorial aspect of the problem. Specifically, we must consider the *Shannon entropy, $H(x)$ defined by equation (4.24). It is the combination of economic behavior ($g(x)$ function) and uncertainty (small β) that generates multiple minima for the potential function, and accordingly multiple equilibria in the economy.* In the stochastic model, if we have multiple equilibria, we do not face the problem of equilibrium selection. Rather, the economy fluctuates stochastically between equilibria as Figures 4.5 and 4.6 show. In this sense, one might say that uncertainty can be a source of fluctuations of the macroeconomy.

The Effectiveness of Policy

Uncertainty also affects significantly the effectiveness of macroeconomic policies. To demonstrate, let us assume once again that $g(x)$ function has a unique stable equilibrium as shown in Figure 4.1. And, for the sake of clarity, consider the case where the real interest rate was reduced. This is equivalent to an upward shift of the $g(x)$ function as shown in Figure 4.3 (B). In the IS/LM model, we draw the conclusion that interest-elastic expenditures such as investment increase, and GDP or Y rises in the new equilibrium. What happens in the present model? The answer depends on the degree of uncertainty, β.

"Policy" is a change in $g(x)$ function in our model. Thus, we change function $g(x)$ in transtion rates (4.6) and (4.7) to

$$g(x) + h(x) \tag{4.27}$$

where

$$h(x) > 0, \qquad h'(x) \cong 0.$$

With this change in $g(x)$ function, ϕ^* which satisfies equation (4.26) or $U'(\phi^*) = 0$, changes to $\phi^* + \delta\phi$. Because $\phi^* + \delta\phi$ is also a root of equation (4.26), it satisfies

$$-2[g(\phi^* + \delta\phi) + h(\phi^* + \delta\phi)] + \frac{1}{\beta} \log\left(\frac{\phi^* + \delta\phi}{1 - \phi^* - \delta\phi}\right) = 0. \tag{4.28}$$

Taking the Taylor expansion of equation (4.28) to the first order, we obtain

$$-2\left[g(\phi^*) + g'(\phi^*)\delta\phi + h(\phi)^*\right] + \frac{1}{\beta}\left[\log\left(\frac{\phi^*}{1 - \phi^*}\right) + \left(\frac{1}{\phi^*(1 - \phi^*)}\right)\delta\phi\right] = 0.$$

$$\tag{4.29}$$

Because ϕ^* satisfies equation (4.26), this equation boils down to

$$-2g'(\phi^*)\delta\phi - 2h(\phi^*) + \frac{1}{\beta}\left(\frac{1}{\phi^*(1-\phi^*)}\right)\delta\phi = 0.$$

This is solved out for $\delta\phi$ as

$$\delta\phi = \frac{2h(\phi^*)}{\frac{1}{\beta}\left(\frac{1}{\phi^*(1-\phi^*)}\right) - 2g'(\phi^*)} > 0. \qquad (4.30)$$

Here we used the assumptions $h'(x) = 0$ (no particular bias in policy) and $g'(\phi^*) < 0$ (ϕ is a stable equilibrium).

It is natural that $\delta\phi$ becomes larger when a change in $g(x)$, $h(\phi^*)$, is greater. Thus, equation (4.30) can be perhaps better rewritten as

$$E = \frac{\delta\phi}{h(\phi^*)} = \frac{2}{\frac{1}{\beta}\left(\frac{1}{\phi^*(1-\phi^*)}\right) - 2g'(\phi^*)} > 0. \qquad (4.31)$$

E defined as $\delta\phi/h(\phi^*)$ in (4.31) gives an increase in ϕ relative to a shift of the $g(x)$ function. It corresponds to the notion of a *multiplier* in deterministic models. E in equation (4.31), therefore, indicates *the effectiveness of macroeconomic policy* in our model.

In an expansionary policy, $\delta\phi$ is positive, that is ϕ^* rises. However, the extent of an increase in ϕ^* depends crucially on β or uncertainty. When uncertainty is negligible, β is so large that $\delta\phi/h(\phi^*)$ or E approaches its maximum value $-1/g'(\phi^*) > 0$. On the other hand, as the degree of uncertainty rises (β declines), E gets smaller approaching zero. This result is quite generic. When uncertainty rises, the effectiveness of macroeconomic policies which affect agents' economic incentives *necessarily* weakens. In the limit, the economy facing infinite uncertainty is trapped in a state in which no economic policy works or, in fact, no economic decision makes sense in that it is no different from tossing a coin.

The result obtained here has broad implications for *elasticity*, a most important concept in economics. Elasticity expresses the responsiveness of agents' actions to a particular change in economic environment. It is theoretically derived from the optimizing behavior of the representative economic agent. Consider demand for apples as a simple example. Demand for apples is a function of the price of an apple. It is derived from the consumer's utility maximization. Under "normal" assumptions, we would obtain demand function for apples as a decreasing function of price. That is, when the price of an apple went down, *ceteris paribus*, people purchase more apples. In our model, a change in economic environment facing agents is expressed as a shift of the function $g(x)$ in transition rates.

Now, we can reinterpret the binary-choice model we have analyzed. Choosing y^* may be interpreted as "buying an apple." And choosing y is now "not buying an apple." Note that the assumption of binary choice is not necessary, but made only for simplification. As long as the number of states is countable, the model works. Thus, we can think of a model of expenditures on apples by generalizing the present binary choice model. In the binary choice framework, the number of apples purchased corresponds to the share of "bulls," x.

Suppose then that the price of apples went down. More people buy apples and/or people buy more apples. In any case, the standard analysis takes it for granted that *individual* elasticity derived theoretically from the microeconomic analysis of the representative agent can translate itself into elasticity in the economy as a whole. The case we consider now corresponds to an upward shift of function $g(x)$ in transition rates (4.6) and (4.7). And price elasticity corresponds to E defined as $\delta\phi / h(\phi^*)$ in (4.31). Because standard analysis ignores uncertainty and the combinatorial aspect, elasticity becomes the value of E when β is infinite. That is, elasticity in standard analysis, E^*, corresponds to

$$E^* = -\frac{1}{g'(\phi^*)} \qquad (4.32)$$

in the present model. However, as we explained earlier, when uncertainty is significant, we cannot ignore the combinatorial aspect of the problem, namely the Shannon entropy $H(x)$. Specifically, elasticity becomes E in (4.31), not E^* in (4.32). In general, E in (4.31) is smaller (in absolute value) than E^* in (4.32). Thus, we obtain the following proposition.

Proposition: *When the degree of uncertainty rises, elasticity E necessarily diminishes (in absolute value). In the limit ($\beta \to 0$), it approaches zero.*

As a corollary, we obtain an important implication for macroeconomic policies.

Proposition: *When the degree of uncertainty rises, the effectiveness of macroeconomic policy necessarily weakens. In the limit ($\beta \to 0$), macroeconomic policy becomes completely ineffective.*

In this sense, we can say that when the degree of uncertainty is extremely high, the economy is caught in an "*uncertainty trap.*"

4.3. The Japanese Economy during the 1990s – A Case Study

To see the relevance of the above proposition, we consider the Japanese economy during the 1990s as a case study. Arguably, Japan was caught by an "uncertainty trap" at a time during the period.

In the buoyant 1980s when some even suggested "Japan as Number One," who would have imagined such gloomy 1990s? As it turned out, amid the worldwide IT revolution, Japan suffered from the decade-long stagnation during the 1990s. After a series of recessions, the interest rate had fallen to zero by the late 1990s.

Facing this unprecedented absolute lower bound for the interest rate, the Bank of Japan (BOJ) apparently lost the most important policy instrument. At the same time, the economy lapsed into deflation – Irving Fisher's curse! Quite naturally, central bankers, policy makers, and economists all began to search for possible policy measures at the zero interest rate bound. *Inflation targeting* was one of the major proposals. In this section, we first briefly survey the Japanese economy during the 1990s. Then we critically examine inflation targeting in relation to uncertainty. This case study should make clear the limits of the standard analysis in macroeconomics.

The Economy

After the asset price bubbles bursted, the Japanese economy officially entered recession in 1991. At first, it appeared as a normal cyclical downturn, but was actually only the beginning of the decade-long stagnation. The average growth rate of Japan during 1992–99 was a mere 1.0 percent. During the same period, the U.S. economy enjoyed the 3 percent growth hailing the New Economy. Even the European Union (EU), suffering from high unemployment, outperformed Japan. The important question is why the Japanese economy was trapped in such a long stagnation.

Table 4.1 shows the record of the Japanese economy during the period. A sensible way to get an overview of the Japanese economy during the 1990s is to look at the demand-decompositon of the growth rate of real GDP. Table 4.1 presents contributions of demand components such as consumption, investment, and exports to growth of GDP. The contribution is defined as the growth rate of each demand component, for example investment, times its share in real GDP. By construction, the figures sum to the growth rate of GDP.

Table 4.1 shows that fixed investment is the most important factor to account for cyclical fluctuations during the period, namely the 1992–93 recession, the 1994–96 recovery, and the 1997–98 recession.[2] In fact, investment is the most important explanatory variable for the Japanese business cycles throughout the postwar period (see Yoshikawa, 1995). This stylized fact applies to the 1990s. When the growth rate fell from 3.8 percent to 0.3 percent during 1991–93, for example, the contribution of investment fell from 1.2 percent to −1.9 percent, accounting for nearly 90 percent of a fall in the growth rate. Similarly, when growth accelerated from 0.3 percent to 5.1 percent during 1993–96, the contribution of investment rose from −1.9 percent to 1.8 percent, again accounting for 80 percent of the recovery. Thus, to explain the long stagnation of the Japanese

---

[2]   The recession which started in May 1997 officially ended in January 1999. According to the government, the Japanese economy subsequently entered the expansionary phase during February 1999–October 2000. Then another recession started in November 2000 which ended in January 2002.

Table 4.1. Contribution of Demand Components to GDP Growth in Japan (%)

	GDP growth	Consumption	Housing investment	Final investment	Inventory investment	Public consumption	Public investment	Exports	Imports
1990	5.1	2.6	0.3	2.0	-0.2	0.1	0.3	0.7	-0.8
1991	3.8	1.5	-0.5	1.2	0.3	0.2	0.3	0.6	0.3
1992	1.0	1.2	-0.3	-1.1	-0.5	0.2	1.0	0.5	0.1
1993	0.3	0.7	0.1	-1.9	-0.1	0.2	1.2	0.2	0.0
1994	0.6	1.1	0.4	-0.9	-0.3	0.2	0.2	0.5	-0.8
1995	1.5	1.2	-0.3	0.8	0.2	0.3	0.1	0.6	-1.4
1996	5.1	1.7	0.7	1.8	0.4	0.2	0.8	0.8	-1.3
1997	1.6	0.3	-0.9	1.5	0.1	0.1	-0.9	1.4	-0.1
1998	-2.5	-0.3	-0.6	-1.4	-0.6	0.1	-0.2	-0.3	0.9
1999	0.2	0.7	0.1	-1.0	0.1	0.1	0.6	0.3	-0.6

economy during the 1990s, we must explain why fixed investment was depressed so much,[3] and why it did not respond to low interest rates.

In addition to fixed investment, depressed consumption is notable. For 1998, we even observe an unprecedented *decline* in consumption. Contrary to common belief, however, a fall in asset prices had relatively little effect on consumption. One might expect that the negative wealth effects depressed consumption after the bubble burst in the early 1990s. Altogether, during the bubble period of 1986–90, households enjoyed almost 1,200 trillion yen worth of capital gains on their assets (200 trillion yen on stock, and 1000 trillion yen on land), but subsequently suffered from the 400 trillion yen worth of capital losses during 1990–92. The analysis of consumption by type of household reveals that capital losses on stock did exert negative wealth effects on consumption of aged retirees and a portion of the self-employed who were major stock owners. The share of these types of households, however, is only 12 percent.

The major capital gains and subsequent losses accrued on land. As one would expect, most land is indivisibly related to housing. Therefore, to the extent that housing service and other consumables are weak substitutes, and land and housing are indivisible, it is not irrational that sizable capital gains and losses on land allowed most households to keep their houses and their consumption intact. Capital gains and losses on stock and land affected household consumption only marginally. Bayoumi (1999) using VARs finds that the effects of land prices on output largely disappears once bank lending is added as an explanatory variable, and concludes that the "pure" wealth effects were quite limited.

Among the factors to explain unprecedentedly depressed consumption is job insecurity. It is well known that the unemployment rate in Japan had been very low by international standards. During the 1980s when the unemployment rate reached 10 percent in many EU countries, it remained 2 percent in Japan. The unemployment rate had been traditionally low in Japan for several reasons. Thanks to bonus payments and the synchronized economy-wide wage settlements called the *Shunto* (Spring Offensive), wages in Japan were believed to be more flexible than in other countries.[4] Besides, the necessary adjustment of labor was once done through changes in working hours per worker rather than changes in the number of workers. On the supply side, cyclical fluctuations in the labor force participation rate were large; in recessions, the "marginal" (typically female) workers who had lost jobs often got out of the labor force rather than remain in the labor force and keep searching for jobs. These factors once

---

[3] For the 1991–94 recession, we must refer to normal stock adjustment after the long boom during the bubble period. And for the 1997–98 recession, the credit crunch played the major role. However, we need to explain why investment stagnated for such a long period *on average*. When demand grows, investment also grows. And if demand stagnates, so does investment. We must, therefore, explain the long stagnation of demand. An answer to this question will be given in Chapter 8, which discusses economic growth.

[4] Taylor (1989), for example, emphasizes the role of *Shunto* for wage flexibility in Japan.

kept the unemployment rate from rising.[5] Even during the 1992–94 recession, the unemployment rate, though rising, did not reach 3 percent.

The long stagnation during the 1990s, however, had thoroughly changed the structure of the Japanese labor market. Most important, with the slogan of "restructuring," firms were now ready to discharge workers. The number of involuntary job losers had more than tripled between 1992 and 1999. In 1999, the unemployment rate in Japan finally became higher than the U.S. counterpart; nobody had expected that would ever happen.

In the autumn of 1997, big financial institutions such as the *Hokkaido Takushoku Bank* and the *Yamaichi Security* went into bankruptcy. These events made an unmistakable announcement that the celebrated lifetime employment in Japan was over. Understandably, job insecurity depressed consumption.[6] In 1998, consumption actually fell. In summary, households faced an unprecedented rise in uncertainty which depressed consumption during the late 1990s.

From another angle, McKinnon and Ohno (1997) attribute the stagnation of the Japanese economy to the appreciation of the yen.[7] However, the appreciation of the yen from 240 per dollar (1985) to 120 (1988) was actually caused by high productivity growth in the Japanese export sector, and broadly followed the purchasing power parity (*PPP*) with respect to tradables (see Yoshikawa, 1990). Thus, it is not plausible to regard the appreciation of the yen as the major *cause* for the long stagnation of the Japanese economy. In fact, as shown in Table 4.1, exports had been the most stable component of GDP throughout the 1990s except for 1998 when the Asian financial crisis rather than the appreciation of the yen hindered exports.

---

[5] For details, see Yoshikawa (1995), Chapter 5.

[6] Nakagawa (1999) demonstrates that uncertainly surrounding the public pension system also depressed consumption.

[7] McKinnon and Ohno (1997) advanced the argument that what they called "fears of ever higher
yen" was the fundamental cause of the long stagnation of the Japanese economy, and that the
introduction of the adjustable peg was the key solution. Their argument rests on the premise that
fluctuations of the exchange rates was the basic cause of the troubles. They even attribute the fall in
the growth rate in the early 1970s to the end of the Bretton Woods system and the introduction of
flexible exchange rates. However, at least for the Japanese economy, the contribution of net exports,
which are naturally most significantly affected by exchange rates, to growth was much *higher* in
the 1970s and 80s when exchange rates were flexible than in the 1950s and 60s when the exchange
rate was fixed (Yoshikawa, 1995, Chapter 2).

McKinnon and Ohno emphasize a possibility of misalignments (deviations from the PPP) under the flexible exchange rate regime. The misalignment does occur. However, for the Japanese
economy, the most important misalignment was the overvaluation of the dollar or *the underval-
uation of the yen* under the Reagan Administration in the 1980s. This misalignment is, therefore,
not consistent with "fears of ever higher yen."

Finally, they argue that responding to the appreciation of the yen, the Bank of Japan initially
eases money, but is, in the medium run, prone to tighten money to produce deflation. This simply
contradicts the facts. The Bank of Japan provides easy money responding to the yen appreciation
not only in the short run but also in the medium run.

In conclusion, the key variables for understanding the long stagnation are corporate investment, and to lesser extent, consumption. We now focus on investment.

Monetary Policy and Investment

Monetary policy is often said to be responsible for the asset price bubbles during the late 1980s, and the subsequent long stagnation during the 1990s. According to this view, during the 80s, low interest rates produced the asset price bubbles, and high land prices, in turn, allowed the liquidity constrained firms to make excessive investment by way of an increase in the collateral values. For the same reason, but now in the opposite direction, the collapse of the asset market entailed the stagnation of investment during the 1990s.

Though the "standard" view contains a bit of truth, it does not actually stand up to careful analyses. There are a number of studies that demonstrate a significant relationship between real variables such as investment and real GDP on the one hand, and asset prices, land prices in particular, on the other. Because asset prices and GDP went up and down in tandem, these findings are not surprising. The problem is interpretation of causality. Most of such analyses interpret their findings as indicating that changes in asset prices affected investment of financially constrained firms by way of changes in their collateral values. Ogawa and Suzuki (1998), for example, find land prices significant in their investment functions, and conclude that financial constraints were significant. Bayoumi (1999) also finds in his vector autoregressions (VARs) that land price changes were an important factor behind the rise in the output gap over the bubble period and the subsequent decline.[8]

However, this is not exactly what happened in Japan during the late 1980s and 90s. During the bubble period, it was believed (falsely, in retrospect) that land-intensive sectors such as holiday resorts and office spaces in Tokyo would command high profits in the near future. These (false) expectations made land prices explode, and *at the same time* induced firms to make *land-intensive* investment. Firms purchased land with money borrowed from banks, and banks, based on their expectations of higher land prices in the future, often allowed more than 100 percent (!) collateral values for land which firms just purchased. Therefore, theoretically, firms could borrow money from banks without any collateral in advance to purchase land. This is different from the standard story explained above, according to which an increase in the price of land which firms had owned *in advance* made it possible for the liquidity constrained firms to borrow more money to make investment. In fact, the ultimate cause of *both* a rise in land prices *and* an extraordinary surge in land-intensive investment was false expectations on future profitability of holiday resorts and office spaces in

---

[8]   Kiyotaki and Moore (1997) offer a theoretical model that suggests that kind of interpretation.

Table 4.2. Interest Rates (percent)

	(1) Call rate	(2) 10-Year government bonds	(3) Long lending rate	(4) Term premium (2)−(1)	(5) Private risk premium: (3)−(2)
1990	7.4	6.8	8.1	−0.6	1.3
1991	7.5	5.8	6.9	−1.7	1.1
1992	4.7	4.8	5.5	0.1	0.7
1993	3.1	3.5	3.5	0.4	0.0
1994	2.2	4.6	4.9	2.4	0.3
1995	1.2	2.9	2.6	1.7	−0.3
1996	0.5	2.8	2.5	2.3	−0.3
1997	0.5	2.0	2.3	1.5	0.3
1998	0.3	1.0	2.2	0.7	1.2
1999	0.03	1.8	2.3	1.8	0.5

Tokyo. Based on such false expectations, the $g(x)$ function shifted to the right meaning that more firms became "bulls" in our model.

After the bubbles burst, the asset prices collapsed, and at the same time investment also fell. However, it is once again not self-evident that this fact suggests that a fall in the asset prices cut investment by way of a fall in the firms' collateral values. For example, investment of large firms and small firms fell during the 1992–94 recession roughly in the same magnitudes. Large firms do not finance their investment by borrowing from banks but rather by issuing bonds, and new equities in capital market. They are *not* financially constrained, and, therefore, the collateral story does not hold true for large firms at the outset. And yet, small firms and large firms cut their investment. Thus, the popular collateral story is doubtful; Meltzer (2001) and Hayashi and Prescott (2002) also express skeptical views against the significance of financial constraints.

Whatever the reasons, investment stagnated. Monetary policy responded to the stagnation of the economy. Table 4.2 shows the record of monetary policy during the period. The BOJ cut the discount rate from 6.0 percent to 5.5 percent in July 1991. Through five successive cuts within a year, it had fallen to 3.25 percent by July 1992.

Despite the further cuts in the interest rates during 1993–94, the economy hardly revived. The annual growth rate of money supply (M2 + CD) which was 12 percent in 1990, had fallen to zero by 1992. Because a sharp decline in bank lending was responsible for this fall in money growth, the problem was why this sharp decline in bank lending occurred. Bayoumi (1999) interprets his finding that bank lending is more important than land price itself in explaining output gap as supporting the financial disintermediation hypotheses. He argues that "undercapitalized banks responded to falling asset prices and other balance sheet pressures by restraining lending to maintain capital adequacy standards." Some Japanese economists also suggested the same, and argued that the credit crunch was responsible for the weak investment. However, as shown in Table 4.2, during 1991–93, the interest rates kept declining. If the credit crunch occurred the interest rate would have risen. Thus, it appears that the major cause of a sharp decline in bank lending during 1991–93 was a downward shift of demand curve (a fall in demand for bank lending) rather than an upward shift of supply curve (the credit crunch or a cut in supply of bank lending). Indeed, responding to successive cuts in the call rate, the diffusion index of "Lending Attitude of Financial Institutions" of *the BOJ Tankan* (Short-term Economic Survey of Corporations) improved during 1992–95 (Figure 4.7). Gibson (1995) also concludes that although a firm's investment is sensitive to the financial health of its main bank, the effect of the problems in the banking sector on aggregate investment during 1991–92 was small. The private risk premium, defined as the difference between the long lending rate and the ten-year government bond rate, also declined during the period (Column (5) of Table 4.2). In summary, the effects of a fall in land prices and consequent bad loans on bank lending were not significant during the 1992/94 recession. By looking at bank-level data, Woo (1999) draws the same conclusion.

Meanwhile, a fall in stock prices created a serious problem for the Japanese banks to meet the BIS capital adequacy standards. The new legislation in April 1996 allowed the authority to step in a bank likely to fail to meet the BIS requirement. This new policy regime was to start in April 1998. In March 1997, the Ministry of Finance (MOF) made clear the new capital adequacy requirements. Unfortunately, this basically correct policy action was taken at the worst timing. Desperate to raise the capital/asset ratio within a short period of time, banks squeezed their assets by cutting lendings. In the autumn, the bankruptcy of big financial institutions such as the *Yamaichi Security* and the *Hokkaido Takushoku Bank* triggered the real credit crunch. Figure 4.7 shows that the *Tankan* DI of lending attitude of banks abruptly worsened during this period despite of the BOJ's efforts to ease money. Note that the *Tankan* DI of lending attitude of banks normally deteriorates at the time of tight money whereas it improves at the time of easy money.

What was the impact of this credit crunch? Motonishi and Yoshikawa (1999) assess the macroeconomic magnitude of the credit crunch by estimating investment functions separately for large/small firms in both the manufacturing/non-manufacturing sectors. The explanatory variables are from *the BOJ's Tankan*, which has the diffusion indices for business conditions and for credit constraints facing firms as shown in Figure 4.7. As one might expect, they find that credit constraints are not significant for investment of large firms, but are significant for small firms, particularly in the nonmanufacturing sector. They conclude that

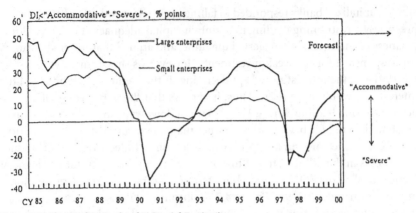

Figure 4.7. Lending Attitude of Financial Institutions.
Source: Bank of Japan, "*Tankan* short-term Economic Survey of Enterprises in Japan."

the credit crunch, by way of depressing investment of financially constrained firms, lowered the growth rate of real GDP by 1.3 percent during 1997–98.[9]

We maintain that the credit crunch not only depressed investment of financially constrained firms but also significantly raised the degree of uncertainty in the economy as a whole. Arguably, the economy was now caught in "uncertainty trap"; β became very low. Amid the credit crunch, the BOJ was forced to lower interest rates further. The call rate became 0.3 percent in 1998, and finally 0.03 percent in 1999. With transaction costs, 0.03 percent effectively means zero interest rate, the absolute minimum for nominal interest rate.

Liquidity Trap and Inflation Targeting

At the zero interest rate bound, the BOJ apparently lost the instrument for traditional monetary policy. The "*liquidity trap*" (Keynes, 1936)[10] was once considered a mere theoretical possibility. However, amid the long stagnation, Japan literally faced this problem. When the short-term policy rate is at zero, the conventional means of effecting monetary ease is no longer feasible. Economists then started discussing how monetary policy could possibly affect the economy with zero interest rate. Krugman (1998) was one of the first economists who proposed an alternative policy. His model lays the basis for subsequent theoretical refinements

[9] Their analysis takes into account only fixed investment, but two thirds of bank lendings is for running costs and inventory investment rather than fixed investment. We can, therefore, reasonably argue that, at the minimum, the credit crunch accounts for one half of the – 2.5 percent growth of real GDP in 1998, the worst record in the postwar Japan.

[10] The concept of the "liquidity trap" was advanced by Keynes (1936) in his *General Theory*. However, the term "liquidity trap" is not his. It is found neither in *General Theory*, nor in the index for his *30-Volume Collected Works*! Instead, the term "liquidity trap" can be found in Robertson (1940) "Mr. Keynes and the Rate of Interest," which is based on his lectures delivered at the London School of Economics in 1939.

and debates. We examine his analysis in detail because it represents the standard approach in macroeconomics; specifically, it ignores the effects of uncertainty, β, on the economy.

In Krugman's model, the representative consumer (!) maximizes the discounted utility sum:

$$V = \frac{1}{1-\rho} \sum_{t=1}^{\infty} C_t^{1-\rho} D^t. \tag{4.33}$$

Here, the inverse of ρ is the elasticity of intertemporal substitution of consumption, C_t, and D is the discount factor $(0 < D < 1)$. With the cash-in-advance assumption, the following inequality must hold in each period:

$$PC \leq M \tag{4.34}$$

where M is the stock of money, and P is the price level.

The assumption is made that all the periods beginning with the second onward are in equilibrium. In equilibrium, both output, Y and C are equal to Y^*, the exogenously given "full-employment" GDP. Money supply is M^*. Thus the price level in equilibrium, P^*, is determined by

$$P^* = M^*/Y^*. \tag{4.35}$$

As a result of the consumer's utility maximization, the interest rate i^* is equal to $(1 - D)/D$.

On this assumption of stationary equilibrium, all the periods beginning with the second onward are conveniently condensed into the future, and the model boils down to the two-period model with the "present" (no asterisk) and the "future" (with asterisk). As we have seen, the "future" is "normal" in that C^* is equal to Y^* and the interest rate is positive. We must also note that the simple quantity equation (4.35) holds so that in the future, the price level P^* is proportionately determined by the money supply M^*.

The consumer's utility maximization leads us to the Euler equation:

$$\left(\frac{C}{C^*}\right)^{-\rho} = D(1+i)\left(\frac{P}{P^*}\right). \tag{4.36}$$

Since we have $C = Y$ and $C^* = Y^*$, we can rewrite (36) as follows:

$$1 + i = \left(\frac{1}{D}\right)\left(\frac{P^*}{P}\right)\left(\frac{Y^*}{Y}\right)^{\rho}. \tag{4.37}$$

Introduce the following definitions:

$$\delta = (1 - D)/D \quad \text{(The subjective discount rate)}$$

$$\Pi = (P^* - P)/P \quad \text{(Inflation)}$$

$$g = (Y^* - Y)/Y \quad \text{(Growth rate),}$$

and we obtain

$$i = \delta + \Pi + \rho g. \tag{4.38}$$

The real interest rate r is

$$r = i - \Pi = \delta + \rho g. \tag{4.39}$$

When the present economy is not caught in the liquidity trap ($i > 0$), the quantity equation holds:

$$M = PY. \tag{4.40}$$

In this case, given the future Y^*, P^*, M^*, and the present M, two equations (4.37) and (4.40) determine the state of the present economy. When the price level P and the nominal interest rate i are freely determined, the full employment is possible. In this case, Y is equal to Y^f. Here, Y^f is the full employment Y in the current period. It may be different from Y^*.

When the nominal interest rate i becomes zero, the story gets complicated. First of all, the cash-in-advance constraints (4.34) no longer hold as equality; only the strict inequality constraint holds:

$$PC = PY < M. \tag{4.41}$$

The crucial link between the price level P and money supply M is broken. However, the Euler equation (4.37) still holds. Thus, in the case of the liquidity trap ($i = 0$), the price level is equal to

$$P = \left(\frac{P^*}{D}\right)\left(\frac{Y^*}{Y}\right)^{\rho}. \tag{4.42}$$

This equation shows that even if the economy is caught in the liquidity trap ($i = 0$), flexible prices can still bring about the full employment ($Y = Y_f$). Specifically, for Y to be equal to the full employment GDP, Y_f, the price level must be equal to P^f:

$$P^f = \left(\frac{P^*}{D}\right)\left(\frac{Y^*}{Y_f}\right)^{\rho}.$$

The trouble occurs when the current P is sticky. Suppose that P is equal to the exogenously given level, $\bar{P}$, which is different from P^f. Then, from (4.42) we know that Y is equal to

$$Y = \left(\frac{P^*}{\bar{P} D}\right)^{\frac{1}{\rho}} Y^*.$$

In general, Y determined this way may be smaller than Y^f:

$$Y < Y_f.$$

Because the link between M and P is broken in the liquidity trap (inequality (4.41)), an increase in M does not help. However, the future economy is *not* caught in the liquidity trap! And there the quantity equation nicely holds (equation (4.35)). Thus, all the BOJ must do is just to persuade the public that M^* *will* increase enough to raise P^* up to P^{**} so as to achieve Y^f in the current period. The level of *future* money supply M^{**} that can achieve P^{**} is given by

$$M^{**} = \bar{P} D Y^{*(1-\rho)} Y_f^\rho.$$

Note that the point of this policy is for central bank (the BOJ) to credibly commit to looser monetary policy *in the future*. As Krugman (1998) puts it, the central bank must "credibly promise to be irresponsible." Surely, toward this goal, the BOJ would have to increase the current money supply, M. It is necessary because an increase in money supply at present can be a strong message, if not the only message, that the BOJ will keep increasing money supply M^* *in the future*. In the Krugman model, the future is not caught in the liquidity trap, and the quantity equation nicely holds. Thus, an increase in M^* in the future is bound to raise P^* if the public really believes that M^* will increase. The expected inflation created this way can get the economy out of liquidity trap by way of lowering the real interest rate.

This is the theoretical basis for Krugman's proposal of inflation targeting. Following Krugman's lead, many economists made similar but slightly different policy recommendations. An array of proposals include announcing a price-level target path, reducing long-term interest rates via commitment to keep the short rate zero for a substantial periods in the future, depreciating the currency by foreign exchange interventions, introducing negative interest on currency (Gessell's solution), and finally, a policy of combining a price level target path, a currency depreciation and a crawling peg and an exit strategy that makes up Svensson's (2003) "Foolproof Way" to escape from liquidity trap.

These are all different policies, of course. However, none of them including the original Krugman model considers uncertainty and the combinatorial aspect we explained in the previous section. For our purpose here, the technical differences of various theoretical models and policy recommendations are secondary; all the proposed policies boil down to a shift of the $g(x)$ function in our analysis in the second section. Therefore, it is enough to consider the efficacy of Krugman's policy recommendation.

In the Krugman's model, inflationary expectations by way of reducing real interest rate stimulate demand. Here, demand is assumed to be interest elastic, of course. However, *interest elasticity depends on the degree of uncertainty.* Our analysis in the second section has shown that greater uncertainty makes the interest elasticity small.[11] All the policy recommendations for overcoming the

---

[11] Dixit and Pindyck (1994) convincingly argue that uncertainty by way of increasing the option value lowers the interest elasticity of irreversible investment. Specifically, they show that a reduction in

liquidity trap and deflation rests on the premise that interest elasticity is high. For example, in Krugman's model, the Euler equation (4.36) gives us $1/\rho$ as the interest elasticity of expenditures. Many economists believe this kind of analysis provides sound microeconomic foundations for macroeconomic policy recommendations. However, it does not actually provide us with any foundations to the extent that the analysis abstracts itself from uncertainty. And the most difficult problem the economy faces in the liquidity trap and deflation is uncertainty. *Uncertainty makes the interest elasticity small.*

Indeed, in the Japanese economy during the 1990s, particularly after the credit crunch in 1997–98, a major problem facing monetary policy was low interest elasticity of demand. Based on the interest elasticity for the U.S. economy, Krugman suggests that to fill the 5 percent GDP gap, the 3–3.75 percent inflationary expectations would be enough. However, with low interest elasticity which appears to have held for the Japanese economy during the 1990s, the necessary expected inflation would have been easily become as high as 30 percent!

Beyond that, in Krugman's model, the "future" is not in a liquidity trap, and the simple quantity theory of money is assumed to hold in the future; price is proportional to money supply in the future. Thus, in theory it is easy for the central bank to generate the expected inflation despite the absence of the current actual inflation. The only thing the central bank must do is to persuade the public *now* to believe that money supply will increase enough to generate inflation *in the future*. However, in reality, the most important factor determining the expected inflation is the current *actual* inflation. Whatever the policy actions of the central bank, who would believe in inflation so easily in the economy actually facing deflation? As long as we believe in the Phillips curve wisdom, namely the story that only high pressure in the real economy produces inflation, then we are likely to be caught by the Catch 22 in our effort to cure recession by generating inflationary expectations.[12]

A large increase in the supply of money coupled with *inflation targeting* was such a popular solution to the problems facing the Japanese economy around the

---

the real interest rate makes the future more important to the present, but this increases not only the present value of the stream of profits, but also the value of waiting (the ability to reduce or avoid the prospect of future losses). The net effect is weak and sometimes even ambiguous. In other words, greater uncertainty lowers the interest elasticity. Their analysis pertains to the behavior of individual firm or consumer. Our analysis is for the economy as a whole.

[12] Blanchard (2000, 190–93) states that "the Phillips curve wisdom remains largely true in modern treatments of the determination of prices, wages, and output: If output is above its natural level, then we are likely to see inflation increase." And yet, he is very optimistic in that the BOJ can easily generate inflationary expectations to lower the real interest rate; "All that is needed is to convince markets that money growth will be cumulatively higher over the next 10 years by 20 percent." He notes that monetary policy affects long-term interest rates "mostly – entirely? – through its effects on expectations," and continues that "the only thing specific to Japan today is that emphasis is not on changes in future expected nominal interest rates, but on the expected future price level. This is not an essential difference." There is an essential difference in the role of expectations in the determination of prices in goods and financial markets, however.

year 2000. Proponents were, among others, Krugman (1998), Bernanke (2000), Blanchard (2000), Rogoff (2002), Eggertsson and Woodford (2003), Bernanke, Reinhart, and Sack (2004), and Auerbach and Obstfeld (2005).

In some circumstances, inflation targeting may be indeed a useful framework to conduct monetary policy. A number of central banks have already adopted inflation targeting which, in some cases, is said to be instrumental in reducing inflation (see Bernanke and Woodford, 2005). Having acknowledged that, we question the efficacy of inflation targeting as a remedy for deflation in the liquidity trapped economy. The point is that in the liquidity trapped economy such as Japan during the late 1990s, the fundamental problem may not have been really deflation and the zero interest rate *per se*, but great uncertainty. We have shown that such uncertainty reduces (interest) elasticity, theoretically to zero in the limit. This makes all the policy proposals in the existing literature for generating inflationary expectations ineffective.

Not only ineffective, such policies may well contribute toward mounting uncertainty. That is, central bank "credibly promising to be irresponsible" may confuse the public, and actually *prolong* the *uncertainty trap* rather than rescuing the economy from the liquidity trap. King (2004) makes an important point that in some circumstances, expectations of monetary decisions within a given policy regime may be less important than expectations of changes in the regime itself, and, therefore, ordinary policy may not work.[13] Our analysis has shown that the "Enemy Number One" in the uncertainty trap is not deflation or zero interest rate *per se*, but low (interest) elasticity and the ensuing policy ineffectiveness. Despite all the technical sophistications, the policy proposals for generating inflationary expectations miss the essential point. The apparently impeccable inflation targeting will not work in the economy facing great uncertainty. This demonstrates the limits of standard macroeconomic analysis, which abstracts itself from uncertainty and the combinatorial problem arising in the macroeconomy.

Some Suggestive Evidence

Before we conclude this chapter, we provide some evidence to suggest that the degree of uncertainty has, in fact, risen in the Japanese economy during the 1990s. We have already referred to job insecurity facing households. Deflation was also a wholly new experience to both households and firms. Arguably, the

---

[13] As an example of such a case, King (2004) shows that interest rate policy did not work to defend exchange rates under the target zone regime in Brazil (1998–99) and the U.K. (1992).

In the literature on target zones for exchange rates, it is assumed that raising interest rates is a successful method for supporting the exchange rate because of uncovered interest parity. But this ignores the possibility that raising interest rates to defend a fixed-exchange-rate regime will simply call into question the durability of the regime itself and raise the probability that the peg or target zone will be abandoned. In such circumstances an increase in interest rates may lead to a fall in the exchange rate (King, 2004, 6).

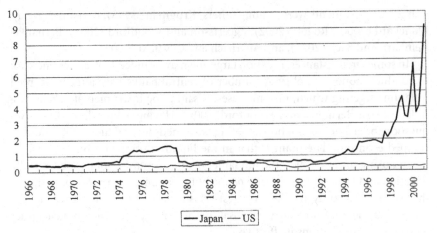

Figure 4.8. CV of Growth Rate of GDP for Japan and United States.
Note: CV= Standard deviation / Mean of quarterly GDP growth rates over the past 5 years.

credit crunch in 1997–98 pushed the economy into uncertainty trap. Having noted that such factors largely contributed to mounting uncertainty, we present some quantitative evidence.

GDP is, of course, the most important macroeconomic variable, and is expected to significantly affect the economic perception of agents. We measure the degree of uncertainty using the GDP growth rates. Figure 4.8 shows the coefficient of variation (standard deviation divided by mean) of the quarterly GDP growth rates for 5 years (20 quarters). For the sake of comparison, we also show it for the United States. We observe that the coefficient of variation has, in fact, risen extraordinarily in Japan during the 1990s, especially in the latter half.

We also estimate AR(2) for quarterly GDP by applying the rolling regression. Uncertainty is now measured by the standard error of regressions (SER). Specifically, we estimate the following equation for the sample period (1961:1–2001:1)

$$\Delta \ln Y_t = \alpha_0 + \alpha_1 \Delta \ln Y_{t-1} + \alpha_2 \Delta \ln Y_{t-2} + u_t,$$

where Y_t is real GDP (quarterly, seasonally adjusted). Figure 4.9 shows the rolling SER divided by the mean. Again, a glance at Figure 4.9 reveals that SER/Mean has risen extraordinarily in Japan during the 1990s.

Note that in Chapter 3, we show that the inverse of β in the model corresponds to the variance of the variable in question. Figures 4.8 and 4.9 suggest that the degree of uncertainty has, in fact, risen in the Japanese economy. Finally, we also note the fact that the amount of cash held by the public had doubled from 35 trillion yen in 1994 to 70 trillion yen by 2001. Even the bank deposits were not taken as safe. It indicates extreme risk perceived by the public, and is consistent with Figures 4.8 and 4.9.

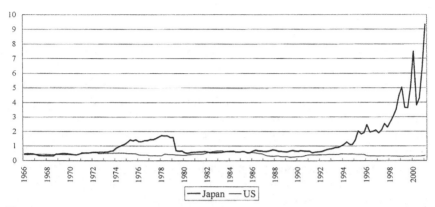

Figure 4.9. SER/Mean of GDP Growth Rate for Japan and United States.
Note: SER = Standard Error of Regression of AR(2) (estimated over the past 5 years) of real GDP growth rate.

4.4. Concluding Remarks

The standard analysis in macroeconomics begins with micreconomic experiment on the assumption of the representative agent. Suppose, for example, that the authority cut the interest rate, or that facing the liquidity trap, it succeeded in generating inflationary expectations. In both cases, the real interest rate is reduced. For the representative household or firm, a lower real interest rate would raise the optimal level of investment and some other expenditures. Translating this result to macroeconomic analysis, the standard analysis concludes that *ceteris paribus,* aggregate demand increases. This kind of analysis is taken by most economists and policy makers as giving sound guidance to macroeconomic policies.

This holds true so long as the degree of uncertainty facing the economy is low. However, when the degree of uncertainty becomes significant, we must depart from the representative agent assumption, and seriously consider that the macroeconomy consists of a large number of economic agents. In this case, a stochastic approach is necessary. The combinatorial aspect of the system plays a crucial role in the analysis of any system, either physical or social, consisting of a large number of entities. The standard economic analysis entirely ignores it. In this chapter, we have shown that it has, in fact, important implications for macroeconomics. Specifically, the effectiveness of policy necessarily weakens as the degree of uncertainty rises. We can call this problem *uncertainty trap.* Whether or not the economy is caught in such uncertainty trap distinguishes a *"depression"* from a normal cyclical *"recession."*

Once the economy falls into this uncertainty trap, textbook macroeconomic policies including monetary policy, which correspond to a change in the $g(x)$ function in the model, become ineffective. We considered Japan's long stagnation during the 1990s as a case study. Many economists argued that the BOJ facing the zero nominal interest rate can still lower the real interest by generating inflationary expectations (Krugman, 1998; Bernanke, 2000; Blanchard, 2000). In our model, their proposed policies change the $g(x)$ function, and induce more economic agents to find a shift from "bear" to "bull" advantageous. When uncertainty is insignificant, or the minimum of the potential function is almost equivalent to the zero of the $g(x)$ function, this certainly helps. It is a normal situation. However, when the degree of uncertainty rises, the combinatorial aspect cannot be ignored, and policies that are effective in normal circumstances do not help. We have provided some suggestive evidences indicating that the degree of uncertainty has, in fact, risen in Japan during the 1990s.

Tobin (1975), in his article "Keynesian models of recession and depression," suggests that "the system might be stable for small deviations from its equilibrium but unstable for large shocks." The same point was also made by Fisher (1933). In our analysis, *uncertainty* plays the key role. When uncertainty is insignificant, the economy fluctuates around the (unique) "natural" equilibrium, and macroeconomic policies are effective. However, when the degree of uncertainty rises above a critical level, the economy may be trapped, and standard policies become ineffective.

5

Slow Dynamics of Macro System: No Mystery of Inflexible Prices

The standard approach such as RBC is based on the premise that the microeconomic behavior of the optimizing agent mimics dynamics of the macroeconomy. In Chapter 1, we explain that this premise is incorrect, and that the macro and micro behaviors are fundamentally different.

In this chapter, we focus on a particular aspect of the macroeconomy, namely the speed of adjustment. The premise of the standard approach is that rational economic agents must respond quickly to any change in economic environment. And it is taken for granted that this micro behavior should translate itself into the macroeconomy. Thus, one expects that the speed of adjustment in the economy as a whole is also fast in normal conditions. In this way, the standard approach does not make any distinction between the speed of adjustment of micro agents and that of the macroeconomy.

Let us take up prices as an example. Since the publication of Keynes's *General Theory* (1936), "inflexibile" or "rigid" prices have been always a focal point of macroeconomics. Modigliani (1944), one of the first economists, coined the proposition that what distinguishes Keynesian economics from neoclassical economics is the assumption of inflexible prices (to be precise, rigid nominal wages in his case).

Many economists take inflexibility of prices as a sign of irrationality. Aside from monopoly power or institutional barriers such as regulations, healthy market forces should make prices flexible. In this chapter, we will explain that slow changes in prices are a *necessity* in the macroeconomy. Slow dynamics is not confined to prices. It is, in fact, a generic property of any complex macro system.

To explain why the behavior of the macroeconomy is "sluggish," this chapter first introduces the notion of "tree" and ultrametrics. The macroeconomy is composed of many agents or sectors of different types. It is organized into hierarchical layers, and has a tree structure in which leaves of trees are basic clusters of agents. We show in Section 5.1 that the dynamics of a large system which has such a structure is *necessarily* sluggish. The macroeconomy is a typical example.

In Section 5.2, we apply the analysis explained in Section 5.1 to the dynamics of prices. We show that given input–output structure of the macroeconomy, there is no mystery in sluggish behavior of prices.

In Section 5.3, we give another explanatian why slow dynamics arises in the macroeconomy. In the standard approach, it is taken for granted that a rational economic agent can swiftly find and move to his first-best or global optimum. This assumption may hold true, as a first approximation, for a well-organized financial market. That there should be no room for arbitrage in efficient market is a cliché. As we explained in Chapter 3, even in such well-organized financial markets, there may be always a room for "arbitrage." Whatever the case for financial markets, in "real" economic activities, agents always face much more complex decision-making problems. Often the problem is not given in advance. To identify the problem is, in fact, an important part of economic activity. Trials and errors then become a source of slow dynamics. Section 5.3 formalizes this idea.

5.1. Tree Models for Spillover of Exogenous Shocks

In a large system, it is usually the case that exogenous disturbances are initially confined to a sector or cluster, and then gradually propagate throughout the system. This holds true not only for *micro shocks*, but also for what are normally taken as *macro shocks*. For example, changes in money supply or oil price are expected to have significant effects on the economy as a whole. However, the initial impacts may be confined to a small number of sectors. Eventually those shocks affect the economy as a whole. In this section, we analyze how the probabilities of such disturbances propagate over time. We also discuss the notion of average distance travelled by disturbances throughout the system over time. For these purposes, we can usefully introduce the notion of a tree structure into our model.

Although we routinely analyze multisector models, we always treat sectors or clusters all on equal footing. That is, we do not usually introduce any notion of similarity, correlations, or distances between sectors or clusters. Typically, sectors or industries are simply indexed by i ($i = 1, \ldots, n$). This tacitly assumes that the distance between any two sectors is the same.[1] To our knowledge, no model with a formal notion of distances among different groups of agents/sectors apparently exists.

For some purposes, it is actually reasonable to introduce the notion of distance between sectors or clusters. For example, one might argue that machinery industry is closer to the iron/steel industry than to agriculture. Leontief's input–output analysis formalizes this idea in a particular way. Magnitudes and speeds with which disturbances originating in one sector spread through the macroeconomy

---

[1]   In some models, agents are assumed to be located at sites of regularly spaced lattices. In such models, agents in nearest lattice sites are assumed to interact in a very crude analogy with Ising models in the ferromagnetics literature in physics.

need be analyzed on such a notion of distance between clusters or sectors. A tree model provides an appropriate measure of distance between sectors or clusters.

Before we explain the tree model, we briefly examine a traditional measure of strength of relationship between two variables, namely *correlation*. The correlation, though popular, is not *transitive*. This fact has been known in the numerical taxonomy literature. Feigelman and Ioffe (1991), for example, have a simple example of three patterns: A = (1, 1, 1, 1), B = (1, 1, −1, 1), and C = (1, 1, 1, −1). Calculating correlations by $\rho = (1/4) \sum_i x_i y_i$ where x's and y's are the components of the patterns above, we see that $\rho_{A,B} = \rho_{A,C} = 1/2$ but $\rho_{B,C} = 0$. To avoid this intransitivity of correlation as a measure of similarity of patterns, we use the notion of *ultrametric* or *tree distance* as a measure of distance between sectors or clusters of agents.

Definition (Ultrametric Distance): *Ultrametric distance denoted as $d(i, j)$ satisfies the following conditions:*

1. $d(i, j) \geq 0$ for any i, j, and $d(i, j) = 0$ only if $i = j$.
2. $d(i, j) = d(j, i)$.
3. $d(i, j) \leq \max_k \{d(i, k), d(j, k)\}$.

The concept of ultrametrics has been used in the literature of mathematics, numerical taxonomy, and physics, especially in spin glass models. For these, see Schikhof (1984), or Mézard, Parisi, and Virasoro (1986), among others. Aoki (1996) has several elementary economic applications of the notion of ultrametrics.

We introduce ultrametric or tree distance into the jump Markov process. Specifically, we make transition rates between clusters or states depend on ultrametric distance between these clusters; the transition rate from state i to state j is small when the ultrametric distance between states i and j is large. We demonstrate that such hierarchical structure of clusters or states *necessarily* produces slow adjustment. Furthermore, we make transition rates between clusters not only functions of ultrametric distances, but also functions of what we call *economic temperature*. As the economic temperature cools, transition rates become smaller from a cluster to another at the same ultrametric distance. In Chapter 4, we have already shown that the aggregate demand plays the role of economic temperature.

Trees

We use upside-down trees to represent hierarchical structures. Figure 5.1 is a simple tree model with two levels or layers, and four clusters or leaves at the bottom. An upside-down tree is commonly used in which the root is on top and the leaves at the bottom of the hierarchy as shown. At the bottom of a tree we

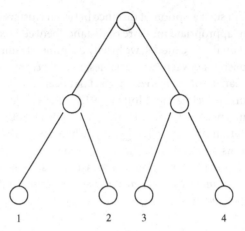

Figure 5.1. Two-level tree.

have leaves, where each leaf represents a state, an agent, or a cluster of agents (sites). It could also be the price of a particular good, as the case may be. The number of the leaves that share a common node of a tree is denoted by m. There are m_1 nodes on level 1 of the tree; they share the top node or the root of a tree. There are then m_2 nodes which branch out from a level 1 node at level two, and so on. In general we have n levels in a tree. Altogether the number of agents, states or sites is $N = m_1 m_2 \cdots m_n$. Agents in the same cluster are alike in some sense. They may be producers of some close substitutes or in the same industry. Or they may represent a group of agents who have a similar reaction function given a disturbance of some kind. The interpretation of cluster, state, or site is flexible.

Without loss of generality, we can assume that an exogenous shock is initially applied at site 1 at time zero. This shock is then transmitted to site i at time t with probability $\Pi_i(t)$. The initial condition is $\Pi_1(0) = 1$, and $\Pi_i(0) = 0, i \neq 1$. We can then calculate the time which it takes for $\Pi_i(i \neq 1)$ to be affected by the initial shock to Site 1, Π_1.

We can also use another measure to gauge the speed with which disturbances travel through the tree. We define the *average distance* travelled by the disturbance by time t,

$$\langle d(t) \rangle = \sum_i d(i, 1) \Pi_i(t)$$

where $d(i, 1)$ is the ultrametric distance between site i and site 1, to be defined shortly. $\langle d(t) \rangle$ indicates how far the disturbances have spread on the average through the model.

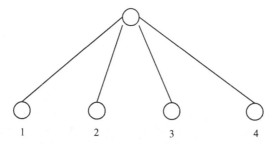

Figure 5.2. One-level tree.

Ultrametric Dynamics of Spillover Probabilities

We are now ready to explain dynamics of propagation of shocks on ultrametric trees. To make our point clear, we compare a simple two-level tree model (Figure 5.1) to the simplest one-level tree model (Figure 5.2). Both models have four sites, which correspond to the number of industries or agents. The difference is that one has two levels whereas the other has only one level.

In the one-level model shown in Figure 5.2, all the sites are symmetric. This one-level model corresponds to the standard model where industries or agents are indexed simply by i ($i = 1, \ldots, n$) with equal distance. In contrast, in the two-level tree model shown in Figure 5.1, four sites are classified into two broad groups. In this case, site 1 is closer to site 2 which belongs to the same group than sites 3 and 4 which belong to a different group.

The dynamics of the tree model is described by the master equation explained in Chapter 2. The probability that shocks are being felt at site i at time t, $\Pi_i(t)$, changes over time as the difference of the influx and outflux of probabilities. Denote the transition rate between site i and j by $w(i, j)$. We assume

$$w(i, j) = w(j, i) \quad \text{for all} \quad i \quad \text{and} \quad j. \tag{5.1}$$

The master equation that describes the dynamics of the probabilities is

$$\frac{d\Pi_i(t)}{dt} = I_i(t) - O_i(t). \tag{5.2}$$

Here, the influx to site i, $I_i(t)$ is

$$I_i(t) = \sum_{j \neq i} \Pi_j(t) w(j, i). \tag{5.3}$$

Similarly, the outflow from site i, $O_i(t)$, is

$$O_i(t) = \Pi_i(t) \sum_{j \neq i} w(i, j). \tag{5.4}$$

For the examples shown in Figures 5.1 and 5.2, we have

$$I_1(t) = \Pi_2(t) w(2, 1) + \Pi_3(t) w(3, 1) + \Pi_4(t) w(4, 1), \tag{5.5}$$

and

$$O_1(t) = \Pi_1(t)[w(1, 2) + w(1, 3) + w(1, 4)]. \qquad (5.6)$$

Now, the transition rate $w(i, j)$ is assumed to depend on two things. One is the ultrametric distance between two sites, and the other is a positive parameter T_e called *economic temperature*. Because the ultrametric distance defined on the tree in the abstract is based on some sense of distance between different sectors in the economy, it is natural to assume that the transition rates $w(i, j)$ depend inversely on the ultrametric distance between sectors i and j. For example, we would expect that technical progress in IC will more directly affect TVs or cameras than food. Then in this example of propagation of new technology, the distance between IC and TV is shorter than that between IC and food. In addition to the ultrametric distance between sectors i and j, all transition rates also depend on the *economic temperature*. Lower temperature uniformly reduces transition rates, and vice versa.

Two-level Tree. We first consider the *two-level* tree shown in Figure 5.1. The ultrametric distance $d(i, j)$ is defined as the number of levels required to "climb up" to reach a common node when one travels from site i to site j. Thus, in the case shown in Figure 5.1, we have the following ultrametric distances:

$$d(1, 2) = d(3, 4) = 1$$

and

$$d(1, 3) = d(1, 4) = d(2, 3) = d(2, 4) = 2.$$

Because the transition rates $w(i, j)$ depends inversely on the ultrametric distance $d(i, j)$, we can assume

$$w(1, 2) = w(3, 4) = q < 1,$$

and

$$w(1, 3) = w(1, 4) = q^2 < q.$$

where

$$q = e^{-1/T_e} < 1 \quad \text{and} \quad q^2 = e^{-2/T_e}.$$

Here, T_e is economic temperature. Lower T_e uniformly reduces all the transition rates. In Chapter 4, we explained that T_e is positively related to the degree of uncertainty in the economy. Note that because the distance between sites 1 and 2 is smaller than that between sites 1 and 3, we set $w(1, 2) = q$ as larger than $w(1, 3) = q^2$.

In this two-level tree model, the probability vector $\Pi(t)$ consists of probabilities at the four leaves:

$$\Pi(t) = [\Pi_1(t), \Pi_2(t), \Pi_3(t), \Pi_4(t)]'.$$

The master equation is

$$\frac{d\Pi(t)}{dt} = W\Pi(t), \tag{5.7}$$

with

$$W = \begin{bmatrix} W_1 & W_2 \\ W_2 & W_1 \end{bmatrix}.$$

Here, W_1 and W_2 are defined as

$$W_1 = \begin{bmatrix} -(q + 2q^2) & q \\ q & -(q + 2q^2) \end{bmatrix} \quad \text{and} \quad W_2 = q^2 e_2 e_2'$$

where

$$e_2 = (1, 1)'.$$

This matrix W has eigenvalues 0, $\lambda_1 = -4q^2 < 0$, and double repeated eigenvalue $\lambda_2 = -2(q + q^2) < 0$, with eigenvectors $u_0 = (1, 1, 1, 1)'$, $u_1 = (1, 1, -1, -1)'$, $u_2 = (1, -1, 0, 0)'$, and $u_2' = (0, 0, 1, -1)'$, respectively. Note that the magnitude of λ_1 is less than that of λ_2 because q is less than one. The speed of dynamics associated with eigenvalue λ_1 is faster than that associated with eigenvalue λ_2. It represents the escape rate of probability from site 1 to site 2.

More explicitly, we have the solution of the master equation corresponding to the initial condition $\Pi_1(0) = 1$, or the condition that an exogenous shock initially occurs at site 1:

$$\Pi(t) = 2^{-2} u_0 + 2^{-1} e^{\lambda_2 t} u_2 + 2^{-2} e^{\lambda_1 t} u_1. \tag{5.8}$$

This equation is equivalent to

$$\Pi_1(t) = \frac{1}{4} + \left(\frac{1}{4}\right) e^{\lambda_1 t} + \left(\frac{1}{2}\right) e^{\lambda_2 t},$$

$$\Pi_2(t) = \frac{1}{4} + \left(\frac{1}{4}\right) e^{\lambda_1 t} - \left(\frac{1}{2}\right) e^{\lambda_2 t},$$

$$\Pi_3(t) = \Pi_4(t) = \frac{1}{4} - \left(\frac{1}{4}\right) e^{\lambda_1 t}. \tag{5.9}$$

Noting that $e^{-4} = .02$ and $e^{-5} = 0.007$, we see that after time $t_1 = 4/2(q + q^2) \approx 2/q$, the term $\exp(\lambda_2 t)$ vanishes. After time $t_2 = 1/q^2$ ($t_2 > t_1$), the term $\exp(\lambda_1 t)$ also vanishes. It means that after time t_2, all four probabilities have approximately reached the equilibrium value of $1/4$ per site. Note that after time t_1 the initial shock to site 1 spills over to site 2, while site 3 and 4 are approximately still nearly untouched. After time t_2 the initial shock has spread over all four sites equally. *In the two-level tree model, to reach the stationary state requires the length of time of order $t_2 = 1/q^2$.*

The average distance travelled by the initial shock $\langle d(t) \rangle$ also summarizes the speed of spill-over.

$$\langle d(t) \rangle = \sum_{j \neq 1} d(1, j) \Pi_j(t)$$

$$= \Pi_2(t) + 2[\Pi_3(t) + \Pi_4(t)]$$

$$= \frac{1}{4} + \left(\frac{1}{4}\right) e^{\lambda_1 t} - \left(\frac{1}{2}\right) e^{\lambda_2 t} + 4\left[\frac{1}{4} - \left(\frac{1}{4}\right) e^{\lambda_1 t}\right]$$

$$= \frac{5}{4} - \left(\frac{3}{4}\right) e^{\lambda_1 t} - \left(\frac{1}{2}\right) e^{\lambda_2 t}. \tag{5.10}$$

Note that $\langle d(0) \rangle = 0$ and $\langle d(\infty) \rangle = 5/4$. The speed of spillover as measured by the average distance traveled by the initial shock $\langle d(t) \rangle$, namely the speed with which $\langle d(t) \rangle$ approaches its asymptotic value $5/4$, is governed by dynamics associated with the eigenvalues of the master equation, or equation (5.7).

One-level Tree. Next, we consider the one-level tree shown in Figure 5.2. In this case, the master equation for the probability vector $\Pi(t)$ consists of probabilities at the four leaves

$$\frac{d\Pi(t)}{dt} = W\Pi(t), \tag{5.11}$$

with

$$W = \begin{bmatrix} W_1 & W_2 \\ W_2 & W_1 \end{bmatrix}.$$

Here, W_1 and W_2 are defined as

$$W_1 = \begin{pmatrix} -3q & q \\ q & -3q \end{pmatrix} \quad \text{and} \quad W_2 = q e_2 e_2'$$

where

$$e_2 = (1, 1)'.$$

This matrix W has eigenvalue 0 with eigenvector $(1, 1, 1, 1)'$, and triple repeated eigenvalue $-4q < 0$ with three independent eigenvectors $(1, 1, -1, -1)'$, $(1, -1, 0, 0)'$, and $(0, 0, 1, -1)'$.

The probabilities evolve with time according to

$$\Pi_1(t) = \frac{1}{4} + \left(\frac{3}{4}\right) e^{-4qt}, \tag{5.12}$$

and

$$\Pi_2(t) = \Pi_3(t) = \Pi_4(t) = \left(\frac{1}{4}\right) - \left(\frac{1}{4}\right) e^{-4qt}. \tag{5.13}$$

Approximately after a time span of $1/q$, the probabilities are all about $1/4$.[2] It takes about this time span for the initial shock to propagate to all the sectors. Hence, this is the time lag for the shock initiated at sector 1 to spread probabilistically to all the other sectors. In the case of prices, this is the time required for the economy-wide price index to fully reflect the price shock which originates in one of its sectors.

The average distance traveled by the initial disturbance $\langle d(t) \rangle$ is as follows:

$$\langle d(t) \rangle = \sum_{j \neq 1} d(1, j) \Pi_j(t) = \Pi_2(t) + \Pi_3(t) + \Pi_4(t) = \frac{3}{4} - \left(\frac{3}{4} \right) e^{-4qt}.$$

(5.14)

Note that $\langle d(0) \rangle = 0$, and $\langle d(\infty) \rangle = 3/4$. Comparing this $\langle d(\infty) \rangle = 3/4$ for the one-level tree with $\langle d(\infty) \rangle = 5/4$ for the two-level tree, we can formally show that the distance traveled is less with the one-level tree than with the two-level tree as we should expect.

To compare dynamic behavior of two models, one the two-level tree model shown in Figure 5.1, and the other the one-level tree model shown in Figure 5.2, we can aggregate the tree by defining a two-dimensional state vector with components

$$S_1(t) = \Pi_1(t) + \Pi_2(t),$$

(5.15)

and

$$S_2(t) = \Pi_3(t) + \Pi_4(t),$$

(5.16)

by defining

$$Q(t) = S\Pi(t),$$

(5.17)

where the aggregation matrix S is given by

$$S = \begin{bmatrix} 1 & 1 & 0 & 0 \\ 0 & 0 & 1 & 1 \end{bmatrix}.$$

The master equation for this aggregated vector $Q(t)$ is

$$\frac{dQ}{dt} = VQ(t)$$

(5.18)

where V is given by

$$V = SWS'(SS')^{-1}.$$

V has eigenvalues 0 and $-4q^2$.

The vector $Q(t)$ has two components $0.5 + 0.5e^{-4q^2 t}$, and $0.5 - 0.5e^{-4q^2 t}$.

To summarize, dynamics of Figure 5.2 is much simpler. It has eigenvalues 0 and $-4q$. We can similarly aggregate the first two sites and the second two sites

---

[2] Note that $e^{-4} = 0.018$.

separately to produce a two node tree. The eigenvalue are still 0 and $-4q$. In other words, after the lapse of time of the order $1/q$, the system of Figure 5.2 has approximately reached its equilibrium state, whereas that in Figure 5.1 has not. Recall that in the two-level tree model, it requires the length of time of order $1/q^2$ which is larger than $1/q$ to reach the stationary state. That is to say, the two-level dynamics is more sluggish than that of the one-level tree of Figure 5.2. Thus, we have established the following proposition.

Proposition: *The two-level tree dynamics is more sluggish than the one-level tree dynamics even if they have the same number of sites.*

This fact remains true when the one-level tree of N sites is compared with the K level tree with $N = 2^K$. We can also group l of N sites into one cluster, and the remaining $N - l$ sites into another. The eigenvalues are 0 and $-Nq$, repeated $N - 1$ times, while those of K level tree are 0 and $-(2q)^K$.

Generally, we can show that the larger the number of levels of tree, the slower the process of disturbance propagation becomes. Ogielski and Stein (1985), among several others, have shown that in the limit of the number of hierarchy going to infinity, the response becomes *power law*, not exponential, decay.

Power Laws

The one-level dynamics corresponds to the standard model in which firms, agents, or sectors are symmetrically treated, typically indexed only by i ($i = 1, \ldots, n$). By construction, it implicitly assumes the fastest adjustment. The implication of the above proposition is that even if the number of firms, agents, or sectors is the same, once we allow the tree structure, dynamics *necessarily* become slower than otherwise. We maintain that tree structure is not an exception but generic in the economy, and, therefore, that slow dynamics is its generic property. There is actually a close relationship between tree dynamics and *power law* which is so universally found not only in nature but also in social and economic phenomena.

In Chapter 10, we will explain that power laws play the central role for understanding financial markets. Here, we briefly explain that power laws also have important implications for the speed of adjustment in dynamics which is the major theme of this chapter. To see the point, we take up a standard equation of motion in physics as an example. Specifically, we consider the following equation of motion with friction:

$$\frac{d^2x(t)}{dt^2} + \mu\left(\frac{dx(t)}{dt}\right) = -U'(x) \quad (\mu > 0). \tag{5.19}$$

Here, $x(t)$ stands for the position, and the second term on the left-hand side stands for friction which is proportional to velocity dx/dt. On the right-hand side is force which is equal to the first derivative of the *potential function* $U(x)$.

We assume that the potential function $U(x)$ is smooth, and that it has a minimum at point zero, $x = 0$. By expanding $U(x)$ around zero, we obtain

$$U(x) = U(0) + U'(0)x + \frac{U''(0)}{2}x^2 + \frac{U'''(0)}{6}x^3 + o(x^4). \qquad (5.20)$$

When friction μ is large, we can ignore acceleration dx^2/dt^2. Consequently, we can approximate (5.19) by

$$\frac{dx}{dt} = -\frac{U'(x)}{\mu}. \qquad (5.21)$$

We consider motion around the stationary point, $x = 0$. Note that because zero is the minimum of $U(x)$, $U'(0) = 0$. Thus, if $U''(0) \neq 0$, we obtain

$$\frac{dx}{dt} = -\frac{U'(x)}{\mu} = -ax. \qquad \left(a = \frac{U''(0)}{\mu} > 0 \right) \qquad (5.22)$$

In this case, we have

$$x(t) = x_0 e^{-at}. \qquad (5.23)$$

The adjustment of x toward its stationary point, $x = 0$, is *exponential*.

However, if $U''(0) = 0$, instead of (5.22), we obtain

$$\frac{dx}{dt} = \frac{-U'(x)}{\mu} = -bx^2 \qquad \left(b = -\frac{U'''(0)}{2\mu} \right). \qquad (5.24)$$

In this case, we have

$$x(t) = \frac{1}{bt + \frac{1}{x_0}} \sim \frac{1}{t}. \qquad (5.25)$$

That is, in this case, we obtain a *power law*. Compared to the exponential adjustment e^{-at}, the power-law adjustment, $1/t$ is much slower. Compare e^{-t} with $1/t$, for example. For $t = 10$, $e^{-10} \cong 4.5 \times 10^{-5}$ whereas $1/10 = 10^{-1}$. For $t = 100$, $e^{-100} \cong 3.7 \times 10^{-44}$ whereas $1/100 = 10^{-2}$. We observe that the exponential adjustment e^{-t} much more quickly approaches the stationary state, namely zero than the power-law adjustment $1/t$. *In general, under power laws, the speed of adjustment is much slower than in the exponential case.* Note that the exponential case is routinely assumed in the standard model in economics.

By way of comparing the two-level tree model with the one-level tree model, we have previously shown that the two-level dynamics is more sluggish than that of the one-level tree. As we noted it, there is actually a close relationship between dynamics of hierarchical trees and power-law behavior.

For example, Ogielski and Stein (1985) derive the expression for the probablity at site 1, $\Pi_1(t)$, as

$$\Pi_1(t) = 2^{-K} + \frac{1}{2} \exp[R^{K+1}t/(1-R)]$$

$$\times \sum_{m=0}^{K-1} \exp[-m\ln 2 - \{(2-R)/(1-R)\}R^{m+1}t]$$

where $R = \exp(-\beta m)$ for a positive parameter β, $m = 0, \ldots K$. Here, K is the number of levels of the hierarchy or tree. By letting $K \to \infty$, the sum is converted into an expression which involves the incomplete gamma function. The result is

$$\Pi_1(t) = \frac{\ln 2}{\beta}[K(2-K/(1-K)]^{-\ln 2/\beta} t^{-\ln 2/\beta} \gamma\left(\frac{\ln 2}{\ln \beta}, \frac{tR(2-R)}{1-R}\right).$$

Here, $R = e^{-\beta}$, and $\gamma(\ ,\ )$ is an incomplete gamma function explained in Appendix 5.1 to this chapter. As $t \to \infty$, we have an asymptotic expression

$$\Pi_1(t) \cong t^{-\ln 2/\ln \gamma}, \qquad (5.26)$$

up to order $O(e^{-t}/t)$. That is, $\Pi_1(t)$ propagates not exponentially as we obtained for the one and two level tree models, but following a *power law*.

As for the $\langle d(t) \rangle$, they show that

$$\langle d(t) \rangle \cong \frac{\ln t}{\ln \beta}. \qquad (5.27)$$

The initial shock to the probability at site 1 decays slowly obeying a power law, and the exogenous shock initiated at site one spreads to other sites with the expected distance of $\ln t/\ln \beta$.

Appendix 5.2 offers two additional examples for further illustration.

Economic Temperature

We have seen the relation between the tree structure of the economy and slow dynamics. Before leaving this section, we propose a notion of *economic temperature*. We often say that economic activities "heat up" or "cool down." Economic temperature formalizes this idea.[3]

Economic activities heat up as agents increase their economic activities by intensifying levels of existing economic transactions, or establishing new links between agents. In terms of hierarchical tree schematics, it means that we introduce more sites and/or more levels are added to hierarchical trees. Conversely,

---

[3]   There is, of course, no precise notion of "temperature" for nonthermal systems especially for macroeconomics despite a section in Sornette (2000, Sec. 7.4).

when economic activities slow down, intensities of existing activities reduce, or some of the existing links between agents are used less frequently or even broken.

One way to formalize these effects is to introduce a parameter that raises or lowers the transition rates. Specifically, we can define the transition rate between two sites, i and j as

$$w(i, j) = \exp\left[\frac{-d(i, j)}{T_e}\right]. \tag{5.28}$$

Then, an increase in T_e uniformly raises $w(i, j)$ while a decease in T_e reduces $w(i, j)$.

In our present tree models, as economic temperature gets lower, $\langle d(t)\rangle$ becomes smaller, and the decay of $\Pi_1(t)$ also becomes slower with time. In addition to the increase in the hierarchy of the model, *uncertainty* also reduces the economic temperature (see Chapter 4). As we argued in Chapter 3, *aggregate demand (relative to factor endowment) plays the role of temperature in economics.*

5.2. Inflexible Prices

One of the most intriguing problems in macroeconomics is to explain why prices are not fully flexible. It is a cliché among economists that if prices are fully flexible, changes in nominal expenditures, or changes in money in particular, will bring about only parallel changes in prices leaving all the real variables unchanged. *New Keynesian Economics* took up this challenge. Mankiw and Romer (1991) wrote

New Keynesian economics arose in the 1980s in response to this theoretical crisis of the 1970s. Much research during the past decade was devoted to providing rigorous microeconomic foundations for the central elements of Keynesian economics. Because wage and price rigidities are often viewed as central to Keynesian economics, much effort was aimed at showing how these rigidities arise from the microeconomics of wage and price setting. (Mankiw and Romer, 1991, 1)

Economists have proposed various explanations of why prices are not fully flexible. A popular argument is that it is to the economic agents' advantage not to change prices and wages so frequently. That is, changes in prices/wages incur significant costs ("menu costs") to economic agents. The "menu cost" model (e.g., Mankiw, 1985; Blanchard and Kiyotaki, 1987) is an example of such an approach. The "efficiency wage" model surveyed by Yellen (1984) and Katz (1986) is another.

Our approach is different. We attribute the slow dynamics of prices to the structure of the macroeconomy, not to a particular micro-behavior of economic agents. In this respect, it shares the spirit with Taylor (1979, 1980) who emphasizes the role of staggered wage setting in the multisector economy as *the* source of slow wage/price dynamics. However, the Taylor model has some problems. For example, based on his model, Taylor (1989) argues that a flexibility of nominal

Table 5.1. Comparison of prewar and postwar Japan: prices, wages, and output, 1905–1938 and 1966–1985

	(1) Mean (%)	(2) S.D. (%)	(3) Coefficient of variation ((2)/(1))	(4) 1st-order autocorrelation	(5) 2nd-order autocorrelation
1905–38					
Nominal price	2.2	12.0	5.45	0.45	−0.01
Nominal wages	4.9	9.8	2.00	0.64	0.30
Real wages	2.4	6.3	2.63	0.39	−0.12
Industrial production	6.8	6.9	1.01	−0.04	−0.15
1966–85					
Nominal price	4.1	7.3	1.78	0.28	−0.16
Nominal wages	10.7	5.6	0.52	0.76	0.54
Real wages	4.4	3.6	0.82	0.56	0.50
Industrial production	6.6	7.1	1.08	0.33	−0.00

Source: Prewar data are taken from Ohkawa et al. (1974–90). Postwar figures are from the Ministry of Labour, *Maitsuki Rodo Tokei Chosa Geppo* (Labour Statistics Monthly), the Bank of Japan, and MITI.

wages accounts for the much smaller size of the fluctuations in real output in Japan compared with United States. According to Taylor, a flexibility of nominal wages, in turn, can be attributed to synchronized union bargaining, called *Shunto* in Japan. Taylor's (1989) sample period is 1972–86. During this period, the variance of real GDP is much smaller in Japan than in the United States as Taylor found it. However, for the 1955–70 period, the variance of real GDP is much *greater* in Japan than in the United States. The synchronized wage bargaining, *Shunto*, began in 1955, and had been there throughout the 1955–70 period. Thus, the Taylor (1989) thesis that a flexibility of nominal wages attributable to synchronized wage bargaining makes variability of real GDP small in Japan does not actually quite stand up to the historical record.

There is another problem. Table 5.1 shows that in Japan, wages were much more flexible in the prewar period when the synchronized wage bargaining did *not* exist than in the postwar period when the *Shunto* was born.[4] Thus, we must conclude that the celebrated Taylor model somehow misses the essential point in explaining inflexible wages/prices. Here, we explore a different explanation.

---

[4]   Kalecki (1939, 1954), Hicks (1965, 1989) and Okun (1981) proposed the two-sector approach to prices: namely, the modern economy consists of two sectors, one "auction markets" and the other "customer markets." In the former, prices are flexible whereas in the latter prices are rigid. Our way to explain why prices/wages became more flexible in the postwar period than in the prewar era would be to show that the share of "customer markets" rose after the Second World War. Hicks (1989) advances this view.

In the Taylor model as well as in virtually all the other multisector models, the distance between a pair of two sectors is assumed to be the same; that is, sectors are symmetric. We focus on the fact that sectors are *not* symmetric or that the distance differs across sectors. Based on this fact, we show that price dynamics is necessarily slow. Using the model of tree dynamics explained in Section 5.1, we will show that "prices" in the macroeconomy necessarily change slowly.

For simplicity, we consider an example that is parallel to the tree model we analyzed in the previous section. Suppose that the economy consists of four sectors. The number of firms (or price makers) in each sector is $N/4$; the total number of firms in the economy is N. The sizes of firms are all equal. The average price of the ith sector is P_i ($i = 1, \ldots, 4$). We define the aggregate price index P as

$$P = \frac{1}{4} \sum_{i=1}^{4} P_i. \tag{5.29}$$

Suppose that responding to an exogenous shock, all the firms in sector 1 raised their prices by δ at time zero. Thus, P_1 increases by δ at time zero. This is an exogenous and permanent shock to P_1. We consider a change in the aggregate price index P over time. The transmission of the disturbance to sector 1, δ, to firms in other sectors, say sector j ($j = 2, 3, 4$), depends on the "distance" between sector 1 and sector j. For example, it is very hard, almost impossible for a steel maker to raise its price even if a subway fare increased. The same steel maker would raise its price when the price of iron increased. There are millions of price makers in the economy, all connected but with different "distances." Thus, the speed of transmission of a disturbance from one sector or price maker to another differs depending on a particular pair. In the present analysis, we assume that the economy has such tree structures as described in Figures 5.1 and 5.2. We assume furthermore that the transmission of a shock among sectors is a jump Markov process, and that the transition rate $w(i, j)$ from sector i to sector j depends inversely on the "tree distance" between sectors i and j. We compare the two-level tree (Figure 5.1) and the one-level tree (Figure 5.2) as we did in the previous section.

To analyze this dynamics, we define $\hat{N}_i(t)$ as the number of firms that have raised their prices by δ in sector i. In this analysis, we assume that a firm either raises its price by δ, or keeps it unchanged; once a firm raises its price by δ, it keeps the price. $\hat{N}_i(t)$ changes stochastically. By assumption, the initial values of $\hat{N}_i(t)$ are as follows

$$\hat{N}_1(0) = \frac{N}{4}, \quad \hat{N}_2(0) = \hat{N}_3(0) = \hat{N}_4(0) = 0. \tag{5.30}$$

We next define $\Pi_i(t)$ as

$$\Pi_i(t) = \frac{\hat{N}_i(t)}{\hat{N}(t)} \tag{5.31}$$

where

$$\hat{N}(t) = \sum_{i=1}^{4} \hat{N}_i(t).$$

$\Pi_i(t)$ is the share of the ith sector in firms which have raised their prices. Namely, it is the conditional probability that given $\hat{N}(t)$, a firm that has raised its price belongs to sector i.

We can then employ the same master equation as equation (5.7) in section 5.1 to analyze the dynamics of $\Pi(t)$:

$$\frac{d\Pi(t)}{dt} = W\Pi(t) \qquad \Pi(0) = (1, 0, 0, 0)'. \qquad (5.32)$$

Here, $\Pi(t)$ is $[\Pi_1(t), \Pi_2(t), \Pi_3(t), \Pi_4(t)]'$, and W is the matrix of transition rates.

On the assumption that the sizes of firms are all equal, we know that the expected value of the *cumulative* change in the aggregate price index up to time t, $\Delta P(t)$ is as follows:

$$\Delta P(t) = \frac{1}{N} \sum_{i=1}^{4} \hat{N}_i(t)\delta$$

$$= \frac{1}{N} \sum_{i=1}^{4} \hat{N}(t)\Pi_i(t)\delta$$

$$= \frac{1}{4} \sum_{i=1}^{4} \left(\frac{\Pi_i(t)}{\Pi_1(t)} \right)\delta. \qquad (5.33)$$

The last equality in (5.33) comes from

$$\Pi_1(t) = \frac{\hat{N}_1(t)}{\hat{N}(t)} = \frac{N}{4}\left(\frac{1}{\hat{N}(t)} \right).$$

Note that $\hat{N}_1(t)$ is $N/4$ for any t. Equation (5.33) shows that the dynamics of $\Delta P(t)$ is determined by the dynamics of $\Pi_i(t)$. The initial value of ΔP, $\Delta P(0)$, is by assumption

$$\Delta P(0) = \frac{N_1(0)\delta}{N} = \frac{\delta}{4}.$$

$\Delta P(t)$ approaches δ as $\Pi_i(t)$, $i = 1, 2, 3, 4$ approaches $1/4$. The master equation of $\Pi(t)$, namely equation (5.32), depends on the structure of tree. We consider the two-level tree model first, and then the one-level tree model.

The four sectors are related to each other with such a tree structure as shown in Figure 5.1. In this case, the transition rate from i to j, w_{ij}, satisfies the following condition:

$$w_{12} = q > w_{13} = w_{14} = q^2 \qquad (0 < q < 1). \qquad (5.34)$$

To reiterate equation (5.9), the expressions for $\Pi's$ are as follows:

$$\Pi_1(t) = \frac{1}{4}\left(1 + e^{-4q^2 t} + 2e^{-2(q+q^2)t}\right)$$

$$\Pi_2(t) = \frac{1}{4}\left(1 + e^{-4q^2 t} - 2e^{-2(q+q^2)t}\right)$$

$$\Pi_3(t) = \frac{1}{4}\left(1 - e^{-4q^2 t}\right)$$

$$\Pi_4(t) = \frac{1}{4}\left(1 - e^{-4q^2 t}\right). \tag{5.35}$$

We will compare this result with the one-level tree case. The one-level tree case is simple with the unique transition rate $w = q$. In this case, we obtain

$$\Pi_1(t) = \frac{1}{4}\left(1 + 3e^{-4qt}\right)$$

$$\Pi_2(t) = \Pi_3(t) = \Pi_4(t) = \frac{1}{4}\left(1 - e^{-4qt}\right). \tag{5.36}$$

Comparing (5.35) and (5.36), we can conclude that the aggregate price dynamics is more sluggish in the two-level tree model than in the one-level tree model.

The four-sector model we have analyzed is a particular example. However, using the analysis explained in the previous section, we can actually show that the larger the number of a levels of a tree is, the slower the dynamics of the aggregate price index P becomes. Figure 5.3 shows the simulation results. In the simulations, the size of price shock δ is assumed to be one. The cumulative change in aggregate price index $\Delta P(t)$, therefore, asymptotically approaches one. The transition rate parameter q is assumed to be $e^{-1} \cong 0.37$. Figure 5.3(A) compares the one-level tree and the two-level tree models with four sectors. Figure 5.3(B) compares the one-level through four-level tree models with 16 sectors. We can observe that the larger the number of levels of a tree is, the slower the change in aggregate price index becomes.

We believe that this result is significant because the tree structure is robust and generic in the macroeconomy. Distances between sectors and price makers all differ in terms of the speed of transmission of shock. And remember, there are actually millions of price makers. The number of the levels of the tree must be, therefore, much larger than two, most likely of greater order. The slow dynamics of the aggregate price necessarily follows.

There is no reason for us to expect that economic agents keep their prices for a fixed interval. They change their prices when they want to. Bils and Klenow (2004) carefully analyze the frequency of price changes for 350 categories of goods and services, and have found frequent price changes, with half of prices lasting less than 4.3 months. On this finding, they reject the popular Calvo–Taylor sticky price models.

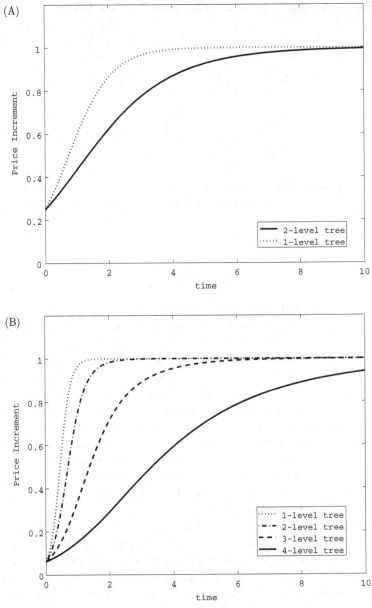

Figure 5.3. Dynamics of Aggregate Price Index in (A) 4 sectors, (B) 16 sectors.
Note: The size of price shock $\delta = 1$ and the transition rate parameter $q = e^{-1}$.

It does not actually make much sense to talk about flexibility or inflexibility *at the micro level*. To change prices is an economic behavior presumably based on some sort of optimization. However, for macroeconomics, the behavior of *aggregate* price index is more important than individual prices. And for the purpose of macroeconomics, changes in individual prices are *stochastic*. Our analysis shows that given the tree structure of the economy, the dynamics of the aggregate price index necessarily becomes sluggish. We believe that it provides better microeconomic foundations for explaining "inflexible" prices *at the macro level* than the analyses in the existing literature.

5.3. "Flat Landscape" Problems and Slow Dynamics

We have shown in the previous section that the tree structure of the economy necessarily produces slow dynamics. This result does not depend on specific assumptions of model, and, therefore, is generic. Before we conclude this chapter, we explain that there is actually yet another reason we should expect slow dynamics in the macroeconomy.

The standard analysis in economics takes it for granted that agents know the global shape of objective functions and constraints. In reality, agents have only local knowledge, and must improve their performances by gradually adjusting some of their decision variables. In doing so, they face complicated and often difficult combinatorial optimization problems. In fact, often the problem is not given in advance. To find problems is an important part of economic activities. This is true particularly in *real* economic activities as distinguished from financial transactions.

In these circumstances, agents who find themselves in a local optimum are not sure if there are other basins corresponding to better local optima, or the global optimum. They may also face nonunique choices because their objectives or criteria may be multivalued. These problems are sources for generating *microeconomic fluctuations*, which we take as essential for understanding the macroeconomy (see Chapter 3). At the same time, they cause slow dynamics in the macroeconomy.

The Metropolis Algorithm

Flat landscape problems are one example for which agents cannot find directions of motion to improve their suboptimal decisions. This may be caused by optimization being too complex with complicated cost surfaces; this case is called "rugged landscapes." The term "landscape" comes from the shape of the potential function which economic agents must minimize for optimization. "Flat landscape," therefore, means that the potential function is flat.

Suppose agents conduct exploratory moves, and evaluate the results with the algorithm proposed by Metropolis et al. (1953).[5] In the Metropolis method, the move is accepted with probability one if it results in lower cost. In order to move *possibly* from a local minimum to a better local or global minimum,

---

[5]   See Ripley (1987) for exposition of the method.

the move is accepted with probability $\exp(-\beta \Delta c)$ even when the cost increases by $\Delta c > 0$, where β is some positive parameter. A trial move, then, is accepted with probability $\min\{1, \exp(-\beta \Delta c)\}$. This algorithm recognizes a possibility that even if a move results in increased cost, the direction of the move may be correct in a more global search scheme; namely, there is a positive probability that leaving the basin associated with the current position, agent eventually reaches a new basin with lower cost.

When an economic agent is confident of the direction of the move, he is ready to choose the move to this direction with high probability. This is the case for situations in which the value of β is small, or the economic temperature is high. On the other hand, if the agent is uncertain whether the move improves his condition or not, this move will be chosen with a small probability. That is, when β is large under great uncertainty or the economic temperature is low, the agent becomes more timid in his moves than otherwise.

In Chapter 4, we showed that the effectiveness of macroeconomic policies, in fact, diminishes as the degree of uncertainty rises. It is important to note that the parameter β may become very large when the macroeconomy is in deep depression. In fact, one may argue that what distinguishes deep *depression* from normal cyclical *recession* is the abnormally high degree of uncertainty. With a very large value of β, any move not resulting in immediate cost reduction is rejected with high probability. This results in agents not revising their current operating modes almost with probability one. This will prolong the depression. Put differently, adjustment paths out of the current state are rarely taken, or become inaccessible once the economy faces great uncertainty (very large β).

Model

We will explain how the flat landscape problem is related to slow dynamics. Toward this goal, we construct a random walk model with endogenous birth rates and an absorbing state. In this model, many agents randomly search for the same optimal solution.

Suppose that agents face "rugged" cost or utility surfaces that are full of local minima (see Figure 5.4). Agents are not sure whether the minima are the true global minimum or they are stuck in some local minimum. They do not know which directions, if any, they should move to improve their performances. They cannot usefully resort to the steepest descent or some gradient procedures to take account of a possiblity that they need to overcome some barriers to leave the current basin of attraction in order to move to another one with smaller costs. Here, we assume that they employ the Metropolis method explained above. We can analyze this model using the jump Markov process.

Suppose there are $K + 1$ "boxes" (clusters, categories, or types). Each agent is in one of the boxes. The $(K + 1)$th box is the absorbing state in that once

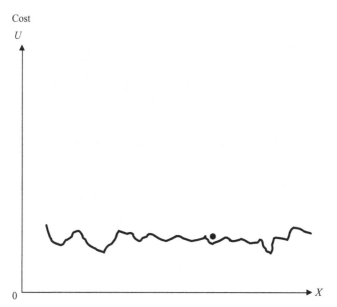

Figure 5.4. Rugged Cost Surface.
Note: The minimum of the U function corresponds to the best state.

economic agents pop into this box, they never leave it. It represents the first best or the global optimum. Other K boxes represent local optima. If an agent is in one of these K boxes, there is a possibility that he will move to another box.

In this model, the global optimum corresponds to a situation in which all K boxes are empty, that is, there is no more room for change. All the agents have reached the absorbing state or the base state. The presence of agents in any of K boxes indicates that not all the agents have achieved their optimal positions. At a given time, we pick an agent at random out of K boxes uniformly, and place it in another box (including $(K+1)$th box) at random. If there are k agents in one of K non-first best boxes, one agent is chosen out of this box with probability k/N. Here, N is the total number of agents in all the boxes excluding $(K+1)$th box. The chosen agent exits or departs from the box he is in, and will go to one of the remaining boxes with probability $1/K$. Call the box he goes to the arrival box; the arrival box is different from the departure box. The configuration of the model is

$$C = (n_1, n_2, \ldots, n_d, \ldots, n_a, \ldots n_k).$$

Here, n_d and n_a are the number of agents in the departure (d) and the arrival (a) boxes, respectively. Omitting the unchanged $n_i s'$ we can summarize C as

$$C = (n_d, n_a).$$

Let us define the *Boltzmann entropy of the configuration*, $S(n_d, n_a)$. Then its difference is

$$\Delta S = S(n_d - 1, n_a + 1) - S(n_d, n_a) \qquad (5.37)$$

when one agent departs box d and goes to box a. We use the Metropolis algorithm explained previously. Its acceptance rate of $(n_d, n_a) \rightarrow (n_d - 1, n_a + 1)$ is a function of ΔS:

$$w\left(n_d - 1, n_a + 1, \mid n_d, n_a\right) = \min\left(1, e^{-\Delta S}\right)$$

where ΔS is defined by

$$\Delta S = -\beta, \qquad\qquad \text{when}\quad n_d = 1, n_a \neq 0,$$

$$\Delta S = \beta, \qquad\qquad \text{when}\quad n_d \neq 1, n_a = 0, \qquad (5.38)$$

and

$$\Delta S = 0 \qquad\qquad\qquad \text{otherwise.}$$

In other words, the entropy changes only when the number of empty boxes changes. When the number of types of unsuccessful agents increases by one ($n_a = 0, n_d \neq 1$), the entropy S increases by β. On the other hand, when the number of empty boxes increases by one, ($n_a \neq 0, n_d = 1$), S decreases by β; Recall that the global optimum corresponds to the state where all the K boxes are empty.

To treat the simplest case, we focus on one of the boxes, called box 1. We denote the number of agents in it by $n_1(t)$, and the probability that $n_1(t) = k$, as $p_k(t)$:

$$p_k(t) = \Pr\left(n_1(t) = k\right). \qquad (5.39)$$

This and related models have been analyzed by several physicists. We follow Godrèche and Luck (1997). We write the master equation for p_k as

$$\frac{dp_k}{dt} = \left(\frac{k+1}{\lambda(t)}\right) p_{k+1} + p_{k-1} - \left[1 + \frac{k}{\lambda(t)}\right] p_k, \qquad k \geq 2,$$

$$\frac{dp_1}{dt} = \frac{2}{\lambda(t)} p_2 + \mu(t) p_0(t) - 2 p_1(t), \qquad\qquad (5.40)$$

and

$$\frac{dp_0(t)}{dt} = p_1(t) - \mu(t) p_0(t).$$

Here, $\lambda(t)$ and $\mu(t)$ are defined as follows:

$$1/\lambda(t) = 1 + (e^{-\beta} - 1) p_0(t),$$

and

$$\mu(t) = e^{-\beta} + (1 - e^{-\beta})p_1(t).$$

See Godrèche, Bouchaud, and Mézard (1995) for more information on this model.

We easily verify that these p's sum to one, and the mean of k is $\sum_k kp_k(t) = N/K := \rho$. We take ρ to be 1 for simplicity.

This set of equations can be used to calculate the generating function

$$F(z, t) = \sum_k p_k(t)z^k, \qquad (5.41)$$

with the initial condition assumed to be $F(z, 0) = z$, that is $p_1(0) = 1$ and all other p's are zero.

This generating function satisfies the partial differential equation

$$\frac{\partial F}{\partial t} = (z - 1)F(z, t) - \frac{z - 1}{\lambda(t)}\frac{\partial F}{\partial z} - (z - 1)Y(t), \qquad (5.42)$$

where $Y(t) = (1 - e^{-\beta})p_0(t) = 1 - 1/\lambda(t)$. See Aoki (2002, 70) for deriving the partial differential equation for the generating function. See also Aoki (2002, App. A.1) for solving the partial differential equation by the method of characteristic curves. The sollution is obtained by solving

$$\frac{dt}{1} = \frac{dz}{(z - 1)/\lambda(t)} = \frac{dF}{(z - 1)(F - Y)}. \qquad (5.43)$$

When $\beta = 0$, which corresponds to a high level of economic activities and a well-behaved cost curve, the equations is especially simple, because $\lambda(t) = \mu(t) = 1$. We obtain

$$F(z, t) = \{1 + (z - 1)e^{-t}\}\exp\{(z - 1)(1 - e^{-t}\}. \qquad (5.44)$$

From (5.44), we finally obtain

$$p_0(t) = (1 - e^{-t})\exp(e^{-t} - 1) = -\frac{1}{e} + \frac{1}{2e}e^{-2t} + \cdots. \qquad (5.45)$$

Equation (5.45) shows that $p_0(t)$ approaches the equilibrium value with time constant $1/2$.

Godrèch and Luck (1997) show that for β *large*, the time constant becomes e^{β}/β^2, a much larger number, indicating a sluggish approach to the equilibrium.

5.4. Concluding Remarks

In this chapter, we have shown that given the tree structure of the macroeconomy, the speed of adjustment necessarily becomes sluggish. This basic result applies to prices. There is no mystery of inflexible prices.

It is a cliché among economists that if prices are fully flexible, changes in nominal expenditures, or changes in money in particular, will bring about only parallel changes in prices leaving all the real variables unchanged. The analysis presented in this chapter demonstrates that such swift changes in prices are, in fact, impossible. Having said that, before we conclude this chapter, we note that rigid prices are not so crucial as is commonly believed for the validity of Keynesian economics. Keynes himself refuted this idea in *General Theory*. Fisher (1933) also regarded deflation not as the savior of, but the menace to, the macroeconomy. As Tobin (1993) puts it, "the central Keynesian proposition is not nominal price rigidity but the principle of effective demand." (Keynes, 1936, Chapter 3)

Table 5.1 shows the means, standard deviations, coefficients of variation, and autocorrelation of the nominal prices, nominal wages, real wages, and production indices in the prewar (1905–38) and postwar (1966–85) periods. As the coefficients of variation clearly show, both nominal and real wages were three to four times more flexible in prewar than in postwar Japan. A comparison of the autocorrelation coefficients shows that the persistence of real wages also increased during the postwar period. Nevertheless, the coefficients of variation of the production index are almost the same for both sample periods.[6] This result leads us to question the widely accepted, yet not fully substantiated proposition that rigid prices are the most important factor leading to output fluctuations. In Chapter 6, we will explore the sources of aggregate fluctuations under the assumption of constant price.

Appendix 5.1. Incomplete Gamma Function

The incomplete gamma function is defined by

$$\gamma(a, x) := \int_0^x t^{a-1} e^{-t} dt.$$

It goes to the usual gamma function $\Gamma(a)$ as x goes to infinity.

It has a series expansion

$$\gamma(a, x) = e^{-x} x^a \sum_{k=0}^{\infty} \frac{\Gamma(a)}{\Gamma(a + k + 1)} x^k.$$

See *Numerical Recipies in C: The Art of Scientific Computation*, Cambridge University Press, or Abramovitz and Stegun (1968, 260).

---

[6]   A glance at the autocorrelation coefficient of the first degree, however, shows that the persistence of changes in the production index increased slightly after World War II. This point remains a subject for further investigation.

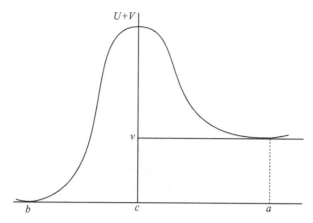

Figure 5.5. Potential Function with Two Basins of Attraction

Appendix 5.2. Examples of Ultrametric Dynamics

Two-State Example

To simplify notation we combine T_e with β and redefine β / T_e as β. So β gets large when T_e becomes small. We consider an example composed of two states, a, b with the transition rates

$$w(a, b) = \exp(-\beta V),$$

and

$$w(b, a) = \exp[-\beta(U + V)],$$

where β is a positive parameter. See Figure 5.5. (For the moment ignore state c.)

Probabilities $P_a(t)$ and $P_b(t)$ are governed by the master equation

$$\frac{dP_a}{dt} = P_b w(b, a) - P_a w(a, b).$$

Substituting $P_b = 1 - P_a$ out in the above, we rewrite it as

$$\frac{dP_a}{dt} = -\gamma(P_a - \Pi_a), \qquad (5.46)$$

where

$$\gamma = w(a, b) + w(b, a),$$

and

$$\Pi_a = \frac{w(b, a)}{\gamma} = \frac{1}{1 + e^{\beta U}}.$$

Suppose that the system is initially in state a, that is, $P_a(0) = 1$. Then, the solution of the master equation gives the expression

$$P_a(t) = e^{-\gamma t} + \Pi_a(1 - e^{-\gamma t}).$$

Substituting this into (A5.2B), we rewrite the master equation as

$$\frac{d P_a(t)}{dt} = -\gamma(1 - \Pi_a)e^{-\gamma t} = -\exp(-\beta V - \gamma t). \qquad (5.47)$$

Suppose we want to change the probability $P_a(t)$ as quickly as possible, and manipulate β / T_e, which we rename β for short, to maximize the right-hand side of this differential equation, or equivalently minimize the exponent with respect to β:

$$V + \frac{\partial \gamma}{\partial \beta} t = 0.$$

This leads to the expression

$$t = -\frac{V}{\dfrac{\partial \gamma}{\partial \beta}} \cong e^{\beta V}.$$

In other words, even when we change β to maximize the speed of adjustment by $\beta \cong \ln t / V$, we have

$$P_a(t) = e^{-\gamma t} + \Pi_a(1 - e^{-\gamma t}) \cong e^{-\beta U} \cong t^{-V/U}.$$

This shows that the probability that the system is in state a reaches the equilibrium value $\Pi_a = 1/(1 + e^{\beta U}) \cong e^{-\beta U}$ at the speed not of an exponential function but that of a power law, that is extremely sluggishly.

Three-State Example

We next examine the same shape as in the previous example by introducing another state and consider a three-state model, with state $\{a, c, b\}$, where state a is a local minimum, b is global minimum, and c is a local maximum. The dynamics has a mode with a long time constant.

The transition rates are

$$w(a, c) = \exp(-\beta V),$$

$$w(c, a) = w(c, b) = \frac{1}{2},$$

and

$$w(b, c) = \exp[-\beta(V + U)].$$

By substituting out $P_c = 1 - P_a - P_b$, the master equation is

$$\frac{dP_a}{dt} = \frac{1}{2} - \left[\frac{1}{2} + e^{-\beta V}\right] P_a - \frac{1}{2} P_b,$$

and

$$\frac{dP_b}{dt} = \frac{1}{2} - \left[\frac{1}{2} + e^{-\beta(U+V)}\right] P_b - \frac{1}{2} P_a.$$

The stationary probabilities are

$$\Pi_a = \frac{1}{1 + e^{\beta U} + 2e^{-\beta V}} \cong \frac{1}{1 + e^{\beta U}} \cong e^{-\beta U},$$

and

$$\Pi_b = \frac{1}{1 + 2e^{-2\beta(U+V)} + e^{-\beta U}} \cong \frac{1}{1 + e^{-\beta U}} \cong 1 - e^{-\beta U}.$$

Solving the differential equations with the initial condition $P_a(0) = 1$, we obtain

$$P_a(t) = \frac{1}{\lambda_1 - \lambda_2}\left[\lambda_1 + \frac{1}{2} + \frac{e^{-\beta(U+V)}}{2}\right] e^{\lambda_1 t}$$

$$+ \frac{1}{\lambda_2 - \lambda_1}\left[\lambda_2 + \frac{1}{2} + e^{-\beta(U+V)}\right] e^{-\lambda_2 t},$$

where λ_i, $i = 1, 2$ are the roots of the characteristic equation, where

$$\lambda_1 \cong -\frac{1}{2}[e^{-\beta V} + e^{-\beta(U+V)}] \cong -\frac{1}{2} e^{-\beta V},$$

and

$$\lambda_2 \cong -1 - \frac{1}{2}[e^{-\beta V} + e^{-\beta(U+V)}] \cong -1 - \frac{1}{2} e^{-\beta V}.$$

In this example λ_1 becomes very small, that is, one of the two time constants associated with this eigenvalue becomes large, and the dynamic mode associated with this eigenvalue is very sluggish, as economic temperature becomes low.

6

Business Cycles: An Endogenous Stochastic Approach

6.1. Introduction

Business cycles, or fluctuations of aggregate economic activities, have long attracted economists' attention. A glance at Haberler (1964) reveals that all kinds of theories had already been advanced by the end of the 1950s.

Some theories consider *monetary* factors, such as changes in money supply, the fundamental factor causing business cycles whereas others consider *real* factors, such as technical progress, fundamental. Some theories emphasize the role played by *exogenous* shocks. The famous theory of Jevons (1884), for example, singled out sun spots as the ultimate factor, and traced the chain of causation from sun spots to weather conditions, weather conditions to harvests, and finally from harvests to general business conditions. In contrast, other theorists purged exogenous factors, and constructed models in which *endogenous* cycles are generated. Goodwin's (1951) model of the nonlinear accelerator is a primary example of such models, Kaldor (1940) is another. More recently, Grandmont (1985) offers another example in which persistent deterministic cycles appear in a purely endogenous fashion without any exogenous shocks. Endogenous cycles produced in these models all rest on the particular nonlinearity of behavior of the representative agent.

Earlier, following the lead of Frisch (1933), Samuelson (1939) demonstrated that the second-order ordinary linear difference equation based on the multiplier and accelerator could generate cycles. Introducing the "ceiling" and the "floor" into such a model, Hicks (1950) ingeniously got around "explosions," and showed that the model could account for a dazzling variety of cycles. Given such an ample accumulation of theories, one might be fed up with theory of business cycles! Yet, even now, new theories keep cropping up. The RBC theory by Kydland and Prescott (1982) is arguably the most influential current theory among the mainstream economists.

As typified by the RBC, a natural research strategy to study business cycles is to explain fluctuations as a direct outcome of the behavior of *individual agents*.

The more strongly one wishes to interpret aggregate fluctuations as something rational or optimal, the more likely one is led to this essentially microeconomic approach. The mission of this approach is to explain fluctuations as responses of individual agents to changes in their economic environments. The consumer's intertemporal substitution, for example, is a device to achieve this goal. This holds true not only for the Kydland–Prescott RBC model but also for endoge-nous competitive models of business cycles such as that of Grandmont (1985). The basically microeconomic approach has been standard in the mainstream economics in the last 20 years or so.

In Chapter 1, we have explained that the common knowledge in science is that we cannot understand the behavior of *macro* system by direct inferences from the behavior of *micro* unit. Plainly, the RBC is in stark contrast to such common knowledge. Business cycles are macro phenomena. We need a different approach.

An alternative approach is based on the fact that the economy consists of a large number of interacting agents or sectors. The population of a large in-dustrialized economy, for example, consists of the order of 10^8 agents. Even if agents intertemporally maximize their respective objective functions, their envi-ronments or constraints all differ, and are always subject to idiosyncratic shocks. The point has been fully explained in Chapters 1 and 3.

The alternative approach which we advance in this chapter is based on the premise that an outcome of interactions of a large number of agents facing such incessant idiosyncratic shocks cannot be described by a response of the representative agent, and calls for a model of stochastic processes. In a seminal work, Slutzky (1937) proposed such a stochastic approach. He asked himself the following question.

Suppose we are inclined to believe in the reality of the strict periodicity of a business cycle, such, for example, as the eight-year period postulated by Moore. Then we should encounter another difficulty. Wherein lies the source of the regularity? What is the mechanism of causality which, decade after decade, reproduces the same sinusoidal wave which rises and falls on the surface of the social ocean with the regularity of day and night? It is natural that even now, as centuries ago, the eyes of the investigators are raised to the celestial luminaries searching in them for an explanation of human affairs. One can dauntlessly admit one's right to make bold hypotheses, but still should not one try to find out other ways? What means of explanation, however, would be left to us if we decided to give up the hypothesis of the superposition of regular waves complicated only by purely random components? The presence of waves of definite orders, the long waves embracing decades, shorter cycles from approximately five to ten years in length, and finally the very short waves, will always remain a fact begging for explanation. The approximate regularity of the periods is sometimes so distinctly apparent that it, also, cannot be passed by without notice. Thus, in short, *the undulatory character of the processes and the approximate regularity of the waves* are the two facts for which we shall try to find a possible source in random causes combining themselves in their common effect. (Slutzky, 1937, 20)

Slutzky then demonstrated that the summation of random variables produces sinusoidal fluctuations.

In the modern literature of probability, Feller explains the idea similar to Slutzky as the *Arc Sine Law* for random walks and coin tossing (Feller, 1968, Vol. I, Ch. III). Consider the following random walk:

$$S_i - S_{i-1} = \epsilon_i = \pm 1 \qquad (i = 1, 2, \ldots, \quad S_o = 0) \qquad (6.1)$$

with the respective probability one half.

The unconditional mean of this process is zero so that one is prone to expect that a realization or a sample path is likely to be always "close" to zero, very often crossing the zero line and spending about a half time in each of two sides of (namely, "above" and "below") the zero line. This natural intuition turns out to be wrong. *The sample path property is quite different from the property of moments.* The Arc Sine Law which is concerned with sample paths shows in a striking fashion that the fraction of time spent on the positive side is much more likely to be close to zero or to one than to the "normal" or "expected" value $1/2$. An implication is that the simple random walk is most likely to produce "cycles" meaning that a fairly long "good time" (above the line) is followed by a fairly long "bad time" (below the line), alternately. Figure 6.1 reproduces Feller's Figure 5 (1968, 84) which records a sample path of 10,000 tosses of an ideal coin for the above random walk.

The strength of Slutzky's approach is its robustness; the weakness of his approach is that the model is devoid of any economic interpretation. Sharing Slutzky's spirit, we build a stochastic model of aggregate fluctuations which has good economic interpretation. We have three main objectives. First, we demonstrate that fluctuations of the aggregate economy arise as an outcome of interactions of many agents/sectors in a simple model. Second, we show that *the level of the aggregate economic activity depends on demand.* In the standard neoclassical equilibrium, where the marginal products of production factors such as labor are equal in all activities and sectors, demand determines only the composition of goods and services to be produced, but *not* the level of the *aggregate* economic activity. As we have explained in Chapter 3, the existence of productivity differentials across sectors leaves demand to play the central role in the determination of the aggregate output. We demonstrate this proposition in a stochastic dynamic model. Third, we show the importance of "allocative disturbances" in business cycles. Our model is a *stochastic multisector model*, and, therefore, fits perfectly the purpose of studying the role of allocative disturbances.

There are two ways for demand to affect the aggregate level of economic activities. One is externality associated with demand which might produce multiple equilibria such as in Diamond (1982). The other is differences in productivity across sectors/activities. In Chapter 3, we have shown that we generically have distribution of production factors across sectors with different productivity in

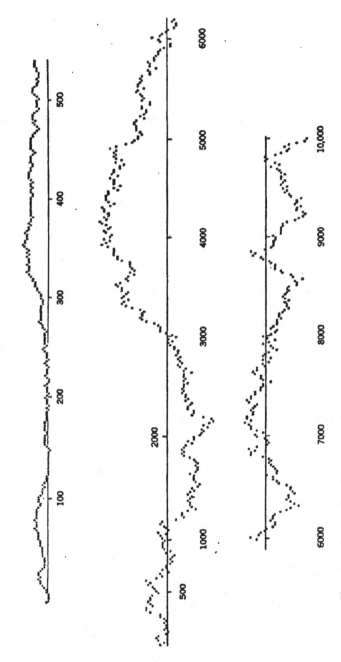

Figure 6.1. Arc Sine Law: The Record of 10,000 Tosses of an Ideal Coin.
Source: Feller's [1957] Figure 5 in Chapter III.

equilibrium. Given this observation, we assume in the subsequent analysis that productivities differ across sectors in the economy.

Although studies of macroeconomy with many agents are not new, dynamic behavior in disequilibrium has not been satisfactorily analyzed. The traditional general equilibrium model focuses on price adjustment with the help of the artificial auctioneer. However, as Clower (1965) and Leijonhufvud (1968) pointed out a long time ago, quantity adjustment might be actually much faster than price adjustment in the real economy.

Before we proceed, it is interesting to compare the behaviors of price and quantity. Figure 6.2 shows frequency distributions of monthly rates of change in price and quantity for the Japanese manufacturing industry and transport machinery industry. Note that the scales of the figures are the same for both price and quantity. Plainly, in both cases, the variance of distribution is much larger for quantity than for price. This means that changes in quantity are, in fact, greater than those in price as suggested by Clower and Leijonhufvud. Their insight spawned a vast literature of the so-called "Non-Walrasian" or "disequilibrium" analysis such as Benassy (1975) and Malinvaud (1977). In these models, as Leijonhufvud (1968) puts it, *quantities determine quantities*. However, the models are static primarily because their purpose is to show the existence of non-Walrasian quantity-constrained equilibrium. Our model shares the spirit of the "Non-Walrasian" approach, but is dynamic to analyze fluctuations of the quantity-constrained economy.

Toward this goal, we consider a very simple quantity adjustment model with a large number of sectors or agents. We assume that sectors have different productivities. Resources are stochastically allocated to sectors in response to excess demands or supplies of the sectors. We show that the total output of such an economy fluctuates, and that the average level of aggregate production (or GDP) depends on demand.

In the main part of the analysis, we keep the number of sectors fixed. Then, we allow the number of sectors to grow in a stochastic way. There we use a method analogous to that of the Ewens sampling formula which is explained in Chapter 2.

6.2. The Model

Suppose that there are K sectors in the economy. We keep the value of K fixed for now. We later briefly consider the case where K is variable. Sectors adjust their outputs by changing the level of input in response to the excess demand or supply of their goods. We model the state of this economy as usual as a continous-time Markov chain or a jump Markov process. We use the notion of holding time to select the sector which adjusts first. See Chapter 2 on holding time.

We assume that productivity differs across firms and sectors. In Chapter 3, we have already explained in detail that productivity dispersion is a necessity in the macroeconomy. In this model, we assume that sector i has productivity

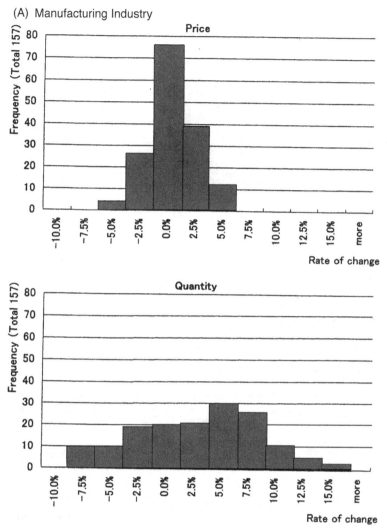

Figure 6.2. Frequency Distributions of Rate of Changes in Price and Quantity (A) Manufacturing Industry, (B) Transport Machinery 1987 (Jan.)–2000(Jan.)
Notes: Price is wholesale price index (WPI)(1995 = 100); quantity is the index of industrial production (IIP)(1995 = 100). Rate of change is to the same month in preceding year.

coefficient c_i ($i = 1, \ldots, K$), which is exogenously given and fixed. Assume, for convenience, that sectors are arranged in decreasing order in productivity:

$$c_1 > c_2 > \cdots > c_K.$$

Sector i uses N_i units of factor of production. It is a nonnegative integer-valued random variable. We call a particular realization of N_i as the "size" of the sector, and denote it by n_i. When the size of sector i is n_i, $i = 1, 2, \ldots, K$, the

(B) Transport Machinery

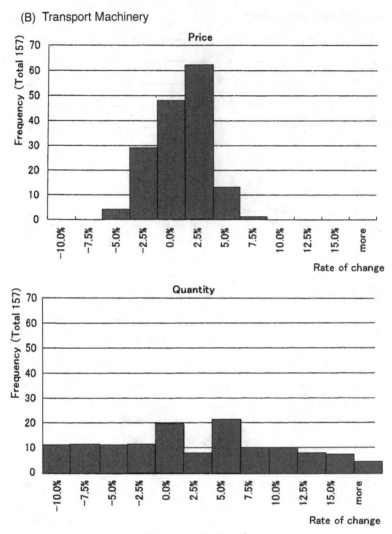

Figure 6.2. *Continued.*

output of sector i is $c_i n_i$, and the total output (GDP) of this economy, Y, is

$$Y(t) := \sum_{i=1}^{K} c_i n_i(t). \qquad (6.2)$$

Demand for the output of sector i is assumed to be $s_i Y(t)$, where $s_i > 0$ is the share of sector i:

$$\sum_{i=1}^{K} s_i = 1.$$

The demand shares s_i are exogeously given and fixed. The excess demand for goods of sector i, $f_i(t)$, is then defined as

$$f_i(t) := s_i Y(t) - c_i n_i(t). \qquad (6.3)$$

Denote the set of sectors with positive excess demand by

$$I_+ = \{i; f_i > 0\},$$

and similarly, the set of sectors with negative excess demand (namely, excess supply) by[1]

$$I_- = \{j; f_j \leq 0\}.$$

To shorten notation, summations over these subsets are denoted as $\sum_+$ and $\sum_-$. Denote by n_+ the sum of n_i's in the set I_+. That is, we write

$$n_+ := \sum_+ n_i,$$

where the subscript $+$ is short for the set I_+. Similarly, we define n_- as

$$n_- := \sum_- n_j,$$

for the sum over the sectors with negative excess demand. By definition, we have $n = n_+ + n_-$. Note that n is not fixed, but endogenously changes.

Sectors with nonzero excess demand attempt to reduce the amount of excess demand by adjusting their size, namely n_i up or down, depending on the signs of the excess demand. Without loss of generality, we can assume that $n_i(t)$ changes by one unit. Thus, the transition rates are such that

$$P(N_i(t + h) = n_i + 1 | N_i(t) = n_i) = \gamma_i h + o(h) \quad \text{for} \quad i \in I_+$$

and

$$P(N_j(t + h) = n_j - 1 | N_j(t) = n_j) = \rho_j h + o(h), \quad \text{for} \quad j \in I_-. \qquad (6.4)$$

The transition rates, γ and ρ, of the jump Markov process will be specified shortly.

The assumptions made here mean that a sector/firm gets ready either to raise or lower the level of its production depending on the sign of excess demand for its product. We can interpret the amount of input used in sector i, n_i, either as the number of workers and machines or as the level of utilization of such production factors in sector i. In the latter interpretation, sector i holds L_i units of capacity of production factor as given, and n_i can change within the limits of 0 and L_i, ($n_i = 1, 2, \ldots, L_i$). n_i / L_i is the capacity utilization rate in this case. Recall that $n = \sum_i n_i$ is not fixed, but endogenously changes.

---

[1]   To be definite we include sectors with zero excess demands as well.

Transition Rates

We assume that γ's and ρ's depend on the total size of the economy, n, and the size of each sector n_i:

$$\gamma_i = \gamma_i(n_i, n),$$

and

$$\rho_j = \rho(n_j, n).$$

There are good theoretical reasons for γ_i to depend only on n_i and n, and similarly for ρ_j. See Zabell (1992) for further references on the statistical reasons for this specification.[2]

The model can allow for the case where the number of sectors K is not fixed, but stochastically increases. We will discuss it later. Here, to accommodate this general case, we specify the entry rate, that is, the rate of size increase, as follows:

$$\gamma_i(n_i, n) = \frac{\alpha + n_i}{K\alpha + n}.$$

When the number of sectors K is fixed, α is zero. In this case, γ_i reduces to n_i/n:

$$\gamma_i(n_i, n) = \frac{n_i}{n}.$$

Similarly, we specify the exit rate, namely, the rate of size decrease by

$$\rho_j(n_j, n) = \frac{n_j}{n}.$$

When γ_i is the same as the fraction n_i/n, ($\alpha = 0$), it is equal to the probability for exit, ρ_j. Then, time histories of n_i are nearly those of near fair coin tosses. We have K such coin tosses available at each jump. The sector that jumps determines which coin toss is selected from these K coins.

For the moment, we set $\alpha = 0$, and discuss the economy with fixed numbers of sectors.

Holding Time

Now, which sector/firm actually changes the level of production depends on the *holding times* of the sectors. We assume that the probability of the time it takes for sector i to adjust its size, either up or down, T_i, is exponentially distributed:

$$P(T_i > t) = \exp(-b_i t),$$

---

[2] This is an example of applying W. E. Johnson's sufficientness postulate. We have discussed specifications of entry and exit probabilities in Aoki (2002). See also Costantini and Garibaldi (1979, 1989), who give clear discussions on reasons for these specifications. As explained clearly by Zabell (1992), there is a long history of statisticians who have discussed this type of problems.

Here, b_i is either γ_i or ρ_j depending on the sign of the excess demand; thus, the holding times are essentially determined by the transition rates specified above. This time is called sojourn time or holding time in the probability literature. We assume that the random variables T's of the sectors with nonzero excess demand are independent.

The sector with the highest probability that it adjusts first is the one with the shortest holding time. And conversely, the sector with the longest holding time has the lowest probability that it adjusts first. With such probabilities, the sector which actually adjusts the level of its input is randomly chosen. We call it the *active* sector. Variables of the active sector are denoted with subscript a.

Let T^* be the minimum of all the holding times of the sectors with nonzero excess demands. Lawler (1995) shows that the probability that the upward jump occurs in sector a is as follows:

$$P(T_a = T^*) = \frac{\gamma_a}{\gamma_+ + \rho_-} \quad \text{for} \quad a \in I_+$$

where $\gamma_+ = \sum_+ \gamma_i$, and $\rho_- = \sum_- \rho_j$. Similarly, the probability that the downward jump occurs in sector a is given by

$$P(T_a = T^*) = \frac{\rho_a}{\gamma_+ + \rho_-} \quad \text{for} \quad a \in I_-.$$

See Lawler (1995, 56) or Aoki (1996, Sec. 4.2). Here, γ_i and ρ_j are the transition rates explained previously.

Output and Excess Demand

After a change in the size of a sector, the total output of the economy changes to

$$Y(t + h) = Y(t) + \text{sgn}\{f_a(t)\}c_a, \tag{6.5}$$

where a is the active sector that jumped first by the time $t + h$.[3] $\text{sgn}(x)$ indicates the sign of x.

After the jump, the active sector's excess demand changes to

$$f_a(t + h) = f_a(t) - c_a(1 - s_a)\text{sgn}\{f_a(t)\}. \tag{6.6}$$

Other nonjumping sectors have the excess demand changed to

$$f_i(t + h) = f_i(t) + \text{sgn}\{f_a(t)\}s_i c_a, \quad \text{for} \quad i \neq a. \tag{6.7}$$

These two equations show the effects of an increase of size in one sector. An increase in output in sector a by c_a raises GDP by the same amount. In this case,

---

[3] For the sake of simplicity we may think of the skeleton Markov chain, in which the directions of jump are chosen appropriately but the holding times themselves are replaced by a fixed unit time interval. Limiting behaviors of the original and the skeletal version are known to be the same under certain technical conditions. They hold for this particular example we are analyzing here. See Cinlar (1975).

sector a experiences an increase in its demand only by $s_a c_a$ which is smaller than c_a, while at the same time, all other sectors experience increases of their demands by $s_i c_a$, $i \neq a$. Equation (6.7) shows a source of externality for this model. Note that the index sets I_+ and I_- also change in general.

Defining

$$\Delta Y(t) := Y(t+h) - Y(t),$$

and

$$\Delta f_i(t) := f_i(t+h) - f_i(t),$$

we rewrite equations (6.5) through (6.7) as

$$\Delta Y(t) = \mathrm{sgn}\{ f_a(t)\} c_a,$$

and

$$\Delta f_a(t) = -(1 - s_a)\Delta Y(t),$$

and

$$\Delta f_i(t) = s_i \Delta Y(t) \quad \text{for } i \neq a.$$

6.3. Stationary Equilibrium

When excess demands of all sectors are zero, no sector changes its output and, therefore, the total output or Y also remains unchanged. For convenience, we call this state *stationary equilibrium*. Before we analyze the dynamics of this model, we study the property of this stationary equilibrium.

By solving K equations of zero excess demand $f_i = 0$, $i = 1, 2, \ldots, K$, we obtain the equilibrium values (denoted by superscript e) of the fractions of sector sizes, n_i^e / n^e for $i = 1, \ldots, K$, and also the ratio of the total output to the total number of production factors, Y^e / n^e. This Y^e / n^e can be interpreted as the average productivity in the economy as a whole.

Specifically, in stationary equilibrium, we obtain the following set of zero excess demand conditions:

$$s_i Y^e = c_i n_i^e, \quad i = 1, 2, \ldots, K$$

or

$$n_i^e = \left(\frac{s_i}{c_i} \right) Y^e.$$

Summing n_i^e over i, we obtain

$$n^e = \sum_{i=1}^{K} n_i^e = \sum_{i=1}^{K} \left(\frac{s_i}{c_i} \right) Y^e.$$

The above two equations give us

$$\frac{n_i^e}{n^e} = \frac{s_i/c_i}{\sum s_i/c_i} \qquad (i = 1, \ldots, K). \tag{6.8}$$

Thus, the *fraction* is uniquely determined; it depends on the ratios of demand share to productivity coefficient, s_i/c_i. Similarly, we can obtain the relation between Y and n in stationary equilibrium as

$$Y^e = \frac{n^e}{\sum_i s_i/c_i}. \tag{6.9}$$

Because of the linearity of the model, the levels of Y and n are indeterminate in stationary equilibrium. We can easily understand this result if we recall the fact that in terms of the textbook Keynesian 45-degree line analysis, the present model corresponds to the case where the demand schedule coincides with the 45-degree line; because $\sum s_i = 1$, both the average and marginal propensities to expend are one. Thus, in the present model, only the average productivity Y/n can be determined *in stationary equilibrium*:

$$\frac{Y^e}{n^e} = \frac{1}{\sum_i s_i/c_i}. \tag{6.10}$$

The level of Y is indeterminate. The dynamic behavior of the model is quite different, however. In what follows, we study dynamics.

6.4. Two-Sector Model

The model explained in the second section is simple. Despite its simplicity, the dynamics produced in this model is actually very complex. Perhaps surprisingly, it is extremely difficult to analyze it in its full generality. To gain insight, we analyze a simple two-sector model in this section.

In the two-sector model, we have $s_2 = 1 - s_1$. This model is characterized by two parameters s_1 and c_2/c_1. (If you wish, c_1 may be set to one with a suitable choice of unit to measure n_1.)

Equation (6.9) shows that

$$\frac{n_2^e}{n_1^e} = \frac{\left(\dfrac{s_2}{c_2}\right)}{\left(\dfrac{s_1}{c_1}\right)}.$$

This, in turn, means that the sign of $(s_2/s_1) - (c_2/c_1)$ determines the relative sizes of the two sectors in equilibrium. Because two sectors are symmetric, it does not matter for dynamics whether n_1^e is larger than n_2^e. For definiteness, we describe the model behavior assuming that this sign is positive, that is $n_2^e \geq n_1^e$. The other case may be examined simply by switching the subscripts.

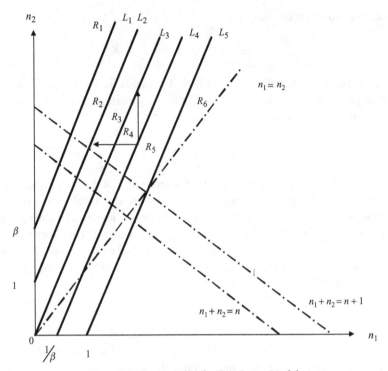

Figure 6.3. Dynamics in the Two-Sector Model.

We suppress time arguments. Consider the nonnegative quadrant of the plane for n_1 and n_2, with the horizontal axis labelled by n_1, and the vertical by n_2. We divide this quadrant into six regions denoted by R_k, $k = 1, 2, \ldots, 6$ (see Figure 6.3). They are bounded by $n_i \geq 0$ ($i = 1, 2$), and five other straight lines with a common slope β:

$$\beta = \left(\frac{c_1}{c_2}\right)\left(\frac{1 - s_1}{s_1}\right). \qquad (6.11)$$

This slope is larger than 1 under our assumptions of parameter values. The intercepts of the five lines are β, 1, 0, -1, and $-\beta$. In Figure 6.3, these five lines are denoted by $L_1, L_2, \ldots, L_5$, respectively. Line 3 cuts the n_1 axis at 0, Line 4 at $1/\beta$, and Line 5 at 1.

In different regions, either the signs of the excess demands, or those after size changes by sector 1 or 2, are different. To see it, we first note that in the two-sector model, $f_1 + f_2 = 0$ holds, and, therefore, that we need consider the sign of only f_1. Let us denote by $f_i^1(\pm)$ the value of the excess demand of f_i after a change of n_1 by ± 1, and by $f_i^2(\pm)$ the excess demand of f_i after a change in n_2 by ± 1, respectively. We then note that $f_1^1(\pm) + f_2^1(\pm) = 0$, and similarly, $f_1^2(\pm) + f_2^2(\pm) = 0$ hold. Recall that only an increase in n_1 is possible when $f_1 > 0$ in sector 1. Similarly, with $f_2 < 0$, $f_1^2(+)$ does not make sense.

Table 6.1. Dynamics of Two-Sector Model

Region	f_1	$f_1^1(+)$	$f_1^1(-)$	$f_1^2(+)$	$f_1^2(-)$
R_1	$+$	$+$	$*$	$*$	$+$
R_2	$+$	$-$	$*$	$*$	$+$
R_3	$+$	$-$	$*$	$*$	$-$
R_4	$-$	$*$	$+$	$+$	$*$
R_5	$-$	$*$	$+$	$-$	$*$
R_6	$-$	$*$	$-$	$-$	$*$

Note: See the text and Figure 6.1 for regions R_1 through R_6. The table shows the signs of f_1, $f_1^1(+)$, and so on. The symbol "$*$" means "no entry," that is, logically impossible combinations.

Now, we note, for example, that in R_1, R_2, and R_3 which are above L_3, $f_1 > 0$. Hence $f_2 < 0$ in these regions. After a change in n_1 by $+1$,

$$f_1^1(+) = s_1 c_2 [n_2 - \beta(n_1 + 1)] > 0,$$

above L_1, and so on. Table 6.1 summarizes signs of the excess demand, and shows how the sign changes by a change in n_i in sector 1 and 2. The five columns from the left to right list signs of f_1, $f_1^1(+)$, $f_1^1(-)$, $f_1^2(+)$ and $f_1^2(-)$ in that order.

The probability of a size increase in sector 2 is larger than that of a size descrease in sector 2 when

$$\gamma_1(n_1, n_2) \leq \rho_2(n_1, n_2).$$

This inequality holds when $n_1 < n_2$.

When state (n_1, n_2) is in R_1, consecutive jumps in sector 1 will bring the state to the boundary L_1 by increasing n_1, and necessarily make the state enter R_2. This is so because f_1 continues to be positive after jumps in R_1. Similarly, consecutive jumps in sector 2 from a state in R_1 also eventually bring the state to the same boundary by decreasing n_2. For that matter, we can calculate the various combinations of jumps in sector 1 and sector 2 to bring the state to the boundary, L_1. We thus see that either way, the state leaves R_1 with probability one. From a state in R_2, consecutive decreases in n_2 make the state enter R_3. Since dynamics is symmetric with respect to the equilibrium state represented by L_3, the state originating in R_6 eventually enters R_4 with probability one. Thus, we focus on R_3 and R_4 in what follows.

We examine the excess demand sign patterns in R_3 and R_4 which border on Line 3. Without loss of generality, we can assume that sector 1 faces excess demand; in other words, we consider region R_3. Then, we have

$$f_1 = \frac{s_1}{\kappa} n^e - c_1 n_1, \tag{6.12}$$

where κ is defined as

$$\kappa = \left(\frac{s_1}{c_1}\right) + \left(\frac{s_2}{c_2}\right). \tag{6.13}$$

Recall equation (6.10), which shows that the inverse of κ is the average productivity Y/n in stationary equilibrium.

In sector 1, n changes from n_1 to $n_1 + 1$. Thus, the change in excess demand in sector 1, Δf_1, is

$$\Delta f_1 = s_1 c_1 - c_1 = -c_1(1 - s_1) < 0.$$

which is negative in sign. Similarly, when n changes from n_1 to $n_1 + 1$ in sector 1, the change in excess demand in sector 2, Δf_2 is

$$\Delta f_2 = c_1 s_2 > 0$$

which is positive.

Therefore, when n increases in sector 1 facing excess demand, either excess demand in sector 1 or excess supply in sector 2 diminishes. In the same fashion, we can show that if n_2 changes, either excess supply in sector 2 or excess demand in sector 1 diminishes. Because the horizontal distance between L_2 and L_3 (or L_4 and L_3) is $1/\beta$ which is less than one, after a unit change in n the state in region R_3 or R_4 necessarily crosses the border L_3. Thus, we obtain *oscillations* around L_3 in regions R_3 and R_4. Figure 6.4 shows a typical sample path.

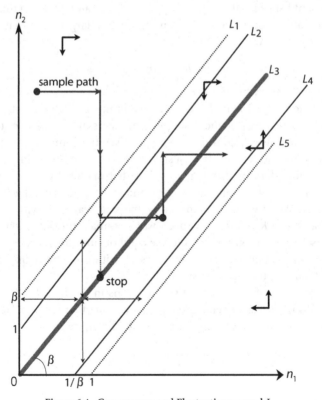

Figure 6.4. Convergence and Fluctuation around L_3.

The Expected Value of GDP

We next derive the stationary probability distribution for the sizes of two sectors, namely (n_1, n_2), and the expected value of Y or GDP. The general discussion of dynamics is conducted via the master (Chapman–Kolmogorov) equation (see the Appendix to this chapter). Here, we explain the derivation of the stationary probability distribution near the equilibrium states represented by L_3. Given the stationary probability distribution, we can calculate the expected value of Y.

Our goal is to demonstrate that *the expected value* of Y depends on demand. Specifically, we show that the sign of the derivative of the expected value of Y with respect to s_1 is positive near the equilibrium (equation (6.9)) in our two-sector model.

Toward this goal, we must first find the stationary probability distribution near L_3. Take the initial state b which is on or just below L_3. ($b \in R_4$). Note that because b is in R_4, sector 2 faces excess demand whereas sector 1 faces excess supply. Let $n(b)$

$$n(b) = (n_1(b), n_2(b))$$

be the state. We define two adjacent positions e and c as follows (see Figure 6.5):

$$n_1(e) = n_1(b) + 1, \quad n_2(e) = n_2(b) + 1,$$

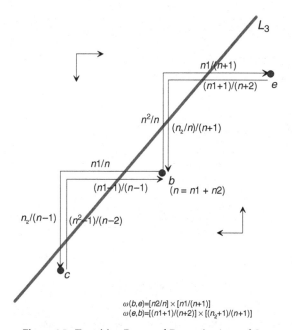

$$\omega(b,e)=[n2/n] \times [n1/(n+1)]$$
$$\omega(e,b)=[(n1+1)/(n+2)] \times [(n_2+1)/(n+1)]$$

Figure 6.5. Transition Rates and Dynamics Around L_3.

and

$$n_1(c) = n_1(b) - 1, \quad n_2(c) = n_2(b) - 1.$$

By the detailed balance conditions between states e and b, and those between b and c, we derive the relations for the stationary probabilities π as

$$\frac{\pi(n(e))}{\pi(n(b))} = \frac{n_1(b)}{n_1(b)+1} \frac{n_2(b)}{n_2(b)+1} \frac{n+2}{n}, \tag{6.14}$$

and

$$\frac{\pi(n(c))}{\pi(n(b))} = \frac{n_1(b)}{n_1(b)-1} \frac{n_2(b)}{n_2(b)-1} \frac{n-2}{n}. \tag{6.15}$$

where

$$n := n_1(b) + n_2(b),$$

By repeating the process of expressing the ratios of probabilities, we obtain[4]

$$\frac{\pi(n_1(b)+k, n_2(b)+k)}{\pi(n(b))} = \left(\frac{n_1(b)}{n_1(b)+k}\right)^2 \frac{n+2k}{n} \quad \text{for } k = 1, 2, \ldots, \tag{6.16}$$

where we use $n_2 = \beta n_1$ on or near L_3.

Similarly, we obtain

$$\frac{\pi(n_1(b)-l, n_2(b)-l)}{\pi(n(b))} = \left(\frac{n_1(b)}{n_1(b)-l}\right)^2 \frac{n-2l}{n}, \quad \text{for } l = 1, 2, \ldots, \bar{l}-1, \tag{6.17}$$

where $\bar{l}$ is the largest positive integer such that $n - 2\bar{l} \geq 0$. Without loss of generality, we treat it as an integer. Noting that

$$n = (1 + \beta)n_1,$$

we can rewrite equations (6.16) and (6.17) as

$$\frac{\pi(n_1(b)+k, n_2(b)+k)}{\pi(n(b))} = \gamma^{-\mu k} \tag{6.18}$$

and

$$\frac{\pi(n_1(b)-l, n_2(b)-l)}{\pi(n(b))} = \gamma^{\mu l} \tag{6.19}$$

where γ and μ are defined as follows:

$$\gamma = \exp(2/n_1(b)),$$

---

[4]   In (16), we assume that k can go to infinity. Actually, there is an upper bound for k which is $\beta/(\beta - 1)$. Here, we implicitly assume that β is close to one. The definition of β is given by (6.11).

and

$$\mu = \frac{\beta}{(1+\beta)}.$$

From now on we write b for $n_1(b)$ because there is no ambiguity.

The stationary distribution is then

$$\pi(b+k) = A\gamma^{-\mu k}, \quad \text{for } k = 1, 2, \dots, \tag{6.20}$$

and

$$\pi(b-l) = A\gamma^{\mu l}, \quad \text{for } l = 1, 2, \dots, \bar{l}-1 \tag{6.21}$$

where A is the normalizing constant defined by

$$A^{-1} = \sum_{0}^{\bar{l}-1} \gamma^{\mu l} + \sum_{k=1}^{\infty} \gamma^{-\mu k} = \frac{\gamma^{\mu\bar{l}}}{(\gamma^{\mu}-1)}. \tag{6.22}$$

This is equivalent to

$$A = \frac{\gamma^{\mu}-1}{\gamma^{\mu\bar{l}}}. \tag{6.23}$$

Now, the expected value of Y, $E(Y)$ is

$$E(Y) = E(c_1 n_1 + c_2 n_2) = (c_1 + c_2\beta)E(n_1). \tag{6.24}$$

We can obtain $E(n_1)$ using the stationary distribution derived above, namely (6.20) and (6.21).

$$E(n_1) = A\left[\sum_{k=1}^{\infty}(b+k)\gamma^{-\mu k} + \sum_{k=0}^{\bar{l}-1}(b-l)\gamma^{\mu l}\right]$$
$$= b + A\left[\sum_{k=0}^{\infty}k\gamma^{-\mu k} - \sum_{l=0}^{\bar{l}-1}l\gamma^{\mu l}\right] \tag{6.25}$$

We calculate (6.24) by means of the generating function

$$G(z) = \sum_{k=1}^{\infty}(\gamma^{-\mu}z)^k - \sum_{l=0}^{\bar{l}-1}(\gamma^{\mu}z)^l = \left[\frac{z}{\gamma^{\mu}-z}\right] - \left[\frac{1-(\gamma^{\mu}z)^{\bar{l}}}{1-\gamma^{\mu}z}\right]. \tag{6.26}$$

We can easily see that

$$G'(1) = \sum_{k=1}^{\infty}k\gamma^{-\mu k} - \sum_{l=0}^{x-1}l\gamma^{\mu l}. \tag{6.27}$$

By a direct calculation, we obtain

$$G'(1) = \frac{1}{(\gamma^{\mu}-1)^2}\left[\bar{l}\gamma^{\mu\bar{l}}(1-\gamma^{-\mu}) + \gamma^{\mu}\gamma^{\mu\bar{l}}\right]. \tag{6.28}$$

Noting

$$\bar{l} = \frac{(1 + \beta)n_1}{2}$$

and (6.23), we obtain from (6.25), (6.27), and (6.28), $E(n_1)$ as

$$E(n_1) = b + AG'(1) = \frac{1}{1 - \gamma^{-\mu}} - \frac{b}{2}(\beta - 1). \tag{6.29}$$

For the value of $\beta = 1$, this is clearly positive. We can show that $E(n_1)$ is positive if $1 \le \beta < \beta^*$ where β^* is defined as

$$\beta^* = \left(\frac{2}{b}\right) \left[\frac{1}{1 - \gamma^{-\mu}}\right] + 1.$$

We assume that this condition is satisfied.

Take the derivative of $E(Y)$ with respect to s_1, and we obtain

$$\frac{d E(Y)}{d s_1} = \frac{d E(Y)}{d \beta} \frac{d \beta}{d s_1}. \tag{6.30}$$

We note that

$$\frac{d \beta}{d s_1} = -\left(\frac{c_1}{c_2}\right) \left(\frac{1}{s_1^2}\right) < 0. \tag{6.31}$$

Hence, $E(Y)$ increases with a small increase in s_1 if and only if

$$\frac{d E(Y)}{d \beta} < 0.$$

To show this inequality, we write $d E(Y)/d\beta$ as follows:

$$\frac{d E(Y)}{d \beta} = [-B_1(\beta)c_1 - B_2(\beta)c_2](\gamma^\mu - 1)^{-2} \tag{6.32}$$

with

$$B_1(\beta) = \frac{2}{b} \frac{1 + \beta^2}{(1 + \beta)^2} + o(1/b),$$

and

$$B_2(\beta) = \frac{2}{b} \frac{2\beta^2(\beta - 1)}{(1 + \beta)^2} + o(1/b).$$

Clearly, both $B_1(\beta)$ and $B_2(\beta)$ are positive. Thus, we have shown the following inequality:

$$\frac{d E(Y)}{d \beta} < 0 \tag{6.33}$$

for all $\beta \ge 1$. Given (6.30), two inequalities (6.31) and (6.33) mean that $d E(Y)/d s_1$ is positive. This establishes the following proposition.

Proposition: *The expected value of Y increases as the demand share for sector 1 goes up in the range of $1 \leq \beta < \beta^*$. Namely, the higher the share of demand for goods and services produced in high productivity sector is, the higher the expected value of GDP becomes.*

Note that as shown in the third section, because of the linearity of the model, the level of GDP is indeterminate in stationary equilibrium. This result of indeterminacy in stationary equilibrium is analogous to the case where the aggregate demand schedule coincides with the 45-degree line in the textbook Keynesian model. Remarkably, this inderminancy of GDP in the deterministic framework does not carry over once the stochastic dynamics in disequilibrium is explicitly considered. The reason is as follows. Suppose that GDP increased by one. How much increase in GDP would this unit increase in Y induce for the next period? It depends on the sectoral demand shares. In the stochastic dynamics, the higher the share of demand for goods/services produced in high productivity sector is, the higher the expected value of an *increase* in GDP would be. As a result, we obtain the higher expected value of GDP in such a case.

Before we leave this section, we note that if we change the linear production function with fixed coefficient c_i to a concave function $c_i n_i^\gamma$, with $0 < \gamma \leq 1$, the pattern of the sign changes of excess demands in response to changes in n_i remains unchanged in the two-sector model; we only need to replace β by $\beta^{1/\gamma}$. For example, the inequality $n_2 > \beta(n_1 + 1)$ is replaced with $(n_2)^\gamma > \beta(n_1 + 1)^\gamma$, which is equivalent to $n_2 > (\beta^{1/\gamma})(n_1 + 1)$.

The regions R_1 through R_6 are analogously defined in Figure 6.3 by lines L_1 through L_5 with slope $\beta^{1/\gamma}$. Arguments for deriving the stationary distribution go through with β replaced by $\beta^{1/\gamma}$. Because the above Proposition holds for all values of β, it also holds for economies with $c_i n_i^\gamma$, $i = 1, 2, \ldots, K$.

6.5. Simulation

Though it is very simple, the model explained in the second section turns out to be very complex. Luckily, we could obtain an interesting result for the two-sector model. We cannot draw analytical results for the general K sector case, however. In what follows, we resort to simulation analysis for studying the case with $K > 2$.

In the simulations, we set the number of sectors equal to ten, namely $K = 10$. Then, we keep fixed the order of productivities as

$$c_j = (10 - j + 1)/10, \quad j = 1, \ldots, 10.$$

In other words, we have $c_1 = 1$ through $c_{10} = 1/10$ at equal intervals; Sector 1 has the highest productivity while sector 10 has the lowest productivity.

We consider four different patterns for the sectoral demand shares, s_i $(i = 1, \ldots, 10)$.

Demand Pattern 1 or $D1$ has $s = (5, 3, 2, 1, 1, 1, 1, 1, 1, 1)/17$
Demand Pattern 2 or $D2$ has $s = (2, 2, 2, 2, 2, 1, 1, 1, 1, 1)/15$
Demand Pattern 3 or $D3$ has $s = (1, 1, 1, 1, 1, 2, 2, 2, 2, 2)/15$
Demand Pattern 4 or $D4$ has $s = (1, 1, 1, 1, 1, 1, 1, 2, 3, 5)/17$

Because the s_i's are the sectoral demand shares, they sum up to one, $\sum_{i=1}^{10} s_i = 1$.

$D1$ has high demand shares for high productivity sectors; to be specific, the share of the demand for the top two high-productivity sectors are almost one half of the total demand share. $D4$ is just the mirror image of $D1$; demand is tilted toward low productivity sectors. $D2$ and $D3$ are in between, the profiles of the demand shares are flatter than $D1$ and $D4$. The sum of the demand shares of the five high productivity sectors in $D1$, $D2$, $D3$, and $D4$ are 0.71, 0.67, 0.33, and 0.29, respectively.

For each case, we tried 400 runs. In every run, we set the initial values of n_i ($i = 1, \ldots, 10$) equal to 100, which means that the initial value of $Y = \sum_{i=1}^{10} c_i n_i = \sum_{i=1}^{10} \left(\frac{i}{10}\right) 100$ is 550. With this initial condition, simulation is done up to 7000 periods. In every case, Y first tends to keep declining, and after these transient periods, enters the closed set of the Markov process; see Feller (1968, XV.4 and 8) for the notions of *closed sets* and *transient states* of Markov process. In the closed set, Y fluctuates without any declining trend. We disregard the transient phase, and focus on the closed set for our study of business cycles. Our simulations have produced several interesting results.

Aggregate Fluctuations

First, our simulations demonstrate that the model explained in the second section generates aggregate fluctuations. Figure 6.6 shows a sample path of Y for demand pattern 1, or $D1$, together with its average over 400 runs as a smooth bold line, and two standard deviations (S.D.) as two dotted lines. Figure 6.6(A) shows the initial transient phase as well as the closed set. In the case of $D1$, the model settles down in the closed set in period 906 which is shown as $T = 906$ in the figure. Figure 6.6(B) shows fluctuations of Y enlarged for a subset of periods between 2000 and 5000.

Plainly, Y fluctuates. The important point is that simple sectoral interactions described in section 2 generate these aggregate fluctuations of Y. We can recall Feller's Arc Sine Law for coin tossing. Our model and simulations demonstrate that simple sectoral interactions described in the second section generically produce the processes similar to coin tossings, and, therefore, *aggregate fluctuations*. Note, however, the crucial difference between our model and coin tossings or random walks. In coin tossings, stochastic disturbances are exogenous. In our model, sectoral interactions are endogenous.

Now, in the case of $D1$ shown in Figure 6.6, the mean of Y is 448.9 while its standard deviation (S.D.) is 9.30; S.D. is 2.1% of the mean of Y. This is a reasonable value for the amplitude of fluctuations of GDP. In Figures 6.7, 6.8, and 6.9, we show sample paths for $D2$, $D3$, and $D4$, respectively. In every case, we observe fluctuations of Y.

Demand, GDP, and Employment

In the fourth section, we show that the expected value of GDP increases as the demand for the high productivity sector increases. This proposition has been shown analytically for the two-sector model. What about for multisector model? Our simulations answer this question.

Figure 6.10 shows the time profiles of Y *averaged over 400 runs* for $D1$, $D2$, $D3$, and $D4$, respectively. The average levels of GDP, $\bar{Y}$, are 448.9, 363.4, 339.1, and 229.8, respectively (Table 6.2). Thus, the simulation results for multisector model bear out the proposition analytically obtained for the two-sector model. *The higher the shares of demand for high productivity sectors are, the higher the expected value of GDP becomes.* This results is remarkable because, as explained in the third section, the level of Y is indeterminate in deterministic stationary equilibrium. However, this indeterminacy of GDP in the deterministic framework does not carry over in the stochastic model. In the stochastic model, the clear relationship between the pattern of demand and the expected value of Y emerges.

We have also studied the effects of temporary demand shocks on aggregate output. To be specific, we put positive temporary *aggregate* demand shock into the model (the $D1$ case) for the periods during 3001 and 3010. The size of the shock is one tenth of Y. It affects all the sectors equally, and thus, it is *aggregate* demand shock. The result is shown in Figure 6.11. The remarkable point is that *temporary* demand shock raises the level of aggregate output *permanently* although its effect is much smaller than the size of the initial temporary shock; the size of temporal demand shock is 10% of Y which is roughly 46 whereas

Table 6.2. Simulation Results – Statistics of Monte Carlo Simulation

Demand pattern	D1	D2	D3	D4
(1) Mean of Y	448.9	363.4	339.1	229.8
(2) S.D. of Y	9.30	9.45	9.67	9.23
(2) / (1)	0.02	0.03	0.03	0.04
Total Number of Employment, n	971	866	1178	1117
$\kappa (= \sum s_i/c_i)$	2.16	2.38	3.47	4.86

Note: (2) S.D. of Y is the average standard deviation of 400 sample paths in the steady state (T $= 2000 - 7000$)

(A) The Entire Sample Period (1–7000)

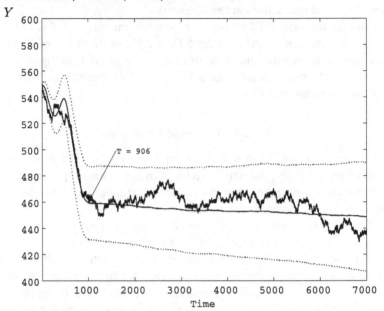

(B) The Enlarged Sub-Sample Period (2000–5000)

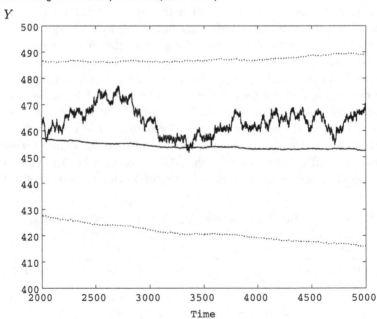

Figure 6.6. Fluctuations of Aggregate Output in Case D1.

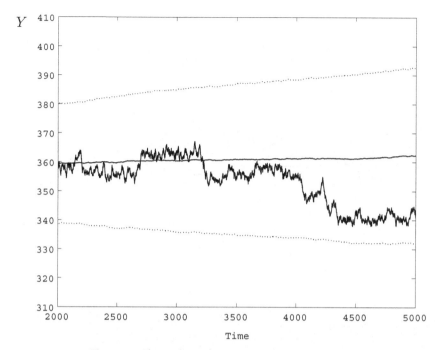

Figure 6.7. Fluctuations of Aggregate Output in Case D2.

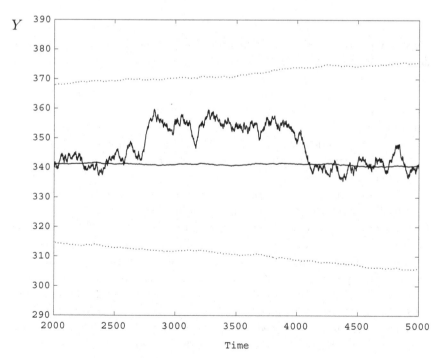

Figure 6.8. Fluctuations of Aggregate Output in Case D3.

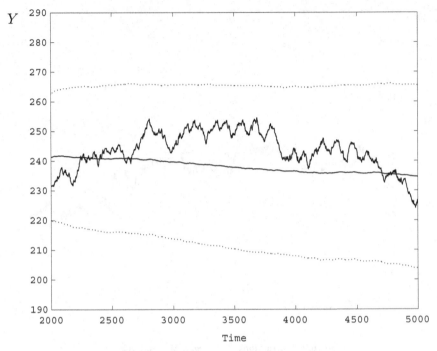

Figure 6.9. Fluctuations of Aggregate Output in Case D4.

the size of permanent effect is about 4 which is less than 1% of Y. This exercise demonstrates once again that the level of aggregate output depends crucially on demand in our stochastic model.

So much for the level of GDP. Now, it is important to recognize that the levels of GDP and employment are different matters. Table 6.2 shows the total employment $n = \sum_i n_i$ for D1, D2, D3, and D4. Note that the total employment n is not fixed but endogenous. We observe that the order of n is not the same as that of Y. Comparing D1 with D4, we observe that total employment n is higher for D4 than for D1. Similarly, total employment is higher for D3 than for D2.

When the shares of demand for high productivity sectors are high, an increase in output is expected to be higher than otherwise because c_i is greater than c_j ($i < j$). Thus, we obtain the proposition in section 4 and the simulation results for the expected value of Y. However, *given demand*, high productivity sectors need *less* employment than low productivity sectors do precisely because those sectors have high productivities. In this sense, in terms of employment, there is always a bias toward low productivity sectors. Figures 6.12, 6.13, 6.14, and 6.15 show employment by sector for D1, D2, D3, and D4, respectively. *Low productivity sectors produce greater employment than high productivity sectors.* This is precisely what we should expect from the Boltzmann–Gibbs distribution

Y

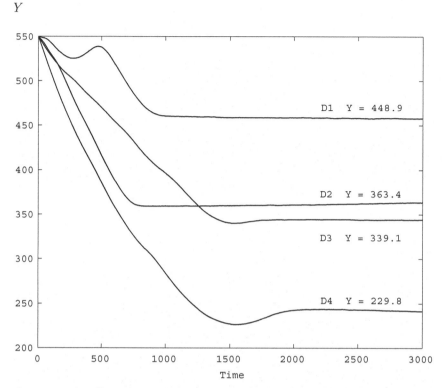

Figure 6.10. The Effects of Demand on the Level of Aggregate Output: Comparison of D1, D2, D3, and D4.

explained in Chapter 3 (see Figure 3.2). And, in fact, the expected value of total employment is higher when demand is tilted toward low productivity sectors.

We can determine how employment should be distributed across sectors. In our model, the share of employment in each sector n_i / n in stationary equilibrium is given by equation (6.8). And equation (6.10) shows that the total employment n is given by

$$n = \left(\sum_{i=1}^{K} \left(\frac{s_i}{c_i} \right) \right) Y = \kappa Y \quad (i = 1, \ldots, K). \tag{6.34}$$

Thus, *ceteris paribus* (namely, given Y), the total employment n depends positively on a crucial parameter κ which is the sum of s_i/c_i ($i = 1, \ldots, K$). However, Y is actually not fixed, but depends on s_i/c_i. It is, therefore, ambiguous how the total employment depends on s_i/c_i. Table 6.2 shows this important parameter, κ for D1, D2, D3, and D4. It turns out that the total employment n is greater in D4 than in D1. Before we proceed to the next simulation, we note once again that despite of this pattern of employment which we have just discussed, the

Y

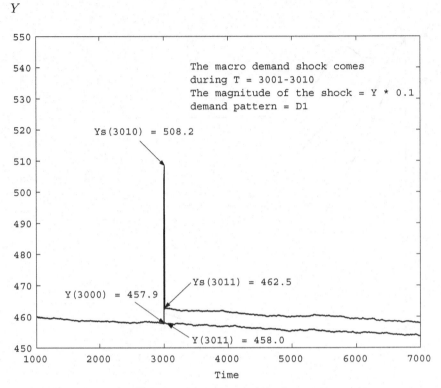

Figure 6.11. The Effect of Temporary Demand Shocks on Aggregate Output.

expected value of *Y* always becomes higher when demand is tilted toward *high* productivity sectors than otherwise.

Allocative Disturbances

Davis, Haltiwanger, and Schuh (1996) draw our attention to the possible importance of *"allocative disturbances"* as distinguished from *aggregate shocks* in business cycles.

In recent years, some economists have begun developing theories to explain the magnitude and cyclical behavior of job and worker flows and their connection to aggregate fluctuations. These theories start from the premise that the economy is subject to a continuous stream of *allocative shocks* – shocks that cause idiosyncratic variation in profitability among job sites and worker–job matches. The continuous stream of allocative shocks generates the large-scale job and worker reallocation activity observed in the data. (p.104) . . .

However, despite the wide diffusion of ideas related to theories of search and reallocation in the economics literature, most analysis of business cycles and aggregate fluctuations ignores or downplays the role of allocative shocks and reallocation frictions. In our view, greater attention to the reallocation process will lead to a firmer understanding of the driving

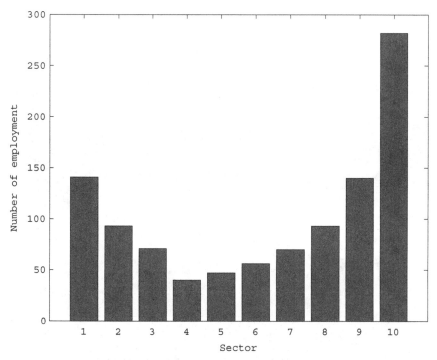

Figure 6.12. Sectoral Distribution of Employment for D1.

forces behind aggregate fluctuations, the mechanisms through which aggregate shocks affect the economy, and the social and economic costs of business cycles. (Davis, Haltiwanger, and Schuh, 1996, 105)

To see the effects of allocative disturbances on aggregate output, we have done two simulations in which the pattern of demand suddenly changes (1) from D1 to D4, and (2) from D4 to D1. The sudden changes in demand pattern cause variation in profitability among sectors, and make reallocation of resources necessary. Note that the propensity to expend in the economy as a whole remains unchanged, namely one, and, therefore, that the changes in demand pattern are *allocative disturbances*. In case (1), the demand pattern changes away from high productivity sectors toward low productivity sectors. And in case (2), we examine the effects of the change to the opposite. What are the consequences of these allocative disturbances on aggregate economic activity, or Y?

The results are shown in Figure 6.16. In both cases, Y responds *negatively* to allocative disturbances, and declines. After a fairly long periods, Y bottoms out, and starts rising but never reaches the level prior to the shocks. It is very interesting to observe that this result holds true not only for case (1) but also for case (2). Recall that the expected value of Y is higher for D1 than for D4. We might expect, therefore, that the effect of the demand pattern changes on Y

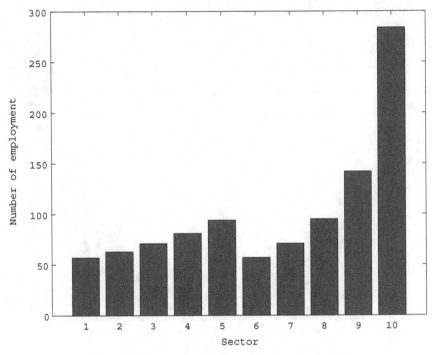

Figure 6.13. Sectoral Distribution of Employment for D2.

is negative when the change is from $D1$ to $D4$ (Case (1)) whereas it is positive when from $D4$ to $D1$ (Case (2)). It turns out that in both cases, the effects of the allocative disturbances on Y are negative.

The reason is as follows. In general, when the demand pattern changes suddenly, profitability among sectors changes; some sectors expand whereas others shrink. These responses are stochastic, and the balance between two opposite forces determines the aggregate outcome. When the demand pattern changes from $D4$ to $D1$, the negative effects of declines in low productivity sectors dominate the positive effects in high productivity sectors. Thus, a decline in Y in the economy as a whole ensues.

We can formally explore the consequences of allocative disturbances in the two-sector model. It clarifies the reason for a rather unexpected consequence of a change in the demand pattern toward high productivity sectors (from $D4$ to $D1$) on the equilibrium level of GDP.

Suppose that in phase 1, a higher demand is placed on the low productivity sector than on the high productivity sector. This leaves the size of the low productivity sector large to meet the demand. Then, the pattern switches. In phase 2, the demand on the low productivity sector is reduced, while that on the high productivity sector increases. Under certain conditions, the effects of reduction in the size of the low productivity sector on Y dominate those of an increase

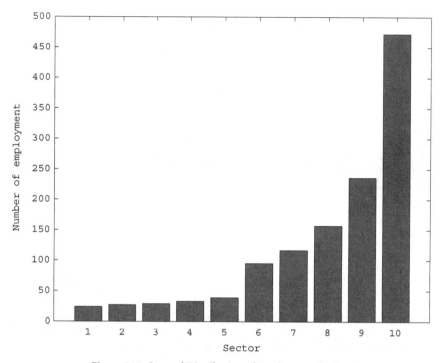

Figure 6.14. Sectoral Distribution of Employment for D3.

in output by the high productivity sector that now faces a higher demand. We should note that an active sector is more likely to come from the low productivity sector with negative excess demand than from the high productivity sector.

Let productivity coefficients be $c_1 = 1$, and $c_2 = c < 1$. In phase 1 of this thought experiment, the initial demand pattern is $s_1 = \sigma$ and $s_2 = 1 - \sigma$ with $\sigma < \frac{1}{2}$, that is, sector 2 (the low productivity sector) has higher demand share. In the stationary state in which excess demand is zero in both sectors, $f_1 = s_1 Y - c_1 n_1 = 0$ and $f_2 = s_2 Y - c_2 n_2 = 0$ hold. We assume that the equilibrium size of sector 2 is larger than that of sector 1, that is,

$$\frac{n_1}{n_2} = \frac{\left(\frac{s_1}{c_1}\right) Y}{\left(\frac{s_2}{c_2}\right) Y} = \frac{\sigma}{1 - \sigma} c < 1. \tag{6.35}$$

Now, suppose that the demand pattern is revised, $s_1' = 1 - \sigma$ and $s_2' = \sigma$ where "$'$" is used to denote this second phase of the thought experiment. Denoting the new equilibrium sizes of the sectors by n_1' and n_2', we obtain

$$\frac{n_1'}{n_2'} = \frac{1 - \sigma}{\sigma} c. \tag{6.36}$$

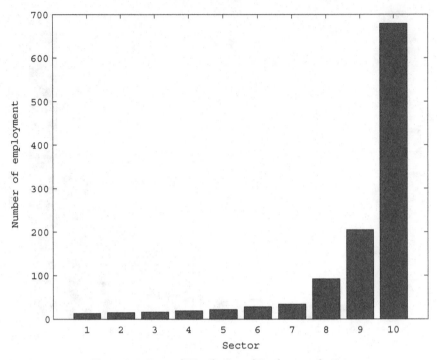

Figure 6.15. Sectoral Distribution of Employment for D4.

From (6.35) and (6.36), we know that the total outputs in stationary equilibrium prior to and after the change, Y and Y' are respectively as follows:

$$Y = c_1 n_1 + c_2 n_2 = n_2 \left(c + \frac{n_1}{n_2} \right) = n_2 \left(\frac{c}{1 - \sigma} \right) \qquad (6.37)$$

$$Y' = c_1 n'_1 + c_2 n'_2 = n'_2 \left(c + \frac{n'_1}{n'_2} \right) = n'_2 \left(\frac{c}{\sigma} \right). \qquad (6.38)$$

Hence

$$\frac{Y'}{Y} = \frac{1 - \sigma}{\sigma} \frac{n'_2}{n_2} < 1 \qquad (6.39)$$

if

$$\frac{n'_2}{n_2} < \frac{\sigma}{1 - \sigma} < 1. \qquad (6.40)$$

and conversely. In other words, if the reduction of the size of sector 2 satisfies inequality (6.40), then GDP is less in phase 2 than in phase 1 despite of the fact that the demand share for high productivity sector increased.

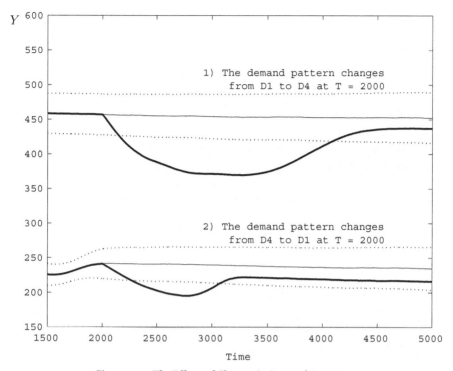

Figure 6.16. The Effects of Changes in Demand Pattern.

Example: *The computer simulation with 10 sectors with demand pattern* $[1, 1, 1, 1, 1, 2, 2, 2, 2, 2]/15$ *correspond to the two-sector model with demand pattern* $\left(\frac{1}{3}, \frac{2}{3}\right)$, *that is,* $\sigma = \frac{1}{3}$. *Then* (6.40) *becomes*

$$\frac{n_2'}{n_2} < \frac{1}{2}$$

that is, when the size of sector 2 shrinks by more than a half of the original size in equilibrium, GDP becomes less in phase 2 than in phase 1. ∎

Probability of Sector Size Changes. To calculate the probability of this change in sector sizes, it is convenient to use the binary tree of the birth-and-death process of this example. The death rate is defined by

$$\mu_n = \frac{n_2}{n} \quad \text{with} \quad n = n_1 + n_2$$

and the birth rate is defined by

$$\lambda_n = \frac{n_1}{n}.$$

Initially, from (6.35), we have $\mu_n > \lambda_n$. μ_n is the probability that an active sector is chosen from sector 2, hence sector 2 shrinks by one unit. Similarly, when an active sector is in sector 1 then the sector 1 grows by one. See Figure 6.3, which shows the associated skeletal Markov chains.

Emergence of New Sectors

So far, we have fixed the number of sectors, K. Our model can actually accommodate the case where the number of sectors K stochastically increases. In what follows, we briefly consider the case where new sectors randomly emerge.

We previously noted that in this general case, the rate of size *increase* is specified as follows:

$$\gamma_i(n_i, n) = \frac{\alpha + n_i}{K\alpha + n}. \tag{6.41}$$

When the number of sectors K is fixed, α is zero. Note that the rate of size decrease remains the same as

$$\rho_j(n_i/n) = n_j/n.$$

Now, if α is much smaller than K, then

$$\gamma_i \approx n_i/(\theta + n) \tag{6.42}$$

where we set

$$\theta := K\alpha. \tag{6.43}$$

Then, we have[5]

$$\gamma_i(n_i, n) \approx \frac{n}{\theta + n}\frac{n_i}{n}. \tag{6.44}$$

A new sector emerges with probability $\theta/(\theta + n)$ in this general case. So long as θ is kept constant, the above expression implies that the choices of K and α do not matter, provided α is much smaller than K. γ_i is the rate of size increase in sector with positive excess demand ($f_i > 0$). On the other hand, in the present case, new sectors emerge at the rate proportional to $\theta/(\theta + n_+)$. This transition rate may be justified as a limiting case in which parameter α goes to zero while $K\alpha$ approaches a positive value θ.

In this extended model, the assumption is either that (1) one of the sectors with positive excess demand increases its size by one with probability $(\alpha + n_a^+)/(K_+\alpha + n_+)$ where K_+ denotes the number of sectors with positive excess demand, and n_+ is the total size of such sectors, or that (2) a new sector emerges with rate proportional to $(K_+ - 1)\alpha/(K_+\alpha + n_+)$. We let α go to zero, and assume that $K_+\alpha$ approaches a common positive value for the sake of simplicity. We have a model in which either one of the existing sectors with positive

---

[5] There is an obvious interpretation of this approximate expression in terms of the Ewens sampling formula (Ewens, 1972).

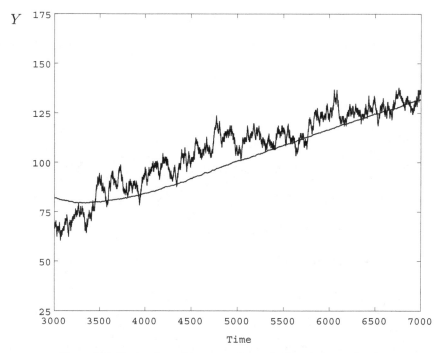

Figure 6.17. Fluctuations of Aggregate Output in Growth Case at $\theta = 1$.

excess demand increases size by one, or a new sector emerges.[6] That is, equation (6.5) must now read that the conditional change in $Y(t + h)$ given $Y(t)$ consist of two terms; the one conditional in the event of the new sector appearing, which occurs with probability $\theta/(\theta + n_+)$, and the second one conditional in the event that no new sector appears.

In the simulations, we assume that a new sector when it emerges inherits characteristics, that is c and s, of the most productive sector. That is, the productivity coefficient of the newly born sector is always 1. As for the demand shares, we assume $D1$, and that each time when the new sector is born, s's are renormalized so that they sum to one. These assumptions are merely for convenience. Other schemes are, of course, possible.

Figures 6.17 and 6.18 show sample paths of total output, Y for $\theta = 1$, and $\theta = 3$, respectively. As the value of θ is increased, the new sectors are borne more frequently. In this generalized model in which the number of sectors randomly increases, as one might expect, the level of Y tends to rise accompanied by fluctuations. That is, we observe growth and fluctuations. The emergence of new

---

[6] We could assume that $K_+\alpha$ converges to θ_+ which may change each epoch. This would lead to a slight modification of the Ewens sampling formula.

Y

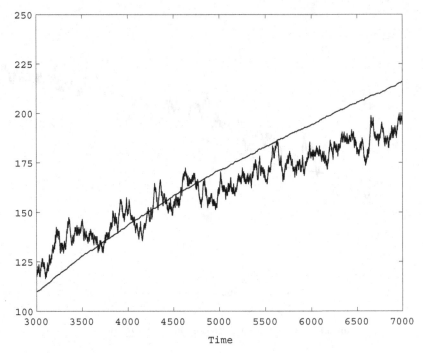

Figure 6.18. Fluctuations of Aggregate Output in Growth Case at $\theta = 3$.

sectors is, in fact, the key factor for economic growth. We will elaborate this idea in Chapter 8.

6.6. Discussion

Our model has established three propositions. First of all, simple reallocation of resources among sectors – an increase in production in sectors facing excess demand and a decrease in production in sectors facing excess supply – endogenously produces quite complex "cycles" of the macroeconomy.

Second, given productivity differentials, the higher the shares of demand for high productivity sectors are, the higher the expected level of GDP becomes. Because our model is linear, and the propensity to expend out of total income is one, the level of GDP is indeterminate in static equilibrium. This result is not surprising if we recall that the model corresponds to the case where the aggregate demand schedule coincides with the 45-degree line in the textbook Keynesian model. However, this indeterminacy of GDP in deterministic framework does not carry over in stochastic dynamics. We have shown that the *expected value* of the level of GDP depends on demand.

Third, "allocative" disturbances as distinguished from macro shocks affect the level of aggregate output, and, therefore, play an important role in business cycles.

As we saw in the first section, Slutzky (1937) demonstrated that simple summation of random variables produced sinusoidal cycles. He mentioned two possibilities for research on business cycles. One is to pursue deterministic equations, and then add random noises to them afterwards. The other is a "purely stochastic approach" so to speak. His own approach was the latter. Our model follows the lead of Slutzky, but has a crucial difference. In Slutzky's model, stochastic disturbances are *exogenous*. In our model, sectoral interactions are endogenous. A stochastic element lies in the fact that we never know which sector/agent "acts" in a particular moment. This problem is handled by the notion of *holding time* in our model. Thus, our model is stochastic, and at the same time endogenous. It is based on a simple but arguably generic assumption that production in sectors facing excess demand expands whereas that in sectors facing excess supply shrinks, both in an appropriately defined stochastic manner. In what follows, we explain the significance of "endogenous stochastic approach" such as ours.

As Slutzky pointed out, one approach in business cycle research is to pursue deterministic equations, though no economist denies the role played by stochastic disturbances. It is actually natural for economists to pursue deterministic equations because these equations are the ones which are meant to describe *economic behaviors*. No wonder, almost all the mainstream theories and models of business cycles take this approach. However, such an approach has a serious weakness.

Let us begin with linear difference equations. With complex characteristic roots, they can produce cycles. Samuelson (1939) showed that simple interactions between the Keynesian multiplier and the acceleration principle can be expressed in terms of a linear second-order difference equation. Depending on parameter values such as the marginal propensity to consume and the acceleration coefficient, the model can produce cycles. However, except for a very special set of parameters – such a set is, in fact, of measure zero in the space of parameters – cycles, if they are present, either diminish or explode over time. Thus, such models cannot be regarded as a self-contained theory of business cycles. That is why Hicks (1950) introduced "ceiling" and "floor" into the model based on a linear difference equation. In his own words, his model is based on the following assumptions:

1. I assume that the investment and saving coefficients are such – and they are distributed in time such a way – that an upward displacement from the equilibrium path will tend to cause a movement away from equilibrium. The divergent movement may not set in immediately; it may be considerably lagged. It may itself have a cyclic character, so that it shows itself in the form of explosive cycles; or it may take the simple (and more

explosive) form of a direct movement away from equilibrium without fluctuation. This is what would happen in the absence of constraints. But I assume

2. that there is a direct restraint upon upward expansion in the form of a scarcity of employable resources. Thus it is impossible for output to expand without limit.

3. There is no such direct limit on contraction. But the working of the accelerator on the downswing is different from its working on the upswing; this difference in mechanism, thought it does not provide a direct check, provides an indirect check which is practically certain, sooner or later, to be effective. (Hicks, 1950, 95)

Hicks is not really concerned whether characteristic roots are complex or real. He assumes an *unstable* difference equation in any case, and at the same time, introduces ceiling and floor into such a model. The problem of this approach is obviously ceiling and floor. For example, Hicks defines ceiling as the state in which "a direct restraint on upward expansion" is present "in the form of a scarcity of employable resources." It would be fine if all the peaks of business cycles were brought about by the limit on resources such as labor. In reality, however, the economy often reaches a peak facing a downturn even though there is still ample stock of unused resources and production factors. For example, consider the case in which the economy went into recession because of a fall in exports despite of high unemployment. Such a case is not exceptional. It is, therefore, doubtful that the economy reaches peaks and troughs at ceilings and floors. Hicks' ceiling and floor, though ingenious, do not provide a generic and robust apparatus for the theory of business cycles.

On theories and models based on the representative agent such as Kydland and Prescott (1982) and Grandmont (1985), we have already pointed out their fundamental problem. Those models and theories require particular *micro* parameter values to produce their own favorite cycles. However, there is actually no justification for translating *micro* parameters characterizing behaviors of the representative agent into *macro* equations. In Chapter 1, we observed that such an attempt often faces difficulties in interpreting parameter values obtained in empirical studies.

After all, can we really trust fairly stable particular parameter values in accounting for macro phenomena called business cycles? Our answer is negative. And we suspect that is why Slutzky (1937) advanced a "purely stochastic approach." Black (1987) echoes Slutzky.

Thus the source of the ups and downs in business and employment can be taken to be uncertainty about the future. Investment decisions must be made with only limited information, and as more information comes in, the values of those investments will fluctuate. Since that is the source of the fluctuations, business will go up and down in a generally random way. The cycles that seem to be there when we look at charts of business fluctuations will be mostly optical illusions. (Black, 1987, 81)

To regard business fluctuations as "mostly optical illusions" is too extreme a view. We do not deny that certain nonstochastic mechanisms always work in the economy generating and amplifying cycles. Hicks (1950, 136) goes far to say that "in the real theory it is the accelerator which is ultimately responsible for producing the cycle." We certainly recognize the importance of the accelerator. The monetary factor that our present analysis does not consider, no doubt, plays an important role in business cycles. Chapter 4 has shown that uncertainty can be a block to the recovery.

Having said that, we suggest the proposition that the fundamental mechanism generating "cycles" in the economy is stochastic *with endogenously determined distribution functions.* Note that this *endogeneity* of noise-generating mechanisms distinguishes our *endogenous stochastic approach* from the run-of-the mill "econometric" approach, that is the approach that adds exogenous noises to deterministic equations. "Cycles" necessarily emerge in the macroeconomy out of stochastic interactions of a large number of agents with countless motives and environments. The strength of the stochastic approach is that it does not require any particular parameter values nor ceiling and floor to account for cycles. Our model has demonstrated that cycles are, in fact, *endogenously* generated on the following arguably generic simple assumptions:

1. Productivity differs across sectors.
2. Sectors facing excess demand expand while sectors facing excess supply shrink.
3. A change in the level of production in one sector, by way of changing GDP, affects demand in all the sectors in an asymmetiric way.

We believe that such sectoral interactions are a fundamental cause for aggregate fluctuations.

Using our simple model, we have established another important proposition. Given productivity differential across sectors/firms, the higher the demand shares of high productivity sectors are, the higher the expected value of GDP becomes. This proposition provides a foundation for the Keynes's principle of effective demand.

Chapter 3 shows that we should expect distribution of productivity across sectors, not a unique level, in equilibrium. Our model is built on this assumption. To appreciate the importance of this assumption in the Keynesian approach, it is useful to recall the textbook Keynesian theory. When aggregate demand increases, total output rises, and the unemployment of labor diminishes. The unemployed are engaged in job search, and their efforts are usually not counted as a part of GDP. If all the unemployment were "natural," however, their "marginal products" in job search, if they were properly measured in markets, would be equal to the marginal product of labor in ordinary production. Thus, in that case, a change in status of worker from unemployment to employment would not change, on the margin, total "output" in the economy. There is no room for the Keynesian theory in such a case.

In Chapter 3, we have shown that the generic assumption for demand to play an important role in the determination of total output is that productivity differs across sectors/activities. For the textbook Keynesian theory, the crucial assumption is that productivity of the unemployed is lower than that of workers engaged in production. In the ordinary Keynesian theory, therefore, an increase in aggregate demand, in effect, mobilizes production factors such as labor to high productivity sectors/activities ("ordinary production" in the textbook explanation). Our analysis demonstrates that in a stochastic dynamic model, the average level of total output depends, in fact, on demand. Note that higher aggregate demand in ordinary Keynesian models corresponds to higher demand shares of high productivity sectors in our model.

Keynes's principle of effective demand tells us only what the *level* of economic activity would be. As Hicks (1950, p. 1) complained, "Keynes did not show us, and did not attempt to show us, save by a few hints, why it is that in the past the level of activity has fluctuated according to so definite a pattern." Our model endogenously produces stochastic cycles. And in this model, the *expected value* of total output depends on demand in the way explained above.

Finally, we have shown by simulations that *allocative disturbances* affect the level of aggregate economic activity. Specifically, sudden changes in the pattern of demand are likely to *lower* GDP in our simulations. Allocative disturbances can be a distress to the macroeconomy. Bernstein (1987), indeed based on his detailed historical study of the American Great Depression during the 1930s, has drawn the following conclusion.

I want to suggest in this study that the difficulty experienced by the American economy in the 1930s was an outgrowth of secular trends in development. By the 1920s, the economy had entered an era characterized by the emergence of dramatically new demand patterns and investment opportunities. These patterns and opportunities foreshadowed and indeed encouraged a shift in the composition of national output. But such a qualitative transformation created impediments to the recovery process in the thirties. These impediments derived from the difficulty of altering technology and labor skills to meet demands for new investment and consumer goods at a time of severe financial instability. In this sense, long-term growth mechanisms played a major role in the cyclical problems of the interwar period. (Bernstein, 1987, 20)

The role of allocative disturbances awaits further study. The jump Markov process is an extremely useful framework for exploring such a problem.

Appendix 6.1: Dynamics of the Two-Sector Model

In this chapter, we presented a two-sector model. This appendix offers more on dynamics of this model.

.Master Equation

The general master equation in R_1 is given by[7]

$$\frac{dP(n_1, n_2)}{dt} = w_1(n_1 - 1, n_1)P(n_1 - 1, n_2) + w(n_2 + 1, n_2)P(n_1, n_2 + 1)$$

$$- P(n_1, n_2)[w_1(n_1, n_1 + 1) + w_2(n_2, n_2 - 1)].$$

Along a path with consecutive size increases in sector 1, n_2 is held fixed, and the master equation simplifies to

$$\frac{dX(n_1; n_2)}{dt} = w_1(n_1 - 1, n_1)X(n_1 - 1; n_2) - X(n_1; n_2)w_1(n_1, n_1 + 1).$$

Along a path of consecutive decrease in sector 2, a similar equation holds. We can solve these equations subject to the boundary condition on L_1, possibly using the generating function method.

By writing $P(n_+, n_-) = P_+(n_+)P_-(n_-)$ we can separate variables

$$\frac{dP_+(n_+)}{dt} = w_+(n_+ - 1, n_+)P_+(n_+ - 1) - w_+(n_+, n_+ + 1)P_+(n_+),$$

and an analogous equation for P_-.

Two-Sector Dynamics

We have shown that states enter in $R_1 \cup R_2$, then they remain in these regions. More precisely, from a state in R_3, we have

$$\frac{d}{dt}P(n_1, n_2; t) = P(n_1, n_2 - 1)w_2(n_2 - 1, n_2) + P(n_1 + 1, n_2)w_1(n_1 + 1, n_2)$$

$$- P(n_1, n_2)[w_1(n_1, n_1 + 1) + w_2(n_2, n_2 - 1)],$$

where we have abbreviated the expressions for the transition rates by suppressing the arguments which do not change. We use subscripts to indicate the arguments that do change.

From a state in R_4, we have an analogous equation in which subscripts 1 and 2 are interchanged.

The detailed balance condition in either regions takes the form

$$\pi_1(m_1 + 1)w_1(m_1 + 1, m_1) = \pi_1(m_1)w_1(m_1, m_1 + 1),$$

and

$$\pi_2(m_2 - 1)w_2(m_2 - 1, m_2) = \pi_2(m_2)w_2(m_2, m_2 - 1).$$

---

[7] We may separate variables into $P(n_1, n_2) = X(n_1; n)Y(n_2 : n)$. Note that the transition rates also depend on $n = n_1 + n_2$, which we do not carry explicitly as arguments in them.

The arguments m's are related to n's within ± 1.

These equations imply the corresponding equation for the sum $n = n_1 + n_2$:

$$\frac{d}{dt}P(n, t) = P(n+1, t)w(n+1, n) + P(n-1)w(n-1, n)$$
$$- P(n, t)[w(n, n+1) + w(n, n-1)],$$

and the corresponding detailed balance condition

$$\pi(n+1)w(n+1, n) = \pi(n)w(n, n+1).$$

We look for the expression for the equilibrium probabilities in these two regions by solving these two algebraic equations. The total units in the economy is the sum of all units in the K sectors, $n := \sum_{i=1}^{K} n_i$. In principle we can write the master equation for the vector (n_+, n_-). However, in our model, the general expression does not seem to be analytically tractable. There are some special cases we can discuss analytically; see for example, in Case 3 introduced above.

In caclulating the total output of the economy, these considerations show that the output is like the cumulative sum in possibly biased coin tosses, with the additional complication that the probability of head or tail may change over time. In the case where $\gamma_i \approx \rho_j$, the time profile of output is nearly that of a fair coin tossing. Some approximate arcsine laws may prevail. That is, there are long swings on which shorter oscillations are superimposed. These seem to be observed in some of our simulation runs to be discussed shortly below.

A jump at sector a occurs with probability

$$\frac{\text{sgn}\{f_a(t)\} + 1}{2}\frac{\gamma_a}{\gamma_+ + \rho_-} + \frac{1 - \text{sgn}\{f_a\}}{2}\frac{\rho_a}{\gamma_+ + \rho_-}.$$

The mean of $Y(t+h)$ conditional on $Y(t)$ is

$$E\{Y(t+h)|Y(t)\} - Y(t)$$
$$= \frac{1}{\gamma_+ + \rho_-}\sum_i \frac{c_i}{2}\left[\frac{n_i}{\theta + n}(1 + \text{sgn}\{f_i\}) - \frac{n_i}{n}(1 - \text{sgn}\{f_i\})\right]$$
$$= \frac{1}{\gamma_+ + \rho_-}\left\{\sum_+ \frac{c_i n_i}{\theta + n} - \sum_- \frac{c_j n_j}{n}\right\}. \tag{6.45}$$

The sign of the right-hand side in the above expression determines if the output is expecte to grow or decay after a jump in a sector size. In the next section we solve for the equilibrium fractions n_i/n. Then, we can put this condition in terms of $\sum_+ s_i$.

Most Likely Path and Stationary Probability Distributions
in Region $R_3 \cup R_4$

In regions $R_3 \cup R_4$ in Figure 6.3, in the intersection of area above the line $n_1 = n_2$, and L_3, the probability for an increase in size in sector 1 is $(\alpha + n_1)/(2\alpha + n)$, and that of a size decrease in sector 2 is n_2/n. Assume that α is neglibibly small compared with n. Then the event in which sector 2 shrinks in size is more probable than sector 1 growth. Therefore, using the maximum likelihood approach, starting from an initial state $n_1(0)$, $n_2(0)$, $n_1(t) = n_1(0)$, but n_2 decreases in size until it hits or enter R_3 by hitting or crossing L_3, or entering R_4. Then, again the most likely behavior is for oscillation of states between n_2^* and $n_2^* + 1$, where $n_2^* = \beta n_1(0) + 1$.

7

Labor Market: A New Look at the Natural
Unemployment and Okun's Law

Unemployment is one of the most important problems in economics. Macroeconomics as a discipline was born through economists' efforts to better understand unemployment. Despite piles of works on the subject, it is still a matter of dispute. Some economists see unemployment as nothing but a particular type of rational economic activity, namely job search. Others take it as a sign of waste of the most important production factor; it costs both the unemployed and the economy as a whole.

This chapter explains that the approach we propose gives us a new perspective on the labor market and unemployment. It follows the tradition of search theory, but differs from the existing literature in one important respect. As explained in Chapter 3, our model is based on the notion of stochastic equilibrium which is conditioned by aggregate demand. In this chapter, extending the model in Chapter 6, we show that unemployment due to demand deficiency and "structural" unemployment cannot be so clearly separated as one might think. This suggests that the natural unemployment may not be defined clearly independent of the level of aggregate demand.

We also show that Okun's law, which puzzles many, can be quite naturally explained. In our analysis, the notion of *equilibrium as distribution* plays the central role. The equilibrium distribution is conditioned by aggregate demand.

7.1. Background

There are different approaches to labor market and unemployment. Let us begin with the assumption that the labor market *were* a single homogeneous market. Then we can apply the standard demand/supply framework. In Figure 7.1, the quantity of labor is measured horizontally while real wages are measured vertically. Plainly, in this framework, unemployment is caused by too high real wages. This was, in fact, Pigou's (1927, 1945) explanation of high unemployment in

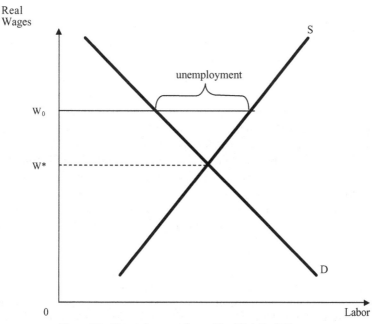

Figure 7.1. Unemployment due to Too High Real Wages.

Britain after World War I.[1] The same idea revived after the first oil shock in 1973/74 when the unemployment rate steadily rose worldwide, particularly in European countries. Malinvaud (1982) called this unemployment due to too high real wages *classical unemployment*. Bruno and Sachs (1985) also attributed a significant part of unemployment in OECD countries to maladjustment of real wages.

The logic behind classical unemployment appears impeccable at first sight. However, to say that real wages are too high presumes that somehow real wages are exogenous. In reality they are, of course, not. As Keynes (1936) emphasized, individual workers and firms do not negotiate about *real* wages but *nominal* wages. Beyond that, many firms are not price takers but price setters. Put another way, firms face demand constraints, or a downward-sloping individual demand curve. Suppose that such a monopolistically competitive firm determines its price, given nominal wages and aggregate demand. In this case, both real wages and employment are endogenously determined conditional on exogenous nominal wages and aggregate demand. Now, employment so determined may fall

---

[1] Despite his own theoretical explanation, Pigou (1927) was cautious enough to refrain from recommending a cut in wages as a policy to cure unemployment. He was rather optimistic having thought that capital accumulation would eventually raise demand for labor (that is, make demand curve shift up), and diminish unemployment. He overlooked the problem of demand deficiency. Thus, he had to have his anticipation betrayed by history, and his theory attacked by Keynes (1936).

short of labor supply, and unemployment ensues if *nominal* wages are too high or aggregate demand is too low (see Solow, 1986). This is the old Keynesian story, of course.

There is a different approach. It emphasizes the fact that the labor market is not a well-organized market, but consists of many segmented markets. The market is segmented in terms of location, industry, worker's skills, and so on. Having incomplete information, both workers and firms must make decisions under uncertainty in such markets. Adjustment in segmented markets must be frictional. Mismatch produces unemployment.

This approach also has a long tradition. On the publication of Pigou's paper, Clay (1928) criticized Pigou's explanation, and attributed high unemployment to slow sectoral adjustments while anticipating an eventual return to the "natural" rate of unemployment. In the *General Theory*, Keynes (1936) also mentioned the kind of unemployment which Clay focused on, and called it "frictional" unemployment.

This postulate (the second postulate of the classical theory) is compatible with what may be called 'frictional' unemployment. For a realistic interpretation of it legitimately allows for various inexactnesses of adjustment which stand in the way of continuous full employment: for example, unemployment due to a temporary want of balance between the relative quantities of specialized resources as a result of miscalculation or intermittent demand: or to time-lags consequent on unforeseen changes; or to the fact that the change -over from one employment to another cannot be effected without a certain delay, so that there will always exist in a non-static society a proportion of resources unemployed 'between jobs'. (Keynes, 1936, 6)

Granted frictional unemployment, Keynes took it as relatively minor, and argued that the core of the matter was "involuntary unemployment" caused by aggregate demand deficiency. His theory of effective demand is meant to explain how the deficiency of aggregate demand arises causing failure to achieve "full employment." He went on to argue that appropriate fiscal and monetary policies can mitigate the problem of high unemployment by maintaining aggregate demand.

The concept similar to frictional unemployment revives time and again. Solow (1964), for example, calls it the "structural unemployment thesis." He criticizes the then popular view that "the economy suffers primarily from 'structural' unemployment that will not yield to – and would indeed frustrate – the standard recipe of expansionary fiscal and monetary policy."

In the realm of economic theory, some thirty years after the publication of the *General Theory*, in the debate on the Phillips curve, Friedman (1968) attacked the Keynesian theory. By so doing, he launched the notion of *natural* rate of unemployment. His definition:

The "natural rate of unemployment," in other words, is the level that would be ground out by the Walrasian system of general equilibrium equations, provided there is imbedded in them the actual structural characteristics of the labor and commodity markets, including market imperfections, stochastic variability in demands and supplies, the cost of gathering information about job vacancies and labor availabilities, the costs of mobility, and so on.

The natural unemployment so defined is obviously akin to Keynes's frictional unemployment. It is "ground out by the Walrasian System of general equilibrium equations." So stated in words, it is ambiguous. Efforts to clarify and make precise the notion of the natural rate of unemployment soon produced the vast literature on the *search theory*.

The notion of the natural rate of unemployment is based on the premise that the labor market is not a single well-organized market as depicted in Figure 7.1, but consists of many segmented markets. No economist denies the importance of this fact surrounding labor market. Even a simple fact such as the coexistence of unemployment and vacancy, the *Beveridge curve*, cannot be explained without resorting to heterogeneity of the labor market. The search theory is a theoretical framework to analyze dynamics and the nature of equilibrium in such labor market. The papers in Phelps (1970) are seminal contributions. More recently, a large body of literature on labor market, both theoretical and empirical, such as Mortensen (1989), Blanchard and Diamond (1990), Davis, Haltiwanger, and Schuh (1996), and Pissarides (2000), all emphasize market segmentation and incomplete information.

Opposite to Keynes, search theorists tend to regard the natural or frictional unemployment as the major component of unemployment. However, most of them admit that the actual unemployment rate often deviates from the natural rate though the reason for that may not be demand deficiency as Keynesians believe. Monetarism, both Mark I (Friedman, 1968) and Mark II (Lucas, 1972), for example, attributes changes in the unemployment rate to unexpected price changes which in turn are to be caused by unanticipated changes in money supply. Whatever the reason for cyclical changes, we have two components in the unemployment rate, one natural and the other cyclical. Thus, it is extremely important to determine how much of observed increases in unemployment are frictional or structural, on the one hand, and cyclical or Keynesian on the other.

Some economists attribute a major part of changes in the unemployment rate to changes in the *natural* rate of unemployment. Lilien (1982), for example, argues that about half of the postwar fluctuations of the U.S. unemployment rate can be accounted for by changes in the natural rate, which are in turn caused by sectoral shifts in labor demand. He proposes the following measure of sectoral shifts.

$$\sigma_t = \left[\sum_{i=1}^{n} \frac{e_{it}}{e_t} (\Delta \log e_{it} - \Delta \log e_t)^2 \right]^{\frac{1}{2}}, \tag{7.1}$$

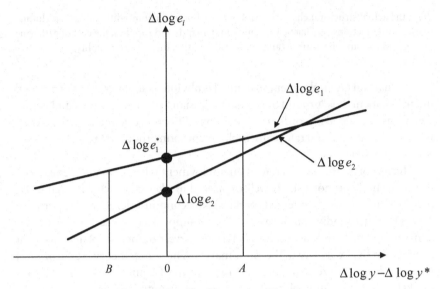

Figure 7.2. Growth of Demand and Employment.

where e_{it} stands for employment in sector i at time t and e_t represents total employment in the economy as a whole. Thus, σ measures the variance of changes in employment across sectors. Lilien shows that the unemployment rate is highly correlated with σ, and then interprets this result as supporting the thesis that sectoral shifts in labor demand have significantly raised the unemployment rate.

Abraham and Katz (1986), however, point out a serious flaw in Lilien's interpretation. The point of their criticism is that a possible negative correlation between aggregate demand and σ may have spuriously produced the observed correlation between the unemployment rate and σ. For example, suppose there are two sectors in the economy. Changes in employment in the two sectors correspond, respectively, to changes in aggregate demand as drawn in Figure 7.2. In sector 1, the growth rate of employment on trend $\Delta\log e_1^*$, which obtains when the growth of aggregate demand $\Delta\log y$ is equal to its natural growth $\Delta\log y^*$, is high, while the cyclical elasticity of growth of employment is small; the line is flatter. The opposite holds in sector 2. One might realistically interpret sectors 1 and 2 as services and manufacturing industry, respectively. Under this assumption, two situations A and B in the figure demonstrate that σ measured by the distance between the two lines increases when the growth of aggregate demand declines and vice versa. Therefore, even if the unemployment rate is determined basically by aggregate demand as traditional Keynesian theory indicates, we would still find a positive correlation between Lilien's σ and the unemployment rate.

To sort out two alternative interpretations, Abraham and Katz calculate the correlation between σ and a measure of job offers. Under Lilien's thesis, σ must be positively correlated not only with the unemployment rate but also the measure of job offers. It turns out that σ is negatively correlated with the measure of job offers. This is what one expects under the Keynesian story. Under Lilien's thesis, the Beveridge curve must frequently shift up and down. The Abraham–Katz finding, however, implies that movements along the stable Beveridge curve dominate.[2]

Beveridge (1944) indeed defined employment as *full* if unemployment is no more numerous than vacancies. According to this definition, the critical level for full employment is the point of intersection of the Beveridge (or the $U - V$) curve and the 45-degree line on the unemployment/vacancy plane. In summary, the movement along a particular Beveridge curve produces a change in the cyclical or Keynesian unemployment. On the other hand, when the Beveridge curve shifts up (northeast) or down (southwest), a change in the natural or frictional unemployment ensues. This is the sort of argument Solow (1964) made to reject the significance of structural unemployment in the United States. Using the same theoretical apparatus, Abraham and Katz also conclude that for the postwar U.S. economy, cyclical or Keynesian unemployment accounts for the major part of actual changes in unemployment.

The separation of the natural or frictional unemployment on the one hand, and unemployment due to demand deficiency on the other, appears conceptually clear-cut to the extent that the Beveridge curve does not depend on demand but only on structural factors such as segmentation of labor market and imperfection of information. However, in this chapter, extending the model in Chapter 6, we demonstrate that the Beveridge curve itself actually depends on demand. It means that we cannot so clearly separate the natural unemployment from unemployment due to demand deficiency as is commonly thought.

We also discuss Okun's law in this chapter. Okun's law (Okun, 1962) is a stable empirical relation between changes in the unemployment rate u and the growth rate of GDP, $\Delta Y / Y$:

$$\frac{\Delta Y}{Y} = \gamma - \alpha(u - u^*) \qquad (\alpha > 0). \qquad (7.2)$$

It means that one percent decrease (increase) in the unemployment rate brings about α percent increase (decrease) in the growth rate of GDP. The value of α varies from country to country and from period to period (see Hamada and Kurosaka, 1984). However, for the United States, α is about 3, and is very stable

---

[2] Hosios (1994), however, points out a theoretical possibility that sectoral disturbances as well as aggregate demand shocks cause a negative correlation between unemployment and vacancy, that is movements along the Beveridge curve. He argues that a job opening involves a commitment of physical capital which is fixed in the short run, and, therefore, that a demand dispersion shock that increases the number of searching workers will increase unemployment and decrease vacancies. We need to explicitly analyze a multisector stochastic model like the one presented in this chapter.

as Okun (1962) first found for this coefficient. To obtain the value greater than one, say 3, we need a sort of increasing returns in labor in the economy as a whole. To the extent that the presence of such strong increasing returns is questionable, Okun's law is a puzzle. We show that Okun's law can be very naturally explained as a *macroeconomic* relation in our stochastic framework.

7.2. The Model

In Chapter 6, using a simple model, we have demonstrated that the level of aggregate output (to be precise its expected value) depends on demand. It is a multisector stochastic model. Thus, this model fits well the purpose of ana-lyzing possible interactions of the natural or frictional unemployment on the one hand, and unemployment due to demand deficiency on the other. Toward this goal, we must extend the model by introducing unemployment and job vacancy.

In the standard search theoretical literature, it is a common assumption that sectors are symmetric in that the distance between any pair of sectors (or islands) is the same. In reality, segmented labor markets are not symmetric in that the distances between various sectors all differ. For example, a worker who left industry or job A may be able to find a new job in industry B much easier than a worker who has worked in industry C, if industry or job A is "closer" to B than to C. Therefore, it is extremely important for full understanding of the labor market to introduce some notion of "distance" between different sectors. For this purpose, we introduce "ultrametric distance" based on the "tree" structure explained in Chapter 5. Chapter 5 shows that the tree structure, in fact, has the fundamental importance for understanding dynamic behavior of the macroeconomy.

Specifically, we treat clusters of different types of unemployed workers as forming a tree structure, and use ultrametric distance to measure similarities of workers in different clusters. When a sector hires a worker it does so randomly from a pool of unemployment composed of different clusters that are suitably weighted by the ultrametric distances. To discuss the Beveridge curve, we also introduce job vacancy into the model. Otherwise, the model in this chapter is basically the same as that analyzed in Chapter 6.

Total Output and Excess Demand

We consider an economy composed of K sectors. Sector i employs n_i workers, $i = 1, \ldots, K$. We make the same assumption as in Chapter 6 that productivities differ across sectors. Production is then characterized by different labor coefficients c_i ($i = 1, \ldots, K$). However, unlike in Chapter 6, here we assume that each sector is in one of two statuses; either in "normal time" or in "overtime." That is, each sector has two capacity utilization regimes ($v_i = 0, 1$).

In normal time, which is indicated by variable $v_i = 0$, n_i workers produce output

$$Y_i = c_i n_i, \tag{7.3}$$

for $i = 1, 2, \ldots, K$.

In overtime indicated by variable $v_i = 1$, n_i workers produce output equal to

$$Y_i = c_i(n_i + 1). \tag{7.4}$$

Each sector can change not only n_i, but also v_i. The firm adjusts its level of production by changing hours of work as well as the number of workers. The labor productivity in sector with $v_i = 1$ is

$$\frac{Y_i}{n_i} = \frac{c_i(n_i + 1)}{n_i} = c_i + \frac{c_i}{n_i} > c_i \tag{7.5}$$

and, therefore, is higher than that in sector with $v_i = 0$ which is simply c_i. This assumption is based on possible underutilization of labor. Okun (1973) explains this phenomenon as follows:

The empirical finding becomes comprehensible once it is recognized that, for a substantial period of time, much of labor input is essentially a fixed cost, reflecting contractual commitments, indivisibilities or complementarity with capital, transaction costs of hiring and firing, and the value of skills that workers have acquired on the job. Thus, in periods of recession or slack, the amount of labor kept on the payroll is greater than the amount technologically required to produce the prevailing depressed level of output. Given the initial presence of such on-the-job underemployment, when demand strengthens, output can be expanded without a commensurate expansion in labor input and a spurt of productivity results. But fixity of labor can explain only a temporary – if perhaps quite lengthy – bonus of productivity from higher output and employment. (Okun, 1973, 212)

The total output (GDP) is given by the sum of all sectors

$$Y = \sum_{i=1}^{K} Y_i. \tag{7.6}$$

Demand for good i is given by $s_i Y$. Here, s_i is the share of the total output Y which falls on goods produced by sector i:

$$\sum_i s_i = 1.$$

Therefore, each sector has the excess demand defined by

$$f_i = s_i Y - Y_i. \qquad i = 1, 2, \ldots, K. \tag{7.7}$$

Changes in Y due to changes in any one of the sectors affect the excess demands of *all* sectors. Changes in the pattern of s's also affect the excess demands of all sectors, of course.

We model the time evolution of this economy as a continous-time Markov chain, as in Chapter 6. At each point in time, each sector belongs to one of two subgroups; one composed of sectors with positive excess demands for their products, and the other with negative excess demands. We denote the sets of sectors with positive and negative excess demands by $I_+ = \{i : f_i \geq 0\}$, and $I_- = \{i : f_i < 0\}$, respectively. For convenience, we call these two groups as profitable and unprofitable sectors, respectively. Profitable sectors wish to expand their production. Unprofitable sectors contract their production.

At the same time, each sector is in either overtime ($v_i = 1$) or normal time ($v_i = 0$) status. Altogether, then, each sector belongs to one of four subgroups: $(I_+, v_i = 1)$, $(I_+, v_i = 0)$, $(I_-, v_i = 1)$, $(I_-, v_i = 0)$.

As is well known for continuous-time models such as the Poisson process, at any given time, only one sector adjusts its production. This is not a special assumption, but a generic property of continuous-time stochastic process. Also, without loss of generality, we can assume a sector adjusts its production up or down by one unit of labor. The sector that has the shortest holding or sojourn time is the sector that jumps first. And only the sector that jumps first succeeds in implementing the desired adjustment. See Chapter 6 for the notion of holding or sojourn time of a continuous-time Markov chain. We call this sector that acts or jumps first as *the active sector*. Variables of the active sector are denoted with subscript a.

State of Each Sector

Sectors adjust their outputs by hiring or firing workers in response to the signs of excess demands. We assume that there are always enough unemployed; the bottleneck does not occur. To increase output, the active sector hires a worker from the pool of the unemployed who were earlier laid off by various sectors. In our model, there is no quitting on the part of workers.

For the active sector, not all the unemployed are homogeneous. Namely, for the active sector that tries to hire a worker, it matters in which sector the worker had a job before entering the pool of unemployment. In other words, the past job experiences of the unemployed matter. This is why we introduce a tree structure.

Each sector has a state vector which has three components: (1) the number of employed, n_i, (2) the number of workers in the pool of unemployed who are laid off by sector i, u_i, and finally, (3) a binary variable v_{ie} (overtime or normal). The state of a sector changes according to the following rules.

1. $v_i = 1$ means that sector i is in overtime status producing $c_i(n_i + 1)$ output with n_i workers. Each sector in overtime status posts one *vacancy* sign. When one of the sectors in overtime status becomes active with positive excess demand, then, it actually hires one additional unit of labor and cancels the overtime sign. Thus in that case, n_a changes to $n_a + 1$, and v_a changes from 1

to 0. When this sector hires the unemployed in its own unemployment pool, u_a changes to $u_a - 1$. Otherwise, u_j changes to $u_j - 1$ ($j \neq a$). In that case, u_a remains unchanged.

2. When a sector in overtime becomes active with negative excess demand, then it cancels the overtime and returns to normal time. The vacancy sign is removed; only v_a changes from 1 to 0.

3. When $v_i = 0$, sector i is in normal time producing $c_i n_i$ output with n_i workers. When one of these sectors in normal time becomes active with positive excess demand, then it posts one vacancy sign and v_a changes from 0 to 1. At the same time, the level of production is raised from the normal level $c_i n_i$ to the overtime level $c_i(n_i + 1)$.

4. If the sector with $v_i = 0$ facing negative excess demand becomes active, it fires one unit of labor. In this case, n_a becomes $n_a - 1$. At the same time, u_a increases to $u_a + 1$.

We implicitly assume that the adjustment of the level of production is swifter by way of firm's changing overtime/normal status (namely hours worked) than by changing the number of workers. To summarize:

1. When $f_a > 0$ and $v_a = 1$, namely, when the sector had a previously posted vacancy sign, then sector a now hires one worker (n_a becomes $n_a + 1$), and cancels the vacancy sign, that is, resets v_a to zero. The number of the unemployed changes from u_i to $u_i - 1$ in some sector i.

2. When $f_a < 0$ and $v_a = 1$, v_a changes from 1 to 0.

3. When $f_a > 0$ and $v_a = 0$, that is, sector a has not previously posted a vacancy sign, then, it now posts a vacancy sign, that is, sets v_a to 1. At the same time, the sector increases its production with existing number n_a of workers by going into overutilization state. Namely, Y_i changes from $c_i n_i$ to $c_i(n_i + 1)$.

4. When $f_a < 0$ and $v_a = 0$, n_a is reduced by one while u_a is increased by one; that is one worker is immediately laid off.

The transition path may be stated, for example, as from $\mathbf{z}$ to $\mathbf{z}'$, where $\mathbf{z} = (n_a, u_a, v_a = 0) \to \mathbf{z}'(n_a, u_a, v_a = 1)$. This transition corresponds to case 3 above where the sector in the normal status facing excess demand posts a vacancy sign, and enters the overtime status. Similarly, the transition from $\mathbf{z} = (n_a, u_a, v_a = 1)$ to $\mathbf{z}' = (n_a + 1, u_a - 1, v_a = 0)$ corresponds to case 1 where the active sector hires a worker. In this example, sector a hires a worker from its own unemployment pool. That is why n_a increases to $n_a + 1$ while at the same time, u_a decreases to $u_a - 1$. If sector a hires a worker from the unemployment pools of other sectors $u_j (j \neq a)$, then we obtain $\mathbf{z} = (n_a, u_a, v_a = 1) \to \mathbf{z}' = (n_a + 1, u_a, v_a = 0)$ and for some $j \neq a$, $\mathbf{z} = (n_j, u_j, v_j) \to \mathbf{z}' = (n_j, u_j - 1, v_j)$. In both cases, the output of the active sector changes to $Y_a' = Y_a + c_a$. These examples should illlustrate the transitions of state of each sector in this model.

Unemployment Pools

In our model, job creation and destruction occur by way of changes in demand for labor. To make our analysis simple, we ignore on-the-job searches and quits. Namely, we assume that only the unemployed get jobs, and also that only laid-off workers get unemployed.

In this model, sectors are differentiated with respect to distance between each other. These distances reflect such factors as geographical differences, differences in technology, and educational qualifications. Workers in different sectors are different in job experiences and human capital. Now, the distance between sectors i and j affects the probability that a worker laid off by sector i gets employed by sector j. This arguably realistic assumption can be modeled on the concept of ultrametric distance explained in Chapter 5. Specifically, the stochastic process of filling a vacancy of sector i by an unemployed worker from the pool of sector j depends on the ultrametric distance between the two sectors of the economy, $d(i, j)$.

Transition of the active sector depends on the sign of the excess demand, f_a as indicated earlier. When the sector in the normal status ($v_a = 0$) faces excess supply ($f_a < 0$), the laid-off worker by definition enters the unemployment pool of sector a, causing the pool to change from u_a to $u_a + 1$.

Hiring a worker occurs only with $f_a > 0$, and $v_a = 1$. Here, we explain how the active sector employs one additional unit of labor. It does not necessarily hire a new worker from its own pool of unemployment. We must distinguish u_a, which denotes the size of sector a's laid-off workers, from the total pool of unemployed from which sector a randomly hires one unit of labor. This pool is composed of u_a and other pools of laid-off workers from sector j, $u_j (j \neq a)$ suitably weighted by ultrametric distance. We denote the latter by $\tilde{u}_a$. Then $u_a + \tilde{u}_a$ is the total size of the pool of the unemployed for sector a, U_a.

The separate sub-pools are organized as a hierarchical tree with ultrametric distance. The unemployed in different unemployment pools have different probabilities of being picked by sector a. The highest probability is for the pool of the workers who are laid off from that sector. Its size is u_a. This assumption accords well with the empirical observation that firms often recall laid-off workers first as they become profitable again. The pools of laid-off workers from other sectors are arranged in increasing order of the ultrametric distance from the pool of size $\tilde{u}_a$.

We illustrate this notion and its use in the case of $K = 3$ with the following ultrametric distances (See Figure 7.3):

$$d(1, 2) = d(2, 1) = 1 \quad \text{and} \quad d(1, 3) = d(2, 3) = 2.$$

In this case, for sector 1, $\tilde{u}_1$ is defined as follows:

$$\tilde{u}_1 = \frac{u_2}{[1 + d(1, 2)]} + \frac{u_3}{[1 + d(1, 3)]} = \frac{u_2}{2} + \frac{u_3}{3}.$$

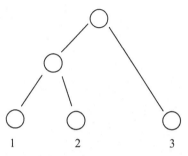

Figure 7.3. An Example of Tree Structure of Three Sectors.

Similarly, we can define $\tilde{u}_2$ and $\tilde{u}_3$ as follows:

$$\tilde{u}_2 = \frac{u_1}{[1 + d(1, 2)]} + \frac{u_3}{[1 + d(2, 3)]} = \frac{u_1}{2} + \frac{u_3}{3}.$$

$$\tilde{u}_3 = \frac{u_1}{[1 + d(1, 3)]} + \frac{u_2}{[1 + d(2, 3)]} = \frac{u_1 + u_2}{3}$$

Suppose sector 1 (with $v = 1$) jumps, and hires a worker. In this case, the conditional probability that a vacancy in sector 1, v_1, is filled with a worker from its own pool of unemployed is $P(u_1$ is reduced by one | sector 1 jumps):

$$P = \frac{u_1}{U_1} = \frac{u_1}{u_1 + \tilde{u}_1} = \frac{u_1}{u_1 + \frac{u_2}{2} + \frac{u_3}{3}}.$$

Similarly v_1 is reduced by one from pool of unemployed of sector 2 with probability, $P(u_2$ is reduced by one | sector 1 jumps):

$$P = \frac{u_2/[1 + d(1, 2)]}{U_1} = \frac{\frac{u_2}{2}}{u_1 + \frac{u_2}{2} + \frac{u_3}{3}}.$$

In the example shown in Figure 7.3, if the size of unemployment pool is the same in all the sectors, namely $u_1 = u_2 = u_3$, then a vacancy in sector 1 will be filled with a worker from its own laid-off pool with probability 6/11, from u_2 with probability 3/11, and from u_3 with probability 2/11. On the same assumption, a vacancy in sector 3 will be filled from u_1 with probability 1/5, from u_2 also with probability 1/5, and from u_3 with probability 3/5.

In this economy, unemployment U

$$U = \sum_{i=1}^{K} u_i$$

and vacancy V

$$V = \sum_{i=1}^{K} v_i$$

coexist. The relation between U and V is the *Beveridge Curve*.

Continuum of Equilibria. Before we turn to simulations of this model, we consider the stationary equilibrium. The equilibrium states of this model are such that all sectors are in normal time, and have zero excess demand, that is,

$$s_i Y_e = c_i n_i^e, \qquad i = 1, 2, \ldots, K, \tag{7.8}$$

where subscript e of Y, and superscript e to n_i denote equilibrium values.
Denote the total equilibrium employment by

$$L_e = \sum_{i=1}^{K} n_i^e. \tag{7.9}$$

Then, we have

$$L_e = \left(\sum_{i=1}^{K} \frac{s_i}{c_i} \right) Y_e = \kappa Y_e, \tag{7.10}$$

where

$$\kappa = \sum_{i=1}^{K} \frac{s_i}{c_i}. \tag{7.11}$$

This equation is the relation between the equilibrium level of GDP and that of employment. Because both Y^e and L^e can take arbitrary values, this model has a continuum of equilibria. As explained in Chapter 6, this indeterminacy of the levels of total output and employment in stationary equilibrium is not surprising. The stationary state in this model corresponds to the case where the aggregate demand schedule coincides with the 45-degree line in the textbook Keynesian model; the "propensity to expend" is one.

7.3. Simulation

The model explained in Section 7.2 is much more complex than that analyzed in Chapter 6 for studying business cycles. It has unemployment and vacancy.

Changes in unemployment in segmented markets are modeled on the concept of ultrametric (tree) distances between sectors. The model is nonlinear and possibly possesses multiple equilibria. Thus, we must use simulations to deduce important properties of the model. We are particularly interested in two relations in the macroeconomy: (1) the relationship between unemployment (U) and vacancy (V) in the economy as a whole, namely the *Beveridge Curve*, and (2) the relationship between changes in the growth rate of GDP and the unemployment rate, namely Okun's law.

In this simulation, the number of sectors K is set to be 8. Productivity differs across sectors. Specifically, we set $c_i = (9 - i)/8$ for $i = 1, \ldots, 8$. Namely, we have $c_1 = 1$ and $c_8 = 1/8 = 0.225$ with equally spaced decrease, in between. Thus, the vector of productivity, C is given by

$$C = \left[1, \frac{7}{8}, \ldots, \frac{1}{8} \right].$$

As in Chapter 6, we are interested in the effects of different demand patterns on the outcomes in the labor market. Two different demand patterns have been tried.

Case $D1$: The demand share vector is $s = [6, 5, 4, 3, 2, 2, 2, 2]/26$. The top-four high productivity sectors share 70 percent of aggregate demand.

Case $D2$: $s = [2, 2, 2, 2, 3, 4, 5, 6]/26$. Opposite to Case 1, the demand share of the top-four high productivity sectors is only 30 percent. The low productivity sectors share 70 percent of aggregate demand.

Given these basic demand patterns, in our simulations, we actually let the demand share vector depend on the level of aggregate output, Y. Specifically, we assume that the demand shares s vary depending on the level of Y in the following way:

$$s_i(t) = s_i(\tau) + \frac{K_i}{500} [Y(t) - Y(\tau)] \qquad \text{for} \qquad t > \tau = 1500. \qquad (7.12)$$

Here, K_i is defined as

$$K_i = (4.5 - i)/8 \qquad \text{for} \qquad t > \tau = 1500 \qquad (i = 1, 2, \ldots 8)$$
$$= 0 \qquad \text{for} \qquad 1 \leq t \leq \tau. \qquad (7.13)$$

Up to time $\tau = 1500$, $K_i = 0$, and s is simply constant demand share vector defined above. As we will see shortly, the Markov chain enters the closed set by $\tau = 1500$. We focus on the period after the Markov chain enters the closed set, namely $t > 1500$. Equation (7.12) means that when the level of output is high ($Y(t) > Y(\tau)$), the demand shares for high productivity sectors (sector 1 through 4) rise whereas those for low productivity sectors (sectors 5 through 8) decline.[3] The extent of an increase (decrease) in s is greatest for sector 1 (sector 8).

---

[3] Given equation (7.12), κ defined by (7.11) actually becomes variable because s_i varies over time.

Conversely, when the level of Y is low ($Y(t) < Y(\tau)$), the demand shares for low (high) productivity sectors rise (decline). Note that $s_i(t)$'s defined by (7.12) sum to one.

Okun (1973) makes the following observation:

One important part of the productivity dividend seems to be associated with shifts of resources toward sectors of higher than average productivity. That portion does not pose the analytical mysteries associated with persistently increasing returns to labor within an industry.

The difference between a high-pressure and a low-pressure economy is not simply a proportionate addition of output and employment across all industries and sectors. The exact distribution of the increments would depend on the source of the added aggregate demand, which might be expansionary monetary policy that would particularly stimulate construction and durable goods; or a wartime military buildup that added especially to the federal sector; or tax cuts and increases in transfer payments that boosted consumer goods industries by an extra margin. Despite these possible differences, history reveals a distinct pattern of resource shifts associated with higher utilization; in particular, the sectoral pattern characteristics of a high-pressure economy is favorable to aggregate productivity. (Okun, 1973, 214)

It turns out that in our simulations, this assumption (equation (7.12)) is crucial for producing the reasonable value of the Okun coefficient.

As for the ultrametric distance between two segmented labor markets which was explained earlier, we assume the following symmetric matrix D:

$$D = \begin{bmatrix} 0 & 1 & 2 & 2 & 3 & 3 & 3 & 3 \\ 1 & 0 & 2 & 2 & 3 & 3 & 3 & 3 \\ 2 & 2 & 0 & 1 & 3 & 3 & 3 & 3 \\ 2 & 2 & 1 & 0 & 3 & 3 & 3 & 3 \\ 3 & 3 & 3 & 3 & 0 & 1 & 2 & 2 \\ 3 & 3 & 3 & 3 & 1 & 0 & 2 & 2 \\ 3 & 3 & 3 & 3 & 2 & 2 & 0 & 1 \\ 3 & 3 & 3 & 3 & 2 & 2 & 1 & 0 \end{bmatrix}.$$

Here, (i, j) element represents the distance between sector i and j. Because the axioms of ultrametric distance,

(I) $d(i, j) = d(j, i)$

(II) $d(i, j) \leq \max_k (d(i, k), d(k, j))$,

are invariant with respect to any positive multiplication, we enlarge the distance by multiplying 10 to emphasize the segmentation of labor market.

The initial conditions are as follows. The labor force in each sector is initially set equal to 100 (the total size of labor force, N, is 800), and the number of employed workers in each sector is 75. Thus, the total size of initial employment

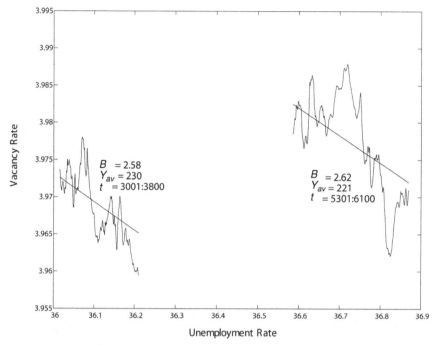

Figure 7.4. **Beveridge Curve for** $D1$.
Notes: Both the unemployment rate (U) and the vacancy rate (V) are the moving averages (MA) of 200 and 500 leads and lags for U and V, respectively.
Two Beveridge curves shown in the figure corresponds to different average levels of Y, one $Y_{av} = 221$ $(t = 5301$–$6100)$ and the other $Y = 230$ $(t = 3001$–$3800)$.
For two sample periods, $V = B + 50/U$ is fitted; Estimated B is also shown in the figure.

is 600 whereas the number of unemployed is 200.[4] The length of simulation is 7000. For each case, we did 400 simulations, and report the average.

Output Y initially keeps declining in the same way as it does in the simulations in Chapter 6. Eventually, the level of Y settles, and afterward its growth rate fluctuates around zero with ± 0.02. Thus, we define the "convergence time" τ as the first time that the growth rate of Y exceeds zero. We obtain $\tau = 353$ for Case $D1$, and $\tau = 805$ for Case $D2$. That is, the convergence is much faster in Case $D1$ where the demand shares are high for high productivity sectors than in Case $D2$. Here, the word "convergence" is used in the sense that the Markov chain enters the closed set of states from which the model does not escape.[5] We take $\tau = 1500$ by which the Markov chain has entered the closed set in both $D1$ and $D2$ cases.

---

[4] The initial unemployment rate is 25 percent. Though this figure may appear too high, in the present model, it turns out to be necessary to keep the unemployment pool from extinction, and to run simulations without serious stacks.

[5] See Feller (1968, XV. 4 and 8) for the notions of "closed sets" and "transient states" of the Markov process.

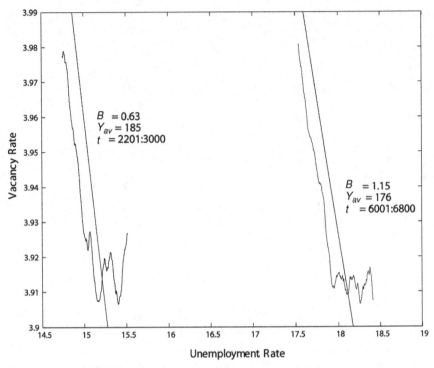

Figure 7.5. Beveridge Curve for D2.
Notes: Both the unemployment rate (U) amd the vacancy rate (V) are the moving averages (MA) of 200 and 500 leads and lags for U and V, respectively.
Two Beveridge curves shown in the figure correspond to different average levels of Y, one $Y_{av} = 176$ ($t = 6001$–6800) and the other $Y_{av} = 185$ ($t = 2201$–3000). For two sample periods, $V = B + 50/U$ is fitted; Estimated B is also shown in the figure.

The simulations done on these assumptions have produced very interesting results. First is the Beveridge Curve. The raw plots of unemployment rate U and the vacancy rate V exhibit a rather nebulous figure in both cases $D1$ and $D2$. However, they consistently show that the relationship between U and V depends on the average level of Y. In other words, the Beveridge Curve shifts up or down when Y goes down or up, respectively. To demonstrate this, we first take moving averages of U and V, and then fit the following curve:

$$V = B + \frac{50}{U}. \tag{7.14}$$

The constant term B in (14) is a parameter to indicate the position of the rectangular Beveridge Curves on the U–V plane. Figures 7.4 and 7.5 show two representative Beveridge Curves for $D1$ and $D2$ Cases, respectively. Each Beveridge Curve corresponds to the average level of Y for that sample period. Both figures show that when Y is high, B is small, and vice versa. That is, when Y declines (goes up), the Beveridge Curve shifts outward (downward).

Table 7.1. Simulation Results

	Case $D1$	Case $D2$
Demand Pattern*	[6,5,4,3,2,2,2,2]/26	[2,2,2,2,3,4,5,6]/26
Demand Share for top 4 sectors	69	31
Average Level of GDP	227	181
Convergence time (τ)	353	805
Number of Employed Workers	509	668
$\kappa^e = \sum_i s_i^e/c_i$	2.2	3.5
$-\Delta Y/\Delta U = 1/[\kappa'(Y^e)Y^e + \kappa(Y^e)]$	3.2	0.5
Okun Coefficient (α)	11.3	2.1

* Demand share vector is actually not constant but dependent on the level of aggregate output Y. See equation (7.12):

$$s_i(t) = s_i(\tau) + \frac{K_i}{500}[Y_i(t) - Y_i(\tau)] \quad \text{for } t > \tau = 1500.$$

At this stage, it is convenient to summarize the results of our simulations (see Table 7.1). The average level of total output Y after convergence depends clearly on the pattern of demand. In Case 1, it is 227 whereas in Case 2, it is 181. The higher the demand shares of high productivity sectors are, the higher the average level of aggregate output is. This confirms the result obtained in Chapter 6.

Figures 7.6 and 7.7 show the average number of employed workers in each sector for Case $D1$ and Case $D2$, respectively. In both cases, sector 8 with the lowest productivity hires the largest number of workers; because of its low productivity, sector 8 needs a large number of workers to meet its demand. We can also observe that the total number of employed workers is larger in Case $D2$ (668) than in Case $D1$ (509). Note that the level of total output Y is higher in Case 1 than in Case 2.

Equation (7.10) shows the total employment is equal to κY. Thus, κ, defined by equation (7.11) as the sum of the ratios of demand share to productivity coefficient in all the sectors, plays the central role for determining the level of total employment. Table 7.1 shows κ for $D1$ and $D2$. κ is 3.5 for $D2$, and is higher than 2.2 for $D1$. Accordingly, total employment is higher for $D2$ than for $D1$.

Our simulations have also produced Okun's law. First, we explain how we can estimate the Okun coefficient α :

$$\frac{\Delta Y}{Y} = \gamma - \alpha(u - u^*).$$

We assume that economy fluctuates about its equilibrium state, and refer to the relation

$$\frac{\Delta Y}{Y_e} = -\alpha \frac{\Delta U}{N} \tag{7.15}$$

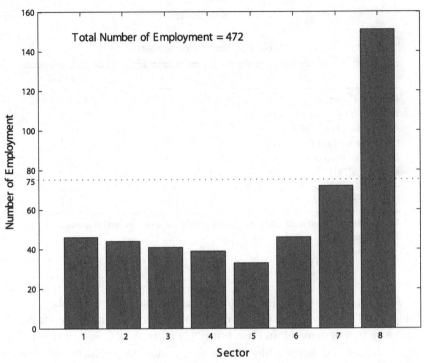

Figure 7.6. Sectoral Distribution of Employment for $D1$.

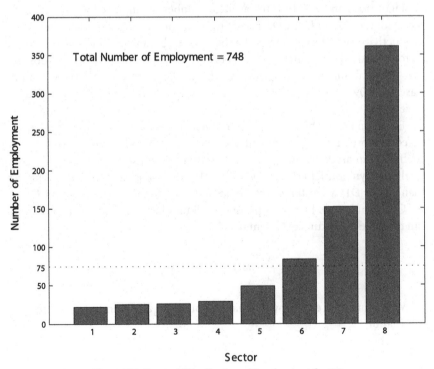

Figure 7.7. Sectoral Distribution of Employment for $D2$.

208

Table 7.2. Simulation Results

	Case $D1$	Case $D2$
Demand Pattern*	[6,5,4,3,2,2,2,2]/26	[2,2,2,2,3,4,5,6]/26
Demand Share for top 4 sectors	69	31
Average Level of GDP	237	176
Convergence time (τ)	353	810
Number of Employed Workers	506	647
$\kappa^e = \sum_i s_i^e / c_i$	2.2	3.7
$-\Delta Y / \Delta U = 1/[\kappa'(Y^e)Y^e + \kappa(Y^e)]$	0.8	1.6
Okun Coefficient (α)	2.9	1.6

* Demand share vector depends on the level of aggregate output Y. In this simulation, the denominator of the adjustment term is 1000, rather than 500:

$$s_i(t) = s_i(\tau) + \frac{K_i}{1000}[Y_i(t) - Y_i(\tau)] \quad \text{for } t > \tau = 1500.$$

as Okun's law. We can then rewrite (7.15) as

$$\alpha = \left(-\frac{\Delta Y_e}{\Delta U_e}\right)\left(\frac{N}{Y_e}\right) = \left(-\frac{\Delta Y_e}{\Delta U_e}\right)\left(\frac{N}{L^e}\right)\kappa. \tag{7.16}$$

Note that in equilibrium, Y_e and L_e are related by the following relation (equation (7.10)):

$$\frac{L_e}{Y_e} = \sum_{i=1}^{K} \frac{s_i}{c_i} = \kappa. \tag{7.17}$$

Differentiating equation (7.17), we obtain

$$-\Delta U_e = \Delta L_e = \kappa'(Y_e) Y_e \Delta Y_e + \kappa(Y_e) \Delta Y_e. \tag{7.18}$$

Equation (7.18) is equivalent to

$$-\frac{\Delta Y_e}{\Delta U_e} = \frac{1}{\kappa'(Y_e) Y_e + \kappa(Y_e)}. \tag{7.19}$$

Thus, from (7.16) and (7.19), we can obtain α as follows:

$$\alpha = \frac{\kappa}{\kappa'(Y_e) Y_e + \kappa(Y_e)}\left(\frac{800}{L_e}\right). \tag{7.20}$$

Using equation (7.12), we can obtain κ and κ' evaluated at the equilibrium level of Y_e. Table 7.1 shows that the obtained Okun coefficient α is 11.3 for Case $D1$ while 2.1 for Case $D2$. We have also conducted simulations in which demand shares are fixed, not depending on the level of Y; namely, vectors of demand share are just $D1$ and $D2$. It turns out that on this assumption, the Okun coefficient becomes much smaller than the ones shown in Table 7.1.

In Table 7.2, we also report the results obtained in the simulations in which the sensitivity of demand shares to the level of Y is small. Specifically, instead of (7.12), we assume

$$s_i(t) = s_i(t) + \frac{K_i}{1000} [Y(t) - Y(\tau)] \qquad \text{for} \qquad t > \tau = 1500. \qquad (7.12)$$

Under this assumption, α is 2.9 for $D1$, and 1.6 for $D2$ (see Table 7.2 for details).

The same assumption that the shares of demand depend on the level of aggregate output Y (equation (7.12)) also produces a high correlation between productivity (Y/L) and the aggregate output (Y). Figure 7.8 shows Y/L and Y. The correlation is 0.99. We will later explain that the point is very important in the controversy surrounding the RBC theory.

We can summarize the qualitative results obtained from these simulations as follows:

1. Larger shares of demand on more productive sectors result in the higher average value of GDP. The major conclusion in Chapter 6 is borne out by the extended model in this chapter.
2. The relation between unemployment U and vacancy V, the Beveridge Curve, depends on demand.
3. The coefficient relating the unemployment rate to the growth rate of GDP is much larger than one as Okun's law claims.
4. The correlation between productivity and aggregate output is positive, possibly very high.
5. The economy reaches equilibrium faster when larger shares of demand fall on more productive sectors. This means that demand affects not only the level of GDP in equilibrium, but also the adjustment speed toward equilibrium.

7.4. Discussion

Economists have long recognized that the labor market is really segmented heterogeneous markets. A stochastic approach is powerful for analyzing dynamics in such markets. It is not an accident that search theory, a stochastic approach, has flourished in the analysis of the labor market.

One of the major insights of stochastic approach is that *macro* relationship or equation is not a direct reflection of *micro* behavior of the representative economic agent. This is precisely the spirit of this book. An early example of such an approach is an attempt to explain the Phillips curve by way of aggregation of stochastic microeconomic behaviors (Lipsey, 1960, Tobin, 1972). Tobin (1972), for example, makes the following remark:

It is an essential feature of the theory that economy-wide relations among employment, wages, and prices are aggregations of diverse outcomes in heterogeneous markets. The myth of macroeconomics is that relations among aggregates are enlarged analogues of relations among corresponding variables for individual households, firms, industries, markets. The myth is a harmless and useful simplification in many contexts, but sometimes it misses the essence of the phenomenon. (Tobin, 1972, 9)

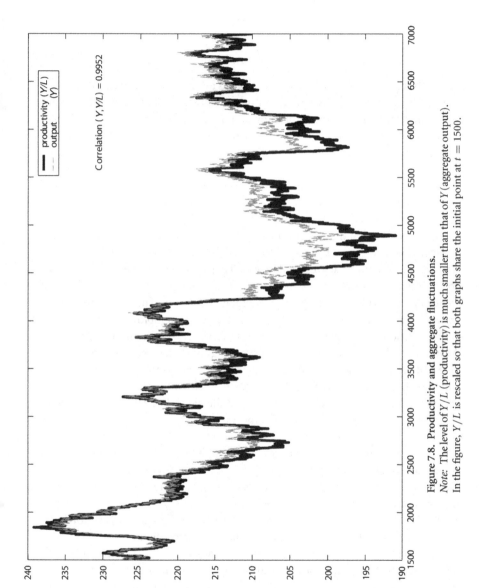

Figure 7.8. Productivity and aggregate fluctuations.
Note: The level of Y/L (productivity) is much smaller than that of Y (aggregate output). In the figure, Y/L is rescaled so that both graphs share the initial point at $t = 1500$.

Using a stochastic dynamic model, we have demonstrated that two important economy-wide relations – the Beveridge Curve and Okun's law – are indeed the outcomes of "aggregations of diverse outcomes in heterogeneous markets." The Beveridge Curve is closely related to the notion of the *natural unemployment*. In what follows, we discuss the implications of our analysis.

Natural Unemployment

If the labor market were a single homogeneous market as illustrated in Figure 7.1, depending on the level of real wages, either unemployment or vacancy exists, but not both of them at the same time. However, in the real labor market, we observe the coexistence of unemployment and vacancy. The relationship between the two is negative. It is called the Beveridge Curve.

Obviously, the Beveridge Curve is borne out of complex interactions of workers and firms in heterogeneous markets. "The actual structural characteristics of the labor and commodity markets," which Friedman (1968) argues generate the "natural unemployment," produce the Beveridge Curve.

It is usually taken that the position of the Beveridge Curve on the $U-V$ plane is determined solely by those "structural" characteristics of the labor market, and is independent of aggregate demand. Then it becomes a very useful device to separate the natural unemployment from unemployment caused by demand deficiency. Beveridge (1944) defined employment as "full" if unemployment is no more numerous than vacancies. The critical level of unemployment is the point of intersection of the Beveridge Curve and the 45 degree line on the U/V plane. Movements along a given Beveridge Curve bring about changes in unemployment due to demand deficiency while keeping the natural unemployment unchanged. On the other hand, shifts of the Beveridge Curve either to the northeast or to the origin on the $U-V$ plane change the level of the natural unemployment rate. In section 1, we reviewed some of the important empirical analyses based on this idea.

Our simulation results, however, indicate a pitfall for this standard approach for, in general, *the Beveridge Curve depends on aggregate demand*. Specifically, as the average level of aggregate output goes up, the Beveridge Curve shifts down to the origin, and vice versa. Figure 7.9 shows the Beveridge Curve for Japan (1980–2000). It is interesting to see that Japan's Beveridge Curve shifts northeast as the economy suffers from the long stagnation during the 1990s.

Why does the Beveridge Curve depend on aggregate demand in our model? The reason is that we have a distribution of productivities in the economy. As explained in Chapter 6, demand affects the level of total output. At the same time, it affects the relationship between vacancy and unemployment.

This result has an extremely important implication. It means that we cannot so clearly separate "structural" unemployment from "cyclical" unemployment due to demand deficiency. It, in turn, means that *the notion of "natural" rate*

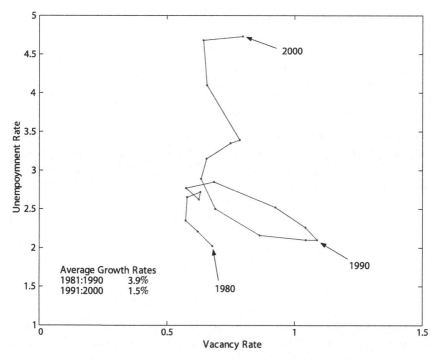

Figure 7.9. Beveridge Curve for Japan from 1980 to 2000.

of unemployment is not well defined. The "natural" unemployment determined solely by "structural" factors makes sense only in the unrealistic imaginary economy where productivities are equal in all the sectors and activities, and demand does not affect the level of total output. As we explained it in Chapter 3, the distribution of production factors among sectors with different productivities depends crucially on aggregate demand. This means that the natural unemployment cannot be defined independent of aggregate demand.

Okun's Law

Okun's law (Okun, 1962) is an empirical relationship between changes in GDP, Y, and the unemployment rate u:

$$\frac{\Delta Y}{Y} = \gamma - \alpha(u - u^*). \tag{7.21}$$

Okun's (1962) original work found that u^* is 4 percent, and α is about 3 for the U.S. economy. Subsequent works have also found that α is about 3. This coefficient is so stable for the United States that the relationship has come to be called Okun's law. This particular number, three, does not universally apply to all the economies, however. Hamada and Kurosaka (1984), for example, report that the Okun coefficient is 13.2 for Japan (1974–82).[6]

The Okun coefficient α is much larger than what one should expect in the the standard neoclassical framework. Take, for example, the Cobb–Douglas production function with capital K and labor L. Then, GDP is given by

$$Y = K^{1-\alpha} L^\alpha \qquad (7.22)$$

with α about 0.7. The total workforce $N = L + U$ is given where L and U are the numbers of employed and unemployed, respectively. When N is given, we have $\Delta U = -\Delta L$. We assume that ΔK is negligible in the short run. The production function then implies that

$$\frac{\Delta Y}{Y} = \alpha \left(\frac{\Delta L}{L} \right) \qquad (7.23)$$

in the short run. This is roughly equal to

$$\frac{\Delta Y}{Y} = -\alpha \frac{\Delta U}{N}. \qquad (7.24)$$

Namely, a decrease in the unemployment rate by 1 percent entails only α percent increase in the growth rate of Y. Thus, the Okun coefficient α which is equal to the labor elasticity of the Cobb–Douglas production function, should be smaller than one, say 0.6 or 0.7. To obtain the number 3, as in Okun's law, we need "increasing marginal product of labor."

To explain Okun's law that the 1 percent decrease (or increase) in unemployment (or employment) raises the growth rate of GDP by α percent with α being much larger than one, we need some sort of increasing returns *in the economy as a whole*. It is very important to recognize that *aggregate* increasing returns do not necessarily mean increasing return technology *in individual firm or sector*. Given distribution of productivities across sectors (or firms), changes in the pattern of demand (s_i in our model) produce all kinds of returns, either increasing or decreasing, in the economy as a whole.

Okun (1973) himself argues that one need to resort to the following factors in explaining the Okun coefficient which is much larger than one:

I stressed then that unemployment was merely the tip of the iceberg that forms in a cold economy. The difference between unemployment rates of 5 percent and 4 percent extends far beyond the creation of jobs for 1 percent of the labor force. The submerged part of the iceberg includes (a) additional jobs for people who do not actively seek work in a slack labor market but nonetheless take jobs when they become available; (b) a longer workweek reflecting less part-time and more overtime employment; and (c) extra productivity – more output per

---

[6]   Hamada and Kurosaka (1984) attribute such a high value of the Okun coefficient as 13 for Japan to several factors: the elastic response in the female participation ratio, flexible working hours, the slow adjustment in employment, and to changes in industrial structures.

manhour – from fuller and more efficient use of labor and capital. In light of the findings of other researchers on various aspects of the output-employment relationship, I shall qualify and modify, but basically reaffirm, the three-to-one relationship that I initially estimated between percentage increments in real gross national product (GNP) and percentage-point reductions in the unemployment rate. (Okun, 1973, 207–208)

A decline in the unemployment rate by 1 percent actually raises labor input by more than one percent. For the U.S. economy during the 1960s, Okun (1973) offers the following estimates:

In light of these other studies, I would now estimate the additional labor input associated with a reduction in unemployment from 5 to 4 percent as follows:

Component	Percent
Jobs for the unemployed	1.05
Lengthened workweek	0.40
Increased labor force pariciparion	0.65
Total addition to labor input	2.10

(Okun, 1973, 211)

These estimates imply that the remaining 1 percent increase in output must come from productivity gains associated with a decline in the unemployment rate by 1 percent. Extra productivity need not arise in individual firm or factory. Okun indeed emphasizes the importance of sectoral shifts.

I now believe that an important part of the process involves a downgrading of labor in a slack economy – high-quality workers avoiding unemployment by accepting low-quality and less productive jobs. The focus of this paper is on the upgrading of jobs associated with a high-pressure economy. Shifts in the composition of output and employment toward sectors and industries of higher productivity boost aggregate productivity as unemployment declines. Thus the movement to full employment draws on a reserve army of the underemployed as well as of the unemployed. In the main empirical study of this paper, I shall report new evidence concerning the upgrading of workers into more productive jobs in a high-pressure economy. (Okun, 1973, 208)

This is precisely the point we have made by means of simulations. Our analysis in this chapter emphasizes the importance of sectoral shifts of resources in generating productivity gains in the economy as a whole. In our first set of simulations reported in Table 7.1, we could obtain the Okun coefficient which is much larger than one, depending on the configurations of demand shares and productivity coefficients; 11.3 for Case $D1$ and 2.1 for Case $D2$. In the second set of simulations reported in Table 7.2, the Okun coefficient α is 2.9 for Case $D1$ and 1.6 for Case $D2$; they are quite close to 3. Note that in either case, we assume *linear* production functions for all sectors in our model so that in this respect, one might expect α close to 1. That the Okun coefficient is much larger than one must, therefore, come from sectoral interactions. It, in turn, means that Okun's

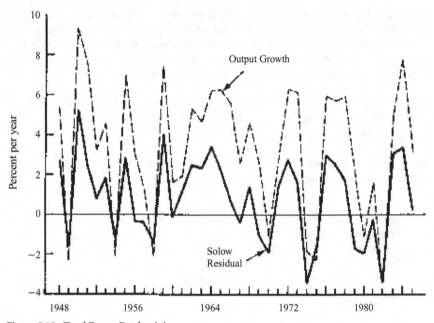

Figure 7.10. Total Factor Productivity.
Source: Mankiw (1989).

law is a macroeconomic phenomenon which arises from aggregations of diverse stochastic outcomes in heterogeneous markets.

Procyclical Productivity

It is a well-established fact that productivity changes procyclically. Figure 7.10 shows changes in TFP (Total Factor Productivity or the Solow Residuals) and output growth for the United States. Measured productivity is highly cyclical.

The interpretation of procyclical productivity changes is a matter of great dispute. RBC theorists take the observed procyclical productivity at face value (Kydland and Prescott, 1982; Prescott, 1986): Procyclical technological distur-bances (or fluctuations in the production function) are indeed the major source of business cycle fluctuations. Critics such as Summers (1986) and Mankiw (1989), on the other hand, argue that observed cyclical productivity merely reflects labor hoarding and other "off the production function" behavior. According to this view, productivity appears to fall in a recession because firms keep unnecessary and underutilized labor. In a boom, the hoarded labor is mobilized entailing an increase in output without an accompanying large increase in measured labor input.

Basu (1996) performed an ingenious test to investigate the relative impor-tance of cyclical fluctuations in labor and capital utilization, increasing returns to scale, and technology shocks (i.e., fluctuations in the production function) as explanations for procyclical productivity. The test is based on the idea that firms may extract unmeasured services from their own capital stocks or hoarded workers, but that in order to produce greater output, they need more materials that do not involve unmeasured efforts or utilizations. His conclusion is that cyclical factor utilization is important, returns to scale are about constant, and technology shocks are small and have low correlation with either output or hours growth. Specifically, "controlling for cyclical utilization reduces the variance of technology shocks by almost 60 percent, their correlation with output growth by 75 percent, and their correlation with hours growth by 85 percent" (Basu, 1996, 749).

Procyclical productivity certainly arises from underutilization of production factors at an individual firm or a production unit. However, given productivity dispersion in the economy, it also arises from mobility of resources across sectors or firms. Our simulation (Figure 7.8) demonstrates that the combination of productivity dispersion and cyclical demand shifts across sectors, in fact, produces highly procyclical productivity *in the economy as a whole*. This is precisely the point Okun (1973, 208) emphasized in his explanation of Okun's law.

8

Demand Saturation–Creation and Economic Growth

In Chapters 3 and 6, we have shown that demand affects the level of total output. As the old Keynesian economics claims, demand is relevant. However, the claim is normally taken to be relevant only for the short run. The long run is the realm of the neoclassical economics, whereby economic growth is determined solely by supply factors. In this chapter, we challenge this standard neoclassical view, and argue that demand actually plays a central role in the process of economic growth.

8.1. Introduction

In the standard literature, the fundamental factor restraining economic growth is diminishing returns to capital in production or R&D technology. In this chapter, we present a model suggesting that "saturation of demand" is another important factor restraining growth.

In the less mathematical literature and casual discussions, the idea of demand saturation has been popular. Every businessman would acknowledge saturation of demand for an individual product. In fact, plot a time series of production of any representative product such as steel and automobiles, or production in any industry, against year, and, with few exceptions, one obtains a S-shaped curve. Figure 8.1, from Rostow (1978), demonstrates this stylized fact. The experiences of diffusion of such consumer durables as refrigerators, television sets, cars, and personal computers tell us that deceleration of growth comes mainly from saturation of demand rather than diminishing returns in technology. Growth of production of a commodity or in an individual industry is bound to slow down because demand grows fast at the early stage but eventually, necessarily slows down. Thus the demand for some products grows much more rapidly than the GDP, while the demand for others grows much more slowly. Products/industries face different income elasticities of demand. The celebrated Engel's Law, based on saturation of demand for food, is an example.

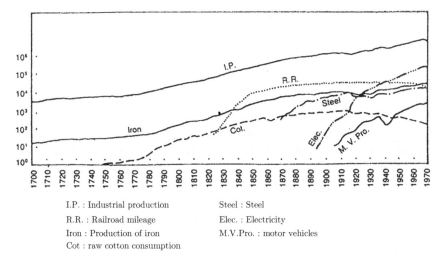

I.P. : Industrial production   Steel : Steel
R.R. : Railroad mileage   Elec. : Electricity
Iron : Production of iron   M.V.Pro. : motor vehicles
Cot : raw cotton consumption

Figure 8.1. Aggregate and Sectoral Growth Patterns Illustrated: British Industrial Production and Six Major Sectors, 1700–1972.
Source: Rostow, W. W., *The World Economy: History and Prospect,* Austin: University of Texas Press, 1978, p. 107.

Keynes (1936) was well aware of the danger of demand saturation. His principle of effective demand is, after all, nothing but a reflection of the law of demand saturation. In the *General Theory,* saying that gold is a special commodity, he argues as follows:

In the second place the result, namely, the increased stock of gold, does not, as in other cases, have the effect of diminishing its marginal utility. Since the value of a house depends on its utility, every house which is built serves to diminish the prospective rents obtainable from further house-building and therefore lessens the attraction of further similar investment unless the rate of interest is falling *pari passu.* But the fruits of gold-mining do not suffer from this disadvantage, and a check can only come through a rise of the wage-unit in terms of gold, which is not likely to occur unless and until employment is substantially better....

Ancient Egypt was doubly fortunate, and doubtless owed to this its fabled wealth, in that it possessed *two* activities, namely, pyramid-building as well as the search for the precious metals, the fruits of which, since they could not serve the needs of man by being consumed, did not stale with abundance. The Middle Ages built cathedrals and sang dirges. Two pyramids, two masses for the dead, are twice as good as one; but not so two railways from London to York. Thus we are so sensible, have schooled ourselves to so close a semblance of prudent financiers, taking careful thought before we add to the 'financial' burdens of posterity by building them houses to live in, that we have no such easy escape from the sufferings of unemployment. (Keynes, 1936, 130–131)

Unfortunately, the existing literature on growth abstracts largely from this important fact that products/industries obey the law of demand saturation and that each product/industry experiences a typical S-shaped life cycle.[1] This, of course, is not to say that the appearance of new products and the disappearance of old ones have not been modeled. In the so-called "creative destruction" and the "quality ladder" literature, Grossman and Helpman (1991), Aghion and Howitt (1992), and Caballero and Jaffe (1993) have analyzed such phenomena in growth models. However, in this line of research, the old products disappear only through the introduction of new products. Unless new products appear, demand for the existing products remains the same. Therefore, it is possible for the economy to keep growing if it succeeds in raising productivity in the production of the *existing* commodities.[2]

In sharp contrast, with saturation of demand as we assume it here, to raise productivity in production of the "mature" products does not help in sustaining economic growth. To put it another way, in the existing R&D-based growth models, the economy can keep growing, if, for example, the automobile industry keeps raising the quality of cars, whereas in our model, it can't because demand for cars saturates in spite of quality improvement.

Likewise, the product life cycle in the existing literature (e.g., Grossman and Helpman, 1991) is based on a production technology or production geography life cycle whereas our model is based on a demand life cycle. In contrast to the "creative destruction" that occurs in the existing literature, growth of demand for the existing commodities in our analysis of "saturation" necessarily slows downs whether or not new commodities appear. It would be absurd to argue that the growth of demand for food decelerated, as Engel found, because manufactured products appeared. The demand for cars did not approach its ceiling because personal computers were invented. Rather the law of demand saturation works for an individual commodity.

Within the same industry, new and old products are often close substitutes like black/white and color TVs or personal computers of different vintage, and old products gradually disappear as new ones appear. Thus, the "creative destruction" story nicely fits the growth of *an industry*. The R&D race among competing firms as it is modeled in the standard endogenous growth literature certainly plays an important role. Technical progress taken up in the existing literature concerns close substitutes, as those models explicitly state. However, as we argued above, the same story does not necessarily hold true for different industries.

---

[1] The volume entitled *Escaping Satiation* edited by Witt (2001) collects interesting papers on "demand-led economic growth." However, in our view, they have not succeeded in advancing any coherent analytical framework.

[2] This point trivially applies to the case where the quality improvement occurs in the production of intermediate goods. It also applies to the case where the creative destruction or the quality improvement occurs in the production of final consumables. See, for example, equation (21) of Caballero and Jaffe (1993). If the number of commodities remains constant ($\dot{N} = 0$), the growth rate of the economy is still positive, which is equal to $\hat{\eta}$, the growth rate of labor productivity in the production of the existing commodities.

Arguably, demand saturation is more relevant for the growth of *the economy as a whole*. In this chapter, we explore the growth model based on demand saturation and innovations which create new demand. To repeat, in the standard creative destruction, quality ladder, or product variety models, the economy can sustain growth if productivity in the population of existing products keeps rising, while in our demand saturation model, it cannot.

We consider the logistic growth of an individual product/industry a stylized fact, and present a formal model of growth built on this stylized fact. An obvious implication of the logistic growth of an individual product/industry is that the economy enjoys high growth if it successfully keeps introducing new products or industries which temporarily enjoy *high growth of demand*. In our model, innovation or technical progress bears new commodities or sectors which enjoy high growth of demand, and, by so doing, sustains the economic growth of the economy as a whole.

The demand-creating innovation in our model is different from the standard total factor productivity (TFP), or an upward shift of the production function. In the standard quality ladder models and the creative destruction literature of Grossman and Helpan (1991), Caballero and Jaffe (1993), and Young (1998), innovation or technical progress raises total factor productivity by way of replacing old commodities with new ones simply because new commodities are assumed to have higher value than old ones. Again, whereas this seems to hold true for the commodities that are basically the same but of different vintages, the same story does not make much sense for wholly different products such as cars and personal computers. Personal computers do not necessarily command higher value added than cars. In short, the standard literature models the dynamics of close substitutes whereas our model stresses the importance of demand saturation and creation of wholly different products or industries for which demand grows transitionally.

The difference between the standard models and our model of demand saturation most clearly shows up in the transitory dynamics. In the standard R&D-based growth models, the efficiency of R&D determines the transitory dynamics, whereas in our model, the pattern of demand saturation is the determinant. As a model of demand constrained growth, our model follows the long line of post-Keynesian literature (e.g., Kaldor, 1957; Robinson, 1962). In the post-Keynesian tradition, income distribution between capital and labor plays a central role in determining aggregate demand. In contrast, our analysis focuses on saturation of demand for an individual good/sector as a factor to generate demand constraints facing the economy. We discuss the transitory dynamics in Section 8.3.

Innovations in the economy facing the law of demand saturation contribute to growth in a different way than an upward shift of the production function does. That TFP does not necessarily capture the significance of technological progress is pointed out by Wright (1997).

The identification of 'technological progress' with changes in total-factor-productivity, or with the 'residual' in a growth-accounting framework, is so widely practised that many economists barely give it a passing thought, regarding the two as more-or-less synonymous and interchangeable. ... Even with extensive quality adjustments, TFP is not generally a good index of technology. If a genuine change in technological potential occurs in a firm, an industry, a sector, or a country, in any plausible model this change will affect the mobilisation of capital and labour in whatever unit is involved. In the new equilibrium, inputs as well as outputs will have changed; the ratio between these may convey little if any useful information about the initiating change in technology. (Wright. 1997, 1562)

We share Wright's concern. The economy always mobilize resources and accumulates capital whenever it finds goods or sectors for which demand grows rapidly. In fact, in our model, the elasticity of capital in the production function is equal to one (the so-called AK model). Therefore, the economy grows whenever capital accumulates. But capital accumulation is constrained by saturation of demand. Innovation creates goods/sectors for which demand grows fast, elicits capital accumulation, and thereby ultimately sustains economic growth.

To substantiate this argument, in Section 8.2, we present a model that incorporates the basic idea that demand for an individual good or sector necessarily faces saturation and thus its growth eventually slows down. We begin with demand for an individual product rather than preferences because the former is more directly related to the stylized fact than the latter. Section 8.3 studies growth of the economy as a whole. Out of the steady state, "vigor of demand" and saturation determine growth whereas the ultimate factor for sustaining economic growth in the steady state is the creation of new products/industries. Under the standard Poisson assumption, successive creation of new products/industries sustains steady-state growth. However, we demonstrate that under the alternative *Polya urn* assumption that the success probability of innovation gets smaller as time goes by, the growth rate of the economy must decelerate and go asymptotically down to zero. This is the same result as that obtained in the standard R&D-based TFP models (e.g., Jones, 1995; Jones and Williams, 1998; Segerstrom, 1998; Young, 1998), though the rate of innovation is a decreasing function of time rather than a function of the R&D capital stock, as is assumed in the existing literature. Section 8.4 provides microeconomic foundations for investment and consumption. For consumption that follows the logistic growth, we present two different microeconomic foundations: the Ramsey model with the representative consumer, and a model with diffusion of goods among different households. The two models suggest different interpretations of saturation of demand. Finally, Section 8.5 offers some concluding discussion.

8.2. The Model

We study an economy in which heterogeneous final goods and an intermediate good are produced. In this section, we take demand for each final product as given, and concentrate on production. We will later consider the firm's behavior which determines investment and also the consumer's behavior which determines consumption in Section 8.4. Let us begin with final goods.

Final Goods

Final goods are produced with an intermediate good as the only input. Production of all the final goods requires the same intermediate good X. The production function is also common.

$$y_k = AX_k \qquad (0 < A < 1). \tag{8.1}$$

We assume perfect competition. Therefore, zero profits ensue:

$$P_k(t) y_k(t) = P_X(t) X_k(t). \tag{8.2}$$

Here $P_k(t)$ is the price of the kth final product, and $P_X(t)$ the price of intermediate good. Because of the common linear production function (8.1), the zero profit condition (8.39) is equivalent to

$$P_k(t) A = P_X(t). \tag{8.3}$$

Thus we can adjust the units of final products in such a way to make all the prices of final goods one. Then

$$P_X = A < 1.$$

The output of each final good is equal to its demand $D_k(t)$ no matter how the latter is determined:

$$y_k(t) = D_k(t). \tag{8.4}$$

In this section, we take a S-shaped life cycle of demand for each product/industry as a stylized fact. To make our analysis tractable, assume that $D_k(t)$ follows the logistic curve:

$$D(t) = \frac{\mu D_0}{[\delta D_0 + (\mu - \delta D_0)e^{-\mu t}]}. \tag{8.5}$$

Because the mechanism is the same for all the products or sectors, for the moment, we drop k and write $D_k(t)$ as $D(t)$. We will explore microeconomic foundations for the logistic growth of demand in Section 8.4. D_0 in (8.42) is the initial value of $D(t)$. Starting with D_0 smaller than μ/δ, $D(t)$ initially increases almost exponentially, but its growth eventually decelerates, and approaching its ceiling μ/δ, the growth rate declines asymptotically to zero. A typical shape of the logistic growth is illustrated and compared with exponential growth in Figure 8.2.

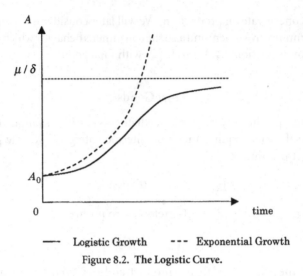

— Logistic Growth   --- Exponential Growth

Figure 8.2. The Logistic Curve.

Though exponential growth is often taken for granted by economists, there is actually ample evidence to show that no *individual* product or industry grows exponentially. Rather demand for or production of a product or an industry typically grows according to the logistic curve. In fact, an eminent mathematician Montroll (1978) goes so far as to suggest that almost all the social phenomena, except in their relatively brief abnormal times, obey the logistic growth. Figure 8.1 above demonstrates this well-known fact of life in our economy.

Growth and saturation of an individual product/sector are here characterized by two parameters μ and δ. They would depend not only on preferences but also on creation of new models and close substitutes of higher quality *in the production of the same commodity*. For example, TV set growth would have certainly reached its ceiling much earlier if there had been only black/white TVs; the emergence of color TVs and small models pushed up the ceiling. We maintain, however, that such technical progress cannot overcome the law of demand saturation in the end.[3] In fact, based on his careful study of the U.S. patent data, Schmookler (1966) even argues that technical progress in one industry is itself very strongly conditioned on the prospects of demand in that industry.

---

[3] Kuznets (1953), for example, argues that

   In the industrialized countries of the world, the cumulative effect of technical progress in a number of important industries has brought about a situation where further progress of similar scope cannot be reasonably expected. The industries that have matured technologically account for a progressively increasing ratio of the total production of the economy. Their maturity does imply that economic effects of further improvements will necessarily be more limited than in the past. (281)

   Based on the American experiences, McLaughlin and Watkins (1939) share this kind of pessimism.

Following the logistic growth of demand, production $y_k(t)$ also satisfies equation (8.5). So far, we have focused on a final good. The number of final products is not given, however. Rather at every moment a new product or sector may arise. The emergence of an utterly new final good or a new sector is the result of innovations. Before we explain it, we turn to production of intermediate goods taking the number of final goods N as if it were constant.

Intermediate Good

To keep our model as simple as possible, we assume that there is only one kind of intermediate good X, and that X is produced by using capital K alone:

$$X = aK. \tag{8.6}$$

Here X is the sum of intermediate goods used in production of final goods:

$$X = \sum_{k=1}^{N} X_k.$$

The capacity utilization a is determined by the firm together with capital accumulation. We will discuss the firm behavior in section 8.4. For the moment, we can imagine that a is constant, which is true in the steady state.

We note that the production function (8.6) has a unitary elasticity of capital, and therefore that as long as capital accumulates, X grows without limit. And given the common production function for final goods (8.1), whenever X grows, production of final goods can also grow. However, X is intermediate good, and as seen previously, the growth of demand for each final good decelerates and declines eventually to zero. In this model, the factor that limits capital accumulation and thereby growth is not diminishing returns on capital but declining growth of demand. We consider how the profit-maximizing firm determines the capital accumulation and the capacity utilization in section 8.4.

Emergence of New Final Goods or Industries

So far we have taken the number of final goods as if it were constant. In fact, new final goods and/or industries emerge as a result of innovations. We can flexibly interpret final goods as sectors or industries if we wish.

Much effort has been made to explicitly analyze R&D activities and inventions in growth models. In fact, the achievement of the endogenous growth theory is to have combined growth models with models of R&D activities. However, as we pointed out above, technical progress in the existing literature basically concerns quality improvement in the production of *close substitutes*. Therefore, it more closely applies to an industry than to the economy as a whole. We maintain that such technical progress "pushes up the ceiling" of demand for the existing products, but cannot overcome the law of demand saturation in the end. Innovations in this model, in contrast, bear wholly new products/sectors/industries for which demand grows fast. Such innovations would depend not only on profit-motivated R&D but also on basic research. In any case, our primary interest is not in microeconomic foundations for R&D activities but in the way in which technical progress or innovation affects the economy.[4]

Specifically we assume that an invention of a new final good or an emergence of a new sector stems stochastically from learning in the process of production of the existing products. To be specific, we assume that the probability that a new final good is invented or a new industry emerges between t and $t + \Delta t$ is $\lambda N \Delta t$ where N is the number of existing final goods ($\lambda > 0$). Because an invention or new sector is a branch off from an existing good or sector, the rate of success probability is proportional to the number of existing final goods/sector N. The more products or sectors in the economy, the more likely a new product or sector emerges. λ is a parameter that represents the strength of innovations or more precisely the probability that a new good or industry emerges in the existing process of production. Innovations are thus accidental, but depend on the prior "knowledge" and experiences which stem from the existing production.

Given this assumption, $Q(N, t)$ the probability that the number of final goods at time t, $N(t)$ is equal to N, satisfies the following equation.

$$\frac{dQ}{dt} = -\lambda N Q(N, t) + \lambda (N - 1) Q(N - 1, t). \qquad (8.7)$$

Without loss of generality, we can assume that the initial number of final goods is one:

$$Q(N, 0) = \delta(N - 1),$$

where the symbol $\delta(.)$ denotes Dirac's delta function. The Appendix shows that the solution of this equation under this initial condition is

$$Q(N, t) = e^{-\lambda t}(1 - e^{-\lambda t})^{N-1}. \qquad (8.8)$$

The probability that there are N goods at time t and the $N + 1$-th good emerges between t and $t + \Delta t$ is then given by

$$\lambda N Q(N, t) \Delta t = \lambda N e^{-\lambda t} \left(1 - e^{-\lambda t}\right)^{N-1} \Delta t. \qquad (8.9)$$

At time t, the production of final good which emerged at $\tau (\tau < t)$, $y_\tau(t)$, has grown to

$$y_\tau(t) = \frac{\mu}{\delta + (\mu - \delta)e^{-\mu(t-\tau)}} \qquad (8.10)$$

---

[4] Thus, the present analysis following Arrow (1962) and Stokey (1988) abstracts from profit maximization in R&D.

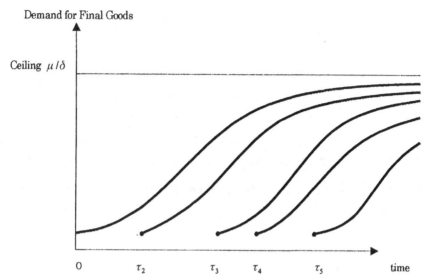

Figure 8.3. Saturation of Demand and Emergence of New Final Goods of Industries.
Note: τ_i is the date of birth of the ith Good/Industry.

because the growth of $y_\tau(t)$ obeys the logistic curve. Again, without loss of generality we can assume the initial production of newly invented good D_0 to be 1 in equation (8.5). Before we provide microfoundations for consumption and investment, we consider the growth of the economy as a whole.

8.3. Growth of the Macroeconomy

In this section, we will analyze the growth of the macroeconomy given the logistic growth of individual final good (Equation (8.10)).

The Basic Result

The aggregate value added or GDP of this economy is stochastic, but in what follows, we will focus on its expected value and denote it by $Y(t)$. $Y(t)$ is simply the sum of production of all the final goods. Because profits in the final good sectors are zero by the assumption of perfect competition, the aggregate value added is equal to the value added (profit) produced by capital K in the intermediate good sector, $P_X X(t)$, which is equal to $\sum_k A X_k = \sum_k y_k = Y(t)$.

Figure 8.3 illustrates this model economy. Each sector once it emerged grows logistically. New sectors emerge stochastically, and the aggregate value added or GDP is simply the sum of outputs of all the then existing sectors.

From equations (8.45) and (8.10), we know that the expected value of GDP of this economy is given by

$$Y(t) = \sum_{N=1}^{\infty} \int_0^t \lambda N e^{-\lambda \tau} (1 - e^{-\lambda \tau})^{N-1} y_\tau(t) d\tau + \frac{\mu}{(\delta + (\mu - \delta)e^{-\mu t})}$$

$$= \sum_{N=1}^{\infty} \int_0^t \lambda N e^{-\lambda \tau} (1 - e^{-\lambda \tau})^{N-1} \frac{\mu}{[\delta + (\mu - \delta)e^{-\mu(t-\tau)}]} d\tau$$

$$+ \frac{\mu}{(\delta + (\mu - \delta)e^{-\mu t})}. \tag{8.11}$$

The second term of the right-hand side is simply the output of the first sector at time t, $y_0(t)$. Using

$$\lambda N e^{-\lambda \tau} (1 - e^{-\lambda \tau})^{N-1} = \frac{d}{d\tau}(1 - e^{-\lambda \tau})^N$$

and

$$\sum_{N=1}^{\infty} (1 - e^{-\lambda \tau})^N = e^{\lambda \tau} - 1$$

we obtain

$$Y(t) = \int_0^t \frac{\left[\frac{d}{d\tau}(e^{\lambda \tau} - 1)\right]\mu}{[\delta + (\mu - \delta)e^{-\mu(t-\tau)}]} d\tau + \frac{\mu}{(\delta + (\mu - \delta)e^{-\mu t})}$$

$$= \lambda \int_0^t \frac{e^{\lambda \tau} \mu}{[\delta + (\mu - \delta)e^{-\mu(t-\tau)}]} d\tau + \frac{\mu}{(\delta + (\mu - \delta)e^{-\mu t})}$$

$$= \lambda \int_0^t \frac{e^{\lambda(t-u)} \mu}{[\delta + (\mu - \delta)e^{-\mu u}]} du + \frac{\mu}{(\delta + (\mu - \delta)e^{-\mu t})}. \tag{8.12}$$

From (8.12), the growth rate of the expected value of GDP, g_t, becomes

$$g_t = \frac{\dot{Y}(t)}{Y(t)} = \lambda + \left(\frac{f(t)}{Y(t)}\right)\left(\frac{\dot{f}(t)}{f(t)}\right)$$

where $f(t)$ is the logistic equation:

$$f(t) = \frac{\mu}{(\delta + (\mu - \delta)e^{-\mu t})}.$$

It is easy to show that g_t satisfies

$$\dot{g}_t = (g_t - \lambda)[2(\mu - \delta)e^{-\mu t} f(t) - \mu - g_t] \tag{8.13}$$

with the initial value g_0:

$$g_0 = \frac{\dot{Y}(t)}{Y(t)} \Big|_{t=0} = \lambda + \mu - \delta.$$

Also, since $e^{-\mu t} f(t)$ approaches zero, we can establish that the growth rate of GDP asymptotically approaches λ.

$$\lim_{t \to \infty} g_t = \lim_{t \to \infty} \frac{\dot{Y}(t)}{Y(t)} = \lambda.$$

Thus, we have established the following proposition.

Proposition: *The rate of economic growth is ultimately determined by the power of demand-creating innovations, λ.*

The growth rate of the economy is initially higher than λ by $\mu - \delta$, but it eventually goes down to λ. In this model, μ and δ have level effects while the ultimate growth rate is determined by λ. The exact time path depends, of course, on all the parameters μ, δ, and λ.

It is important to recognize that not only the steady-state growth, but also the out-of-steady-state growth, is generated by the successive emergence of new products/industries. The growth of older industries keeps declining, whereas newer products/industries enjoy high growth. How high depends on μ and δ.

From the perspective of this model, it is easy to understand that historians have identified the leading or key industries in the process of economic growth. The best known example would be perhaps Rostow (1960, 261–62) who argues that

The most cursory examination of the growth patterns of different economies, viewed against a background of general historical information, reveals two simple facts:

1. Growth-rates in the various sectors of the economy differ widely over any given period of time;
2. In some meaningful sense, over-all growth appears to be based, at certain periods, on the direct and indirect consequence of extremely rapid growth in certain particular key sectors.

Vigor of the leading sectors depends on μ and δ in the model. For the sake of illustration, we show a simulation result (Table 8.1 and Figure 8.4). In this example, we assume that λ, μ, and δ are 0.03, 0.12, and 0.02, respectively. Table 8.1 and Figure 8.4 show both the growth rate of GDP and the average growth rate defined as $\Sigma_{\tau=1}^{t} g_\tau / t$ for each period (year). For the first ten years, the growth rate of the economy is higher than 9 percent. In year 20, it is still 5.7 percent. By year 40 the growth rate has slowed to 3.2 percent which is close to the assumed asymptotic rate 3 percent. The average growth rate, of course, decelerates much more slowly than the growth rate itself. The average growth rate for the first thirty years, for example, is 7.5 percent, although the growth rate in the year 30 is 3.9 percent. This example demonstrates that depending on μ and δ, the economy

Table 8.1. *A simulation result* ($\lambda = 0.03$, $\mu = 0.12$, $\delta = 0.02$)

Time	GDP	Growth rate (%)	Average growth rate (%)	Time	GDP	Growth rate (%)	Average growth rate (%)
0	1.00			51	18.82	3.0	5.8
1	1.14	12.8	12.8	52	19.40	3.0	5.7
2	1.28	12.3	12.5	53	20.00	3.0	5.7
3	1.45	11.8	12.3	54	20.62	3.0	5.6
4	1.62	11.4	12.1	55	21.25	3.0	5.6
5	1.81	11.0	11.9	56	21.90	3.0	5.5
6	2.01	10.6	11.6	57	22.57	3.0	5.5
7	2.23	10.2	11.4	58	23.26	3.0	5.4
8	2.46	9.8	11.2	59	23.98	3.0	5.4
9	2.70	9.4	11.0	60	24.71	3.0	5.3
10	2.95	9.0	10.8	61	25.46	3.0	5.3
11	3.22	8.7	10.6	62	26.24	3.0	5.3
12	3.50	8.3	10.4	63	27.04	3.0	5.2
13	3.79	7.9	10.2	64	27.87	3.0	5.2
14	4.09	7.6	10.1	65	28.72	3.0	5.2
15	4.39	7.2	9.9	66	29.59	3.0	5.1
16	4.71	6.9	9.7	67	30.50	3.0	5.1
17	5.03	6.6	9.5	68	31.43	3.0	5.1
18	5.35	6.3	9.3	69	32.38	3.0	5.0
19	5.68	6.0	9.1	70	33.37	3.0	5.0
20	6.01	5.7	9.0	71	34.39	3.0	5.0
21	6.35	5.4	8.8	72	35.44	3.0	5.0
22	6.69	5.2	8.6	73	36.52	3.0	4.9
23	7.03	5.0	8.5	74	37.63	3.0	4.9
24	7.37	4.8	8.3	75	38.78	3.0	4.9
25	7.72	4.6	8.2	76	39.96	3.0	4.9
26	8.07	4.4	8.0	77	41.17	3.0	4.8
27	8.42	4.2	7.9	78	42.43	3.0	4.8
28	8.77	4.1	7.8	79	43.72	3.0	4.8
29	9.13	4.0	7.6	80	45.05	3.0	4.8
30	9.48	3.9	7.5	81	46.42	3.0	4.7
31	9.85	3.8	7.4	82	47.84	3.0	4.7
32	10.21	3.7	7.3	83	49.30	3.0	4.7
33	10.59	3.6	7.2	84	50.80	3.0	4.7
34	10.96	3.5	7.0	85	52.34	3.0	4.7
35	11.35	3.4	6.9	86	53.94	3.0	4.6
36	11.74	3.4	6.8	87	55.58	3.0	4.6
37	12.14	3.3	6.7	88	57.27	3.0	4.6
38	12.54	3.3	6.7	89	59.02	3.0	4.6
39	12.96	3.2	6.6	90	60.82	3.0	4.6
40	13.38	3.2	6.5	91	62.67	3.0	4.5
41	13.81	3.2	6.4	92	64.58	3.0	4.5
42	14.26	3.2	6.3	93	66.54	3.0	4.5
43	14.71	3.1	6.3	94	68.57	3.0	4.5
44	15.18	3.1	6.2	95	70.66	3.0	4.5
45	15.66	3.1	6.1	96	72.81	3.0	4.5
46	16.15	3.1	6.0	97	75.03	3.0	4.5
47	16.66	3.1	6.0	98	77.31	3.0	4.4
48	17.18	3.1	5.9	99	79.67	3.0	4.4
49	17.71	3.1	5.9	100	82.09	3.0	4.4
50	18.26	3.1	5.8				

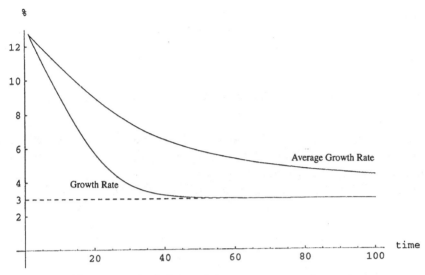

Figure 8.4. **A simulation result** ($\lambda = 0.03$, $\mu = 0.12$, $\delta = 0.02$).

can sustain a much higher growth rate than the equilibrium rate for a very long period. The transitionary dynamics is determined by the pattern of demand saturation.

Everyone knows that no economy grows at 10 percent indefinitely. Some economies, however, actually experienced 10 percent growth for a decade, and this decade-long high growth is often crucial for their growth experiences. Japan, for example, experienced 10 percent growth for a decade and a half, from 1955 through 1970. The era of high economic growth had transformed a semi-traditional economy into a modern industrial nation. We will later explain Japan's experience as a case study. The point is that we cannot dismiss "out of steady state" merely as transitory, but must attach equal importance to it as to the steady state.

The out-of-steady-state growth path illustrated in Figure 8.4 is qualitatively similar to that obtained in the old Solow (1956) model and also in the more recent R&D-based growth models such as Jones (1995), Young (1998), and Segerstrom (1998). Namely, the growth rate decelerates over time. The mechanism is fundamentally different, however. In the Solow model, diminishing returns to capital in ordinary production is the factor which brings about slower growth. In the R&D-based models, diminishing returns in R&D leads to slower growth. In contrast, in the present model the deceleration of the out-of-steady-state growth rate comes from saturation of demand. To be specific, as equation (8.13) shows, the out-of-steady-state growth path depends on μ and δ, which determine how vigorous the growth of demand is, or, conversely, how soon demand reaches its saturation. When δ is very small, and, therefore, the ceiling of demand is very high, the pace of deceleration can be slow. This out-of-steady note-state growth is basically constrained by demand. In this sense, the present model follows the long tradition of post-Keynesian literature mentioned in Section 8.1.

An Extension: The Non-Poisson Polya Urn Model

In the model above, we assumed that a new good or sector emerged as a branch off in the production of N existing goods and that it followed the Poisson birth process with the parameter λN. Under this assumption, the long-run growth rate is sustained by the rate of innovation λ.

In the standard R&D-based growth models, Jones (1995), Jones and Williams (1998), Segerstrom (1998), and Young (1998), among others, showed that if R&D was subject to diminishing returns due, for example, to congestion in research, the "finishing out" effect, and increasing difficulty, then the growth rate decelerated to zero in the steady state unless some exogenous factor such as population growth sustained it.

We will examine a similar problem in our model. In the existing literature mentioned above, all of which use the Poisson model, the Poisson parameter, which is λ in our model, is the success probability of R&D, and, therefore, the birth rate is naturally taken as a function of the stock of R&D, which corresponds to N in our model. The deceleration of the long-run growth rate occurs when the birth rate $\lambda = f(N)$ shows diminishing returns, namely when $f(N) / N$ is a decreasing function of N.

In our basic model, the birth of a new goods/sector is a branch off from the production of N existing goods. Therefore, we assumed that the birth rate was λN. However, we model the emergence of wholly new goods/industries rather than close substitutes to the existing goods. It is not directly linked to R&D but is strongly conditioned on the advancement of basic scientific knowledge. One might like to assume, therefore, that if opportunities for innovations narrow over time, the probability of the emergence of new goods/sectors be a decreasing function of time rather than N. Specifically, in place of the Poisson distribution, we assume that the probability that a new good or sector emerges at τ, p_τ, is

$$p_\tau = \frac{\omega}{\omega + \tau} \qquad (\omega > 0, \tau = 1, 2, \ldots)$$

This probability decreases in τ, and declines asymptotically to zero. This kind of model, often called Polya-like urns, is extensively used in population genetics (e.g., Hoppe, 1984). The existing literature in economics all rely on the Poisson distribution, and, to our knowledge, this non-Poisson model is new.

Now, we assume that a new good is invented exogenously with p_τ rather than as a branch off from the existing goods, namely, that p_τ is independent of the number of existing goods. In this case, when we denote the probability that there are N goods at τ by $Q(N, \tau)$ as we did previously, then $Q(N, \tau)$ satisfies

$$Q(N, \tau + 1) = (1 - p_\tau) Q(N, \tau) + p_\tau\, Q(N - 1, \tau)$$

$$= \left(\frac{\tau}{\omega + \tau}\right) Q(N, \tau) + \left(\frac{\omega}{\omega + \tau}\right) Q(N - 1, \tau) \quad \text{for } \tau = 1, 2, \dots$$

with the following boundary conditions:

$$Q(1, \tau) = \left(\frac{1}{\omega + 1}\right)\left(\frac{2}{\omega + 2}\right) \cdots \left(\frac{\tau - 1}{\omega + \tau - 1}\right)$$

and

$$Q(\tau, \tau) = \frac{\omega^\tau}{\omega(\omega + 1)(\omega + 2) \cdots (\omega + \tau - 1)} = \frac{\omega^\tau}{[\omega]^\tau}$$

where $[\omega]^\tau$ is defined by the equation.

The solution of this equation is

$$Q(k, \tau) = \frac{c(k, \tau)\omega^k}{[\omega]^\tau}$$

where $c(k, \tau)$ is the absolute value of the Sterling number of the first kind; see Aoki (1997, 279) or Abramovitz/Stegun (1968, 825). Using the generating function

$$[x]^k = \sum_{j=0}^{k} c(k, j)x^j$$

we obtain the expected value of GDP, $Y(t)$, as

$$Y(t) = \sum_{\ell=1}^{t} \sum_{j=1}^{\ell} \frac{c(\ell - 1, j - 1)\omega^{j-1}}{[\omega]^{\ell-1}} \left(\frac{\omega}{\omega + \ell}\right) y(t - \ell)$$

$$= \sum_{\ell=1}^{t} \left(\frac{\omega}{\omega + \ell}\right) y(t - \ell).$$

Here $y(t - \ell)$ is the production of the final good which emerged at time ℓ. Note that $y(t - \ell)$ follows the logistic curve, and therefore, that its growth rate eventually declines to zero.

For simplicity, take ω as an integer. Then we have

$$\sum_{\ell=1}^{t} \left(\frac{\omega}{\omega + \ell}\right) = \omega \left[\sum_{m=1}^{\omega+t} \frac{1}{m} - \sum_{m=1}^{\omega} \frac{1}{m}\right] \cong \log\left[\frac{\omega + t}{\omega}\right].$$

Therefore we have shown that in the present case, GDP grows drawing the logarithmic curve.

$$Y(t) \sim \log(t + \omega)$$

The growth rate of the economy is $1/t + 1/(t \log(t + \omega))$ and goes asymptotically down to zero.

Thus, the result similar to Jones (1995), Young (1998), and Segerstrom (1998) holds in our model. If the opportunities for innovations diminish over time, the long-run growth is not sustained. Note that in the existing literature, λ is a (possibly) decreasing function of N whereas in the present analysis, λ is independent of N and is a decreasing function of time.

8.4. Foundations for the Logistic Growth of Demand

Having found the growth rate of GDP, we next turn to the general equilibrium of this model. We have already explained production of both final goods and an intermediate good. In what follows, we first consider the firm behavior which determines investment in the intermediate good sector, and then the consumer behavior which determines consumption/saving. The consumer behavior must be consistent with growth of income or GDP (equation (8.13)) and the logistic growth of demand for an individual final good. Also saving must be equal to investment; final goods are not only consumed but also used for investment.

In this model, consumption leads to the logistic growth of individual final goods. We suggest two different models, one the standard Ramsey model with the representative consumer and the other with diffusion of final goods among different households. Because the model of investment is common, we begin with the firm's investment.

The Firm's Investment Decisions

The intermediate good is produced by the representative firm using capital K (see equation (8.6)). The firm is constrained by demand, and the capacity utilization rate a is variable. Capital accumulates so as to maximize the value of this firm (industry). Profit of this firm, which stems from selling intermediate goods to firms producing final goods, is $P_X X$.

Gross investment I requires finished goods as an input. For simplicity, we assume that final goods are perfect substitutes for increasing K. I consists of two parts, one the net investment inclusive of the standard adjustment costs, and the other the depreciation, which depends positively on the capacity utilization rate (a in equation (8.6)) of the existing capital stock K. Specifically, we assume:

$$I = \varphi(z)K + d(a)K \qquad (8.14)$$

with $z = \dot{K}/K$.

$\varphi(z)$ satisfies

$$\varphi'(z) > 0 \text{ for } z = \dot{K}/K > 0, \qquad \varphi'(z) < 0 \text{ for } z < 0,$$

$$\varphi''(z) > 0 \text{ for any } z, \quad \text{and} \quad \varphi(0) = 0, \varphi'(0) = 1. \qquad (8.15)$$

We assume the convex adjustment cost for negative z to rule out disaccumulation of capital. Depreciation $d(a)$ is also a convex function of the capacity utilization rate (Smith, 1969):

$$d'(a) > 0, \quad d''(a) > 0, \quad \text{and} \quad d(0) = 0. \tag{8.16}$$

The value of this firm S is then given by

$$S_t = \int_t^\infty [P_X X_\tau - I_\tau] \exp\left(-\int_t^\tau \rho_u \, du\right) d\tau$$

$$= \int_t^\infty [P_X X_\tau - \varphi(Z_\tau) K_\tau - d(a_\tau) K_\tau] \exp\left(-\int_t^\tau \rho_u \, du\right) d\tau. \tag{8.17}$$

We note that S_t satisfies

$$\rho_t = \frac{\dot{S}_t}{S_t} + \frac{P_X X_t - I_t}{S_t} \tag{8.18}$$

and observe that ρ is the rate of return on stock of this firm or the interest rate. The stock of this firm is owned by the consumer (or consumers). It will be explained shortly.

The firm is constrained by demand X. Because capital stock K is also given, the capacity utilization rate $a = X/K$ is given at each moment in time. The firm maximizes its present value with respect to investment. If the pace of capital accumulation is short of the growth rate of sales, the capacity utilization rate rises, and so does depreciation. On the other hand, when the firm raises the rate of capital accumulation, it incurs higher adjustment costs. The firm must balance the two so as to maximize its present value. This decision depends crucially on the growth rate of demand $g = \dot{X}/X$ facing the firm.

A change in the capacity utilization rate $a = X/K$ must by definition satisfy the following equation:

$$\dot{a}_t = (g_t - z_t) a_t. \tag{8.19}$$

It can be shown that the optimal capital accumulation z and capacity utilization rate a must satisfy (8.19) and (8.20):

$$\dot{z}_t = \left(\frac{1}{\varphi''(z)}\right) [(\rho - z)\varphi'(z) + \varphi(z) - r(a)] \tag{8.20}$$

where

$$r(a) = d'(a) a - d(a), \quad r'(a) > 0. \tag{8.21}$$

$r(a)$ measures a marginal increase in the firm's value when the rate of capital accumulation z rises by way of lowering the capacity utilization, and accordingly depreciation. $r(a)$ is, therefore, the profit rate on capital K in this model. Given capital stock K, the profit rate r is an increasing function of the firm's demand

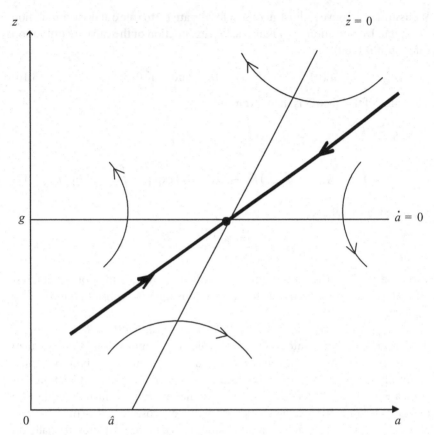

Figure 8.5. The Determination of Capital Accumulation z and Capacity Utilization Rate a.
Note: $\hat{a}$ is defined by $\rho = d''(\hat{a}) - d(\hat{a})$.

X. The rule for the optimal capital accumulation (equation (8.20)) is basically equivalent to the one in Uzawa (1969).

This optimal path can be most clearly seen with the help of Figure 8.5 when g is constant as in the steady state. The capital accumulation z approaches the growth rate of sales g from above when the initial capacity utilization is higher than its equilibrium level a^* which satisfies $r(a^*) = (\rho - g)\varphi'(g) + \varphi(g)$, and vice versa. When g becomes higher, so does the long-run profit $r(a^*)$, and higher $r(a^*)$ induces higher capital accumulation. The firm's prospects for demand basically determine investment. Investment also depends negatively on the interest rate ρ.

So much for the investment of the demand-constrained firm. In what follows, we will consider the consumer behavior which determines consumption/saving. We will present two alternative stories, one the Ramsey model and the other a model of diffusion of consumption goods among different households.

The Consumer's Consumption/Saving Decisions

The Ramsey Model. In the neoclassical approach, the queen of the economy is the consumer. Demand for final goods must be, therefore, consistent with the consumer's utility maximization. In what follows, we demonstrate that demand for final goods which obeys the logistic equation is in fact consistent with the intertemporal utility maximization of the Ramsey consumer with a particular utility function.

For convenience, we consider the representative consumer's utility maximization at time 0. At time 0, there is only one final good as is assumed in Section 8.3. This assumption is made for simplicity. The assumption that there are n goods ($n > 0$) at time 0 merely deprives our presentation of its simplicity without giving us any additional insight.

Starting with one final good at time 0, new goods keep emerging. The probability that there are N goods at time t and the $N+1$-th good emerges during t and $t + \Delta t$ is given by (8.13). Thus as of time 0, the consumer faces uncertainty concerning the timing of the emergence of new goods. We assume that the consumer maximizes the expected utility U:

$$U = \int_0^\infty \left\{ \int_0^t \sum_{N=1}^\infty [\lambda N e^{-\lambda \tau}(1 - e^{-\lambda \tau})^{N-1} u_\tau^t(C_{N+1}(t))] \, d\tau + u_0^t(C_1(t)) \right\} e^{-\theta t} dt$$

$$(8.22)$$

where θ is the subjective discount rate and $C_j(t)$ is the consumption of the j-th good. In (8.22), the expected value is taken with respect to the probability of the emergence of new goods. A similar assumption is made in Aghion and Howitt (1992).

To obtain the logistic demand function, we assume that the utility coming from consumption of a certain final good at time t depends not only on t but also on τ ($\tau < t$), the time when this final good emerged. To be specific, we assume that the utility function $u_\tau^t(C_N(t))$ is common for all the $C_N(t)$ ($N = 1, 2, \cdots$) and is

$$u_\tau^t(C_N(t)) = \left[\frac{\mu}{(\delta + (\mu - \delta)e^{-\mu(t-\tau)})} \right] \log(C_N(t)).$$

$$(8.23)$$

The logistic growth of demand (8.14) characterized by two parameters μ and δ translates itself into the utility function (8.23). It is actually more accurate to say that μ and δ, which characterize the time-dependent utility function, lead us to the logistic growth of demand for an individual final good. The logistic part of utility function (8.23) implies that the (marginal) utility coming from consumption of a particular final good depends crucially on how long a time has passed since this final good first emerged. Though it monotonically increases over time, its growth rate eventually decelerates and is bound to approach zero.

The consumer owns the stock (capital) of the intermediate good industry, S_t, which earns the rate of return ρ_t. Thus his/her budget constraint is

$$\dot{S}_t = \rho_t S_t - \sum_{i=1}^{\infty} C_i(t). \tag{8.24}$$

The consumer maximizes (8.22) subject to (8.24) and S_0. Introducing the costate variable (shadow price of capital stock) $v(t)e^{-\theta t}$, we obtain the necessary conditions for optimality as follows:

$$C_1(t) = \left(\frac{1}{v(t)}\right)\left[\frac{\mu}{\delta + (\mu - \delta)e^{-\mu t}}\right] \tag{8.25}$$

$$C_{N+1}(t) = \int_0^t \lambda N e^{-\lambda \tau}(1 - e^{-\lambda \tau})^{N-1}\left(\frac{1}{v(t)}\right)\left[\frac{\mu}{\delta + (\mu - \delta)e^{-\mu(t-\tau)}}\right]d\tau$$

$$\text{for } N \geq 1 \quad (8.26)$$

$$\frac{\dot{v}(t)}{v(t)} = \theta - \rho_t \tag{8.27}$$

and

$$\lim_{t\to\infty} v(t)e^{-\theta t}S(t) = 0. \tag{8.28}$$

Because $S(t)$ grows asymptotically at the rate of $g(t)$ and $v(t)$ satisfies (8.27), the transversality condition (8.28) is equivalent to

$$\lim_{t\to\infty} \exp\left\{-\int_0^t (\rho_\tau - g_\tau)d\tau\right\} = 0. \tag{8.29}$$

Condition (8.29) is satisfied when the optimal solution (8.20) exists for investment decisions.

From (8.25) and (8.26), we obtain

$$C(t) = \sum_{j=1}^{\infty} C_j(t) = \left(\frac{1}{v(t)}\right)\left\{\frac{\mu}{\delta + (\mu - \delta)e^{-\mu t}}\right.$$

$$\left. + \sum_{N=1}^{\infty} \int_0^t \lambda N e^{-\lambda \tau}(1 - e^{-\lambda \tau})^{N-1}\left[\frac{\mu}{\delta + (\mu - \delta)e^{-\mu(t-\tau)}}\right]d\tau\right\} \tag{8.30}$$

for total consumption $C(t)$ at time t. Thanks to (8.11), we can rewrite (8.30) as

$$C(t) = \frac{Y(t)}{v(t)}. \tag{8.31}$$

$1/v(t)$ is simply the average propensity to consume.

Given (8.27), equation (8.31) is equivalent to

$$\theta - g_t + \frac{\dot{C}(t)}{C(t)} = \rho_t \qquad (8.32)$$

Equation (8.32) is nothing but the Euler equation or the Keynes/Ramsey rule. It requires that for optimality, the marginal rate of substitution defined by the left-hand side of equation (8.32) must be equal to the interest rate ρ. The optimal saving decisions satisfy (8.32).

As we have already seen, the optimal investment decisions satisfy (8.20). Note that both the optimal saving and investment decisions, (8.32) and (8.20), depend on the time paths of the growth rate of Y, g_t, and the interest rate ρ_t. The interest rate ρ_t, the growth rate of capital z_t, and the capacity utilization a_t are simultaneously determined by (8.19), (8.20), and (8.32) in such a way that g_t satisfies (8.13) in Section 8.3.

The goods market equilibrium, namely

$$Y = C + I = \sum_i C_i + \phi(z)K + d(a)K, \qquad (8.33)$$

is, as usual, assured by the appropriate change in the interest rate. Formally, the time path of this equilibrium interest rate ρ can be found by considering the "command economy" corresponding to the market economy. Maximize the consumer's utility (8.22) under the constraint (8.19) and (8.33). The time path of Y_t is given by (8.13) and sets a constraint for this problem. Call the Lagrange multiplier for the goods market equilibrium constraint (8.33) $\omega_t e^{-\theta t}$. Then

$$\rho_t = \theta - \left(\frac{\dot{\omega}}{\omega}\right)$$

is the equilibrium interest rate.

In this model, the capacity utilization rate a, and accordingly, the profit rate $r(a) = d'(a)a - d(a)$ are endogenously determined. The higher the growth rate determined by δ, μ and λ, the higher the profit rate r. This can be seen most clearly for the steady state. In the steady state, $\dot{C}/C$ is g, and the interest rate ρ becomes equal to the consumer's discount rate θ. The relation between the growth rate g and the profit rate r in this case is shown in Figure 8.6. When the strength of innovations to create new sectors/goods λ gets higher, the steady-state growth rate becomes higher. Higher investment is induced by higher profit which is in turn generated by the higher capacity utilization rate.

To equilibrate the goods market, higher investment (or a shift up of the investment function) generated by high growth of demand brings about a high interest rate. The high interest rate in turn makes the consumer find high growth of consumption desirable (the Euler equation). It accordingly generates high saving which must be equal to investment in equilibrium. The ultimate factor to determine the growth rate is the vigor of demand characterized by three parameters μ, δ and λ.

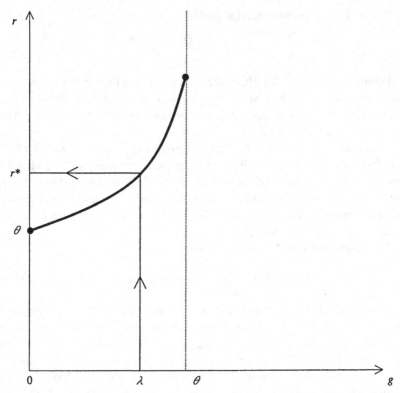

Figure 8.6. The Determination of the Profit Rate r Corresponding to the Steady State Growth Rate λ.
Note: The relation between g and r is given by $r = (\theta - g)\phi'(g) + \phi(g)$. Thus $r^* = (\theta - \lambda)\phi'(\lambda) + \phi(\lambda)$.

In standard growth models, such as Romer (1990), Grossman and Helpman (1991), Aghion and Howitt (1992), and Jones (1995), the rate of innovation raises the long-run growth rate of the economy by increasing TFP. In the present model, the rate of innovation λ raises the growth rate of the economy by increasing aggregate demand. Technical progress elicits investment of the demand-constrained firm both by increasing the number of goods produced over time, and transitionally, by reducing the average age of products in the market, favoring products on faster growth segments of their demand life cycles.

Diffusion of Final Goods among Different Households. The Ramsey model is the most standard approach in macroeconomics. However, as argued in Chapter 1, it is a bad idea to use the Ramsey model as a descriptive model. The main theme of this book is that the model built on the representative agent is not a good framework for analyzing the macroeconomy. This basic idea applies to the present case. In many economies, for many periods in history, a declining growth of demand for a particular product has been closely related to diffusion of the product among *different* households. Some households own the product

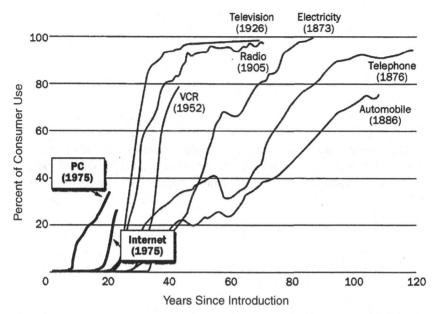

Figure 8.7. Diffusion of Consumer Durables. *Source:* W. Michael Fox and *Forbes* magazine Bill Gates [1999].

whereas others do not. It is particularly true for such consumer durables as televisions, refrigerators, cars, and personal computers. For these consumer durables, it makes more sense to analyze their growth in a model with different households than in a model with the representative consumer. Diffusion of consumer goods among households, in fact, plays an important role in the logistic growth.[5] Bill Gates notes this fact (Figure 8.7; Gates, 1999, 118). In this section, we consider such a model.

Suppose there are M households in the economy. Without loss of generality, we can assume that M is equal to μ/δ. Households are indexed by i $(i = 1, 2, \ldots, M = \mu/\delta)$. We define $f_{iN}(t)$ functions:

$f_{iN}(t) =$ 1 if household i purchases the Nth product at time t.

$f_{iN}(t) =$ 0 if household i does not purchase the Nth product at time t.

We assume that the number of households which consume the Nth product at time t, $m_N(t)$, follows a birth and death process with the birth rate μ and the death rate δm_N. Note the following relation:

$$\sum_{i=1}^{M} f_{iN}(t) = m_N(t). \tag{8.34}$$

---

[5] Yoshikawa (1995) explains the high growth of the Japanese economy during the 1950s and 60s emphasizing diffusion of consumer durables. We will briefly explain it later.

This process leads us to the logistic equation for the expected value of $m_N(t)$, $\hat{m}_N(t)$. Thus if the N-th product emerged at τ, $\hat{m}_N(t)$ satisfies the following equation:

$$\hat{m}_N(t) = \frac{\mu}{(\delta + (\mu - \delta)e^{-\mu(t-\tau)})} \qquad \text{for each } N. \qquad (8.35)$$

The (expected) diffusion rate or the percentage of households which consume the Nth product is $\hat{m}_N(t)/M$.

For simplicity we assume that a household purchases $1 - s$ unit of any final product if it consumes this product. s is the saving rate. As in Solow (1956), the present analysis abstracts from the determination of s. The saving rate is assumed to be common for all the households ($i = 1, 2, \ldots, M$), and depends positively on the interest rate ρ_t. It also depends on time t. Note that the consumption of a final good by each household is constant. This assumption seems to hold, as an approximation, for many consumer durables.

Then, with the expected income of household i, $I_i(t)$, the budget constraint for household i at time t becomes

$$I_i(t) = \sum_{N=1}^{\infty} \int_0^t \lambda N e^{-\lambda\tau}(1 - e^{-\lambda\tau})^{N-1}(1 - s) f_{iN+1}(t)d\tau$$

$$+ (1 - s) f_{i1}(t) + s I_i(t)$$

$$= \sum_{N=1}^{\infty} \int_0^t \lambda N e^{-\lambda\tau}(1 - e^{-\lambda\tau})^{N-1} f_{iN+1}(t)d\tau + f_{i1}(t). \qquad (8.36)$$

Thanks to (8.34) and (8.35), incomes of all the households (8.36) sum up to GDP, $Y(t)$:

$$\sum_{i=1}^{M} I_i(t) = \sum_{N=1}^{\infty} \int_0^t \lambda N e^{-\lambda\tau}(1 - e^{-\lambda\tau})^{N-1} \sum_{i=1}^{M} f_{iN+1}(t)d\tau + \sum_{i=1}^{M} f_{i1}(t)$$

$$= \sum_{N=1}^{\infty} \int_0^t \lambda N e^{-\lambda\tau}(1 - e^{-\lambda\tau})^{N-1} \frac{\mu}{(\delta + (\mu - \delta)e^{-\mu(t-\tau)})}d\tau$$

$$+ \frac{\mu}{(\delta + (\mu - \delta)e^{-\mu t})}$$

$$= Y(t).$$

The goods market equilibrium is then

$$s(\rho_t) = \frac{\varphi(z_t) K_t + d(a_t) K_t}{Y_t} = \frac{\varphi(z_t) + d(a_t)}{a_t}. \qquad (8.37)$$

Just as in the Ramsey model, the interest rate ρ_t, the growth rate of capital z_t, and the capacity utilization rate a_t are simultaneously determined by equations

(8.19), (8.20), and (8.37) in such a way that g_t satisfies equation (8.13) in Section 8.3. In the steady state, we obtain

$$s(\rho^*) = \frac{\varphi(\lambda) + d(a)^*}{a^*}$$

and

$$\varphi'(\lambda) = \frac{r(a^*) - \varphi(\lambda)}{\rho^* - \lambda}.$$

The steady-state growth rate is λ. The steady-state values of the interest rate ρ^* and capacity utilization rate a^* are different from those of the Ramsey model. The effects of an increase in λ on the equilibrium interest rate and the capacity utilization rate are, however, qualitatively the same as in the Ramsey model provided that the interest elasticity of the saving rate is high enough.

In the Ramsey model with the representative consumer, the S-shaped growth of each product derives directly from the assumption (8.23) that the marginal utility coming from consumption of a particular final good depends on how long a time has passed since the good first emerged. In the second model, a household is assumed to purchase a given unit of each product. The S-shaped growth derives from diffusion of each product among different households. In both cases, growth of demand induces capital accumulation by the demand-constrained firm, and thereby economic growth. Growth, on the other hand, creates higher income which makes more households able to purchase goods. Equation (8.36) defines income distribution which generates diffusion of final goods among households. Because the amount of a final good which each household purchases is bounded, growth of production of an individual good necessarily decelerates parallel to diffusion of the good among households. Creation of wholly new goods/sectors is the ultimate factor to sustain growth in such an economy. In the next section, we will explain that diffusion of consumer durables played a very important role in Japan's postwar economic growth.

8.5. Discussion

In the standard literature, the fundamental factor restraining economic growth is diminishing returns to capital in production or R&D technology. We presented a model in which the factor restraining growth was saturation of demand. Our analysis began with a common observation that for individual products/industries, there was a history of logistic development with initial acceleration and eventual retardation of growth. Taking this as a stylized fact, we presented a formal model of growth consistent with this important fact.

This model provides new perspectives to several important problems addressed by the economics of growth. The first new perspective pertains to out-of-steady-state dynamics. Despite the controversy surrounding conditional convergence, for many economies, and for advanced economies in particular, we observe the eventual deceleration of growth rates. In the Solow model, diminishing returns to capital in production is the factor to bring about slower growth. In the R&D-based models, it is diminishing returns in R&D. Thus, in both approaches, diminishing returns in technology is the factor that brings about a slowing of economic growth. In contrast, in our model, saturation of demand (μ and δ) is the factor that leads the economy to slower growth.

The second new perspective relates to the nature of technical progress or innovations. In the standard analysis, technical progress brings about higher value added given the same level of inputs. It is basically equivalent to an upward shift of the production function. The so called product variety, quality ladder, or creative destruction model (e.g., Grossman and Helpman, 1991; Caballero and Jaffe, 1993) using the Dixit/Stiglitz production/utility function, successfully endogenizes this kind of technical progress. Empirically, technical progress has been measured by growth accounting as TFP (total factor productivity).

In the model presented here, the aggregate production function is $Y = AK$. Because A is constant, there is no TFP growth; for the economy to grow, capital must accumulate. However, saturation of demand constrains capital accumulation and leads the economy to deceleration of growth. Innovation or technical progress in this model creates a major new product or industry which commands high growth of demand and thereby elicits capital accumulation and so sustains economic growth. In his famous book, Schumpeter (1934) distinguishes five types of *innovations*: (1) the introduction of a new good, (2) the introduction of a new production method, (3) the opening of a new market, (4) the conquest of a new source of supply of raw materials, and (5) the new organization of industry. His first and third types of innovations as an engine for growth seem to be most naturally interpreted in terms of the kind of model presented here.

The distinction between the conventional TFP and demand-creating technical progress is not only theoretically important but is also empirically relevant. Young (1995), for example, in his careful study of growth accounting, demonstrates that TFP growth in the newly industrializing countries (NICs) of East Asia (e.g., Hong Kong, Singapore, South Korea, and Taiwan) is not extraordinarily high, but actually comparable to those in other countries. The very high average growth rate (8–10%) of East Asian NICs for such a long period as 25 years must be, therefore, explained by extraordinary injection of capital and labor rather than extraordinary TFP growth. These facts have become widely known throughout the world via Krugman's (1994) famous article "The Myth of Asia's Miracle."

The basic question remains: Why did the economy grow so fast in these countries? The analysis of this paper suggests that in these countries, new sectors that command high growth of demand vigorously emerged (high μ/δ and λ). TFP growth may not be extraordinarily high, but it does not necessarily mean there is an absence of demand-creating innovations. Young, in fact, reports that in East Asian NIEs the industrial structure has drastically changed. A change in the industrial structure in the course of economic growth is likely to reflect demand-creating innovations which are conceptually different from TFP. To the extent that exports happen to have commanded high growth (i.e., high μ/δ), we can easily understand that the high growth of East Asian NIEs often looked to be export-led. Nelson and Pack (1999) make a similar argument emphasizing the importance of productive assimilation for the success of Asian NIEs. Productive assimilation is related to λ in our model.[6]

To repeat, our analysis shows that technical progress has a different aspect from the conventional TFP represents, namely demand creation, and that it is demand creation that sustains economic growth. It may shed light not only on "the Asian Miracle" but also on the high growth of the American economy during the 1990s in which, despite remarkable progress in information technology (IT), TFP growth was not so high as one might expect at least until the late 1990s (Gordon, 1999). Advancement of information technology may not only increase productivity on the supply side, but also create new markets and mediate demand-led growth.

Demand-creating technical progress is most likely to entail changes in industrial structure. Yoshikawa and Matsumoto (2001) indeed demonstrate that changes in industrial structure and economic growth are positively related for Japan. To see this, we need a measure of changes in industrial structure, of course. Suppose the economy consists of n sectors, and that the share of the ith sector at time t is w_i^t. Then our measure of changes in industrial structure from t_1 to t_2, σ, is

$$\sigma = \frac{\sqrt{\sum_{i=1}^{n} \left(w_i^{t_2} - w_i^{t_1} \right)^2}}{T} \qquad \text{where } T = t_2 - t_1.$$

The shares of industries w_i sum to one, and, therefore, a vector of sectoral shares in a certain period can be represented by a point on the $n - 1$ dimensional simplex. This measure σ is nothing but a distance between two points on this simplex. σ so defined rises when some industries declined, and, therefore, is not necessarily positively correlated with the growth rate. However, to the extent that changes in industrial structure are brought about by innovations and births of growing sectors, the positive correlation between σ and the growth rate is expected. Figure 8.8 shows σ and the growth rate of real GDP ρ for Japan. Here σ is calculated by rolling for the ten year period, namely for 1955–65, 1956–66, and so on up to 1988–98. The correlation of σ with the growth rate is 0.84. A piece of evidence shown in Figure 8.8 suggests that changes in industrial structure

---

[6] Nelson and Pack (1999) discuss only the general importance of productive assimilation. From the perspective of the present paper, Asian NIEs could grow rapidly because they succeeded in productive assimilation in those sectors where growth of demand was very high.

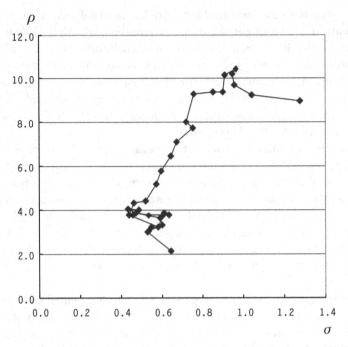

Figure 8.8. σ (Measure of Changes in Industrial Structure) (Ten-Year Case) and ρ, (GDP Average Growth Rate), Japan.
Note: see text for definitions of ρ and σ.

accompany growth. And given the law of demand saturation, it, in turn, suggests the importance of *demand-creating innovations.*

Our model also provides different policy implications than the standard R&D-based growth models. The standard literature amply demonstrates the importance of R&D. However, these models ignore differences in the age of products/industries. In our model, R&D in the mature product/industry does not promote economic growth *not* because efficiency in R&D diminished but primarily because demand approached saturation. Any policy to promote growth must seriously consider the age of the product or the prospect of demand.

The ultimate factor in sustaining growth λ which creates wholly new products/industries would depend, not only on profit-motivated R&D, but also heavily on basic scientific research. In fact, λ is not necessarily confined to supply-side factors. Growth and saturation of demand often parallel diffusion among different households, as we discussed in the second model in Section 4.2. Thus appropriate income distribution policy which triggers diffusion of major product can be taken as a demand-creating innovation. This point may be important for growth of developing countries. It was certainly important in the postwar Japanese growth during the 1950s and 60s.

We have argued that even the long-run growth is strongly conditioned by demand. However, we can not expect that there is any general answer to the question of how growth is conditioned by demand. The process of growth is historical, and therefore, to gain insight into the pattern of growth, historical case study is necessary (Rostow, 1960). Drawing on Yoshikawa (1995), we shall briefly explain the rapid economic growth of the Japanese economy during the 1950s and 60s, and how economic growth was conditioned by demand in this particular episode.

The Postwar Japanese Experience: A Case Study

The Japanese economy enjoyed an average of 10 percent growth for almost two decades beginning in the mid-1950s. Several factors are believed to have contributed to this growth. The abundance of importable foreign technology is often mentioned as one such factor. However, it is not obvious that the stock of available foreign technology was much greater in the 1950s and 1960s than in the 1920s and 1930s, or for that matter in the nineteenth century. One might plausibly expect that such a stock was greatest when Japan opened its doors to the West in the late nineteenth century. Yet the growth rate during the 1950s and 1960s was much higher than that in the prewar period.

A sharp decline in natural resource costs is also often mentioned. Technical progress in marine transportation is believed to have contributed to this effect. A sharp decline in marine transport costs in the postwar era has made natural resources commodities, rather than part of the "factor endowment" of individual countries. This has naturally given leverage to the resource-poor Japanese economy. Total factor productivity in the industry, in fact, grew at the annual rate of 10 percent in the postwar era as against 2–3 percent in the prewar period. Wright (1990) suggests that the origin of U.S. industrial success during 1879–1940 lay in the country's resource abundance. It should not be surprising, then, that resource-poor Japan benefited greatly from the postwar changes which made natural resources easily tradable commodities.

Granted that these factors are very important, we suggest that (1) internal migration and accompanying household formation, and (2) diffusion of consumer durables, namely "catch up of demand," played a particularly important role in the process of rapid economic growth.

Recall that the Japanese economy in the 1950s and 1960s was a two-sector economy consisting of a rural agricultural sector and an urban manufacturing sector. In 1950, nearly half of the country's total labor force was still engaged in agriculture. Population continuously flowed from the former sector into the latter in the process of economic growth (Figure 8.9). The dual structure of the economy enabled the manufacturing sector to hire enough labor at a level of real wages that, determined in the agricultural sector by "disguised" unemployment, were lower than the marginal product in the industrial sector. Growth of the manufacturing sector therefore entailed high profits rather than an increase in real wages. The high profits, in turn, were supposed to induce high investment.

All this is, of course, what Lewis (1954) describes as a typical process of growth in an underdeveloped dual economy. Indeed, the Lewisian model has

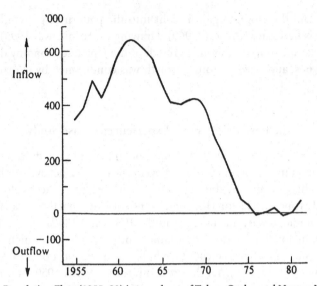

Figure 8.9. Population Flow (1955–80) into and out of Tokyo, Osaka, and Nagoya Metopolitan Area.
Source: Annual Report on Internal Migration, Statistical Bureau, Management and Coordination Agency.

been successfully applied to the century-long development of the Japanese economy by a number of economists (see Ohkawa and Rosovsky, 1973; Minami, 1968; Inada, Sekiguchi, and Shoda, 1992). In the Lewisian model, however, population flow between two sectors is taken to be solely a result of the growth of the modern manufacturing sector. Minami (1968) and others demonstrate that internal migration was in fact quite sensitive to the growth of the manufacturing sector; More people left rural agricultural areas for urban industrial cities in booms and vice versa. Yearly fluctuations in population flow was therefore a *result* of industrial growth. In the Lewisian model, the key factor behind this industrial growth is low real wages made possible by the existence of disguised unemployment in the agricultural sector. In contrast to the Lewisian model, in the case of the *postwar* Japanese economic growth (1955–70), population flow between the two sectors was in fact the major factor in generating high demand for products of the industrial sector. In our view, population flow was a *cause* as well as a result of economic growth.

According to the Lewisian theory, population is supposed to flow continuously from the rural agricultural sector to the urban industrial sector, as actually happened in Japan. Among Asian developing countries, however, this Lewisian population flow occurred to a substantial extent only in a few NIEs.[7] The basic problem of the theory is that the growth of a modern industrial sector is sustained by high profits, which are guaranteed by repressed real wages, whereas demand for products is assumed to emerge automatically as production grows.

[7]   The Lewisian population flow has been now happening in China since the late 1990s.

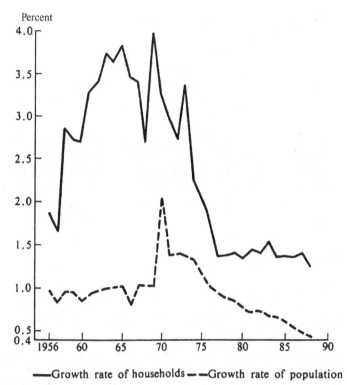

—Growth rate of households — —Growth rate of population

Figure 8.10. Growth Rate of Households and Population, 1956–90.
Note: The figure for 1970 is an outlier; Okinawa prefecture was returned to Japan by the United States in 1970.

In reality, demand does not emerge automatically. Demand is precisely the factor that divides prewar and postwar Japan.

The postwar Japanese growth during the period 1955–70 was led by domestic demand. For example, the contribution of net export to growth was on average –0.2 percent for the high-growth period.[8] In the process of domestic demand-led growth, population flow and household formation played a crucial role. Because of the large-scale population flows, *household formation* dramatically accelerated during the period of high economic growth, 1955–70 (Figure 8.10). We underline the fact that in this period the growth rate of households forms a hump shape at a high-level parallel to the growth of real GDP, while the growth rate of population was quite stable at a much lower level of about 1 percent. Population growth or the growth of the labor force, which plays such an important role in the standard growth theory, has little explanatory power for the high growth of the Japanese economy during the 1950s and 60s.

As one might expect, traditional three-generation-merged households hardly increased during this period. Instead, the "core" households consisting of a

---

[8] This is reflected in another fact that Japan's current account was basically in balance during the 1950s and 60s.

married couple, possibly with unmarried children, and/or an unmarried adult, dramatically increased, particularly in urban industrial areas. Where three generations of family members kept a traditional single household in rural villages, they needed only one of each consumer durable such as refrigerator, television set, washing machine, and car. But when young people giving up agriculture left their rural villages for urban industrial areas, they formed new, separate households. This additional household formation necessarily generated additional demand for houses, consumer durables and electricity. In this way, population flow sustained high domestic demand in the period of high economic growth, 1955–70.

Along with the creation of a large number of households, the high-growth period also saw the *diffusion process* of newly available consumer durables; Here, we can usefully recall S-shaped curves in Figure 8.3. Now, the diffusion of consumer durables was facilitated by a steady decline in prices of those products on the one hand, and an increase in income on the other. Electric washing machines, for example, first appeared in the Japanese market in 1949. At the time, a machine cost ¥54,000 while the average annual labor income was about ¥50,000. Understandably, only 20 machines per month were sold! By 1955, however, only six years later, the price of a washing machine had fallen to ¥20,000 while the average annual income had risen to above ¥200,000. By then, about a third of households could afford to own a washing machine. The same story holds for other consumer durables. Because urban cities led this diffusion process, urbanization not only created new households but also sustained high demand for consumer durables. This is precisely the story that the second diffusion model, not the Ramsey model, tells us. By the end of the 1960, however, most of the then-available consumer durables were facing a saturation of the Japanese domestic market.

This whole process of domestic-demand-led high economic growth (1955–70) is schematically summarized in Figure 8.11. Channels 1 and 2 in the diagram are easily recognized: capital accumulation in the industrial sector, raising labor demand, brings about population flow from rural agricultural areas to urban cities. In addition to these well-recognized channels, we must emphasize the oft-neglected and yet very important fact that such population flow in turn, with its creation of new households and raising demand for consumer durables and electricity, ultimately sustained profitability of investment in manufacturing industry (channels 3, 4, 5). We must stress that the role of newly available consumer durables was not confined to a demand for those products themselves. Through an input–output interrelationship, they augmented demand for intermediate goods such as steel and electricity, and accordingly high investment in those sectors.

In this virtuous circle for high economic growth, low real wages were not as instrumental as Lewis (1954) emphasized. Rather, it was growth in domestic demand that sustained profitability of investment. And to such growth a steady rise in real wages, rather than low repressed wages, is a contributing factor. In fact, in the prewar period, except for 1920–21 and 1929-30, real wages saw little increase, while in the postwar period they enjoyed steady growth. A steady rise in

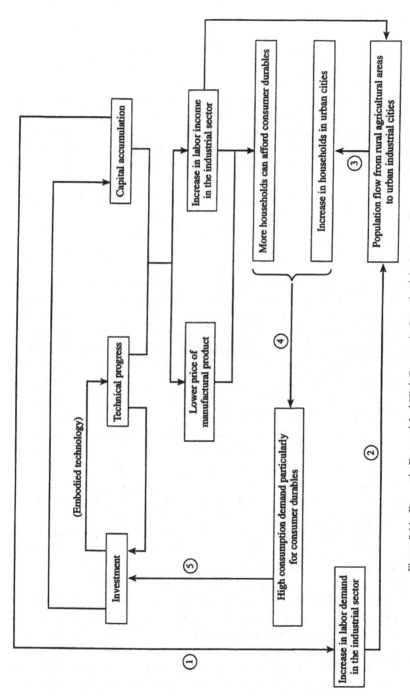

Figure 8.11. Domestic-Demand-Led High Economic Growth of the Japanese Economy, 1955–70.

real wages sustained effective demand for the postwar Japanese economy because the key product was consumer durables which, not yet being internationally competitive, had to find a domestic market.

The domestic-demand-led virtuous circle for economic growth based on the Lewisian dual structure is not unique to the postwar Japanese economy. Kindleberger (1967, 1989), for example, discusses the postwar growth of the European economy in a Lewisian model. In any case, in the Japanese economy during 1955–70, population flows and the consequent household formation, by diffusing newly available consumer durables, continuously stimulated economy-wide investment demand.

The situation changed dramatically around 1970. By then the pool of the so-called disguisedly unemployed in the agricultural sector had been largely exhausted. Therefore, the population flow from the rural sector and the associated urban household formation both sharply decelerated. At the same time, the then available consumer durables saw saturation in the domestic market. For these reasons, the domestic-demand-led virtuous circle for high economy growth was broken. We believe that this structural change occurred around 1970, *a few years in advance of the first oil embargo in 1973.*

Some economists such as Bruno and Sachs (1985) attribute a fall in the rate of economic growth in the 1970s ultimately to the oil shock in 1973. However, they cannot explain why the second oil shock, which occurred in 1979, did not bring about a similar fall in the rate of economic growth; the average growth rates of real GDP for 1973–80 and 1981–90 were 4.1 percent and 4.2 percent, respectively. During the first oil crisis (1973–74) the oil price quadrupled, while in the second oil crisis (1979–80) it only doubled; so it might be argued that the first oil crisis hit the Japanese economy harder than the second one. But transfer payments to OPEC necessitated by an increase in the oil price, when seen as relative to GDP, were actually comparable during two oil crises: 3.8 percent and 4.1 percent, respectively. The supply-side analyses that attribute a fall in the rate of economic growth to the first oil crisis are therefore inconsistent with the fact that the second oil crisis did not entail a similar fall in the growth rate. Nor can they explain why the growth rate of the oil-importing South Korean economy fell so sharply during the second oil crisis while the effect of the first oil crisis was relatively small there, just the opposite of the Japanese case. Yoshikawa (1995, Chapter 4) shows that demand is, in fact, an indispensable part of any reasonable explanation of the oil crises in the 1970s.

We do not mean to argue that the oil crisis did not affect the supply side of the Japanese economy at all, but we do maintain that a permanent fall in the rate of economic growth beginning in the early 1970s was caused by a *domestic structural change*, as explained earlier, rather than by the first oil crisis. In this way, demand played a central role in the high economic growth of the Japanese economy and its end. We believe that this story of the Japanese economy can be easily understood by the growth model explained in this chapter. At the same time, the postwar Japanese experience shows that economic growth is a historical phenomenon in that no model can encompass whole history; in particular how demand conditions economic growth must be studied case by case. ■

The relation between demand and growth is an unresolved problem. For example, Solow (1997) emphasizes the importance of "the medium-run" analysis as a challenge to modern macroeconomics:

> One major weakness in the core of macroeconomics as I have represented it is the lack of real coupling between the short-run picture and the long-run picture. Since the long-run and the short-run merge into one another, one feels they cannot be completely independent. There are some obvious, perfunctory connections: every year's realized investment gets incorporated in the long-run model. That is obvious. A more interesting question is whether a major episode in the growth of potential output can be driven from the demand side. (Solow, 1997, 231–232)

That is, the integration of the Keynes's principle of effective demand for the short run and growth theory for the long run remains a central theme in macroeconomics. Our model may provide a constructive step toward solving this problem.

Finally, in the model presented here, to make our analysis tractable, we inevitably made an unrealistic assumption that μ, δ, and λ were constant. We hope that the assumption is justified for the purpose of studying economic growth. However, in the short/medium run, μ, δ, and λ would all fluctuate. Giving the μ, δ, and λ shocks to the model economy, as is done in the standard RBC literature, one would be able to generate fluctuations of the growth rate. Such simulation exercises with demand shocks might generate a more realistic explanation of short-run fluctuations than those based on TFP shocks.

Appendix 8.1

Equation (8.7) in the text can be solved in the following way. First we define the generating function $G(z, t)$ as

$$G(z, t) = \sum_{n=N_0}^{\infty} z^n Q(n, t).$$

Multiplying (8.7) by z^n, and taking its sum over $n = N_0, N_0 + 1, \ldots$, we obtain the partial differential equation:

$$\frac{\partial G(z, t)}{\partial t} = \lambda z(z - 1)\frac{\partial(G, t)}{\partial z} \tag{8.38}$$

with the initial condition

$$G(z, 0) = z^{N_0}. \tag{8.39}$$

To solve this partial differential equation, we introduce the artificial variable called s for which the following ordinary differential equations hold.

$$\frac{dt}{ds} = 1 \tag{8.40}$$

$$\frac{dz}{ds} = -\lambda z(z - 1). \tag{8.41}$$

With the initial condition $(s, t) = (0, 0)$, (8.40) can be solved immediately to give

$$t = s.$$

Similarly, with the initial condition $(s, z) = (0, m)$, (8.41) can be solved to give

$$\lambda s = \log\left(\frac{z}{z-1}\right)\left(\frac{m-1}{m}\right). \tag{8.42}$$

Since $s = t$, from (8.42) we obtain

$$m = \frac{e^{-\lambda t}z}{[1 - (1 - e^{-\lambda t})z]}. \tag{8.43}$$

On the other hand, from (8.38), (8.40) and (8.41) we know that $G(z(s), t(s))$ satisfies

$$\frac{dG}{ds} = \frac{\partial G}{\partial z} \cdot \frac{dz}{ds} + \frac{\partial G}{\partial t} \cdot \frac{dt}{ds}$$

$$= -\lambda z(z-1)\frac{\partial G}{\partial z} + \frac{\partial G}{\partial t} = 0,$$

and therefore that G as a function of s is constant. Since z is m when s is zero, from (8.39) we find that this constant is m^{N_0}. Using (8.43), we see that $G(z, t)$ is

$$G(z, t) = \frac{e^{-\lambda N_0 t}z^{N_0}}{[1 - (1 - e^{-\lambda t})z]^{N_0}}. \tag{8.44}$$

The denominator of (8.44) can be expanded as

$$\frac{1}{[1 - (1 - e^{-\lambda t})z]^{N_0}} = \sum_{\ell=0}^{\infty}\binom{-N_0}{\ell}(-1)^{\ell}(1 - e^{-\lambda t})^{\ell}z^{\ell}$$

$$= \sum_{\ell=0}^{\infty}\binom{N_0+\ell-1}{\ell}(1 - e^{-\lambda t})^{\ell}z^{\ell}.$$

Thus

$$G(z, t) = \sum_{\ell=N_0}^{\infty}\binom{\ell-1}{\ell-N_0}e^{-\lambda N_0 t}(1 - e^{-\lambda t})^{\ell-N_0}z^{\ell}. \tag{8.45}$$

The probability that the number of final goods at t is N, $Q(N, t)$ is the coefficient of z^N of this generating function (8.45), and is given by

$$Q(N, t) = \binom{N-1}{N-N_0}e^{-\lambda N_0 t}(1 - e^{-\lambda t})^{N-N_0}.$$

Without loss of generality, we can take N_0 as 1. Then $Q(N, t)$ becomes

$$Q(N, t) = e^{-\lambda t}(1 - e^{-\lambda t})^{N-1}.$$

This is equation (8.8) in the main text, and is called the negative binominal distribution.

9

The Types of Investors and Volatility in Financial Markets: Analyzing Clusters of Heterogeneous Agents

Thoughtout this book, we have focused on the real economy. The methods explained in Chapter 2 are extremely useful, not only for analyzing the real economy, but for analyzing financial markets. In this chapter, we analyze the combinatorial problem that is so crucial in a market with many heterogeneous investors. It has important implications for volatility in the financial market.

9.1. Introduction

We have repeated time and again that the behavior of macroeconomic variables emerges as an outcome of aggregation of micro behavior of a large number of interacting agents. Financial markets are no exception. In fact, there has been a veritable explosion of empirical and simulation studies of financial markets – prices, returns, or volumes of transactions – based on the explicit assumption of heterogeneous investors (see Gopikrishnan et al., 1998; Lux and Marchesi, 1999; Mantegna and Stanley, 1994; Takayasu and Sato, 1997). Reported simulation studies of financial markets by multiagent models apparently mimic well many, if not all aspects of the actual behavior of asset returns (see Lux and Marchesi, 1999).

Investors in the markets employ various strategies or trading rules. For convenience, we identify investors with the strategies or the rules they employ, and say that investors of the same type form a *group* or *cluster*. Clusters evolve over time as agents switch their decision rules or behavioral patterns in response to changing economic environments. They also change as agents enter or exit. It is impossible to say in advance how many clusters will be present at any given time. We can only sample some numbers of agents and count the number of different strategies being used at a particular time. There can be, in principle, infintely many potential strategies. For example, random combinations of two basic algorithms in different proportions produce different strategies, because they will have different expected performance and variances or risk characteristics. In such a case, there are infinitely many strategies.

Moreover, new decision or trading rules will be continuously invented over time. Knowing the types of agents present in market is analogous to or formally identical with the so-called *sampling of species problem* faced by statisticians concerned with the evolution of biological species (see Zabell, 1992). The purpose of this chapter is to apply such mathematical theory to the interactive agent problem in financial markets. We first describe a jump Markov process to examine the distribution of the sizes of clusters of agents by strategy types.

To analyze the behavior of such markets, we consider *order statistics* of shares by types. That is, we derive distributions of the sizes of the clusters in non-increasing order. If the size distributions are such that most probabilities are concentrated on the first few order statistics, we can reasonably concentrate on the first several largest clusters or groupings of agents. Examining a few such large clusters will give us the approximate behavior of markets as a whole. This is especially true when agents/investors are positively correlated.

We are interested in situations in which a few of the large fractions of the types of agents, whatever the types may be, dominate and approximately determine the market excess demand for the stocks. The joint distribution for the largest r clusters of the agents classified by their trading rules is derived. It is used to characterize the market excess demand, and the price movements. In our analysis, r is taken to be two.[1] We then show in a model in which there are two types of investors, one "fundamentalist" and the other "chartist," the distribution of stock prices becomes a *power law*.

9.2. Cluster Formation in Financial Markets

In this section, we first explain the mathematical method which is outlined in Section 2.2 of Chapter 2. Using this method, we demonstrate that under certain conditions, a relatively small number, say two or three, of types of agents emerge by way of their stochastic interactions.

Distribution of Agent Types

We have two alternative characterizations of *state* of the market. We begin with the more familiar of the two. It is the *empirical distribution* mentioned in Chapter 2. The other is based on the *partition vector* introduced in Section 2.2. Here, we give an example of jump Markov process which naturally leads to the second method.

Suppose there are a large number, K, of agents who participate in a market. For the moment suppose that the value of K is known. Then, the vector $\mathbf{n} = (n_1, n_2, \ldots, n_K)$ describes how n agents are distributed over K types,

---

[1] Our approach provides a stochastic generalization of a deterministic model of share market such as Day and Huang (1990). Their model is deterministic and discrete-time with two types of agents of fixed number, namely one of each.

$n = n_1 + n_2 + \cdots + n_K$. In this section we use this vector as the state vector. We use jump Markov processes as our model. Jump Markov processes are uniquely determined by transition rates.

We assume an *open model* in which the total number of agents (investors) n is not fixed, but can vary over time[2]; that is, we assume that the total number of agents of all types is random by allowing entries and exits, in addition to changes of types of agents (changes in strategies employed by existing agents).

In our open model, we need to specify entry rates, exit rates and rates of type changes. The transition rate

$$w(\mathbf{n}, \mathbf{n} + \mathbf{e}_k) = c_k(n_k + h_k), \tag{9.1}$$

specifies entry rate to the market by agents of type k, for $n_k \geq 0$, where $\mathbf{e}_k$ is the vector with unit element in the kth position and zero elsewhere. In this specification of the entry transition rate, the term $c_k n_k$ stands for attractiveness of a large group, such as network externality which makes it easier for others to join the cluster or group. The other term, $c_k h_k$, represents new entry to the market which is independent of cluster size, and is similar to the immigration term in the literature of birth-and-death-with-immigration models.

The second transition rate is that of the exit or departure from the market by type j agents:

$$w(\mathbf{n}, \mathbf{n} - \mathbf{e}_j) = d_j n_j, \tag{9.2}$$

for $n_j \geq 1$. Finally, the transition rate of changing types by agents from type j to type k, that is, switching of trading rules from j to k by agents, is

$$w(\mathbf{n}, \mathbf{n} - \mathbf{e}_j + \mathbf{e}_k) = \lambda_{jk} d_j n_j c_k(n_k + h_k). \qquad (j, k = 1, 2, \ldots K) \tag{9.3}$$

We assume that $d_j \geq c_j > 0$, and $h_j > 0$, and

$$\lambda_{jk} = \lambda_{kj} \quad \text{for all } j, k \text{ pairs.}$$

The jump Markov process specified this way has the steady state or stationary distribution

$$\pi(\mathbf{n}) = \prod_{j=1}^{K} \pi_j(n_j), \tag{9.4}$$

where

$$\pi_j(n_j) = (1 - g_j)^{-h_j} \binom{-h_j}{n_j} (-g_j)^{n_j}$$

---

[2] There is an important reason for this assumption. One feature of the actual financial markets, that is not apparently adequately modeled in most existing simulation models, is *volatility*. Volatility of prices (returns) tends to decrease and become too small in a closed model as the total number of agents is increased. One reason for this perplexing result seems to be the use of a closed model in the simulations, that is, the assumption that the total number of agents, n, is held fixed in conducting a simulation.

and

$$g_j = c_j/d_j.$$

These expressions are derived straightforwardly by applying the detailed balance conditions to the transition rates (see Chapter 2 for further explanation). Unfortunately, the model in this form ignores the possibility of *correlation* in agent behavior.[3] To allow for that, we proceed to a method for deriving the size distribution of strategy clusters.

Size Distribution of Strategy Clusters

To consider *correlation* among agents (investors), we now introduce the second state vector, called the *partition vector* explained in Chapter 2. It is defined as

$$\mathbf{a} = (a_1, a_2, \ldots, a_n)$$

where a_k is *the number of types or clusters with exactly k agents*. Consequently we have an inequality

$$\sum_{i=1}^{n} a_i = K_n \leq K. \tag{9.5}$$

Here, K_n is the number of groups or clusters formed by n agents. We also have the following equality:

$$\sum_{i=1}^{n} i a_i = n. \tag{9.6}$$

This is an accounting identity.[4]

To further simplify our presentation, let us suppose that $h_j = h$ and $g_j = g$ for all j. Because there are a_j of the n's which equal j, it follows that

$$\pi(\mathbf{n}) = \binom{-Kh}{n}^{-1} \prod_{j=1}^{K} \binom{-h}{j}^{a_j}. \tag{9.7}$$

Now let K become very large to allow for the possibility of an indefinite number of types. To keep the mean finite we keep h very small, while the product Kh approaches a positive constant θ. We note that the negative binomial expression

$$\binom{-h}{j}^{a_j}$$

---

[3]   Lack of correlation among agent behavior are assumed in other economic models. For example, Sutton (1997) noted this in connection with Gibrat's law.

[4]   The partition vector is originally introduced by Kingman under a different name. We use the name introduced by Zabell because it is appropriate in our applications. The set of agents is partitioned into subsets, each of which is composed of agents of the same type. What we call clusters correspond to the exchangeable random partitions in Kingman (1978a, b).

approaches $(h/j)^{a_j}(-1)^{ja_j}$ as h becomes smaller. Suppose $K_n = k < K$. Then, there are

$$\frac{K!}{a_1!a_2!\cdots a_n!(K-k)!}$$

many ways of realizing the **a** vector. Hence

$$\pi(\mathbf{a}) = \binom{-\theta}{n}(-1)^n\frac{K!}{a_1!a_2!\cdots a_n!(K-k)!}\prod_j\left(\frac{h}{j}\right)^{a_j}. \qquad (9.8)$$

Noting that $K!/(K-k)! \times h^k$ approaches θ^k in the limit of K becoming infinite, and h approaching 0 while keeping Kh at θ

$$\theta = Kh, \qquad (9.9)$$

we arrive at the probability distribution known as *the Ewens distribution,* or *Ewens sampling formula*:[5]

$$\pi_n(\mathbf{a}) = \frac{n!}{\theta^{[n]}}\prod_{j=1}^{n}\left(\frac{\theta}{j}\right)^{a_j}\frac{1}{a_j!}, \qquad (9.10)$$

where

$$\theta^{[n]} := \theta(\theta+1)\cdots(\theta+n-1). \qquad (9.11)$$

This is called an ascending factorial of θ introduced in Chapter 2. We next examine some of its properties following Watterson (1976).

Number of Clusters and Value of θ

The Ewens sampling formula has a single positive-valued parameter θ. Its value influences the number of clusters formed by the agents. Smaller values of θ tends to produce a few large clusters, while larger values produce a large number of clusters of smaller sizes.

To obtain quickly some intuitive understanding of the effects of the value of θ on the cluster size distributions, take $n = 2$ and $a_2 = 1$. All other a's are zero. Then

$$\pi_2(a_1 = 0, a_2 = 1) = \frac{1}{1+\theta}. \qquad (9.12)$$

This shows that two randomly chosen agents are of the same type with high probability when θ is small, and with small probability when θ is large.

---

[5]   This distribution is very well known in the genetics literature; see Ewens (1972), Kingman (1978a, b), or Johnson, Kotz, and Balakrishnan (1997).

     This distribution has been investigated by Arratia, Barbour, and Tavaré (1992), or Hoppe (1987) among several others. Kingman (1980) states that this distribution arises in many applications. There are other ways of deriving this distribution. See Costantini and Garibaldi (1999).

Two extreme situations also reveal connections between the value of θ and the number of clusters. One is the probability of n agents forming a single cluster, given by

$$\pi_n(a_j = 0, 1 \leq j \leq n-1, a_n = 1) = \frac{(n-1)!}{(\theta+1)(\theta+2)\cdots(\theta+n-1)}. \tag{9.13}$$

The other is the probability that n agents form n singletons given by

$$\pi_n(a_1 = n, a_j = 0, j \neq 1) = \frac{\theta^{n-1}}{(\theta+1)(\theta+2)\cdots(\theta+n-1)}. \tag{9.14}$$

With θ much smaller than one, the former probability is approximately equal to 1, whereas the latter is approximately equal to zero. When θ is much larger than n, the latter probability is close to 1.

Recall the definition of the ascending factorials in (9.11). From (9.11), Hoppe (1987) has shown that the probability of n agents forming k clusters is given by

$$\Pr(K_n = k) = \frac{1}{\theta^{[n]}} c(n,k)\theta^k \tag{9.15}$$

where $c(n,k)$ are the polynomial coefficients[6] in the expansion of $\theta^{[n]}$:

$$\theta^{[n]} = \sum_{1}^{n} c(n,k)\theta^k. \tag{9.16}$$

We can use this formula to verify that the expected number of types increases with θ. As θ goes to infinity, the expected number of types approaches n, namely, total fragmentation of agents in the sample by types. For small values of θ, Ewens has shown that the mean number of clusters formed by n agents is

$$E(K_n) = \sum_{j=0}^{n-1} \frac{\theta}{\theta+n-j} \approx 1 + \theta[\log(n-1) + \gamma] \tag{9.17}$$

where $\gamma = .577$ is Euler's constant.

Fractions

The expected value of a_j is given by

$$E(a_j) = \sum_{w(n)} a_j \pi_n(a) = \frac{\theta}{j} \frac{n!}{(n-j)!} \frac{\theta^{[n-j]}}{\theta^{[n]}}, \tag{9.18}$$

---

[6] These are known as the signless Stirling numbers of the first kind. Stirling numbers are discussed in van Lint and Wilson (1992, p. 104) for example. This number is the number of permutations of n symbols with exactly k cycles. In Hoppe, his urn model of the Ewens distribution makes the occurence of this number natural.

where

$$w(n) := \{\mathbf{a} : \sum_j j a_j = n\}. \tag{9.19}$$

A quick way to see this is to recognize that the multiplication of π_n by a_j is equivalent to changing the partition vector from $\mathbf{a}$ to $\mathbf{a}'$ where the jth component is changed from a_j to $a_j - 1$ and the sum $\sum i a_i = n$ is changed to $\sum i a_i' = n - j$, because $a_i' = a_i$, $i \neq j$, but $a_j' = a_j - 1$. We can evaluate the effects of increasing correlations or mutual dependence on the size of $E a_j$, by taking the partial derivative of it with respect to θ: as θ increases, $E a_j$ for j much smaller than n increases linearly in θ.

Watterson (1976) shows how to calculate the variance and covariances by using the relation

$$E\{a_j(a_j - 1)\} = \left(\frac{\theta}{j}\right)^2 \frac{n!}{(n - 2j)!} \frac{\theta^{[n-2j]}}{\theta^{[n]}} \tag{9.20}$$

and for $i \neq j$

$$E\{a_i a_j\} = \frac{\theta^2}{ij} \frac{n!}{(n - i - j)!} \frac{\theta^{[n-i-j]}}{\theta^{[n]}}. \tag{9.21}$$

A characteristic of this distribution is that the standard deviations of a_i's are of the same order of magnitude as the means.

The Expected Share of the Largest Fraction

We define x_i as

$$x_i = \frac{n_i}{n} \quad (i = 1, \dots, K).$$

By definition, we have

$$\sum_{i=1}^{K} x_i = 1. \tag{9.22}$$

We relabel x's with $x_{(i)}$ in decreasing order of size:

$$x_{(1)} \geq x_{(2)} \geq \cdots \geq x_{(K)}.$$

Note that $x_{(i)'}s$ are stochastic variables. We follow Watterson (1976), and Watterson and Guess (1977) to sketch how the probability density function of the largest order statistics of x's, namely $x_{(1)}$, is derived.[7] Following an entirely analogous procedure, we can calculate the joint probability density for r order statistics of the fractions.

---

[7] See Arratia, Barbour, and Tavaré (2003) for rigorous derivation.

Start with a finite K. Without loss of generality, we can assume that x_K is $x_{(1)}$, namely that the share of the Kth type of agents is largest. Thus,

$$0 \le x_i \le x_K = 1 - x_1 - \cdots - x_{K-1} \qquad \text{for } i = 1, \ldots, K - 1.$$

Then, we have

$$
\begin{aligned}
E(x_{(1)}) &= K \int \cdots \int x_K \phi(x_1, \ldots, x_K) dx_1 dx_2 \cdots dx_{K-1} \\
&= K \int \cdots \int (1 - x_1 - x_2 - \cdots - x_{K-1}) \phi(x_1, \ldots, x_K) \\
&\quad \times dx_1 dx_2 \cdots dx_{K-1}.
\end{aligned}
\tag{9.23}
$$

where ϕ is the joint density function of xs, and is the symmetric Dirichlet distribution[8] with parameter ϵ, that is

$$\phi(x_1, x_2, \ldots, x_K) = \frac{\Gamma(K\epsilon)}{(\Gamma(\epsilon))^K} \prod_{i=1}^{K} x_i^{\epsilon - 1}. \tag{9.24}$$

We show how $E\left(x_{(1)}\right)$ is calculated in Appendix 2.

The order statistics of the fractions, $x_{(1)} \ge x_{(2)} \ge \cdots$, are important in markets with highly correlated agents. With θ smaller than 1, the sum of two or three largest fractions can be shown to be nearly one. See Table III of Watterson and Guess (1977) where numerical values of the expected values of the largest fraction is tabulated for different values of θ.[9] For example, with $\theta = .3, .4$, and $.5$, the expected values of the largest fraction are $E(x_{(1)}) = .84, .79$, and $.76$, respectively. They obtained these numbers numerically.

The marginal probabilty density of the share of the largest fraction $x_{(1)} = x$ is

$$f(x) = \theta x^{-1} (1 - x)^{\theta - 1} \qquad (1/2 < x \le 1). \tag{9.25}$$

When $x_{(1)}$ is not greater than $1/2$, the expression is more complex:

$$f(x) = \Gamma(\theta + 1) e^{\gamma \theta} x^{\theta - 2} g(x^{-1} - 1) \qquad (0 \le x \le 1/2), \tag{9.26}$$

where $g(\cdot)$ is the density of the random variable and characterized in terms of its Laplace transform. See Appendix 9.1 for the expression of $g(\cdot)$.

See Appendix 9.1 for the joint probability density for the first r largest fractions. The expression for $r = 2$ is used in Section 9.3. For a mathematically more

---

[8]   The appearance of Dirichlet distributions here may seem arbitrary. Actually there is a deep mathematical relation between the exchangeable random partitions introduced by Kingman (1978a, b) and its representation using the Dirichlet measures, see Zabell (1992). We do not stop here to explain these but go directly to calculate the expected size of the largest fraction goverened by the Dirichlet distribution. Also see Kingman (1993).

[9]   See also the table in Griffiths (2004). The entries in his table is calculated by using the Poisson–Dirichlet distribution. We do not discuss this distribution here, however.

streamlined exposition using Poisson–Dirichlet processes, see Griffiths (2004) or Pitman (2002).

Two Largest Fractions

We can also obtain the lower bound for $E(x_{(2)})$. Let $E(x)$ and $E(y)$ be the expected values of the two laragest fractions, $x = x_{(1)}$ and $y = x_{(2)}$. Watterson (1976) shows that

$$E(y) \geq \theta E(x) B_{1/2}(0, \theta + 1) \approx \theta E(x)(\log 2 - \theta/2) \qquad (9.27)$$

where $B_{1/2}$ is an incomplete beta function, see Abramovitz and Stegun (1968, 26.5). Using this formula, $E(x_{(2)}) \approx .16$ with $\theta = .4$, hence $E(x_{(1)}) + E(x_{(2)}) \approx .95$. Similarly, we have $E(x_{(1)} + x_{(2)}) = .97$, and .92 for $\theta = .3$, and .5, respectively. We may therefore think of θ about 0.4. With $\theta = .4$, the expected numbers of clusters are $E(K_{10}) = 2.1$, $E(K_{100}) = 3.0$, $E(K_{1000}) = 4.0$, $E(K_{10^5}) = 5.8$, and $E(K_{10^7}) = 7.7$. These figures indicate that there are several small fractions in addition to the two large ones when the number of participants are $n \geq 100$.

Watterson also has bounds for other moments of $x = x_{(1)}$ and $y = x_{(2)}$ with k and l nonnegative integers

$$E(x^k y^l) \geq G\theta^2 \Gamma(\theta) e^{\gamma\theta} B_{1/2}(k, l + \theta) \qquad (9.28)$$

with

$$G = E(x)/\theta\Gamma(\theta)e^{\gamma\theta}.$$

Here, $B_{1/2}(a, b)$ is the incomplete beta function. The inequality comes from approximation he used to evaluate some integrals. Abramovitz and Stegun have some series expansions for the incomplete beta functions. Unfortunately the bounds are not sharp enough to give precise bounds on the variances of x. If we use $y \approx .95 - x$, then

$$E(xy)/E(x) = \theta B_{1/2}(1, 1 + \theta) \approx [\theta/(1 + \theta)] \left[1 - \left(\frac{1}{2}\right)^{1+\theta} \right], \qquad (9.29)$$

may be used to estimate the coefficient of variation

$$\sqrt{\text{var}(x_{(1)})}/E(x_{(1)}) \approx .21. \qquad (9.30)$$

In other words, the standard deviation of the largest fraction is about 1/5 of its mean. See Watterson (1976) and Watterson and Guess (1977) for more precise calculation procedures.

The above analysis can be summarized as follows.

Proposition: *If n is large, some small number of configurations account for the majority of possible patterns. That is, a relatively small number of clusters or groups are most likely to be realized or observed.*

This feature has been noticed in other disciplines as well; Mekjian (1991) compares genetic and physics examples. The proposition justifies studying markets with a small number of strategy clusters. In what follows, we focus on the two largest fractions.

9.3. Market Volatility

As we pointed out earlier, in many of existing simulation studies using closed models, the volatility of prices (returns) tends to become too small when the total number of agents (investors) is large. Thus, models with exogenously fixed number of investors often face difficulty in explaining volatility. Here, we show that our model has nonvanishing volatility even if the number of participants goes to infinity.

Market Excess Demand

We first derive an approximate expression for the market excess demands with two large fractions $x = x_{(1)}$ and $y = x_{(2)}$. We have shown above that about 95 percent of the total market participants belong to the two largest subgroups of agents by types. With two largest clusters, there are two regimes; one with a cluster of investors with strategy 1 is the largest share, and the other with a cluster of investors using strategy 2 being the largest. These two alternate assignments contribute to sudden changes of volatility when the strategies are switched.

For convenience, we use the same individual excess demand functions as in Day and Huang (1990). The investors who follows strategy 1 has the excess demand

$$d_1(P) = (u - P)h(P) \tag{9.31}$$

while investors with strategy 2 has the excess demand

$$d_2(P) = -(u - P). \tag{9.32}$$

Here, we have

$$h(P) = [(P - m)(M - P)]^{-1/2}. \tag{9.33}$$

This specification corresponds to the case where $a = b = 1$ in Day and Huang (1990). We can set $u = (M + m)/2$ without loss of generality. In the language of Day and Huang, investors with strategy 1 are the *fundamentalists*, and those with strategy 2 *chartists*. We note that the two excess demands are of opposite sign, that, the two types of agents are on the opposite side of the market.

Let P denote the stock price, and let $d_x(P)$ denote *individual* excess demand of the type that happens to be the largest fraction x. Similarly for $d_y(P)$. Note that x and y are fractions of the investors in the larger and smaller clusters, respectively. We have two regimes, then.

Regime 1: A cluster of investors with strategy 1 has the largest share. Namely, fundamentalists dominate in the market.

Regime 2: A cluster of investors with strategy 2 has the largest share. Namely, chartists dominate in the market.

Market Equilibrium

The market excess demand, D, is then given by summing over individual excess demands

$$\frac{D(P)}{n} = xd_x(P) + yd_y(P). \tag{9.34}$$

Because we have two regimes, equation (9.34) actually takes the following form:

$$\frac{D(P)}{n} = \begin{cases} x\,[(u - P)h(P)] + y\,[-(u - P)] & \text{for Regime 1} \\ x\,[-(u - P)] + y\,[(u - P)h(P)] & \text{for Regime 2.} \end{cases}$$

We set the right-hand side of this equation to zero to define the equilibrium prices at which the zero market excess demand is realized.

We first consider Regime 1 where the investors in the largest cluster are using strategy 1. In Regime 1, when the inequality

$$\frac{(M - m)}{2} > \left(\frac{x}{y}\right) \tag{9.35}$$

holds, there are three prices at which the market excess demand becomes zero. One is

$$P = u, \tag{9.36}$$

and, the other two are given by the roots of

$$h(P) = \frac{y}{x}, \tag{9.37}$$

or

$$-P^2 + 2uP - Mm = \left(\frac{x}{y}\right)^2. \tag{9.38}$$

Denote them by P^* and P_*, where

$$P_* < u < P^*. \tag{9.39}$$

We call P^* and P_* *high* and *low* equilibrium prices, respectively. These equilibrium prices depend on x and y, as shown below.

If

$$\frac{(M-m)}{2} < \frac{x}{y},$$

then $P = u$ is the only price which produces the zero excess demand. To be definite, in what follows, we assume that $(M - m)/2$ is sufficiently large so that inequality (9.35) holds, and the three equilibrium prices exist.

In Regime 2 where the investors in the largest cluster are using strategy 2, there are also three equilibirum prices if inequality (9.35) holds with y/x replacing x/y.[10] We examine the case with three equilibrium prices in both regimes; Namely, we assume that $(M - m)/2$ is larger than both x/y and y/x.

Noting that

$$P^* = u + \sqrt{(M-m)^2/4 - (x/y)^2} \qquad \text{for Regime 1}$$

and

$$P^* = u + \sqrt{(M-m)^2/4 - (y/x)^2} \qquad \text{for Regime 2,}$$

the two equilibrium prices P^* and P_* are further apart in Regime 2 than in Regime 1:

$$m < P_*(2) < P_*(1) < u < P^*(1) < P^*(2) < M. \tag{9.40}$$

Here, $P^*(2)$ denotes the high equilibrium price under Regime 2, and so on. These inequalities establish the following proposition.

Proposition: *The range of equilibrium prices is wider in Regime 2 than in Regime 1. In this sense, the fluctuations of stock price become greater when chartists dominate than when fundamentalists dominate in the market.*

We can easily show that of these three critical points, only $P = u$ is locally unstable. The derivative of the market excess demand with respect to P is

$$\frac{D'(P)}{n} = y - \left(\frac{M-m}{2}\right)^2 h(P)^3 x \tag{9.41}$$

in Regime 1. In particular, for $P = u$ we obtain

$$\frac{D'(u)}{n} = -\frac{2}{M-m}x + y, \tag{9.42}$$

for Regime 1. This is positive, and less than 1, when $M - m$ is sufficiently large. Thus, the equilibrium price $P = u$ is locally unstable.

---

[10]   Thus, if $y/x \leq (M-m)/2 \leq x/y$, then Regime 1 has a unique $P = u$, but in Regime 2 there are three critical points.

The difference equation is locally stable at the other two equilibrium prices because the following inequalities:

$$D'(P^*) = -x(u - P^*)^2 h(P^*)^3 < 0 \tag{9.43}$$

and

$$D'(P_*) = -x(u - P_*)^2 h(P_*)^3 < 0 \tag{9.44}$$

hold again for sufficiently large $M - m$.

Power Laws for the Distribution of Prices

In Chapter 5, we explain that *Power Laws* are an extremely important concept for understanding behavior of macro systems. Indeed, power laws play a crucial role in understanding financial markets. We will explain it in Chapter 10. Here, we discuss large changes in market prices and returns in heuristic term (see also Sornette, 1998; Takayasu and Sato, 1997, among others).

We fix the time interval Δ and write the difference equation for market price as

$$P_{t+\Delta} = P_t + \frac{\kappa D(P_t, \xi_t)}{n} \tag{9.45}$$

where $\kappa = c\Delta$ is an adjustment constant, and ξ_t stands for the two-dimensional vector with components x_t and y_t, that is,

$$\xi_t = (x_t, y_t).$$

Let ρ_t be the price difference $P_t - P_{t-\Delta}$ for some small Δ:

$$\rho_t = P_t - P_{t-\Delta}. \tag{9.46}$$

Then, the price difference is governed by the difference equation

$$\rho_{t+\Delta} = A_t \rho_t + B_t \tag{9.47}$$

with

$$A_t = 1 + \frac{\kappa D'(P_{t-\Delta}, \xi_{t-\Delta})}{n}. \tag{9.48}$$

Here, prime indicates partial derivative with respect to P. We define B_t as

$$B_t = \frac{\kappa D_\xi(P_{t-\Delta}, \xi_{t-\Delta})(\xi_t - \xi_{t-\Delta})}{n} \tag{9.49}$$

where the subscript ξ indicate the gradient vector with respect to x and y.

In the present case, (A_t, B_t) is not *i.i.d.* (independently and identically distributed) but is ergodic stationary so that we can appeal to Brandt (1986) to analyze the above system.[11] Brandt demonstrates that under certain technical conditons, a stationary distribution exists for

$$\rho_\infty = A_\infty \rho_\infty + B_\infty. \tag{9.50}$$

Furthermore, the probability distribution of ρ_∞ is shown to be as follows:

$$\rho_\infty \sim \sum_{j=0}^{\infty} \left\{ \left(\prod_{i=-j}^{-1} A_i \right) B_{-j-1} \right\}.$$

Because a pair of A_∞ and B_∞ are independent of ρ_∞, we can apply the Kesten–Goldie Theorem to be explained in Chapter 10. It establishes that a stationary probability distribution of ρ_∞ is a power law; that is, we obtain

$$\Pr(|\rho_\infty| > z) = C z^{-\gamma} \tag{9.51}$$

with some constants C and γ under some technical conditions. The index γ of the power distribution is determined by

$$E\left(A_t^\gamma\right) = 1. \tag{9.52}$$

We will explain this condition, a part of the Kesten–Goldie Theorem, in greater detail in Chapter 10. It determines γ by[12]

$$\gamma = 1 + \frac{2}{\kappa} \frac{E(-D'/n)}{E(D'^2/n^2)} \tag{9.53}$$

where

$$\frac{E(-D')}{E(D'^2)} = \frac{\Theta E(x) - E(y)}{\Theta^2 E(x^2) - 2E(xy)\Theta + E(y^2)}$$

$$\approx \frac{\Theta - .18}{.18(\Theta + 2/3)^2 - (4/3)\Theta - .35} \tag{9.54}$$

with

$$\Theta = E\left\{ \left(\frac{M - m}{2} \right)^2 [h(P_t)]^3 \right\}. \tag{9.55}$$

In Chapter 10, we will see that growing evidence now amply demonstrates that changes in asset prices obey the power distribution with the exponent close to 3. Thus, it is extremely important to check whether γ in (9.53) can be close to 3.

---

[11] Because (A_t, B_t) is not i.i.d. (B_t is serially correlated), we cannot apply the theorem due to Kesten (1973), Vervaat (1979), Letac (1986), Goldie (1991), or de Haan et al. (1989) to the above system. In Chapter 10, we will explain this theorem.

[12] With a large Θ, we have an approximate expression of γ:

$$\gamma \approx 1 + 10/\kappa\Theta.$$

Recall that κ measures the adjustment speed of the price dynamics. Faster adjustment, other things being equal, will give smaller γ values.

Toward this goal, we first note that $E(D'^2/n^2)$ is positive. Therefore, if $E(-D'n)$ is positive, γ is greater than one. Now, if we evaluate the expected value of D' in the neighborhood of stable equilibrium prices, P^* and P_*, $E(-D'/n)$ is positive; recall two inequalities (9.43) and (9.44). Thus, we conclude that γ is greater than one.

An interesting question is whether γ is greater or smaller in Regime 1 than in Regime 2. First, we can show

$$E(-D'/n)|_{Regime1} > E(-D'/n)|_{Regime2}. \qquad (9.56)$$

Furthermore, if Θ defined by (9.55) is less than one; that is, if

$$\Theta < 1 \qquad (9.57)$$

holds, then we obtain

$$E(D'^2/n^2)|_{Regime1} < E(D'^2/n^2)|_{Regime2}. \qquad (9.58)$$

From (9.53), (9.56), (9.58), we conclude that under condition (9.57), γ is greater in Regime 1 than in Regime 2. In summary, we have obtained the following proposition.

Proposition: *The model with two types of investors, "fundamentalists" and "chartists," produces a power distribution of changes in stock price. The exponent γ is greater than one. It is greater in Regime 1 where fundamentalists dominate in the market than in Regime 2 where chartists dominate.*

A great anomalous change in price has a smaller probability when the exponent of the power distribution γ is greater. Note that the probability *density* function corresponding to (9.51), $f(x)$, is proportional to $x^{-(\gamma+1)}$. Thus, the above proposition makes sense. When chartists dominate in the market, stock prices become more "unstable" than otherwise. In other words, an anomalous change in price like a "crash" has higher probability when chartists dominate in the market.

9.4. Concluding Remark

In this chapter, we used an open model formalized as a jump Markov process to theoretically examine a multiagent model of financial markets. First, we have shown that when investor behaviors are positively correlated, that is, when the parameter θ in the Ewens distribution takes on a small positive value, two largest clusters to which most agents belong are likely to emerge.

Is there any justification for expecting that behaviors of the investors are positively correlated? Keynes (1936) gave an emphatic answer YES to this question by resorting to an ingenious metaphor:

Or, to change the metaphor slightly, professional investment may be likened to those newspaper competitions in which the competitors have to pick out the six prettiest faces from a hundred photographs, the prize being awarded to the competitor whose choice most nearly corresponds to the average preferences of the competitors as a whole; so that each competitor has to pick, not those faces which he himself finds prettiest, but those which he thinks likeliest to catch the fancy of the other competitors, all of whom are looking at the problem from the same point of view. (Keynes, 1936, 156)

We have analyzed a model in which there are two types of investors, "fundamentalists" and "chartists." The model produces a *power distribution* of changes in stock price *with the exponent greater than one*. This is a significant result. Its level of significance is explained in Chapter 10.

Appendix 9.1: Joint Probability Density for r Largest Fractions

In Section 9.2, we have shown how the probability density function of the largest order statistics of x's, $x_{(1)}$ is derived ($r = 1$). In this appendix, we will derive the joint probability density for the largest r fractions on the K-dimensional simplex, $x_{(1)} \geq x_{(2)} \geq \cdots \geq x_{(r)}$. Here, x_i, $i = 1, 2, \ldots, K$ are the fractions.

Denote the Dirichlet probability density on the K dimensional simplex by $\phi(x_1, x_2, \ldots, x_k) = \mathcal{D}(\epsilon, K)$. Then, the probability density for the first r order statistics is given by

$$f(x_1, x_2, \ldots, x_r) = K(K-1)(K-2)\cdots(K-r+1)$$

$$\times \int \phi(x_1, x_2, \ldots, x_k) dx_{r+1} \cdots dx_{K-1},$$

where $1 \geq x_1 \geq x_2 \cdots \geq x_r > 0$, and where we subsitute $x_K = 1 - x_1 - \cdots - x_{K-1}$. Carrying out the integral

$$f(x_1, \ldots, x_r) = \frac{K!}{(K-r)!} \frac{\Gamma(K\epsilon)}{\Gamma(\epsilon)^K} (x_1 \cdots x_r)^{\epsilon-1} x_R^{(K-r)\epsilon-1} I,$$

where

$$I = \int \cdots \int \prod_{r+1}^{K-1} y_j^{\epsilon-1} [1 - a - x_r(y_{r+1} + \cdots + y_{K-1})]^{\epsilon-1} dy_{r-1} \cdots dy_{K-1},$$

where the integration is carried out in area A:

$$A = \{0 \leq y_j \leq 1, r+1 \leq j \leq K-1; (1-a-x_r)/x_r$$

$$\leq y_{r+1} + \cdots + y_{K-1} \leq (1-a)/x_r\}$$

where $a := x_1 + x_2 + \cdots + x_r$.

As in the case of the largest fraction, introduce random variable Z with the density function g_{K-r-1} which is the $(K - r - 1)$-fold convolution of the density $\epsilon y_j^{\epsilon-1}$, $j = r+1, \ldots, K-1$.

The integral is approximately given by

$$I = \frac{\epsilon^{-(K-r)}}{x_r} g_{K-r-1}\left(\frac{1-a}{x_r}\right).$$

Letting $K\epsilon$ approach θ, while K goes to infinity and ϵ to zero, we note that $K(K-1)\cdots(K-r+1)$ approaches K^r, and

$$\Gamma(\epsilon)^K = \left[\frac{\Gamma(1+\epsilon)}{\epsilon}\right]^K$$

which approaches $\epsilon^{-K}e^{-\gamma\theta}$, where we use the fact

$$\Gamma(1+\epsilon) \approx 1 - \gamma\epsilon,$$

where γ is Euler's constant, $\gamma = .5772\cdots$.

Combining them, we arrive at

$$f(x_1, x_2, \ldots, x_r) = \theta^r e^{\gamma\theta}\Gamma(\theta)x_r^{\theta-1}g\left(\frac{1-a}{x_r}\right)(x_1 x_2 \cdots x_r)^{-1},$$

in the range $1 \geq x_1 \geq \cdots \geq x_r > 0$, and $\sum_1^r x_i \leq 1$.

We know from our result for the largest fraction that $f(x_1) = \theta x_1^{-1}(1 - x_1)^{\theta-1}$ for x_1 between 1/2 and 1, that is

$$\Gamma(1+\theta)e^{\gamma\theta}g\left(\frac{1-x_1}{x_1}\right) = \theta\left(\frac{1-x_1}{x_1}\right)^{\theta-1},$$

for x_1 between 1/2 and 1.

To obtain the expression for the density in the range $0 \leq x \leq 1/2$, we follow Watterson (1976) and differentiate the Laplace transform for the random variable Z:

$$E(e^{-sZ}) = \exp\left[\theta\int_0^1 (e^{-sz} - 1)z^{-1}dz\right]$$

with respect to s. Recall that this transform is derived in connection with the largest fraction. Then, divide the result by $-\theta$ to see

$$(1/\theta)\int_0^\infty e^{-sz}zg_\theta(z)dz = \int_0^\infty I_{(0,1]}(y)e^{-sy}dy\int_0^\infty e^{-sz}g_\theta(z)dz.$$

The right-hand side is the product of two Laplace transforms. Hence the integrand of the left-hand side is the convolution of the uniform function on the unit interval and g_θ:

$$(1/\theta)zg_\theta(z) = \int_{z-1}^z g_\theta(y)dy.$$

Setting z to 1, we obtain

$$g_\theta(1) = e^{-\gamma\theta}/\Gamma(\theta).$$

Differentiating the integral equation with respect to z, we derive the differential equation which determines the function recursively

$$zg_\theta'(z) + (1-\theta)g_\theta(z) = -\theta g_\theta(z-1),$$

where $z \geq 0$. In the range $z \in [0, 1)$, this integro-differential equation yields the result we obtained above. In the next range $z \in [1, 2)$ we have

$$g_\theta(z) = z^{\theta-1} \left[g_\theta(1) - \theta \int_1^z g_\theta(u-1) u^{-\theta} du \right].$$

Changing the variable of integration to $v = 1/u$, we note that the integration above becomes

$$\int_{1/z}^1 v^{-1}(1-v)^{\theta-1} dv.$$

The joint density for the first two largest fractions is given by

$$f_\theta^{(2)}(x, y) = \frac{e^{\gamma\theta}\theta^2 \Gamma(\theta) y^{\theta-1}}{xy} g_\theta\left(\frac{1-x-y}{y}\right) = \frac{\theta^2}{xy}(1-x-y)^{\theta-1}.$$

This expression is valid for the range $0 < y < x < 1, 0 < x + y < 1$, and $x + 2y > 1$, that is $y > (1-x)/2$.

We know that

$$g(z) = \frac{z^{\theta-1}}{\Gamma(\theta)e^{\gamma\theta}},$$

for z between 0 and 1. For other values of z, we have a recursion

$$\frac{zg(z)}{\theta} = \int_{z-1}^z g(y)dy;$$

see Watterson and Guess (1977). Alternatively, we have

$$g(z) = z^{\theta-1} \left[g(n)n^{1-\theta} - \theta \int_n^z g(y-1)y^{-\theta} dy \right],$$

in the range $n \leq z < n+1$. This can be verified by direct subsitution into the differential equation for g_θ.

With the joint probability densities for the largest 2 or 3 fractions in the case of a large number of correlated agents in a market, we are in a position to approximately obtain the macroeconomic behavior of the market prices and quantities.

Appendix 9.2: The Calculation of the Expected Share of the Largest Fraction

We change variables from x's to y's:

$$y_i = x_i/(1 - x_1 - x_2 - \cdots - x_{K-1}) \leq 1.$$

Noting that

$$1 - x_1 - \cdots - x_{K-1} = \left(1 + \sum_{j=1}^{K-1} y_j\right)^{-1},$$

and that the Jacobian is

$$\frac{\partial(x_1 \ldots x_{K-1})}{\partial(y_1 \ldots y_{K-1})} = \left(1 + \sum_{j=1}^{K-1} y_j\right)^{-K} = (1 + Z_{K-1})^{-K}$$

where

$$Z_{K-1} = \sum_{j=1}^{K-1} y_j$$

we rewrite

$$E(x_{(1)}) = \frac{K\Gamma(K\epsilon)}{(\Gamma(\epsilon))^K} \int \cdots \int \prod_{j=1}^{K-1} y_j^{\epsilon-1}(1 + Z_{K-1})^{-1-K\epsilon} dy_1 \cdots dy_{K-1}.$$

The range of integration is over the cube, $0 \le y_j \le 1$, $j = 1, \ldots, K - 1$. By multiplying the numerator and denominator by ϵ^{K-1}, we can rewrite this integral as

$$E\left(x_{(1)}\right) = \frac{K\Gamma(K\epsilon)}{(\Gamma(\epsilon))^K}\left(\frac{1}{\epsilon^{K-1}}\right)$$

$$\times \int \cdots \int \prod_{j=1}^{K-1} \left(\epsilon y_j^{\epsilon-1}\right)(1 + Z_{K-1})^{-1-K\epsilon} dy_1 \ldots dy_{K-1}.$$

To calculate this expected value, $E\left(x_{(1)}\right)$, we first give the Laplace transform of Z_{K-1} on the assumption that y's are $i.i.d.$:

$$E(e^{-sZ_{K-1}}) = \{E(e^{-sY_1})\}^{K-1} = \left\{\int_0^1 e^{-sy}\epsilon y^{\epsilon-1} dy\right\}^{K-1}.$$

Write the integrand as

$$\epsilon e^{-sy} y^{\epsilon-1} = \epsilon\{y^{\epsilon-1} + (e^{-sy} - 1)y^{\epsilon-1}\}.$$

And consider the following limit.

$$E(e^{-sZ_{K-1}}) \to \exp\left\{\theta \int_0^1 (e^{-sy} - 1)y^{-1} dy\right\} \quad \text{as} \quad K \to \infty, \epsilon \to 0, K\epsilon \to \theta.$$

Denote by Z the limiting random variable of Z_{K-1}. Then

$$E(x_{(1)}) = e^{\gamma\theta}\Gamma(\theta + 1)E\{(1 + Z)^{-1-\theta}\}.$$

In deriving this expression we used the fact that $\Gamma(K\epsilon) \to \Gamma(\theta)$, $\Gamma(\epsilon) = \Gamma(1+\epsilon)/\epsilon$, and $\Gamma(1+\epsilon) \approx \Gamma(1) + \Gamma'(1)\epsilon = 1 - \gamma\epsilon$, where $\gamma = -\Gamma'(1)$ is Euler's constant. See Abramovitz and Stegun (1968, 5.1.1 and 5.1.11).

By definition

$$\Gamma(1+\theta) = \int_0^\infty x^\theta e^{-x} dx,$$

and we note that

$$\Gamma(\theta + 1)(1 + Z)^{-1-\theta} = \int_0^\infty s^\theta e^{-(1+Z)s} ds.$$

Taking expectation with respect to Z, we finally obtain

$$E(x_{(1)}) = e^{\gamma\theta} \int_0^\infty s^\theta e^{-s} E(e^{-sZ}) ds = \int_0^\infty e^{-s} e^{-\theta E_1(s)} ds.$$

Here, we use the relation

$$E(e^{-sZ}) = \exp\{-\gamma\theta - \theta \ln s - \theta E_1(s)\},$$

and define $E_1(s)$ as

$$E_1(s) = \int_s^\infty e^{-x} x^{-1} dx = -\gamma - \ln s - \sum_{n=1}^\infty \frac{(-s)^n}{nn!}$$

$$= -\gamma - \ln s - \int_0^1 \left(\frac{e^{-sy} - 1}{y}\right) dy.$$

10

Stock Prices and the Real Economy:
Power-Law versus Exponential Distributions

This final chapter explores the relationship between stock prices and the real economy. The standard approach – the so-called consumption-based asset pricing model – attempts to explain it based on the assumption of the representative agent. In this chapter, we argue once again that the representative agent assumption is fundamentally flawed. Drawing on the recent advancement of *"econophysics"* on financial markets,[1] we argue that in contrast to the neoclassical view, there is in fact a wedge between financial markets, the stock prices in particular, and the real economy.

10.1. Introduction

Stock prices depend necessarily on the real economy. Their "correct" prices or the fundamental values are the discounted present values of a stream of future dividends/profits. Because business activities, profits in particular, are significantly affected by the state of the real economy, the stock prices are also affected by the real economy. More precisely, in the standard neoclassical theory, stock prices are simultaneously determined with all the supplies and demands in general equilibrium (Diamond, 1967). Thus, like production and consumption, the stock prices depend ultimately on preferences and technologies.

However, there is a long tradition in economics which questions whether the stock prices are really determined in the way stated above. Many believe that "bubbles" are possible in the market. And whether or not they are "rational," extraordinary changes in the stock prices (either up or down) *by themselves* may do harm to the real economy They are not a mere mirror image of the real economy. In history, depressions were often accompanied by falls in the stock prices. As early as the nineteenth century, economists were talking about "financial crises." More recently, Minsky (1957, 1975) highlighted the importance of stock prices in the macroeconomy, and advanced the "financial accelerator"

---

[1] See Mantegna and Stanley (2000) for the introduction to econophysics.

thesis. It was revived in the 1990s, and bore a vast literature. Today, most central banks closely monitor asset prices in the conduct of monetary policy.

The crucial problem is whether the stock prices are always equal to their fundamental values. Shiller (1981) in his seminal work performed the ingenious "variance-bound tests" on this issue, and drew the following conclusion:

We have seen that measures of stock price volatility over the past century appear to be far too high – five to thirteen times too high – to be attributed to new information about future real dividends if uncertainty about future dividends is measured by the sample standard deviations of real dividends around their long-run exponential growth path. (Shiller, 1981, 433)

Naturally, Shiller's seminal work[2] spawned the debate over alleged excess volatility of stock price. Rather than accepting that stock prices are too volatile to be consistent with the standard theory, a majority of economists have attempted to reconcile the alleged volatility with efficiency or "rationality" of market.

One way to explain volatility of stock prices is to allow significant changes in the discount rate or the required return on stocks. In fact, in the neoclassical macroeconomic theory, the following relationship between the rate of change in consumption, C, and the return on capital, r, must hold in equilibrium (see, for example, Blanchard and Fischer, 1989):

$$-\left[\frac{u''(C)C}{u'(C)}\right]\left(\frac{\dot{C}}{C}\right) = \frac{1}{\eta(C)}\left(\frac{\dot{C}}{C}\right) = r - \delta. \qquad (10.1)$$

Here, the elasticity of intertemporal substitution η is defined as

$$\frac{1}{\eta(C)} = -\frac{u''(C)C}{u'(C)} > 0.$$

In general, η depends on the level of consumption, C. Equation (10.1) says that the rate of change in consumption over time is determined by η and the difference between the rate of return on capital, r, and the consumer's subjective discount rate, δ. This equation, called the *Euler equation*, is derived as the necessary condition of the representative consumer's maximization of the Ramsey utility sum.

The return on capital, r, in equation (10.1) is the return on capital equity or stocks, which consists of the expected capital gains/losses and dividends. Thus, according to the neoclassical macroeconomics, the return on stocks must be consistent with the rate of change in consumption over time in such a way that equation (10.1) holds.

Now, the results of the tests of Shiller (1981) and LeRoy and Porter (1981) imply that the volatility of stock prices must come from the volatility of the discount

---

[2] The variance bound test for the volatility of stock prices was also performed by LeRoy and Porter (1981).

rate or the return on capital, r, rather than that of dividends. And yet, consumption C is not volatile. If anything, it is *less* volatile than dividends or profits. Thus, given equation (10.1), the volatility of stock prices or their rate of return r must be explained ultimately by sizable fluctuations of the elasticity of intertemporal substitution η which depends on consumption. Consequently, on the representative agent assumption, researchers focus on the "shape" of the utility function in accounting for the volatility of stock prices (Grossman and Shiller, 1981). It is not an easy task, however, to reconcile the theory with the observed data if we make a simple assumption for the elasticity of intertemproral substitution, η; η must change a lot despite of the fact that changes in consumption are small.

A slightly different assumption favored by theorists in this game is that the utility, and therefore, this elasticity η depend not on the current level of consumption C_t but on its deviation from the "habit" level, $\hat{C}_t$, namely, $C_t - \hat{C}_t$. By assumption, the habit $\hat{C}_t$ changes much more slowly than consumption C_t itself so that at each moment in time, $\hat{C}_t$ is almost constant. The trick of this alternative assumption is that although C_t does not fall close to zero, $C_t - \hat{C}_t$ can do so as to make the elasticity of intertemporal substitution η, now redefined as

$$\frac{1}{\eta} = -\frac{u''(C - \hat{C})(C - \hat{C})}{u'(C - \hat{C})} > 0, \qquad (10.2)$$

quite volatile. Campbell and Cochrane (1999) is a primary example of such an approach. Though ingenious, the assumption is not entirely persuasive. Why does the consumer's utility become minimal when the level of consumption is equal to the habit level even if it is extremely high? In any case, this is the kind of end point we are led to as long as we keep the representative agent assumption in accounting for the volatility of stock prices.

Meanwhile, Mehra and Prescott (1985), using the representative agent model, present another problem for asset prices. They considered a simple stochastic Arrow–Debreu model. The model has two assets, one the equity share for which dividends are stochastic, and the other the riskless security. Again, on the representative agent assumption, the "shape" of the utility function and the volatility of consumption play the central role for prices of or returns on two assets. For the reasonable values of η, which may be more appropriately called the relative risk aversion in this stochastic model, and the U.S. historical standard deviation of consumption growth, Mehra and Prescott calculated the theoretical values of the returns on two assets. The risk premium, namely the difference between the return on the equity share and the return on the riskless security implied by their model, turns out to be mere 0.4 percent. In fact, the actual risk premium for U.S. stocks (the Standard and Poor's 500 Index, 1889–1978) against short-term securities such as the Treasury Bills, is 6 percent. Thus, the standard model with the representative consumer fails to account for such a high risk premium that is actually observed. Mehra and Prescott posed this result as a puzzle. Since then, a number of authors have attempted to explain this puzzle (e.g., Campbell and Cochrane, 1999).

The "puzzles" we have seen are, of course, puzzles conditional on the assumption of the representative agent. Indeed, Deaton (1992) laughs away the so-called "puzzles" as follows:

There is something seriously amiss with the model, sufficiently so that it is quite unsafe to make any inference about intertemporal substitution from representative agent models. . . .

The main puzzle is not why these representative agent models do not account for the evidence, but why anyone ever thought that they might, given the absurdity of the aggregation assumptions that they require. While not all of the data can necessarily be reconciled with the microeconomic theory, many of the puzzles evaporate once the representative agent is discarded. (Deaton, 1992, 67, 70)

We second Deaton's criticism. Having said that, here, we note that the standard analyses all focus on the *variance* or the *second moment* of asset prices or returns (see e.g., Cechetti, Lam, and Mark, 2000, and the literature cited therein). As we will see shortly, a number of empirical studies actually demonstrate that the variance or standard deviation may *not* be a good measure of *risk*. Kiyono et al. (2006), in fact, demonstrates that the probability density function of the U.S stock returns is non-Gaussian for the period including the Black Monday in October, 1987. We must, therefore, consider probability distributions, not just moments. In what follows, we will critically examine the consumption-based asset pricing model, and argue that financial markets, stock prices in particular, and the real economy are, in fact, different creatures.

10.2. The Power-Law Behavior of Stock Prices and Returns

Toward this goal, we must begin with the story of the power-law probability distribution. It may appear too technical at first, but is essential for our understanding of the workings of financial markets on one hand, and the real economy on the other. Although economists routinely adopt the normal or the Gaussian distribution, it turns out that it is actually not so generic as they believe. Specifically, the *power law* plays a central role for understanding financial markets.[3] Despite its fundamental importance, the power law is relatively unknown among mainstream economists. We first give its definition.

Definition (Power-Law Distribution): *A stochastic variable x is said to obey a power-law distribution when it is characterized by a probability density function* $p(x)$ *with power-law tails:*

$$p(x) \propto x^{-(1+\alpha)} \quad (\alpha > 0).$$

---

[3] See Chapters 4 and 6 of Sornette (2000), and Mandelbrot and Hudson (2004) for the introduction of power-law distributions.

Normal Distribution

To appreciate the importance of the power-law distribution, we need to compare it with the normal distribution. The probability density function of the standard normal distribution $\phi(x)$ is well known:

$$\phi(x) = \frac{1}{\sqrt{2\pi}} \exp\left(-\frac{x^2}{2}\right).$$

Economists, like scientists in other disciplines, have long believed that the normal distribution is the norm, the deviation from which serves only for curiosity of mathematicians. There are several justifications for this belief. The most important one is, of course, *the central limit theorem*. The random walk model is another.

A version of the central limit theorem states as follows.

The Central Limit Theorem: *Suppose that x_i is an identically and independently distributed (i.i.d.) random variable with mean zero and a finite variance σ^2. Then the probability density function $f_n(s)$ of the (normalized) sum of x_i, $s_n = \sum_{i=1}^{n} x_i / [\sigma\sqrt{n}]$, converges to a normal distribution with unit variance, as n becomes large:*

$$f_n(s) \to \phi(s) = \frac{1}{\sqrt{2\pi}} \exp\left(-\frac{s^2}{2}\right) \quad \text{when} \quad n \to \infty.$$

See any textbook on probability such as Feller (1968) for technical details. The point is that the theorem allows *any* distribution for x_i, as long as the second moment exists.

The normal distribution can be also seen as a limit of the *random walk model*. Consider a random walk model on a one-dimensional lattice. Starting from the origin, a "ball" moves to the right by one with probability one-half, and to the left by one with probability one-half. The position of the ball after N moves is then

$$n - (N - n) = 2n - N \qquad (n = 0, \ldots, N)$$

where n is the number of moves to the right. Thus, the position of the ball corresponds to n.

The probability that the number of moves to the right is n after N moves, $P(N, n)$, is then

$$P(N, n) = \binom{N}{n}\left(\frac{1}{2}\right)^n \left(\frac{1}{2}\right)^{N-n} = \binom{N}{n}\left(\frac{1}{2}\right)^N = \frac{N!}{(N-n)!n!}\left(\frac{1}{2}\right)^N.$$

Just as we obtained the Boltzmann–Gibbs distribution in Chapter 3, we take the logarithm of $P(N, n)$ and use the Stirling formula

$$\log x! \cong x \log x - x.$$

Then, we obtain

$$\log P(N, n) = (N - n)\log\left(\frac{N}{N-n}\right) + n\log\left(\frac{N}{n}\right) - N\log 2.$$

Define x, which is the deviation of n from $N/2$, as follows:

$$n = N\left(\frac{1}{2} + x\right) \quad \left(-\frac{1}{2} \le x \le \frac{1}{2}\right).$$

And we obtain

$$\log P(N, n) = -N\left(\frac{1}{2} - x\right)\log(1 - 2x) - N\left(\frac{1}{2} + x\right)\log(1 + 2x).$$

Using the expansion

$$\log(1 + \alpha) = \alpha - \frac{\alpha^2}{2} + o(\alpha^3)$$

we obtain

$$P(N, n) = \exp\{-2Nx^2\} \quad \text{where} \quad x = \frac{1}{N}\left(n - \frac{N}{2}\right).$$

Because $P(N, n)$ is a probability density function, its sum (integral) must be one. Define y as

$$y = n - \frac{N}{2} = Nx.$$

With y, we have

$$P(N, n) \sim \exp\left(-\frac{2y^2}{N}\right) \quad y \in (-\infty, \infty).$$

Using the well-known formula

$$\int_{-\infty}^{\infty} e^{-\alpha x^2}\, dx = \sqrt{\frac{\pi}{\alpha}}$$

and noting $\alpha = 2/N$ in our case, we finally obtain *the density function for the normal distribution*:

$$P(N, n) = \sqrt{\frac{2}{N\pi}}\exp\left(-\frac{2y^2}{N}\right)dy \quad \text{where} \quad y = n - \frac{N}{2}.$$

Thus, to the extent that the random walk model is generic, the normal distribution is the norm. In passing, we note that the standard deviation of $P(N, n)$, σ is

$$\sigma = \frac{\sqrt{N}}{2}.$$

In other words, the standard deviation (fluctuation) of the random walk σ is proportional to the square root of the step size, $\sqrt{N}$. Because the step size is expected to be proportional to the length of time, t, σ is also proportional to the square root of time, $\sqrt{t}$.

The central limit theorem, and the fact that the normal distribution can be seen as the limit of a random walk, are well known. These facts suggest strongly that the normal distribution is very generic; we should expect the normal distribution everywhere in nature. However, it turns out that the normal distribution may not be so generic as we might believe. A crucial assumption of the central limit theorem is that the probability distribution of x_i has the finite variance. What happens if the variance or the second moment does not exist?

Power Laws and Lévy Flight

The normal distribution actually belongs to a group of distributions called a *stable distribution*. A stable distribution is a specific type of distribution encountered in the sum of n i.i.d. random variables with the property that it does not change its functional form for different values of n. It is known that the normal distribution is the only stable distribution having all its moments finite. Now, there exists a limit theorem stating that, under certain conditions, the probability density function (pdf) of a sum of n i.i.d. random variables x_i converges in probability to a stable distribution. Note that the central limit theorem is a special case of this more general limit theorem. When the pdf of x_i has a finite variance, it becomes the usual central limit theorem. The limit distribution is the normal distribution. On the other hand, when the variance or the second moment does not exist (namely, it becomes infinite) for the underlying stochastic process, a sum of n i.i.d. random variables converges to a distribution with power-law tails which is also a member of the group of stable distribution.

The random walk which leads us to the normal distribution has been regarded as a very generic model with wide applications. However, it is also restrictive in the sense that the length of a jump of a "ball" is constant. Generally, we can consider a random walk with the following probability distribution of the lengths of a jump of a ball:

$$
\begin{array}{lll}
\pm a & \text{with probability} & C \\
\pm \lambda a & \text{with probability} & C/M \\
\vdots & & \vdots \qquad\qquad (a > 0,\ C > 0,\ \lambda > 1,\ M > 1) \\
\pm \lambda^j a & \text{with probability} & C/M^j \\
\vdots & & \vdots
\end{array}
$$

In this generalized random walk model, a ball can fly to any point on a one-dimensional lattice with power-law probabilities: a small jump is more likely than a big jump. This is a one-dimensional example of a *Lévy flight*.[4] Now, this generalized random walk, or a Lévy flight, is much "wilder" than the ordinary random walk model, and can lead us to power-law distributions rather than to the normal distribution.[5]

In summary, a stable distribution is more general than the normal distribution. In this group of probability distributions we have strong contenders to the normal distribution, namely power-law distributions.

In addition to the kind of limit distribution, we must also take into account the speed of convergence. The problem can be best illustrated by an example. Consider the *truncated* Lévy flight defined by the following distribution:

$$P(x) = \begin{array}{lll} 0 & \text{for} & 0 < m < x \\ c\,P_L(x) & \text{for} & -m \leq x \leq m \\ 0 & \text{for} & x < -m \end{array}$$

where $P_L(x)$ is the symmetric Lévy flight. Unlike the Lévy flight, in which the length of a jump is unbounded, the truncated Lévy flight has a limit ($m > 0$) on the length of a jump. Since the truncated Lévy flight has a finite variance, the probability distribution of the sum of n random variables form this distribution, $P(S_n)$ converges to the normal distribution. The question is how quickly $P(S_n)$ will converge. Obviously, when n is small, the Lévy flight well approximates $P(S_n)$. Thus, there exists a crossover value of n, n^* such that

$$\begin{array}{lll} \text{For} & n \ll n^*, & P(S_n) \sim \text{The Lévy Flight} \\ \text{For} & n \gg n^*, & P(S_n) \sim \text{The Normal Distribution} \end{array}$$

This example illustrates the point that in general, the kind of probability distribution we obtain in practical applications depends on n (see section 8.4 of Mantegna and Stanley, 2000 for further details).

In fact, more and more evidence has been gathered to the effect that natural phenomena are characterized by power-law distributions (see, for example, Sornette, 2000). In economics, empirical size distributions of many variables of interest have been actually known for long to obey a power-law distribution. For example, Pareto (1896) found that the distribution of income y was of the following form:

$$N(y > x) \sim x^{-\left(\frac{3}{2}\right)}$$

where $N(y > x)$ is the number of people having income x or greater than x. The Pareto distribution is nothing but a particular form of power-law distribution (see Chatterjee et al., 2005 for recent studies on this theme).

More recently, electronic trading in financial markets has enabled us to use rich high-frequency data with the average time delay between two records being

---

[4] The model is not restricted to a one-dimensional model. Mandelbrot (1983) coined the term "Lévy flight" for the generalization of random walks in continuous space.

[5] The reader can usefully refer to Figure 4.7 of Sornette (2000, 93) to appreciate the point that Lévy flight is much "wilder" than the ordinary random walk. For Lévy flights and power laws, see also Chapter 4 of Paul and Baschnagel (1999).

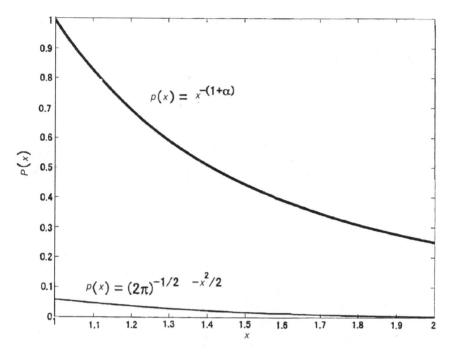

Figure 10.1. Tail comparison of Standard Normal Distribution and Power Law ($\alpha = 1$).
Notes: The Normal Distribution $N(x) = \frac{1}{\sqrt{2\pi}} \exp\left(-\frac{x^2}{2}\right)$; Power-Law Distribution $f(x) = x^{-(1+\alpha)}$ $(0 < \alpha < 2)$.

as short as a few seconds. By now, a number of empirical analyses based on such data have amply demonstrated that most financial variables such as changes in stock price or foreign exchange rates are, in fact, characterized by power-law distributions, *not* by the normal distribution.

What is the significance of these results? The significant difference between the normal and power-law distributions shows up in the tails of distributions as shown in Figure 10.1. Under power laws, large deviations from the mean have much larger probability (dubbed *fat tails*) than under the normal distribution. Put it another way, given the normal distribution, some of the big earthquakes which actually occurred would not have reasonably occurred whereas they are quite possible under power laws. Likewise, under the normal distribution, drops in stock price like the October 1987 crash would have insignificant probability whereas under power laws, the probability becomes significant. Power laws have, therefore, important implications for our understanding of financial markets.

Asset Prices

Growing evidence dating back to Mandelbrot (1963) now amply demonstrates that changes in asset prices do not obey the normal distribution but the power law. For our present purpose, it is enough to cite Gabaix et al. (2003).

Stylized Fact 1: *The probability distribution of changes in stock prices r is the following power law with the exponent $\alpha = 3$:*

$$P\,(|r| > x) \propto x^{-\alpha}, \qquad \alpha = 3 \tag{10.3}$$

where r is defined as follows:

$$r_t = \log P_t - \log P_{t-\Delta t}.$$

The probability density function, $f(r)$ corresponding to (10.3) is

$$f(r) \propto x^{-(\alpha+1)} = x^{-4}, \tag{10.4}$$

that is, in terms of density function $f(r)$, r obeys the power law with the exponent $\alpha + 1 = 4$.

See also Mandelbrot (1997) and Mantegna and Stanley (2000) for the above stylized fact.

That exponent α is about 3 is the standard result. The value of the exponent has far-reaching implications. First of all, when the exponent of the power-law *density function* is 3, the variance or the second moment does not exist. In general, suppose a random variable X has a power-law *density* $f(x)$ in the range $1 \leq x \leq \infty$ with exponent $\mu + 1$:

$$f(x) = x^{-(\mu+1)} \quad (1 \leq x \leq \infty).$$

The nth moment M_n of X is then defined as

$$M_n = \int_1^\infty x^n f(x)dx = \int_1^\infty x^{-(\mu+1-n)}dx.$$

Thus, the nth moment of X, M_n exists if and only if

$$\mu + 1 - n > 1 \quad \text{or} \quad \mu > n.$$

In other words, the nth moment of the random variable X does not exist for $\mu \leq n$.

Though it appears that the second moment or variance *does* exist for financial returns (see Chapter 9 of Mantegna and Stanley, 2000), it is still a matter of dispute. If the variance does not exist, the standard theory of asset prices faces a serious problem because it rests on the basic assumption that the distribution of returns is normal (Gaussian), and that *risk* can be measured by the variance or standard deviation of the rate of return; (see Mandelbrot and Hudson, 2004 for very readable and forceful criticism of the standard theory of asset prices and finance).

Whether or not the second moment exists, compared to the normal distribution, power-law distributions have *fat tails* meaning that large deviations from the mean have the significant probabilities (Figure 10.1). Mandelbrot, a founder of new approach, contrasts two broad classes of probability distributions, one the "mild," the other the "wild." The normal distribution belongs to the "mild" one whereas power-law distributions are "wild." To appreciate the point, following Sornette (2000), we can think of the distribution of height. The probability that someone has twice your height is virtually zero because the distribution of height is normal, and "mild." In contrast, in the case of the distribution of wealth which Pareto (1896) first explored, there is a nonvanishing fraction of the population twice, ten times, or even 100 times as wealthy as you are. The reason is that unlike height, wealth is distributed under the power law. "Wild" probability distributions are, in fact, found to well approximate the size frequency distributions of a wide range of natural phenomena such as earthquakes, hurricanes, and floods. And now, changes in stock prices have been found to obey a power-law distribution. Dismissing the "equity premium puzzle" mentioned earlier, Mandelbrot draws the important implication for power-law distributions for *risk* as follows:

Why is it that stocks, according to the averages, generally reward investors so richly? The data say that, over the long stretch of the twentieth century, stocks provided a massive "premium" return over that of supposedly safer investments, such as U.S. Treasury Bills. Inflation-adjusted estimates of that premium vary, depending on the dates you examine, between 4.1 percent and 8.4 percent. Conventional theory calls this impossible. Only two things, the theory says, could so inflate stock prices: Either the market is so risky that people will not invest otherwise, or people merely *fear* it is too risky and so will not invest otherwise. Now, when studying this, economists typically measure the real market risk by its volatility – quantified by their old friend, the bell-curve standard deviation. . . . But these papers miss the point. They assume that the "average" stock-market profit means something to a real person; in fact, it is the extremes of profit or loss that matter most. Just one out-of-the-average year of losing more than a third of capital – as happened with many stocks in 2002 – would justifiably scare even the boldest investors away for a long while. The problem also assumes wrongly that the bell curve is a realistic yardstick for measuring the risk. As I have said often, real prices gyrate much more wildly than the Gaussian standard assume. In this light, there is no puzzle to the equity premium. Real investors know better than the economists. They instinctively realize that the market is very, very risky, riskier than the standard models say. So, to compensate them for taking that risk, they naturally demand and often get a higher return. (Mandelbrot and Hudson, 2004, 230–231)

At this stage, we return to the standard consumption-based theory of asset pricing, namely equation (10.1). According to the basic equation of the consumption-based asset pricing model, the equity return r and the rate of change in consumption must be closely related. Now, the standard empirical analyses which attempt to reconcile the neoclassical theory with the observed data all focus on the *moments* of the relevant variables. However, given the stylized fact that equity returns obey the power law for which the second moment may not even exist, the standard approach is highly questionable. *The valid approach is to compare the probability distributions – not just the moments – of consumption growth and the stock prices or returns*, namely the left-hand and the right-hand sides of the Euler equation (equation (10.1)).

Growth of Real Variables

The return on equity obeys the power-law distribution with exponent $\alpha = 3$ (the stylized fact 1 above). What about the rate of change in consumption? Changes in consumption and aggregate income or GDP are similar. Canning et al. (1998) shows that the distribution of the growth rates of GDP, g, is exponential.

$$P(g) \sim \exp(-\gamma \mid g \mid). \tag{10.5}$$

Stanley et al. (1996), analyzing all U.S. publicly traded manufacturing companies within the years 1975–91 (taken from the Compustat database), drew the conclusion that the distribution of the growth rates of companies is also exponential.

Stylized Fact 2: *The probability distributions of growth rates of real variables such as GDP, consumption, and the size of firm are exponential. They are fundamentally different from the probability distributions of the asset prices or returns which are power laws.*

This fact implies that *the standard Euler equation (equation (10.1)) based on the representative agent assumption for explaining asset prices is fundamentally flawed.*

It is important then to identify and compare the underlying mechanisms which generate power-law distributions for the returns of financial assets on one hand, and exponential distributions for the real economic activities such as the growth of real GDP on the other. Before we proceed to this interesting problem, in the next section, we first show that the standard (not necessarily consumption based) asset pricing model has also a fundamental problem.

10.3. The Problem with the Standard Asset Pricing Model

In this analysis, *multiplicative process* plays an essential role.

Definition (Multiplicative Process): *Y_t is said to follow a multiplicative process when it satisfies the following stochastic difference equation:*

$$Y_t = M_t Y_{t-1} + Q_t \quad (t = 1, 2, \ldots) \tag{10.6}$$

where $\{M_t, Q_t\}$ is a pair of i.i.d. real-valued random variables.

For the relation between multiplicative process and power laws, the following theorem (attributed to Kesten, 1973; Goldie, 1991) is fundamental.

Theorem (Kesten–Goldie): *Consider the multiplicative process defined by equation (10.6).*

A. *If*

$$E\left[\log(|M_t|)\right] < 0 \quad (t = 1, 2, \ldots) \tag{10.7}$$

holds, then Y_t converges in distribution, and has a unique limiting distribution.
B. *If in addition to (10.7), $Q_t/(1 - M_t)$ is nondegenerate,[6] and there exists some $\alpha > 0$ such that:*

$$0 < E\left[|Q_t|^\alpha\right] < \infty, \tag{10.8}$$

$$E\left[|M_t|^\alpha\right] = 1 \tag{10.9}$$

and

$$E\left[|M_t|^\alpha \ln^+ |M_t|\right] < \infty, \tag{10.10}$$

then the tails of the limiting distribution are asymptotic to a power law, that is, they obey a power law of the type

$$P\left(|Y_t| > x\right) \approx c \cdot x^{-\alpha}. \ \blacksquare$$

Note that as we will see shortly, equation (10.9) gives the power exponent α of the distribution of Y_t. Using this theorem, we first explain Lux and Sornette's (2002) analysis of "rational bubbles." It turns out that beyond bubbles, this analysis actually makes clear the fundamental difficulty faced by the standard model of asset prices.

Model of "Rational Bubbles"

Blanchard (1979), and Blanchard and Watson (1982) present the model of rational bubbles. In this model, the "bubbles" B_t is assumed to follow an explosive path with probability $\pi (0 < \pi < 1)$, while collapse to zero with probability $1 - \pi$. To allow for the start of a new bubble after the collapse, an *i.i.d.* stochastic disturbance ϵ_t is added. Thus, B_t follows the following process:

$$B_t = a_t B_{t-1} + \epsilon_t \tag{10.11}$$

where

$$a_t = a > 1 \quad \text{with probability } \pi$$

and

$$a_t = 0 \quad \text{with probability } 1 - \pi.$$

Therefore, $\{a_t\}$ is also *i.i.d.* Because $\{a_t, B_t\}$ is a pair of *i.i.d.* random variables, B_t is a multiplicative process.

Rational expectations require B_t to satisfy

$$B_t = \beta E\left[B_{t+1}|\Omega_t\right] \qquad (0 < \beta < 1) \tag{10.12}$$

---

[6] Here, "nondegenerate" means that Q_t is not a constant times $(1 - M_t)$, and the notation $\ln x^+$ denotes max $(0, \log x)$.

where Ω_t is the information set available to investors at time t, and β is the discount factor. It is easy to show that because of equation (10.12), the following condition must hold for the multiplicative process determined by equation (10.11):

$$a = \frac{1}{\pi \beta} > 1. \tag{10.13}$$

The rate of "bubble explosion" is determined by π and β in such a way that equation (10.13) holds.

Now, we apply the Kesten–Goldie theorem to this model. Because B_t satisfies the conditions which the theorem requires, the tails of the limiting distribution of B_t follow a power-law:

$$\text{Prob}\,(B_t > x) \propto x^{-\alpha}$$

Using equation (10.9), we can determine the power exponent α of this distribution. In the present case, equation (10.9) reads as follows:

$$E\left[a_t^\alpha\right] = \pi a^\alpha = 1. \tag{10.14}$$

This is equivalent to

$$\alpha = \frac{\log\,(1/\pi)}{\log a}. \tag{10.15}$$

Using (10.13), we can rewrite (10.15) as

$$\alpha = \frac{\log\,(1/\pi)}{\log\,(1/\pi) + \log\,(1/\beta)} < 1.$$

The Blanchard–Watson model of "rational bubbles," therefore, leads us to the power-law distribution of stock prices with the power exponent which is *less than one*. However, as we have seen in the previous section, it is well established that the probability distribution of stock prices and their returns[7] follows the power laws with *the exponent close to 3* (see equation (10.4)). Thus, using the Kesten–Goldie theorem, Lux and Sornette (2002) have shown that the Blanchard–Watson model of rational bubbles fails in accurately characterizing the behavior of stock prices.

Difficulty Faced by the Standard Model

More broadly, Sornette's (2002) analysis implies that the standard (not necessarily consumption–based) asset pricing model also faces the same fundamental

---

[7] The difference between stock prices themselves and their rates of change is inessential in that distributions of both variables are basically the same (see Lux and Sornette, 2002).

difficulty.[8] According to the standard model, the price of stock, P_t satisfies the following relation:

$$P_{t+1} = a_t P_t - D_t. \tag{10.16}$$

Here, the dividend D_t is equal to

$$D_t = e^{gt} d_t \tag{10.17}$$

where d_t satisfies

$$0 < E(d_t) = d < \infty. \tag{10.18}$$

The term e^{gt} reflects the growth of the firm or the economy. Rational expectations require that

$$\frac{E(P_{t+1}) - P_t}{P_t} + \frac{E(D_t)}{P_t} = r. \tag{10.19}$$

Here, r is the rate of return on stock or the discount rate. Equation (10.19) is equivalent to

$$E(P_{t+1}) = (1+r)P_t - E(D_t). \tag{10.20}$$

Comparing (10.20) with (10.16), we see that

$$E(a_t) = 1 + r = \beta^{-1} > 1 \tag{10.21}$$

where β is the discount factor:

$$\beta = \frac{1}{1+r} \cong e^{-r}. \tag{10.22}$$

Now, equations (10.17) and (10.18) imply that condition (10.8) of the Kesten–Goldie Theorem is not satisfied: $E[|-D_t|^\alpha] = d^\alpha e^{\alpha gt}$ diverges as t goes to infinity. Thus, we cannot apply the theorem to equation (10.16) for P_t. To get around this problem, we follow Sornette (2002), and divide both sides of equation (10.16) by e^{gt} to obtain

$$\hat{P}_{t+1} = e^{-g} a_t \hat{P}_t - e^{-g} d_t \tag{10.23}$$

where

$$\hat{P}_t = e^{-gt} P_t. \tag{10.24}$$

Equation (10.23) satisfies the conditions for the Kesten–Goldie Theorem. We note that except for a constant term, g, the rates of change in P_t and $\hat{P}_t$ are basically equal:

$$\frac{\hat{P}_{t+1} - \hat{P}_t}{\hat{P}_t} = \frac{P_{t+1} - P_t}{P_t} - g \tag{10.25}$$

---

[8] Sornette (2002) considers the problem of "bubbles." In our view, his analysis applies more usefully to the fundamental valuation formula.

and, therefore, that the probability distributions of $\hat{P}_t$ and P_t are the same. Thanks to the theorem, the distributions of P_t and $\hat{P}_t$ are power laws. Using equation (10.9), we can find the power exponent α :

$$E\left[\left(e^{-g}a_t\right)^{\alpha}\right] = 1 \qquad (10.26)$$

Sornette (2002) considers the case where multiplicative factor a_t follows the *log-normal distribution* such that

$$E\left[\log a_t\right] = \log a_0 \qquad (10.27)$$

with variance σ^2. Then

$$E\left[\left(e^{-g}a_t\right)^{\alpha}\right] = \exp\left[-g\alpha + \alpha \log a_0 + \alpha^2 \left(\frac{\sigma^2}{2}\right)\right]. \qquad (10.28)$$

Substituting (10.28) into (10.26), we obtain

$$\alpha = \frac{2\left(g - \log a_0\right)}{\sigma^2}. \qquad (10.29)$$

In the case of the log-normal distribution,

$$E(a_t) = a_0 e^{\frac{\sigma^2}{2}} \qquad (10.30)$$

holds. From (10.21), (10.22), and (10.30), we obtain

$$e^r = a_0 e^{\frac{\sigma^2}{2}}. \qquad (10.31)$$

This equation is equivalent to

$$\frac{\sigma^2}{2} = r - \log a_0. \qquad (10.32)$$

We substitute (32) into (29) to obtain

$$\alpha = \frac{g - \log a_0}{r - \log a_0} = 1 + \frac{g - r}{r - \log a_0}. \qquad (10.33)$$

Thus, we can conclude that as long as r is greater than g, the power exponent α of the probability distribution of stock returns is *less than one*. Note that unless the discount rate r is greater than the growth rate of dividends g, the standard valuation formula does not make sense.

Proposition: *The standard (not necessarily consumption-based) asset pricing model leads us to the result that the probability distribution of stock prices or returns is a power law with the exponent α less than one. This contradicts the stylized fact that α is about 3.*

In this way, the standard theory of asset prices faces a serious difficulty. In fact, by detailed study of microscopic fluctuations in prices on the London Stock

Exchange, Farmer et al. (2004) demonstrate that large price changes occur when there are *gaps* in the occupied price levels in the order book.[9] It suggests that in a market where participants place many small orders uniformly across prices, such large price fluctuations as we actually observe would not happen. In other words, *differences in opinion* as indicated by *gaps* in placed prices play the crucial role in causing large price fluctuations. *Thus, any theory of asset prices built on the representative agent assumption is fundamentally flawed.*

Farmer et al. (2004) has also found that the probability distributions of the stocks which are more lightly traded (or have lower event rates) tend to display fatter tails, with more extreme risks than otherwise. This finding poses another difficulty to the representative agent model. At this stage, we can usefully recall that the model we analyzed in Chapter 9 with two different types of investors, "fundamentalists" and "chartists," has produced a power-law distribution of changes in stock price *with the exponent greater than one.*

We need a theory that starts from stochastic microeconomic behaviors. Within such a theoretical framework, we can compare financial markets with the real economy. The stylized fact is that stock prices and returns obey the power law with the exponent close to 3, whereas the probability distribution of real variables such as GDP and consumption is exponential.

10.4. Underlying Mechanism: A Truncated Lévy Flight Model

We now come back to the fundamental problem, what is the underlying mechanism that generates power-law distributions for returns of financial assets and exponential distributions for real economic variables such as growth rate of real GDP.

As we explained in Section 10.2, the random walk the leads us to the normal (or Gaussian) distribution. Unlike the standard random walk, the *truncated Lévy flight*, explained earlier, depending on parameters, can generate a wide class of probability distributions including power laws and exponential distributions. In what follows, we will consider a particular model of truncated Lévy flight which nests both power laws and exponential distributions. The model is an adapted or modified version of Huang and Solomon (2001).

The Real Economy

We first consider a model of the real economy. The economy consists of N sectors or units. For the sake of expositional convenience, we call the variable of interest "consumption." It may be "production," and in that case, the aggregate variable is GDP. N sectors or units may be interpreted either as N types of consumers,

---

[9] Farmer et al. (2004) documentents that even for actively traded stocks, the number of occupied price levels on either "sell" or "buy" side of the book at any given time is typically only 30.

or as N types of consumption goods. Interpretation of the model can be very flexible.

The aggregate consumption at time t, $C(t)$, is nothing but the sum of the individual consumptions:

$$C(t) = c_1(t) + \cdots + c_N(t). \tag{10.34}$$

Here, $c_i(t)$ is the consumption of type i good or the ith consumer's consumption. The argument t stands for calendar or real time. We interpret the period from t to $t + 1$ as one month, one quarter or one year as the case maybe.

We are interested in the growth rate of the *aggregate* consumption $C(t)$ over $[t, t + 1]$. We define $r(t)$ as

$$r(t) = \frac{C(t+1) - C(t)}{C(t)}. \tag{10.35}$$

Our goal is to derive the probability distribution of r.

The growth of aggregate (or macro) consumption arises from the aggregation of growths of the N individual (or micro) consumptions. We think of this *micro* growth in the form of a (large) number of *elementary events*. The number of elementary events within a period (namely over $[t, t + 1]$) is τ. One elementary event is that a sector, sector i, say, being randomly chosen from the set $\{1, 2, \ldots, N\}$ between t and $t + 1$, experiences growth of consumption. We use the term "sector," but it can be any micro unit such as agent, individual or firm. A sector may be chosen either uniformly with probability $1/N$ or with some other probabilities possibly dependent on the size of the sector. If sector i is chosen, $c_i(t)$ grows by a random factor λ:

$$c_i'(t) = \lambda c_i(t). \tag{10.36}$$

Here, $c_i'(t)$ is defined as c_i immediately after the elementary growth. At this event, no other sector ($j \neq i$) experiences growth.

For simpler exposition, we assume that

$$\lambda = 1 + g, \quad \text{for } \forall\, i, t \tag{10.37}$$

where

$$g = \pm\gamma \quad (0 < \gamma < 1).$$

Note that this is a particular type of multiplicative process for c_i. As we mention later, the probability distribution of λ does not matter at all.

It is extremely important to keep in mind the difference between t and τ. One is the *calendar time*, t, and the other is τ, the number of *elementary (micro) events* within a given period of time. When there are a total of τ such elementary events undergone by some or all of the N sectors, each sector is most likely to experience more than one elementary events on the average. We denote the resultant growth rate of aggregate consumption as $r(t; \tau)$. That is, $r(t; \tau)$ is the growth rate of $C(t)$

between t and $t + 1$ when the number of elementary micro events during the period is τ. Although τ is a random number, we use its expected value and denote it by τ.

With τ random selections out of N sectors in one period, we can write the rate of growth of aggregate consumption as

$$r(t; \tau) = \sum_{i,k} g_{i,k}, \qquad (k = 1, \dots \tau) \tag{10.38}$$

where

$$g_{i,k} = \frac{(c_{i,k+1} - c_{i,k})}{C} = \frac{\pm \gamma c_i(t; k)}{C}. \tag{10.39}$$

Here, $g_{i,k}$ indicates the kth elementary growth that has occurred to $c_i(t)$. The total change that defines the growth rate of aggregate consumption $C(t)$ is the sum of these elementary growths that occured to $c_1, \dots, c_N$. The total number of the elementary events that have occurred is equal to τ.

In this model, the size of a jump of a micro unit is constant (equation (10.37)). Thus, the micro behavior is described by the ordinary random walk. However, such micro growths occur τ times within a period. As a consequence, the growth of *aggregate* consumption $C(t)$ follows the *truncated Lévy flight* explained in Section 10.2. It is a "truncated" Lévy flight because τ is finite.

We make an important assumption that there is a lower bound constraint to the elementary micro growth process. That is, the sector size after an elementary (micro) growth must be above the minimum, $c_{\min}(t)$ defined by

$$c_{\min}(t) = q c_{\text{av}}(t), \qquad (0 < q < 1) \tag{10.40}$$

where

$$c_{\text{av}}(t) = \frac{C(t)}{N}. \tag{10.41}$$

Here, q is the fraction of the average consumption that serves as the lower bound to all of c's. Thus, we actually obtain $c_i'(t)$ not as (10.36) but as

$$c_i'(t) = \max \{\lambda c_i(t), c_{\min}(t)\} = \max \{(1 \pm \gamma) c_i(t), q c_{\text{av}}(t)\}. \tag{10.42}$$

By scaling c_i by $c_{\text{av}}(t)$ we define the fraction $y_i(t)$:

$$y_i(t) = \frac{c_i(t)}{c_{\text{av}}(t)}.$$

It satisfies the normalization condition that the average of the fractions is 1:

$$\bar{y} = \frac{1}{N} \sum_i y_i(t) = 1. \tag{10.43}$$

By changing variables into

$$Y_i = \log y_i, \tag{10.44}$$

we observe that the basic dynamics defined by (10.42) becomes a kind of random walk with varying step sizes, that is, a *truncated Lévy flight* explained earlier with a lower reflecting barrier:

$$Y_i'(t) = Y_i(t) + \log \lambda. \tag{10.45}$$

Here again, the prime indicates *the value after one elementary event*, not *the calender time* derivative.

The master equation is

$$P(Y'(t)) - P(Y(t)) = \frac{1}{N} \left[\int dF(\lambda) P(Y - \log \lambda, t) - P(Y, t) \right] \tag{10.46}$$

where F is the probability distribution for λ.[10] Each sector is assumed to be selected with equal probability $1/N$, here. It is shown by Choquet (1960), and Choquet and Deny (1960), and Levy and Solomon (1996) that the asymptotic stationary distribution of Y, $P(Y)$ defined by

$$\int_q^N dF(\mu) P(Y - \mu) d\mu = \Lambda P(Y) \qquad (\Lambda \quad \text{is a constant}) \tag{10.47}$$

is exponential. That is, we obtain

$$P(Y) \propto e^{-\alpha Y}. \tag{10.48}$$

Because Y is defined as $\log y$ (equation (10.44) above), we have the probability density function of y as

$$p(y) = K y^{-1-\alpha}. \tag{10.49}$$

This constant K is determined by the fact $p(y)$ is the probability density that integrates to 1:

$$\int p(y) dy = 1. \tag{10.50}$$

At the same time, the normalization noted earlier requires that the mean of y is 1 (equation (10.43)):

$$\int y p(y) dy = 1. \tag{10.51}$$

From (10.50) and (10.51), we can derive an implicit relation between q, α and N (See Malcai, Biham, and Solomon, 1999);

$$N = \left(\frac{\alpha - 1}{\alpha} \right) \left[\frac{(q/N)^\alpha - 1}{(q/N)^\alpha - (q/N)} \right]. \tag{10.52}$$

---

[10] In our present model, $\lambda = 1 \pm \gamma$ (equation (10.37)). Thus, λ is assumed to take only two values. More generally, if a probability density function $f(\lambda)$ exists for λ, then $dF(\lambda)$ in (10.46) should be replaced by $f(\lambda) d\lambda$.

This equation is solved approximately as

$$\alpha \approx \frac{1}{1-q},\tag{10.53}$$

when $N \gg e^{1/q}$.

Denote by $R(r;\tau)$ the cumulative distribution function of r, that is, the probability that the growth rate is less than or equal to r with τ elementary growths. We also define

$$\bar{R}(r;\tau) = 1 - R(r;\tau).\tag{10.54}$$

For $\tau = 1$, we define

$$\bar{S}(r) = R(r, 1)\tag{10.55}$$

and

$$\bar{S}(r) = 1 - S(r).\tag{10.56}$$

Note that the distribution function S refers to one elementary change to only one of the N sectors.

From the asymptotic solution of the master equation, we obtain

$$\bar{S}(r) \sim \left(\frac{r}{r_{\min}}\right)^{-\alpha}\tag{10.57}$$

where

$$r_{\min} = \frac{\gamma c_{\min}}{C} = \frac{\gamma q c_{\mathrm{av}}}{C} = \gamma q \left(\frac{C}{N}\right)\left(\frac{1}{C}\right) = \frac{\gamma q}{N}.\tag{10.58}$$

There are many ways how the growth rate of *aggregate* consumption, r is realized.[11] The same aggregate growth rate, r, may be due either to a small number of elementary micro growths with large step size such as $r/2$ and $r/3$, or to a large number of small micro growths each with small step size. This makes a difference to the emerging probability distribution of r.

Exponential Distribution

In what follows, we will derive an exponential distribution for the aggregate growth rate r, under the condition that the number of micro events τ does not exceed a critical level, $\bar{\tau}$, which is defined shortly. It is simpler to explain this by way of a concrete example.

Suppose there are $2k$ events out of τ with magnitude $\gamma/2$ rates each, and that the rest of τ (that is $\tau - 2k$) steps make almost zero net contribution to the

---

[11] A positive r and a negative r can be treated in almost identical ways. We focus on positive r.

aggregate growth. In this case, the aggregate growth rate r is achieved by way of

$$r = 2k \left(\frac{\gamma}{2}\right) = k\gamma. \qquad (\text{k} = 1, 2, \dots) \qquad (10.59)$$

The probability that the aggregate growth rate is equal to or greater than $k\gamma$ with τ elementary events is given by

$$\bar{R}(r = k\gamma, 2k) = \binom{\tau}{2k} \left[\bar{s}\left(\frac{\gamma}{2}\right)\right]^{2k} \cong \tau^{2k} \left[\bar{s}\left(\frac{\gamma}{2}\right)\right]^{2k}. \qquad (10.60)$$

Here, we have used the fact that the number of combinations of taking $2k$ out of τ, that is $_\tau C_{2k} = \tau(\tau - 1)\dots(\tau - 2k + 1)/(2k)!$ can be approximated by τ^{2k}. We know from (10.57) and (10.58)

$$\left[\bar{s}\left(\frac{\gamma}{2}\right)\right]^2 = \left(\frac{N}{2q}\right)^{-\alpha}. \qquad (10.61)$$

Thus, we can rewrite the above probability (10.60) as

$$\bar{R}(r = k\gamma, \ 2k) = \left[\left(\frac{N}{2q}\right)^{2\alpha} \frac{1}{\tau^2}\right]^{-\frac{r}{\gamma}}. \qquad (10.62)$$

If we define

$$\bar{\tau} = \left(\frac{N}{2q}\right)^{\alpha}, \qquad (10.63)$$

we can rewrite equation (10.62) more compactly as follows:

$$\bar{R}(r = k\gamma, 2k) = \left[\frac{\bar{\tau}^2}{\tau^2}\right]^{-\frac{r}{\gamma}}. \qquad (10.64)$$

When $\tau < \bar{\tau}$ is satisfied, then this probability distribution is exponential. It is given by

$$\bar{R}(r = \gamma k, 2k) = \exp\left[-\left(\frac{\log A}{\gamma}\right)r\right] \qquad (10.65)$$

where

$$A = \left(\frac{\bar{\tau}}{\tau}\right)^2. $$

Its density function is of the form

$$f(r) = -\frac{d\bar{R}(r, 2k)}{dr} = \frac{\log A}{\gamma} \exp\left[-\left(\frac{\ln A}{\gamma}\right)r\right]. \qquad (10.66)$$

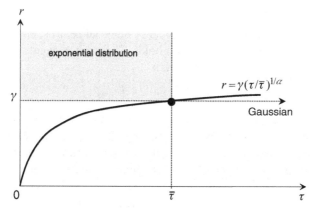

Figure 10.2. Exponential distribution for the real economy.
Note: See Huang and Solomon (2001) for further details of this diagram.

We note that the peak value of this density is

$$f(0) = \frac{\log A}{\gamma} \qquad (10.67)$$

The probability of the rate r being achieved as $r = bk \times \gamma/b$, $(b = 1, 2, \ldots)$ can be calculated similarly. No substantial changes are involved.

Thus, we have established the following proposition.

Proposition: *To obtain an exponential distribution for the growth rate of aggregate consumption, the number of elementary events within a given calender time period, τ, cannot exceed a critical level $\bar{\tau}$. This maximum number $\bar{\tau}$ is given by*

$$\bar{\tau}(b) \cong (N/bq)^{\alpha}$$

for some small positive integer b. The probability density function of r is then the following exponential distribution:

$$f(r, b) \propto \exp\left[-\frac{b}{\gamma} \log\left(\frac{\bar{\tau}}{\tau}\right) r\right]. \qquad (10.68)$$

The probability distribution of r depends on parameters. In particular, it depends crucially on τ and γ. Figure 10.2 shows the region where we obtain exponential distribution in terms of τ and γ. For $\tau < \bar{\tau}$, and r larger than γ, we obtain the exponential distribution of r. Note that in our example, r is $k\gamma$ (equation (10.59) ($k = 1, 2, \ldots$) and, therefore, is necessarily greater than γ. γ is the growth rate of "elementary events" (equation (10.37)) so that we can conceptually take it as small as we wish.

The implication of this proposition is that to obtain an exponential distribution for the growth rate of *aggregate real* variables as we actually do, the number of micro growths within a short period of time τ must be sufficiently "small."

Financial Returns

In this section, we study a similar model of financial returns, and characterize the case where power law distribution holds. There are N agents or assets each with financial resources or wealth, $w_i(t)$:

$$W(t) = w_1(t) + \cdots + w_N(t). \tag{10.69}$$

As in the real-sector model, one of N sectors (or stocks) are randomly selected for an elementary event, that is, a micro change. This random selection could be uniform with probability $1/N$, or could be modified to favor large sectors (or investors). There are τ such micro or elementary events within a unit interval of time.

When sector i is selected, it undergoes the change

$$w_i'(t) = (1 + g)w_i(t) \tag{10.70}$$

where

$$g = \pm\gamma.$$

Again, $w_i'(t)$ indicates the value of w_i immediately after the elementary growth in the ith asset or agent's wealth. It is *not* the time derivative of $w_i(t)$.

The rate of return on financial assets or wealth over a calender period from t to $t + 1$, $r(t)$, is defined, analogously to the rate of growth of consumption, by

$$r(t) = \frac{W(t + 1) - W(t)}{W(t)}. \tag{10.71}$$

We are interested in the case where the probability distribution of r becomes a power-law distribution. When there are τ elementary events during $[t, t + 1]$, r is denoted by $r(t, \tau)$. By definition, $r(t, \tau)$ is as follows:

$$r(t, \tau) := \sum_{i,k} f_{i,k} \tag{10.72}$$

where

$$f_{i,k} = \frac{\pm\gamma w_i(t; k)}{W(t)}.$$

As in the real sector model, we obtain

$$\bar{S}(r) = 1 - R(r; 1) \sim \left(\frac{r}{r_{\min}}\right)^{-\alpha} \tag{10.73}$$

where

$$r_{\min} = \frac{\gamma w_{\min}}{W} = \frac{\gamma q w_{av}}{W} = \frac{\gamma q W}{WN} = \frac{\gamma q}{N}.$$

Equation (10.73) corresponds to (10.57) for the real economy.

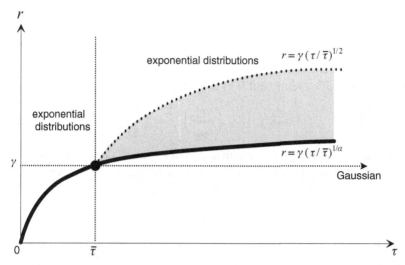

Figure 10.3. Power-Law distribution ($\alpha > 2$) for the financial markets.

Again, the probability distribution of r depends on parameters, τ and γ. Huang and Solomon (2001) demonstrate that depending on parameters, a power-law distribution emerges. The region in which power laws *with the exponent α close to 3* emerge[12] in the financial model is shadowed in Figure 10.3. The boundaries of the region are determined by two curves on the $\tau - r$ plane.

One is

$$r = \gamma \left[\frac{\tau}{\bar{\tau}} \right]^{1/\alpha} \tag{10.74}$$

where

$$\bar{\tau} = \left(\frac{N}{2q} \right)^{\alpha}. \tag{10.75}$$

The other curve is defined by

$$r = \gamma \sqrt{\frac{\tau}{\bar{\tau}}}. \tag{10.76}$$

Equation (10.74) can be derived as follows. For a given aggregate growth rate r, we compare two cases. In case one, r is attained by two elementary growths, each of which has the size of $r/2$, whereas in case two, r is attained by just one elementary growth. We consider the condition that the former is more likely than

---

[12] Huang and Solomon (2001) demonstrate by their simulations that the exponent α becomes close to 3.

the latter, that is

$$_\tau C_2 \left(\bar{S} \left(\frac{r}{2} \right) \right)^2 > \tau \bar{S}(r). \tag{10.77}$$

Here, $_\tau C_2$ is the combination of taking two elementary events with net contribution to r out of τ events, and $\bar{S}(r)$ is

$$\bar{S}(r) = \bar{R}(r, 1) = \left(\frac{r}{r_{\min}} \right)^{-\alpha} = \left(\frac{rN}{q\gamma} \right)^{-\alpha}. \tag{10.78}$$

Recall that $\bar{S}(r)$ is the probability that at least r growth rate is attained by one elementary event. By substituting (10.78) into (10.77), and approximating $_\tau C_2 \simeq \tau^2$, we can rewrite the above inequality (10.77) as

$$r < \bar{r} \equiv \frac{2q}{N} \gamma \tau^{\frac{1}{\alpha}}. \tag{10.79}$$

In this region, power-law distributions are less likely to hold because the effects of the initial power law for a single step, $\bar{S}(r)$, on the distribution of r weakens. Recall that the inequality (10.77) means that r is more likely to be obtained by two steps than a single step. In other words, power laws emerge in the region whose boundary is

$$r = \frac{2q}{N} \gamma \tau^{\frac{1}{\alpha}}. \tag{10.80}$$

With $\bar{\tau}$ defined by (10.75), equation (10.80) can be rewritten as equation (10.74).

Likewise, we can derive the other boundary, equation (10.76) (see Huang and Solomon, 2001 for details). Here, we focus on the region[13] where $\tau > \bar{\tau}$ and $r > \gamma$ hold. Recall that we obtain the exponential distribution when $\tau < \bar{\tau}$ and $r > \gamma$ hold (for the real economy).

As for power laws, we can also derive them by way of using Langevin equation. This alternative approach is explained in Appendix 10.1. The merit of the Huang–Solomon model is that it nests both power laws and exponential distributions. We can summarize the results of our analysis as follows.

Proposition: *In a truncated Lévy flight model in which the aggregate growth rate, r is composed of a number of micro or elementary growths within a unit interval of time, the probability distribution of r depends crucially on the number of such micro events, τ. Specifically, when τ is smaller than a critical value $\bar{\tau}$, the exponential distribution emerges while we can obtain power laws with the exponent α close to 3 for $\tau > \bar{\tau}$. To the extent that the number of micro growths within a period is small in the real economy whereas it is large in financial markets, we can explain the stylized*

---

[13]   We note that as τ becomes much larger than $\bar{\tau}$, the probability distribution eventually approaches the Gaussian distribution via intermediate Lévy like distributions (see Huang and Solomon, 2001).

fact that we observe the exponential distribution for "real" growth whereas power laws with the exponent α close to 3 for financial returns.

10.5. Concluding Remarks on Real and Financial Markets

People often think or perhaps feel that real and financial markets are different. It rarely happens that our salaries and wages are doubled within a relatively short period of time, say a year. In contrast, we know that, if not very often, the price of a stock can double in a year. This difference is formally reflected in two different probability distributions; one is exponential distribution for the growth rate of *real* variable such as GDP or consumption, while the other is power-law distribution for asset prices and returns.

We began with the observation that a particular type of multiplicative process, the *truncated Lévy flight*, nests a broad range of growth processes including real and financial activities. The preceding analysis has shown that within this framework, the crucial parameter is the number of elementary micro growth events within a given period, say a month (τ in the model). When the number of micro growth events within a period is small, an exponential distribution can emerge. Conversely, when the number of micro growth events within a period is large, then power-law distributions can emerge.

Thus, given the present model, to account for the stylized fact that we have exponential distributions for the growth rate of real GDP whereas power-law distributions for asset prices and returns, we must assume that within a given period, the number of micro growth events is relatively small in the case of real economic activities whereas it is large in the case of asset prices. Here, we must take this proposition as an *assumption*, and leave it for further research. We maintain that this is a plausible assumption, though. Note that what matters is not *additive* disturbance but multiplicative disturbance. We believe that we can reasonably argue that the frequency of multiplicative shocks is much higher for asset prices than for real micro economic activities.

Think of it this way. In your "real" life, the costs of transportation and food today is more or less the same as yesterday, and will be about the same tomorrow. In contrast, in stock market, you must be always aware of the presence of "multiplicative shocks." Our analysis shows that the frequency of multiplicative shocks is a crucial determinant of different probability distributions of aggregate growth rate; one exponential distribution for the real economy, and the other power laws for financial returns. In any case, it is an important research agenda to ascertain this proposition. For the moment, we conclude that we have a good deal of empirical observation to reject the standard asset price model based on the representative consumer, and at the same time, a plausible theoretical reason to believe that the real economy and asset markets are different creatures.

Appendix 10.1: Power Laws Derived from the Langevin Equation

In this appendix, we sketch an alternative approach based on the *Langevin equations*. This approach is known to be equivalent to the Fokker–Planck equation, and describes the stationary distributions of returns. This approach is not so helpful to our understanding the mechanisms generating financial returns and real economic activities as the one in the main text, but is theoretically clear cut. We follow Richmond and Solomon (2001).

Let $\phi(t)$ be the instantaneous return of some financial asset. We assume that its dynamics is given by the Langevin equation:

$$\frac{d\phi(t)}{dt} = F(\phi(t)) + G(\phi(t))\eta(t),$$

where η is a mean zero and finite variance noise:

$$E(\eta(t)) = 0, \quad \text{and} \quad E[\eta(t)\eta(t')] = 2D\delta(t - t').$$

Richmond has shown that the probability distribution of ϕ satisfies the generalized Fokker–Planck equation[14]

$$\frac{\partial P}{\partial t} = D\frac{\partial}{\partial \phi}\left[G\left(\frac{\partial(GP)}{\partial \phi}\right)\right] - \frac{\partial}{\partial \phi}(FP).$$

He shows that this equation has the steady-state solution

$$P(\phi) = \frac{1}{Z|G(\phi)|}\exp(-\Psi(\phi))$$

where Z is the normalization constant, and

$$\Psi(\phi) = -\frac{1}{D}\int^{\phi}\frac{F}{G^2}d\phi.$$

For a simple example, suppose that

$$G(\phi) = \phi + \epsilon,$$

and

$$F(\phi) = -J\phi,$$

with $J > 0$. Then, by taking $\epsilon \longrightarrow 0$, we obtain

$$P(\phi) = \frac{1}{Z}|\phi|^{-1-J/D}.$$

With a cubic

$$F(\phi) = -J\phi + b\phi^2 - c\phi^3,$$

---

[14]   See Aoki (2002, Sec. 8.7) or Honerkamp (1998, chapter 6), for example.

there is a correction term $\exp(2b\phi - c\phi^2)/D$. Thus in regions where the exponential correction is nearly 1, we have an approximate power law.

Next, partially following Solomon and Richmond (2001), we apply this basic tool in developing a financial model with N agents with resources $w_i(t)$, $i = 1, 2, \ldots, N$.

The aggregate asset is

$$W(t) = \sum_j b_j w_j$$

where

$$\sum b_j = 1.$$

We focus on the fraction

$$x_i(t) = \frac{w_j(t)}{W(t)}.$$

Its Langevin equation is

$$dx_i(t) = \frac{dw_i(t)}{W(t)} - \frac{w_i(t)du}{W^2(t)}$$

$$= (\epsilon_i(t)\sigma_i - a)x_i(t) + a_i$$

where

$$a = \sum_i b_i a_i(t).$$

We assume that the evolution of financial asset of type i agents is given by

$$dw_i(t) = \epsilon_i(t)\sigma_i w_i(t) + a_i W(t), \quad i = 1, 2, \ldots, N.$$

We take without loss of generality that the mean of ϵ is 0 and variance 1. The Langevin equation becomes

$$dx_i(t) = \epsilon\sigma_i x_i(t) - ax_i(t).$$

From the formula developed above of Richmond, the steady-state solution is

$$P(x_i) = \frac{1}{(\sigma_i x_i)^2} \exp\left(2\int \frac{[-ax_i + a_i]}{(\sigma_i x_i)^2} dx_i\right).$$

In the range where $2a_i/x_i\sigma_i^2 \ll 1$, this distribution is approximately a power law:

In other words, we have

$$P(x_i) \approx x^{-1-\alpha_i}, \tag{10.81}$$

where

$$\alpha_i = 1 + 2a/\sigma_i^2.$$

Appendix 10.2: Examples of Power Laws in Clusters

In the main text, we have considered a truncated Lévy flight model in which a power law distribution is generated. In that model, lower bounds or lower reflective boundaries play the essential role for generating power laws. There are different models. This appendix assembles such models in which power laws are generated without the assumption of lower bounds.

1. Large Deviations and Power Laws

For i.i.d., Poisson random variables $X_i, i = 1, 2, \ldots$, the sum possesses a power-law relation. Let $S_n = X_1 + \cdots + X_n$. By the Markov or Chernoff inequality

$$\Pr(S_n/n > a) = \Pr(e^{\theta S_n} \geq e^{na\theta}) := e^{-nI(a)},$$

where θ is nonnegative, and

$$I(a) := \sup[\theta a - \log M(\theta)],$$

where $M(\theta) = E(e^{\theta X_1})$.

When x is Poisson distributed with mean λ, then $M(\theta) = \exp[\lambda(e^{\theta} - 1)]$, and $I(a) = a \log(a/\lambda) - (a - \lambda)$. We have a power-law relationship

$$\Pr(S_n/n > a) \approx a^{-na}.$$

2. Yule Process

In a Yule process a cluster starts with a single agent. New agents arrive as a linear birth process with rate λ. These agents are all of the same type. Let $N(t)$ be the number of agents at time t. Its probability generating function is

$$G(z, t) = \sum_{i=0}^{\infty} p_i z^i = [ze^{-\lambda t}/(1 - z + ze^{-\lambda t})]^{n_0},$$

where p_i is the probability that $N(t) = i$, and n_0 is the initial number of agents, which is set to 1. (See Cox and Miller, 1965 for example.) From this generating function we retrieve

$$p_n(t) = e^{-\lambda t}(1 - e^{-\lambda t})^{n-1}.$$

Aldous (2001) has an example which modifies this basic Yule process model by assuming that new types of agents appear within each cluster at a constant rate μ, so that the number of types grows exponentially. The number of agents in a randomly chosen cluster is given by

$$p(n) = \int_0^{\infty} \mu e^{-\mu t} e^{-\lambda t}(1 - e - \lambda t)^{n-1} dt.$$

Changing variable from t to $x = e^{-\lambda t}$, we recognize this integral to be that of a beta integral, hence

$$p(n) = \frac{\Gamma(1 + \rho^{-1})}{\rho} \frac{\Gamma(n)}{\Gamma(n + 1 + \rho^{-1})} \approx n_1 - \rho^{-1},$$

with $\rho = \lambda/\mu$.

3. Birth–Death process with second-order balanced rates

A model related to this arises in the birth-death process when their rates are

$$\frac{\lambda_{i-1}}{\mu_i} = 1 - \frac{a}{i} +_O (1/i^2) = [1 + a/i]^{-1} +_O (1/i^2),$$

where λ_{i-1} is the birth rate in a cluster of size $i - 1$, and μ_i is the death rate of a cluster of size i. This assumption says that clusters of small sizes have higher death rates than larger clusters.

Let μ be the entry rate of a singleton. We can write down the master equation for this model and look for stationary solutions by means of the detailed balance condition. We also assume that the maximum size is N.

The last of the master equation is then

$$\frac{dp_N(t)}{dt} = \lambda_{N-1} p_{N-1}(t) - \mu_N p_N(t).$$

The total number of clusters is given by

$$F_N = \sum_{i=1}^{N} p_i(t)$$

and the fraction of clusters of size i is

$$a_i(N) = \frac{p_i}{F_{N,}}$$

where p_i is the stationary state value of $p_i(t)$ as t goes to infinity.

It is straightforward to verify that

$$a_i(N) \prod_{j=2}^{i} (1 + a/j)^{-1} \approx i^{-a}.$$

This is the power law for this model. See Karev, Wolf, Rzhetsky, Berezovskaya, and Koonin (2002).

4. Yule–Simon Model

A Ewens distribution yields a Zipf distribution and not a more a general power law, because the expected number of clusters of size i in the presence of n agents in the model, $E(a_i(n))$, is given by

$$z_i(n) := E(a_i(n)) = \frac{\theta}{i}\left(1 - \frac{i}{n}\right)^{\theta-1} \approx \frac{\theta}{i}.$$

See Aoki (2002, 156). The Ewens model has the entry rate of new type $\theta/[\theta + n]$ which depends on n.

Costantini, Donadio, Garibaldi, and Viarengo (2005) has introduced an entry rate which is independent of n in their reformulation of Yule (1924) and Simon (1955).

Let u be the probability of starting a new cluster by an entrant. Then, $1 - u$ is the probability of a new entrant joining one of the existing clusters.

Denoting the expected value of $a_i(n)$ by $z_i(n)$ as above, we have, recalling that an entry into a cluster with n changes the number of clusters of i and $i - 1$,

$$z_i(n + 1) - z_i(n) = (1 - u)[(i - 1)z_{i-1}(n) - iz_i(n)]/n,$$

and

$$z_i(n + 1) - z_i(n) = u - (1 - u)z_1(n)/n.$$

We focus on a stationary relation of these recursive relations

$$\frac{z_i^*(n + 1)}{n + 1} = \frac{z_i^*(n)}{n}.$$

We derive the relation

$$z_i^*(n) = \left(\frac{i - 1}{\rho_i}\right)z_{i-1}^*(n),$$

where $\rho = 1/(1 - u)$.

The stationary solution has the Yule distribution

$$f_i = \frac{z_i^*(n)}{nu} = \rho B(i, \rho + 1), \qquad i = 1, 2, \ldots.$$

The fraction sums to one and we have

$$f_i \approx i^{-1-\rho}.$$

5. The Chinese Restaurant Process and Its Variants

Dubins and Pitman proposed a construction for cluster formation which is known as the Chinese restaurant process. A restaurant has an infinite number of tables and each table can seat an infinite number of customers (agents). The first agent sits at a table. Call it table 1, or cluster 1. After n agents have been seated, there are k_n occupied tables, with $n = n_1 + \cdots + n_{k_n}$. This is the random partition of n into k_n subsets. The next customer either sits at one of the already occupied tables with equal probability, or starts a new table.

There is a one-parameter version and a two-parameter version. In the two-parameter version the probability of starting a new table is $(\theta + k_n\alpha)/(\theta + n)$, and the probability of sitting at a table with n_i guests already seated is $(n_i - \alpha)/(n + \theta)$. In the one parameter version $\alpha = 0$, and θ is some positive number. See Aoki (2006) for an important qualitative difference between models with $\alpha > 0$ and those with $\alpha = 0$.

Agents i and j are of the same type, that is, they belong to the same partitioned subset of $[n]: = \{1, 2, \ldots, n\}$, if seated at the same table.

Pitman (2002) has shown that the sequence $x_1, x_2, \ldots$ defined as the fraction of the partitioned subsets divided by n converges to the Poisson–Dirichlet distribution as n goes to infinity, denoted by $PD(\alpha, \theta)$. The kth term of the sequence is given by $D_k \prod_{j=1}^{k-1}(1 - D_j)$, where D_j is distributed as $B(1 - \alpha, \theta + j\alpha)$.

Durrett and Schweinsberg (2005) modified this process by assuming that the $(n + 1)$st cluster (table) is started with a constant probability r.

Generally, they prove that the cluster size distribution is given by power laws.

References

Abraham, K., and L. Katz (1986) "Cyclical Unemployment: Sectoral Shifts or Aggregate Disturbances?," *Journal of Political Economy*, Vol. 94, No. 3, 507–522.

Abramovitz, M., and I. A. Stegun, (1968) *Handbook of Mathematical Functions*, New York: Dover.

Aghion, P., and P. Howitt (1992) "A Model of Growth through Creative Destruction," *Econometrica*, Vol. 60, 323–351.

Aldous, D. J. (2001) "Stochastic Models and Descriptive Statistics for Phylogenetic Trees, from Yule to Today," *Stat. Sci.* Vol. 16, 23–34.

Andersen, S.P., A. de Palma, and J.F. Thisse (1993) Discrete Choice Theory of Product Differentiation, Cambridge, MA: MIT Press.

Aoki, M. (1976) *Optimal Control and System Theory in Dynamic Economic Analysis*, New York: North-Holland.

―――― (1995) "Economic Fluctuations with Interactive Agents: Dynamic and Stochastic Externalities," *Japanese Economic Review*, Vol. 46, 148–165.

―――― (1996) *New Approaches to Macroeconomic Modeling*, New York: Cambridge University Press.

―――― (1997) "Shares in Emergent Markets: Dynamics and Statistical Properties of Equilibrium Classification of Agents in Evolutionary Models," in T. Katayama and S. Sugimoto (eds.), *Statistical Methods in Control and Signal Processing*, New York: Marcel Dekker.

―――― (1998) "Simple Model of Asymmetrical Business Cycles: Interactive Dynamics of a Large Number of Agents With Discrete Choices," *Macroeconomic Dynamics*, Vol. 2, 427–442.

―――― (2002) *Modeling Aggregate Behavior and Fluctuations in Economics: Stochastic Views of Interacting Agents*, New York: Cambridge University Press.

―――― (2002) "Open Models of Share Markets with Two Dominant Types of Participants," *Journal of Economic Behavior & Organization*, Vol. 49, Issue 2, 199–216.

―――― (2006) "Long-run Behavior of Macroeconomic Models with Heterogeneous Agents: Asymptotic Behavior of One- and Two-Parameter Poisson-Dinichlet Distribution" Proc. Wehia 06 Conference, Bologna Italy.

Aoki, M., and Y. Shirai (2000) "A New Look at the Diamond Search Model: Stochastic Cycles and Equilibrium Selection in Search Equilibrium," *Macroeconomic Dynamics*, Vol. 4, 487–505.

Aoki, M., and H. Yoshikawa (2002) "Demand Saturation/Creation and Economic Growth," *Journal of Economic Behavior and Organization*, Vol. 48. 127–154.

Arratia, R., A.D. Barbour, and S. Tavaré (1992) "Poisson Process Approximation for Ewens Sampling Formula," *Annales of Applied Probability,* Vol. 2, 519–535.

———— (2003) *Logarithmic Combinatorial Structures: A Probabilistic Approach, EMS Monographs in Mathematics, 1,* Zurich: European Mathematical Society Publishing House.

Arrow, K. (1962) "The Economic Implications of Learning by Doing," *Review of Economic Studies,* Vol. 29, No. 3, 155–173.

Attanasio, O., and G. Weber (1993) "Consumption Growth, the Interest Rate and Aggregation," *Review of Economic Studies,* Vol. 60, No. 3, 631–649.

Auerbach, A. J., and M. Obstfeld (2005) "The Case for Open-Market Purchases in a Liquidity Trap," *American Economic Review,* Vol. 95, No. 1, 110–137.

Baily, M. N. (1978) "Stabilization Policy and Private Economic Behavior," *Brookings Papers on Economic Activity 1,* 11–50.

Ball, L., N. G. Mankiw, and D. Romer (1988) "The New Keynesian Economics and the Output-Inflation Tradeoff," *Brooking Papers on Economic Activity,* No. 1, 1–82.

Basu, S. (1996) "Procyclical Productivity Increasing Returns or Cyclical Utilization," *Quarterly Journal of Economics,* Issue 3, 719–751.

Bayoumi, T. (1999) "The Morning After: Explaining the Slowdown in Japanese Growth in the 1990's," *Journal of International Economics,* Vol. 53, 241–259.

Bellman, R. E. (1961) *Adaptive Control Processes: A Guided Tour,* Princeton, NJ: Princeton University Press.

Benassy, J. P. (1975) "Neo-Keynesian Disequilibrium Theory in a Monetary Economy," *Review of Economic Studies,* Vol. 42, 503–523.

Bernanke, B. S. (2000) "Japanese Monetary Policy: A Case of Self-Induced Paralysis," in Ryoichi Mikitani and Adam S. Posen (eds.), *Japan's Financial Crisis and its Parallels to U.S. Experience,* Washington DC: Institute for International Economics, 149–166.

————, V. R. Reinhart, and B. S. Sack (2004) "Monetary Policy Alternatives at the Zero Bound; An Empirical Assessment," *Brooking Papers on Economic Activity,* Washington DC.: The Brookings Institution, 1–100.

————, and M. Woodford (2005) (eds.) *The Inflation–Targeting Debate,* Chicago: University of Chicago Press.

Bernstein, M. A. (1987) *The Great Depression,* Cambridge: Cambridge University Press.

Beveridge, W. (1944) *Full Employment in a Free Society,* London: Allen and Unwin.

Bils, M., and P. J. Klenow (2004) "Some Evidence on the Importance of Sticky Prices," *Journal of Political Economy,* Vol. 112, No. 5, 947–985.

Black, F. (1987) *Business Cycles and Equilibrium,* Oxford and Cambridge, MA: Basil Blackwell.

Blanchard, O. J. (1979) "Speculative Bubbles, Crashes and Rational Expectations," *Economics Letters,* Vol. 3, 387–389.

————, and M. W. Watson. (1982) "Bubbles, Rational Expectations and Financial Markets." *Crises in the Economic and Financial Structure,* edited by Paul Wachtel, 295–316, Lexington, MA: D.C. Heath and Company.

———— (2000) "Discussions of the Monetary Response – Bubbles, Liquidity Traps, and Monetary Policy," in Ryoichi Mikitani and Adam S. Posen (eds.), *Japan's Financial Crisis and its Parallels to U.S. Experience,* Washington DC: Institute for International Economics, 185–193.

————, and P. Diamond (1990) "The Aggregate Matching Function" in Diamond' P. (ed.) *Growth, Productivity, Unemployment,* Cambridge, MA: MIT Press.

————, and S. Fischer (1989) *Lectures on Macroeconomics,* Cambridge, MA: MIT Press.

————, and N. Kiyotaki (1987) "Monopolistic Competition and the Effects of Aggregate Demand," *American Economic Review*, Vol. 77, 647–666.

Brandt, A. (1986) "The Stochastic Equation $Y_{n+1} = A_n Y_n + B_n$ with Stationary Coefficients," *Adv. Appl. Prob.*, Vol. 18, 211–220.

Breiman, L. (1969) *Probability and Stochastic Processes: With a View Toward Applications*, New York: Houghton Mifflin.

Bruno, M., and J. Sachs (1985) *Economics of Worldwide Stagflation*, Cambridge, MA: Harvard University Press.

Caballero, R., and A. Jaffe (1993) "How High Are the Giant's Shoulders? An Empirical Assessment of Knowledge Spillovers and Creative Destruction in a Model of Economic Growth," in Blanchard, O. and S. Fischer (eds.), *NBER Macroeconomics Annual 1993*, Cambridge MA: MIT Press.

Campbell J. Y., and J. H. Cochrane (1999) "By Force of Habit: A Consumption-Based Explanation of Aggregate Stock Market Behavior," *Journal of Political Economy*, Vol. 107, 205–251.

Canning, D., L. A. N. Amaral, Y. Lee, M. Meyer, and H. E. Stanley (1998) "Scaling the Volatility of GDP Growth Rates," *Economic Letters*, Vol. 60, 335–341.

Carroll, C. D. (2000) "Solving Consumption Models with Multiplicative Habits," *Economics Letters*, Vol. 68, 67–77.

Caselli, F., and J. Ventura (2000) "A Representative Consumer Theory of Distribution," *American Economic Review*, Vol. 90, No. 4, 909–926.

Cecchetti, S. G., P. S. Lam, and N. C. Mark (2000) "Asset Pricing with Distorted Beliefs: Are Equity Returns Too Good to Be True?," *American Economic Review*, Vol. 90, No. 4, 787–805.

Chamayou, J-F., and G. Letac (1991) "Explicit Stationary Distributions for Compositions of Random Functions and Products of Random Matrices," *Journal of Theoretical Probability*, Vol. 4, 3–36.

Choquet, G. (1960) "Le Théorème de Représentation Intégrale dans les Ensembles Convexes Compacts," (French) *Ann. Inst. Fasrier Grenoble*, Vol. 10, 333–344.

Choquet, G., and J. Deny (1960) "Sur léquation de convolution $\mu = \mu^* \sigma$," C. R. Acad. Sci. Paris, 1 Math. Vol. 250, 799–801.

Cinlar, E. (1975) *Introduction to Stochastic Processes*, Englewood Cliffs, NJ: Prentice-Hall.

Clay, H. (1928) "Unemployment and Wage Rates," *Economic Journal*, Vol. 38, No. 149, 1–15.

Clower, R. (1965) "The Keynesian Counterrevolution: A Theoretical Appraisal," in F. Hahn and F. Brechling (eds.), *The Theory of Interest Rates*, London: Macmillan.

Costantini, D. et al. "Herding and Clustering: Ewens vs Simon-Yule Models," *Physica A*, forthcoming.

Costantini, D., and U. Garibaldi (1979) "A Probabilistic Foundation of Elementary Particle Statistics. Part I," *Studies in History and Philosophy of Modern Physics*, Vol. 28, Issue 4, 483–506.

———— (1989) "Classical and Quantum Statistics as Finite Random Processes," *Foundations of Physics*, 19, 743–754.

———— (1999) "A Finitary Characterization of the Ewens Sampling Formula," Mimeo, Univ. Bologna, Depart. Statistics.

————, S. Donadio, U. Garibaldi, and P. Viarengo (2005) "Herding and Clustering: Ewens vs. Simon–Yule models," *Physica A: Statistical Mechanics and Its Applications*, Vol. 355, 224–231.

Costello, D. (1993) "A Cross-Country, Cross-Industry Comparison of Productivity Growth," *Journal of Political Economy,* Vol. 101, 207–222.

Cox, D. R., and H. D. Miller (1965) *The Theory of Stochastic Processes,* London: Chapman & Hall.

Davis, S. J. (1987) "Allocative Disturbances and Specific Capital in Real Business Cycles Theories," *American Economic Review,* Vol. 77, 326–332.

———, J. C. Haltiwanger, and S. Schuh (1996) *Job Creation and Destruction,* Cambridge, MA: MIT Press.

Day, R., and W. Huang (1990) "Bulls, Bears and Market Sheep," *J. Econ. Behavior Organization,* Vol. 14, 299–330.

Deaton, A. (1992) *Understanding Consumption,* Oxford: Oxford University Press.

de Haan, L., S. I. Resnick, H. Rootzén, and C. de Vries (1989) "Extremal Behavior of Solutions to a Stochastic Difference Equation with Applications to Arch Processes," *Stoch. Proc. Appli.* Vol. 32, 213–24.

Derrida, U. B. (1981) "Random-Energy Model: An Exactly Solvable Model of Disordered Systems," *Physical Review B: Condensed Matter,* Vol. 24, 5, 2613–2626.

Diamond, P. (1967) "The Role of a Stock Market in a General Equilibrium Model with Technological Uncertainty," *American Economic Review,* Vol. 57, No. 4, 759–776.

——— (1982) "Aggregate Demand Management in Search Equilibrium," *Journal of Political Economy,* Vol. 90, 881–894.

——— (1990) (ed.), *Growth, Productivity, Employments,* Cambridge, MA: MIT. Press.

Dixit, A. K., and R. S. Pindyck (1994) *Investment under Uncertainty,* Princeton, NJ: Princeton University Press.

Durrett, R., and J. Schweinsberg (2005) "Power Laws for Family Sizes in a Duplication Model," arXiv:math.Pr/0406216 v3.

Eggertsson, G. B., and M. Woodford (2003) "The Zero Bound on Interest Rates and Optimal Monetary Policy," *Brookings Papers on Economic Activity,* Washington, DC: The Brookings Institution, 139–233.

Ewens, W. J. (1972) "The Sampling Theory of Selectively Neutral Alleles," *Theoretical Population Biology,* Vol. 3, 87–112.

——— (1990) "Population Genetic Theory – The Past and the Future," S. Lessard (ed.), *Mathematical and Stochastic Developments of Evolutionary Theory,* London: Kluwer Academic Pub.

Fagnart, J-F., O. Licandro, and F. Portier (1999) "Firm Heterogeneity, Capacity Utilization and the Business Cycle," *Rev. Econ. Dynamics,* 2, 433–455.

Farmer J. D., L. Gillemot, F. Lillo, S. Mike, and A. Sen (2004) "What Really Causes Large Price Changes?" *Quantitative Finance,* Vol. 4, 383–397.

Fair, R. C. (1989) Book Review of R. E. Lucas, *Models of Business Cycles,* London and New York: Blackwell, *Journal of Economic Literature,* Vol. 27, 104–105.

Feigelman, M. V., and L. B. Ioffe (1991) "Hierarchical Organization of Memory," in *Models of Neural Networks,* edited by E. Domany et al., Berlin: Springer-Verlag.

Feller, W. (1957) *An Introduction to Probability Theory and Its Applications, Vol. I,* New York: Wiley.

Feng, S. and J. Hoppe (1998) "Limiting Behavior of Some Combinational Structures in Population Genetics," *C.R. Mathematics Academy Science,* Vol. 20–3, 65–70.

Fisher, I. (1933) "The Debt Deflation Theory of Great Depressions," *Econometrica,* Vol. 1, 337–357.

Frisch, R. (1933) "Propagation Problems and Impulse Problems in Dynamic Economics," in *Economic Essays in Honour of Gustav Cassel,* London: George Allen and Unwin, 172.

Friedman, M. (1968) "The Role of Monetary Policy," *American Economic Review*, Vol. 58, No. 1, 1–17.

Gabaix, X., P. Gopikrishnan, V. Plerou, and H. E. Stanley (2003) "A Theory of Power-Law Distriburions in Financial Market Fluctuations," *Nature*, Vol. 423, 267–270.

Gates, B. (1999) *Business@The Speed of Thought*, New York: Warner Books.

Gibson, M. (1995) "Can Bank Health Affect Investment? Evidence from Japan," *Journal of Business*, 281–308.

Godrèch, C., J. P. Bouchaud, and M. Mézard (1995) "Entropy Barriers and Slow Relaxation in Some Random Walk Models," *Journal of Physics A: Mathematical and General*, Vol. 28, No. 23, 603–611.

———, and J. M. Luck (1997) "Non-Equilibrium Dynamics of a Simple Stochastic Model," *Journal of Physics A: Mathematical & General*, Vol. 30, 6245–6272.

Goldie, C. M. (1991) "Implicit Renewal Theory and Tails of Solutions of Random Equations," *The Annals of Applied Probability* 1, 126–166.

Good, I. J. (1965) *The Estimation of Probabilities: An Essay on Modern Bayesian Methods Research Monograph; No. 30*, Cambridge, MA: M.I.T. Press.

Goodwin, R. (1951) "The Nonlinear Accelerator and the Persistence of Business Cycles," *Econometrica*, Vol. 19, No. 1, 1–17.

Gopikrishnan, M., M. Meyer, L. A. N. Amaral, and H. E. Stanley (1998) "Inverse cubic law for the distribution of stock price variations," *European Physical Journal B*, Vol. 3, 139–140.

Gordon, R. (1999) "Monetary Policy in the Age of Information Technology: Computers and the Solow Paradox," IMES Discussion Paper, No. 99-E-12, Bank of Japan.

Grandmont, J. M. (1985) "On Endogenous Competitive Business Cycles," *Econometrica*, Vol. 53, 995–1045.

Griffiths, R. C. (2004) "The Frequency Spectrum of a Mutation, and Its Age, in a General Diffusion Model," *Theoretical Population Biology*, Vol. 64, 2, 241–251.

Grossman, G. M., and E. Helpman (1991) *Innovation and Growth in the Global Economy*, Cambridge, MA: MIT Press.

Grossman, S. J., and R. J. Shiller (1981) "The Determinants of the Variability of Stock Market Prices," *American Economic Review*, No. 71, 222–227.

Habakkuk, H. J. (1962) *American and British Technology in the Nineteenth Century*, Cambridge: Cambridge University Press.

Haberler, G. (1964) *Prosperity and Depression, 5th ed*, Cambridge, MA: Harvard University Press.

Hamada, K., and Y. Kurosaka (1984) "The Relationship between Production and Unemployment in Japan: Okun's Law in Comparative Perspective," *European Economic Review*, Vol. 25, Issue 1, 71–94.

Hansen, L. P., and K. J. Singleton (1982) "Generalized Instrumental Variables Estimation of Nonlinear Rational Expectations Models," *Econometrica*, Vol. 50, No. 5, 1269–1286.

——— (1983) "Stochastic Consumption, Risk Aversion, and the Temporal Behavior of Asset Returns," *Journal of Political Economy*, Vol. 9, No. 2, 249–265.

Hayashi, F. (1986) "An Extension and Tests of the Permanent Income Hypothesis," (in Japanese), Economic Planning Agency, *Keizai Bunseki*, No. 101, 1–23.

———, and E. Prescott (2002) "The 1990's in Japan: A Lost Decade," *Review of Economic Dynamics*, Vol. 5, 206–235.

Hicks, J.R. (1950) *A Contribution to the Theory of the Trade Cycle*, Oxford: Oxford University Press.

——— (1965) *Capital and Growth*, London: Oxford University Press.

_____ (1989) *A Market Theory of Money*, New York: Oxford University Press.

Honerkamp, J. (1998) *Statistical Physics: An Advanced Approach with Applications*, Berlin: Springer.

Hoppe, F. M. (1984) "Pólya–like Urns and the Ewens Sampling Formula," *Journal of Mathematical Biology*, Vol. 20, 91–94.

_____ (1987) "The Sampling Theory of Neutral Alleles and an Urn Model in Population Genetics," *J. Math. Biology* Vol. 25, 23–59.

Hosios, A. J. (1994) "Unemployment and Vacancies with Sectoral Shifts," *American Economic Review*, Vol. 84, No. 1, 124–144.

Hubbard, G. (1998) "Capital-Market Imperfections and Investment," *Journal of Economic Literature*, Vol. 36, 193–225.

Huang, Z. F., and S. Solomon (2001) "Power, Lévy, Exponential and Gaussian-Like Regimes in Autocatalytic Financial Systems," *The European Physical Journal B*, Vol. 20, 601–607.

Hwang, H. (1995) "Asymptotic Expansions for the Stirling Numbers of the First Kind," *Journal of Combinatorial Theory, A*, Vol. 71, 343–351.

Inada, K., S. Sekiguchi, and Y. Shoda (1992) *The Mechanism of Economic Development*, Oxford: Oxford University Press.

Ingber, L. (1982) "Statistical Mechanics of Neocortical Interaction," *Physica D*, Vol. 5, 83–107.

Iwai, K. (2001) "Schumpeterian Dynamics: A Disequilibrium Theory of Long Run Profits," in L. F. Punzo, (2001) *Cycle, Growth and Structual Change*, London and New York: Routledge.

Jevons, W. S. (1884) *Investigations in Currency and Finance*, London: Macmillan.

Johnson, N., S. Kotz, and N. Balakrishnan (1997) *Multivariate Discrete Distributions*, New York: Wiley.

Jones, C. (1995) "R&D-Based Models of Economic Growth," *Journal of Political Economy*, Vol. 103, 759–784.

_____, and John Williams (1998) "Measuring the Social Return to R&D," *Quarterly Journal of Economics*, Vol. 113, 1119–1135.

Jovanovic, B. (1982), "Selection and the Evolution of Industry," *Econometrica*, Vol. 50, 649–670.

Kaldor, N. (1940) "A Model of the Trade Cycle," *Economic Journal*, Vol. 50, No. 197, 78–92.

_____ (1957) "A Model of Economic Growth," *Economic Journal*, Vol. 68, 591–624.

Kalecki, M. (1939) *Essays in the Theory of Economic Fluctuations*, London: George Allen and Unwin.

_____, (1954) *Theory of Economic Dynamics*, London: George Allen and Unwin.

Karev, G. P., Y. I. Wolf, A. Y. Rzhetsky, F. S. Berezovskaya and E. V. Koonin (2002) "Birth and Death of Protein Domains: A Simple Model of Evolution Explains Power Law Behavior," *BMC Evolutionary Biology*, Vol. 2:18.

Katz, L. F. (1986) "Efficiency Wage Theories: A Partial Evaluation," *NBER Macroeconomics Annual*, Vol. 1, 235–276.

_____ (1954) *Theory of Economic Dynamics*, London: George Allen and Unwin.

Kelly, F. D. (1976) "On Stochastic Population Models in Genetics," *J. Appl. Probab.* Vol. 13, 127–131.

_____ (1979) *Reversibility and Stochastic Network*, New York: Wiley.

_____ (1983) "Invariant measures and the Q-matrix," in J. F. C. Kingman and G. E. H. Reuter (eds.) *Probability, Statistics, and Analysis*, Cambridge: Cambridge Univ. Press.

Kendall, D. G. (1975) "Some Problems in Mathematical Genealogy," in J. Gani (ed.) *Perspective in Probability and Statistics*, New York: Academic Press.

Kesten, H. (1973) "Random Difference Equations and Renewal Theory for Products of Random Matrices," *Acta Mathematica*, Vol. 131, 207–248.

Keynes, J. M. (1936) *The General Theory of Employment, Interest, and Money*, London: Macmillan.

Kindleberger, C. (1967) *Europe's Postwar Growth*, Cambridge, MA: Harvard University Press.

—— (1989) "The Iron Law of Wages," in his *Economic Laws and Economic History*, Cambridge: Cambridge University Press.

King, M. (2004) "The Institutions of Monetary Policy," *The American Economic Review*, Vol. 94, No. 2, 1–13.

Kingman, J. F. K. (1969) "Markov Population Processes," *Journal of Applied Probability*, Vol. 6, 1–18.

—— (1978a) "Random Partitions in Population Genetics," *Proceedings of Royal Society*, Vol. 361, 1–20.

—— (1978b) "The Representation of Partition Structure," *Journal of London Mathematical Society*, Vol. 18, 347–380.

—— (1980) *Mathematics of Genetic Diversity*, Philadelpha: SIAM.

—— (1993) *Poisson Processes*, Oxford: Clarendon Press.

Kirman, A. P. (1992) "Whom or What Does the Representative Individual Represent?," *Journal of Economic Perspectives*, Spring Vol. 6, No. 2, 117–136.

—— (1993) "Ants, Rationality, and Recruitment" *Quarterly Journal of Economics*, Vol. 108, 137–156.

Kiyono, K., Z. R. Struzik, and Y. Yamamoto (2006) "Critical and Phase Transition in Stock-Price Fluctuations" *Physical Review Latters*, Vol. 96.

Kiyotaki, N., and J. Moore (1997) "Credit Cycles," *Journal of Political Economy*, Vol. 105, No. 2, 211–248.

Krugman, P. (1991) "History versus Expectations," *Quarterly Journal of Economics*, Vol. 106, 651–667.

—— (1994) "The Myth of Asia's Miracle," *Foreign Affairs*, Vol. 73, No.6, 62–78.

—— (1998) "It's Baaack: Japan's Slump and the Return of the Liquidity Trap," *Brookings Papers on Economic Activity 2*, 137–203.

Kuznets, S. (1953) *Economic Change*, New York: Norton.

Kydland, F., and E. Prescott (1982) "Time to Build and Aggregate Fluctuations," *Econometrica*, Vol. 50, 1354–1370.

Lamont, O. A., and R. H. Thaler (2003) "The Law of One Price in Financial Markets," *Journal of Economic Perspectives*, Vol. 17, No. 4, Fall, 191–202.

Lawler, G. (1995) *Introduction to Stochastic Processes*, London: Chapman & Hall.

Leijonhufvud, A. (1968) *Keynesian Economics and Economics of Keynes*, Oxford: Oxford University Press.

LeRoy, S. F., and R. D. Porter (1981) "The Present-Value Relation: Tests Based upon Implied Variance Bounds," *Econometrica* Vol. 49, 555–574.

Letac, G. (1986) "A Contraction Principle for Certain Markov Chains and Its Applications," *Contemporary Mathematics*, Vol. 50, 263–273.

Levy, M., and S. Solomon, (1996) "Dynamical Explanation for the Emergence of Power Law in a Stock Market," *International Journal of Modern Physics C*, Vol. 7, 65–72.

Lewis, W. Arthur (1954) "Economic Development with Unlimited Supplies of Labor", *Manchester School of Economic and Social Studies*, Vol. 5, 139–191.

Lilien, D. (1982) "Sectoral Shifts and Cyclical Unemployment," *Journal of Political Economy*, Vol. 90, No. 4, 777–793.

Lipsey, R. G. (1960) "The Relation Between Unemployment and the Rate of Change of Money Wage Rates in the United Kingdom, 1862–1957: A Furthermore Analysis," *Econometrica*, Vol. 27, 1–31.

Lucas, R. E. (1972) "Expectation and the Neutrality of Money," *Journal of Economic Theory*, Vol. 4, Issue 2, 103–124.

———— (1987) *Models of Business cycles,* London and New York: Blackwell.

Lux, T., and M. Marchesi (1999) "Scaling and Criticality in a Stochastic Multi-Agent Model of a Financial Market," *Nature* Vol. 397, 498–500.

Lux, T., and D. Sornette (2002) "On Rational Bubbles and Fat Tails," *Journal of Money, Credit and Banking* Part 1, Vol. 34, No. 3, 589–610.

McKinnon, R., and K. Ohno (1997) *Dollar and Yen*, Cambridge MA: MIT Press.

Malcai, O., O. Biham, and S. Solomon (1999) "Power-Law Distributions and Levy-Stable Intermittent Fluctuations in Stochastic Systems of Many Autocatalytic Elements," *Physical Review E*, Vol. 60, 1299–1303.

Malinvaud, E. (1977) *Theory of Unemployment Reconsidered*, Basil Blackwell, Oxford.

———— (1982) "Wages and Unemployment," *Economic Journal*, Vol. 92, No. 365, 1–12.

Mandelbrot, B. B. (1963) "The Variation of Certain Speculative Prices," *Journal of Business*, Vol. 36, 394–419.

———— (1983) *The Fractal Geometry of Nature*, Freeman: New York.

———— (1997) *Fractals and Scaling in Finance: Discontinuity, Concentration, Risk*, Springer Verlag: New York.

————, and R. L. Hudson (2004) *The (MIS) Behavior of Markets*, New York: Basic Books.

Mankiw, N. G. (1985) "Small Menu Costs and Large Business Cycles: A Macroecononic Model of Monopoly," *Quarterly Journal of Economics,* Vol. 100, 529–539.

———— (1989) "Real Business Cycles: A New Keynesian Perspective," *Journal of Perspectives*, Vol. 4, No. 3, 79–90.

————, and D. Romer (1991) *New Keynesian Economics*, Cambridge, MA: MIT Press.

————, and S. P. Zeldes (1991) "The Consumption of Stockholders and Non-Stockholders," *Journal of Financial Economics*, Vol. 29, 97–112.

Mantegna, R. N., and H. E. Stanley (1994) "Stochastic Process with Ultraslow Convergence to a Gaussian: The Truncated Lēvy Flight," *Phy. Rev. Lett*, Vol. 73, 2946–2949.

———— (1995) "Scaling Behavior in the Dynamics of an Economic Index," *Nature*, Vol. 376, 46–49.

———— (2000) *An Introduction to Econophysics: Correlations and Complexity in Finance*, Cambridge UK: Cambridge University Press.

Marshall, A. (1898) "Distribution and Exchange," *Economic Journal*, Vol. 8, 37–59.

———— (1920) *Principles of Economics*, 8th ed. London: Macmillan.

Matsuyama, K. (1995) "Complementarities and Cumulative Process in Models of Monopolistic Competition," *Journal of Economic Literature*, Vol. 33, 701–729.

McFadden, D. (1974) *The Measurement of Urban Travel Demand*, Berkeley, CA: Institute of Urban and Regional Development.

McLaughlin, G., and R. Watkins (1939) "The Problem of Industrial Growth in a Mature Economy," *American Economic Review*, Vol. 29, 1–14.

Mehra, R., and E. C. Prescott (1985) "The Equity Premium," *Journal of Monetary Economics*, 15, 145–161.

Mekjian, A. Z. (1991) "Cluster Distributions in Physics and Genetic Diversity," *Physical Review A*, Vol. 44, Issue 12, 8361–8374.

Meltzer, A. (2001) "Monetary Transmission at Low Inflation: Some Clues from Japan in the 1990's," *Monetary and Economic Studies*, Vol. 19, No. S-1 (February), 13–34.

Metropolis, N., A. W. Rosenbluth, M. N. Rosenbluth, A. H. Teller, and E. Teller (1953) "Equation of State Calculations by Fast Computing Machines," *Journal of Chemical Physics*, Vol. 21, 1087–1092.

Mézard, M., G. Parisi, and M. A. Virasoro (1986). "SK Model: The Replica Solution without Replicas," *Europhysics Letters*. Vol. 1, 77–82.

Mill, J. S. (1844) "Of the Influence of Consumption upon Production," in his *Essays on Some Unsettled Questions of Political Economy*, London: John W. Parker.

Minami, R. (1968) "The Turning Point in the Japanese Economy," *Quarterly Journal of Economics*, August, Vol. 83, 380–402.

Minsky H. P. (1957) "Monetary Systems and Accelerator Models," *American Economic Review*, 47, 859–883.

———— (1975) *John Maynard Keynes*, New York: Columbia University Press.

Modigliani, F. (1944) "Liquidity Preference and the Theory of Interest and Money," *Econometrica*, Vol. 12, No. 1, 45–88.

Montroll, E. W. (1978) "Social Dynamics and the Quantifying of Social Forces," *Proceedings of National Academy of Sciences U.S.A.*, Vol. 75, No. 10.

Mortensen, D. T. (1989) "The Persistence and Indeterminacy of Unemployment in Search Equilibrium," *Scandinavian Journal of Economics,* 91, 347–60.

———— (2003) *Wage Dispersion*, Cambridge, MA: MIT Press.

Motonishi, T., and H. Yoshikawa (1999) "Causes of the Long Stagnation of Japan During the 1990s: Financial or Real?," *Journal of the Japanese and International Economies*, Vol. 13, 181–200.

Murphy, K., A. Shleifer, and R.Vishny (1989) "Industrialization and the Big Push," *Journal of Political Economy*, Vol. 97, 1003–1026.

Neftci, S. (1984) "Are Economic Time Series Asymmetrical Over the Business Cycles?" *Journal of Political Economy*, 92, 307–328.

Nelson, R., and H. Pack (1999) "The Asian Miracle and Modern Growth Theory," *Economic Journal*, Vol. 109, 416–436.

Ogawa, K., and K. Suzuki (1998) "Land Value and Corporate Investment: Evidence from Japanese Panel Data," *Journal of Japanese and International Economies*, Vol. 12, 132–49.

Ogielski, A. T., and D. L. Stein (1985) "Dynamics on Ultrametric Spaces," *Physical Review Letters,* Vol. 55, 1634–1637.

Ohkawa, K., and H. Rosovsky (1973) *Japanese Economic Growth*, Stanford: Stanford University Press.

Ohkawa, K., N. Takmatsu, and Y. Yamamoto (1974) *National Income: Estimates of Long-Term Economic Statistics of Japan since 1868* (in Japanese), Tokyo: Toyo Keizai Shimposha.

Okun, A. M. (1962) "Potential GNP: Its Measurement and Significance," *Proceedings of the Business and Economic Statistics Section,* American Statistical Association, 98–104, reprinted in Okun's *The Political Economy of Prosperity*, Washington DC: The Brookings Institution, 1970.

———— (1973) "Upward Mobility in a High-Pressure Economy," *Brooking Papers on Economic Activity*, Vol. 1, 207–261.

———— (1981) *Prices and Quantities: A Macroeconomic Analysis*, Washington DC: Brookings Institution.

Pareto, V. (1896) *Cours d'Economie Politique*, Lausanne.

Paul, W., and J. Baschnagel (1999) *Stochastic Processes: From Physics to Finance*, Springer: Berlin.

Phelps, E. S. et al. (1970) *Microeconomic Foundations of Employment and Inflation Theory*, New York: W.W. Norton.

Pigou, A. (1927) "Wage Policy and Unemployment," *Economic Journal*, Vol. 37, No. 147, 355–368.

———— (1945) *Lapses from Full Employment*, London: Macmillan.

Pissarides, C. (2000) *Equilibrium Unemployment Theory*, Blackwell, Oxford.

Pitman, J. (2002) *Combinational Stochastic Processes*, Lecture Notes for St. Elour Summmer School.

Prescott, E. C. (1986) "Theory Ahead of Business Cycle Measurement," *Federal Reserve Bank of Minneapolis Quarterly Review* Fall, 9–22.

Ramsey, F. (1928) "A Mathematical Theory of Saving," *Economic Journal*, December, Vol. 38, 543–559.

Richmond, P., and S. Solomon (2001) "Power Laws Are Disguised Boltzmann Laws," *International Journal of Modern Physics C*, Vol. 12, No. 3, 333–343.

Ripley, B. (1987) *Stochastic Simulation*, New York: Wiley.

Robertson, D. H. (1940) "Mr. Keynes and the Rate of Interest," in his *Essays in Monetary Theory*, London: Staples Press.

Robinson, J. (1962) *Essays in the theory of Economic Growth*, London: Macmillan.

Rogoff, K. (2002) "Stop Deflation First for the Revival of the Japanese Economy," *Nikkei Shimbun*, October 7.

Romer, P. M. (1990) "Endogenous Technological Change," *Journal of Political Economy*, Vol. 98, 71–102.

Rostow, W. W. (1960) *The Process of Economic Growth*, Oxford: Oxford University Press.

———— (1978) *The World Economy: History and Prospect*, Austin: University of Texas Press.

Sachkov, Y. L. (1996) "Controllability of Hypersurface and Solvable Invariant Systems," *Journal of Dynamical and Control Systems*, Vol. 2, 1, 55–67.

Salter, W. E. G. (1960) *Productivity and Technical Change*, Cambridge: Cambridge University Press.

Samuelson, P. (1939) "Interactions between the Multiplier Analysis and the Principle of Acceleration," *Review of Economic Statistics*, Vol. 21, No. 2, 75–78.

Schikhof, W. H. (1984). *Ultrametric Calculus: An Introduction to p-adic Analysis*, London: Cambridge University Press.

Schmookler, J. (1966) *Invention and Economic Growth*, Cambridge, MA: Harvard University Press.

Schumpeter, J. (1934) *Theory of Economic Development*, Cambridge, MA: Harvard University Press.

Schrödinger E. (1944) *What is Life?*, Cambridge: Cambridge University Press.

Segerstrom, P. (1998) "Endogenous Growth without Scale Effects," *American Economic Review*, Vol. 88, 1290–1310.

Shiller, R. J. (1981) "Do Stock Prices Move Too Much to be Justified by Subsequent Changes in Dividends?," *The American Economic Review*, Vol. 71, No. 3 421–436.

Simon, H. A. (1955) "On a Class of Skew Distribution Functions," *Biometrika*, Vol. 42 425–440.

Slutzky, E. (1937) "The Summation of Random Causes as the Sources of Cyclic Processes," *Econometrica*, Vol. 5, 105–146.

Smith, K. (1969) "The Effect of Uncertainly on Monopoly Price, Capital Stock and Utilization of Capital," *Journal of Economic Theory*, Vol. 1, Issue 1, 48–59.

Solomon, S., and P. Richmond (2001) "Power Laws of Wealth, Market Order Volumes and Market Returns," *Physical A: Statistical Mechanics and its Applications*, Vol. 299 (1–2), 188–197.

Solow R. M. (1956) "A Contribution to the Theory of Economic Growth," *Quarterly Journal of Economics*, Vol. 70, 65–94.

———— (1957) "Technical Change and the Aggregate Production Function," *Review of Economics and Statistics*, Vol. 39, 312–320.

———— (1964) *The Nature and Sources of Unemployment in the United States*, Stockholm: Almqvist and Wicksell.

———— (1986) "Unemployment: Getting the Questions Right," *Economica*, Vol. 53, S23–S34.

———— (1997) "Is There a Core of Usable Macroeconomics We Should All Believe In?" *The American Economic Review*, Vol. 87, 230–232.

Sornette, D. (1998) "Multiplicative Processes and Power Laws," *Phy. Rev*, E57, 4811–13.

———— (2000) *Critical Phenomena in Natural Sciences*, Berlin: Springer.

———— (2002) "Slimming" of Power Law Tails by Increasing Market Returns, *Physica A* 309, 403–418.

Stanley, M. H. R., L. A. N. Amaral, S. V. Buldyrev, S. Havlin, H. Leschhorn, P. Maass, M. A. Salinger, and H. E. Stanley (1996) "Scaling Behavior in the Growth of Companies," *Nature*, Vol. 379, 804–806.

Stokey, N. (1988) "Learning by Doing and the Introduction of New Goods," *Journal of Political Economy*, Vol. 96, No. 4, 701–717.

Summers, L. H. (1986) "Some Skeptical Observation on Real Business Cycle Theory," *Federal Reserve Bank of Minneapolis Quarterly Review*, Vol. 10, 23–27.

———— (1991) "The Scientific Illusion in Empirical Macroeconomics," *Scand. J. of Economics* 93(2), 129–148.

Sutton, J. (1997) "Gibrat's Legacy," *Journal of Economic Literature*, Vol. 35, 40–59.

Svenson, L. (2001) "The Zero Bound in an Open Economy: A Foolproof Way of Escaping from a Liquidity Trap," *Monetary and Economic Studies*, Vol. 19, No. S-1 (February) 277–312.

Takayasu, H., and A. Sato (1997) "Stable Infinite Variance Fluctuations in Randomly Amplified Langevin Systems," *Physical Review Letters*, Vol. 79, 966–969.

Tavaré, S., A. D. Barbour, and R. Arratia (1997) "Approximating Random Combinatorial Structures," Mimeo Univ. Southern Calif., Dept. Math.

Taylor, J.B. (1979) "Estimation and Control of a Macroeconomic Model with Rational Expectations," *Econometrica*, Vol. 47, No. 5, 1267–1286.

———— (1980) "Aggregate Dynamics and Staggered Contracts," *Journal of Political Economy*, Vol. 88, No. 1, 1–23.

———— (1989) "Differences in Economic Fluctuations in Japan and the US: The Role of Nominal Rigidities," *Journal of Japanese and International Economies*, Vol. 3, 127–144.

Tobin, J. (1972) "Inflation and Unemployment," *American Economic Review*, Vol. 62, 1–18.

———— (1975) "Keynesian Models of Recessions and Depression," *American Economic Review*, 65(2), 195–202.

———— (1993) "Price Flexibility and Output Stability: An Old Keynesian View," *Journal of Economic Perspectives*, Vol. 7, 45–65.

Uzawa, H. (1969) "Time Preference and the Penrose Effect in a Two-Class Model of Economic Growth," *Journal of Political Economy*, Vol. 77, No. 4, Part 2, 628–652.

Van Kampen, N. G. (1992) *Stochastic Processes in Physics and Chemistry* (Revised and enlarged edition), Amsterdam: Elsevier.

Van Lint, J. H., and R. M. Wilson (1992) *A Course in Combinatoric,* Cambridge: Cambridge Univ. Press.

Vervaat, W. (1979) "On a Stochastic Difference Equation and a Representation of Nonnegative Infinitely Divisible Random Variables," *Adv. Appl. Prob.* Vol. 11, 750–83.

Watterson, G. A. (1974) "Models for the Logarithmic Species Abundance Distributions," *Tho. Pop. Bio.* Vol. 6, 217–50.

_____ (1976) "The Stationary Distribution of the Infinity–Many Neutral Alleles Diffusion Model," *Journal of Applied Probability,* Vol. 13, 639–651.

_____, and H. A. Guess (1977) "Is the Most Frequent Allele the Oldest?" *Theoretical Population Biology,* Vol. 11, 141–160.

Weitzman, M. L. (1982) "Increasing Returns and the Foundations of Unemployment Theory," *The Economic Journal,* Vol. 92, 787–804.

Witt, U. (ed.) (2001) *Escaping Satiation,* Berlin: Springer.

Woo, D. (1999) "In Search of 'Capital Crunch': Supply Factors behind the Credit Slowdown in Japan," IMF Working Paper No. 9913.

Wright, G. (1990) "The Origin of American Industrial Success, 1879–1940," *American Economic Review,* Vol. 80, 651–668.

_____ (1997) "Towards a More Historical Approach to Technological Change," *Economic Journal,* Vol. 107, 1560–1566.

Yellen, J. L. (1984) "Efficiency Wage Models of Unemployment," *American Economic Review.* Vol. 74, 200–205.

Yoshikawa, H. (1990) "On the Equilibrium Yen-Dollar Rate," *American Economic Review,* Vol. 80, 576–583.

_____ (1993). "Monetary Policy and the Real Economy in Japan," in K. J. Singleton (ed.) *Japanese Monetary Policy,* Chicago: University of Chicago Press, 121–159.

_____ (1995) *Macroeconomics and the Japanese Economy,* Oxford: Oxford University Press.

_____ (2003) "The Role of Demand in Macroeconomics," *Japanese Economic Review,* Vol. 54, No. 1, 1–27.

Yoshikawa, H., and K. Matsumoto (2001) "Change in Industrial Structure and Economic Growth," (in Japanese), Japanese Ministry of Finance, *Financial Review,* Vol. 58, 121–138.

Young, A. (1995) "The Tyranny of Numbers: Confronting the Statistical Realities of the East Asian Growth Experience," *Quarterly Journal of Economics,* Vol. 110, 641–680.

_____ (1998) "Growth without Scale Effects," *Journal of Political Economy,* Vol. 106, 41–63.

Yule, G. U. (1924) "A Mathematical Theory of Evolution, Based on the Conclusions of Dr J. C. Wills, F. R. S." *Philosophical Transactions of the Royal Society of London, B.* Vol. 213, 21–87.

Zabell, S. L. (1992) "Predicting the Unpredictable," *Synthese,* Vol. 90, 205–232.

Author Index

Van Kampen, N. G., 39, 41
van Lint, J. H., 260
Ventura, J., 60
Vervaat, W., 268
Viarengo, P., 306
Virasoro, M. A., 123

Walras, L., 2
Watkins, R., 224
Watson, M. W., 287
Watterson, G. A., 43, 259, 261, 262, 263, 271, 272
Weitzman, M. L., 75
Williams, J., 222, 232

Wilson, R. M., 260
Witt, U., 220
Wolf, Y. I., 305
Woo, W., 111
Woodford, M., 116–117
Wright, G., 23–222, 247

Yellen, J. L., 133
Yoshikawa, H., 21, 78, 84–85, 107, 108, 241, 245, 247, 252
Young, A., 23, 220, 222, 231, 232, 233–234, 244
Yule, G. U., 306

Zabell, S. L., 43, 46, 156, 256, 261–262

Subject Index

325

business cycles (*cont.*)
  periodicity of, 149
  productivity and, 216–217
  random variables and, 183
  random walks and, 150
  RBC theory. *See* real business cycle theory
  representative agents. *See* representative agents
  sectoral analysis. *See* sectoral analysis
  sinusoidal cycles, 183
  stochastic processes and. *See* stochastic
    processes
  sun spots and, 148
  technology and. 148, 216–217, *See* technical
    development,
  uncertainty and, 185. *See also* uncertainty
  wave structure of, 149

Calvo–Taylor models, 137
capacity utilization rate, 235
capital accumulation, optimal, 235
cash-in-advance constraints, 114
Cauchy's formula, 54
causality, interpretation of, 109
central limit theorem, 279
Chapman–Kolmogorov equation, 32
  aggregate dynamics and, 33, 163
  death process and, 34
  Diamond model and, 71
  employment and, 69
  equilibrium and, 13, 59. *See* equilibrium
  Fokker–Planck equation and, 33. *See*
    Fokker–Planck equation
  Markov theory and, 26, 93–95. *See* Markov
    Process
  moments of, 33
  solutions to, 34. *See also* specific *forms*
  stochastic dynamics and, 29. *See also*
    stochastic processes
characteristic curves, method of, 143
chartists, 264, 266, 269, 291
Chernoff inequality, 304
Chinese restaurant process, 306
cluster formation, 44–48
  balance condition for, 45
  in financial markets, 256–264
  generating functions and, 52
  internal states and, 54
  partition vector, 49
  shares of, 52
Cobb–Douglas production function, 84, 214
coin tossings, 150, 168–169, 188
combinatorial effects, 29
  binary choices and, 42, 98

Shannon entropy, 29, 104. *See also specific
  topic*
community preference, 65
configurations. *See* states
consumption
  demand and. *See* demand
  durable goods and , 7
  exponential distribution and, 297
  income and individual. *See* representative
    agents
  Ramsey consumers, 4, 11. *See also specific topic*
continuous-time models, 28, 198. *See* jump
    Markov processes
correlations, between variables, 123
creative destruction model, 219–220, 231–244
  saturation and, 22
  technical progress and, 221
cumulant generating function, defined, 37

death process, 34, 36, 38, 40
deflation, 87, 89
demand
  Aoki–Yoshikawa model and, 23. *See also*
    Aoki–Yoshikawa model
  Beveridge curve and, 27, 195, 205, 210,
    212
  economic growth and, 21–24, 27
  economic temperature and, 82, 133
  effective. *See* effective demand principle
  excess demand, 157, 264, 265
  innovation and, 229
  law of, 221–222
  logistic growth, 234–237, 243
  macroeconomics and, 13, 14
  Okun's law and, 27. *See also* Okun's law
  productivity and, 75, 86–87, 211
  saturation and, 21–22, 24, 218–253
  shocks and, 169, 195
depression, 26, 275–276
  Great Depression, 89
  recession and, 119, 140
detailed balance condition, 50, 305
deterministic models, 100, 103, 167
Diamond model, 63, 68–73
  Aoki–Shirai model and, 72
  dynamic optimization and, 70, 71
  equilibrium model, 66
  reservation cost in, 71
  as search model, 72
digamma function, 57
Dirichlet distribution, 53, 261–262, 270
discrete choice models, 65
  binary choice. *See* binary choice models

Printed in the United States
By Bookmasters